BECOMING OPEN SOULS

ANTONIO A. FELIZ

BECOMING OPEN SOULS

~~~~~~~~~

Transcending Institutional
Seduction & Cultural Rape

~~~~~~~~~

By

ANTONIO A. FELIZ

An Open Souls Publication
From
**CONCORD PRESS, INTERNATIONAL
& CONCORD CIRCLES INSTITUTE**

Library of Congress Cataloging in Publication Data
Becoming Open Souls, *Transcending Institutional Seduction & Cultural Rape*
Antonio A. Feliz
1943—

ISBN: 0-929582-01-2   Library of Congress Control Number: 2004110216

1. Church of Jesus Christ of Latter-day Saints—Controversial Literature
2. Ethnic Studies   3. Gay/Lesbian Studies   4. Mormon Church—Controversial Literature
5. New Age   6. Peace Studies   7. Philosophy   8. Political Science   9. Spirituality

Becoming Open Souls, *Transcending Institutional Seduction & Cultural Rape,* is an
Open Souls Publication from Concord Circles Institute ®. This California non-profit aims
to increase public awareness of principles represented by "pyramids of agreement" of the
ancient *Mexica/Toltec* tradition of *circles of peace* or "power of one" ceremonies that
derive from the pre-Columbian ancestors of most modern Mexican nationals. This is done
with events sponsored by *Concord Circles*, Of Reconciliation & Education. These events
affirm the human Mass Mind, together with all other mass minds, as The Creative Force for
securing an enduring peace among all creatures of planet Earth.

Web-Site: www.concordcirclesinstitute.org
E-mail author: losfeliz@concordcirclesinstitute.org
For event registration information on *Concord Circles*, Of Reconciliation & Education
Or, for information on other Open Souls Publications, e-mail:
concordcircles@concordcirclesinstitute.org

Cover photograph: "Sunset At Laguna Beach" © by Antonio A. Feliz. Recurring themes
throughout this book make mention of the sun, of the surface reflections of sunlight on
bodies of water and of their mutual relationship to sacred stories of the Christian Bible.
While, this particular photograph by the author was not taken at the time it happened, it
reflects the author's deeply personal experience—wherein a *Mexica/Toltec* wise man first
taught him to "follow the sun" in Becoming Open Souls, Chapter Seven, "Transcending
My Religious Abuse."

First Edition

ALSO BY ANTONIO A. FELIZ

Out of the Bishop's Closet
A Call To Heal Ourselves, Each Other and Our World
1992 Second Edition paperback ISBN: 0-9624751-7-3
[Alamo Square Press; San Francisco, CA 1992]

The Issue Is Pluralism
An Urgent Call To Greater Pluralism In Civil Marriage Law
2000 Edition paperback ISBN: 0-9703314-0-1
[Editorial Los Feliz; Los Feliz Village, Los Angeles, CA 200]

"PERSONAL DICHOTOMIES"
A spiritual auto-biography in

Searching For Your Soul
Writers of Many Faiths
Tell Their Stories of Spiritual Discovery
An anthology of spiritual biography, including contributions from:
Gandhi, Malcolm X and Dr. Martin Luther King, Jr. with an
Introduction by and, Edited by Katherine Kurs
1999 paperback ISBN: 0-8052-1111-X
[Schocken Books, a division of Random House Inc. New York, NY 1999]

"PERSONAL DICHOTOMIES"
Also in

Wrestling With The Angel
Faith and Religion in The Lives of Gay Men
Edited by Brian Bouldrey
Lambda "Book of The Year" Award For Religion in 1996
[Villard Books, Inc. New York, NY 1999]

A Mi Familia
To Los Feliz, Acosta, Tafolla, Yorba, Peralta, Cota and Los Lugo
who were original to 20th century California
An essay sent to the author's extended family; whose ancestors were
original to early 20th century Anaheim, CA February 2, 2002
An Open Souls Publication from Concord Press, International

"Such is the concreteness of existence that a situation may come under several rules at once, forcing us to choose outside of any rule, and from inside ourselves…"

—Kierkegaard

ACKNOWLEDGMENTS

At the risk of failure to mention someone because of a lack of memory, I express my profound gratitude in the following paragraphs to persons who have assisted me in significant ways that have each, resulted in this book. To any, that I may have inadvertently omitted, I ask that you consider the source and, forgive my neglect. My honest intent is to here acknowledge all contributors to this book's publication.

I must acknowledge one of the few novels that I've read in my life; Patricia Nell Warren's groundbreaking bestseller, The Frontrunner. It was one of my college students who, literally, *threw* a paperback first edition of this now globally famous work on my desk when; as Director of Residential Life in 1982, at Park College—now, a university—I was not yet out of my closet as a Gay man. It was the *context* of the character Harlan in Warren's The Frontrunner that had strongly paralleled my personal story. That single synchronicity first led me to write my story and, this book continues that same story, which began in my first book.

My profoundest appreciation also goes to Concord Press, International, especially to my publisher, Robert Webster and editor, Debra Marshall. Without the financial and technical support of these, this book would not have become the reality it now has become. I'm also grateful for the Concord Circles Institute which has fostered the introduction of Concord Circles, as I know them, to the public world. I recommend the Concord Circles Institute to philanthropic donations from all individuals and groups involved in movements toward peace, justice and global community. Concord Circles Institute is a good place for articulate and insightful, yet unpublished, other writers of spiritual biography to seek publication of their best work.

I'm grateful to Judy Ballantyne, for allowing me to house sit for her the year that I first began the writing of this book. The tremendous hospitality of her neighbors; Craig Miller and Joseph Pentheroudakis, was also a welcome blessing to me during that important phase of the book project. The many hours of conversation with Claire Summerhill –also, afforded by my living in her Sandy, Utah family home– created new awarenesses during the early days when the idea of this book first lodged itself in my "enfolded" reality.

I am also equally indebted to Phyllis Baker, another good friend who graciously made her home available to me during the initial research stages of this work. Another, without whose initial financial assistance this work never would have even been initiated, is my good friend, A. Stanton. Whether contributions were in cash or in kind, they are all very appreciated—including those who asked that I not mention their names. All of these teach me that, of all relationships, *friend* is the sacred one.

Additionally, others have read many drafts transcribed from my journals, and their open frankness responding editorially is much appreciated. For their empathic response in this most tedious process, I extend my sincerest heartfelt thanks to: Phyllis Baker; Brace Suvelius; Joel S. Federman; A. Stanton; Patricia Warren and Mary Jane. Because the stories I tell in this book are all non-fiction, I need to say that this book would not have been written, if it had not been for key L.D.S. and R.L.D.S. (CofC) relationships. I am deeply grateful to Jon Butler; Mel Barber; Leon Berg; the man whom I refer to as "Don" and the late, Bob Swoffer [of Kansas City, Missouri's G.A.L.A.] for all of their sincere views and opinions on key theological issues discussed in this book.

There are others, not mentioned here, but whose way of inter-relating with me has equally impacted the direction of this work. For personal reasons of privacy, they have asked for anonymity. For this reason, those with whom I have inter-related in the past, who are, by request, represented by a pseudonym in the text, remain anonymous to the reader. Their choice to allow me to publish how I experienced the experience of our inter-relating is a gift that I hold sacred.

The following voluntarily lent their views on various ideas and theories discussed herein as influenced by their, respective, discipline. This was done through numerous conversations with me over a period of years: Dr. Judy Ballantyne, a geologist; Dr. Joel S. Federman, a social theorist; Dr. David Knowlton, a social anthropologist; Dr. Cynthia Mothersole, a clinical pshchologist; Dr. M. Ortiz, a professor of organizational behavior; Dr. Joseph Pentheroudakis, a linguist; Dr. D. Michael Quinn, a Mormon historian; Dr. Joseph Rivetto, a clinical psychiatrist; Dr. Robert G. Strickley, a pharmaceutical bio-chemist; Dr. Phillip Wannamaker, a geophysicist; Claire (Sandra) Summerhill, an attorney; Paul Toscano, a lawyer / author and Margaret Toscano, an educator / author; David White, Sergio Clough and the late Jimm Kinney--all three of whom are gifted mystics. To another group of unnamed friends, whose highly significant work is in the Search for Extra-Terrestrial Intelligence, I equally extend a special thanks for our conversations that stimulated ways of envisioning that are reflected in the last parts of this book. Some of my most energized times in life have been the honest conversations with all of the above persons. This has largely been because of the regeneration, which I always gain from their educated insight and the uncommon wisdom of each one's, respective and diverse, professional expertise. The collective wisdom of this entire group, their individual intelligent application of the academic discipline in which they have each been trained and their sharing helped to define the ideas discussed by me herein. I am genuinely grateful for the generous gift of their collective scientific and mystical vision.

Along this line, I also extend my sincere gratitude to all those who were my school teachers in my formative years. I am, especially, indebted to: Mrs. White, my first journalism teacher, of whom I write in Chapter One, and my high school Principal, Mr. Kennedy, who took an interest in my education in public speaking. First, by coaching my competition in the 1960 Lions Club Student Speaking Contest and; second, I will always be grateful to him for deciding to let me speak at our 1961 Strathmore Union High School graduation, in spite of those who opposed it. That graduation experience, was my first experience in discovering my rather divergent personal views on competition *per se*; i.e.: *What really is* competition, anyway? How do we each usually respond to competition? What does *what we each actually do when we encounter competition in others and in one-self* say to us about all of us?

In more recent years, I've experienced powerful new mentors in the leaders of the *Mexica* Movement in Los Angeles, California: Dr. Olin Tezcatlipoca; as in Pomona, California's Raymond Ramirez; and Los Angeles based *Dona* Maria and Gabriel Castaneda—all of whom I consider modern warrior priests of the *Mexica*. To all of these *Mexica*, I am most grateful for sharing their wisdom of ancient ceremonies and sacred tradition with me. These are all sacred relationships.

The specific *Mexica* Indigenous people, to whom I owe the most for the perspectives discussed throughout this book, asked that they not be individually named by me in my work. Nevertheless, their tradition to be represented publicly "in only collective ways" does not change the pivotal place some of them have in my phenomenology. For example, the two men who first held out their arms in open greeting to me by saying, "I am Another Yourself" in their Indian language as we introduced ourselves to each other, are both soulful names in my world of dream and memory. And, there are other special ones also…

Many of these—although not named—are still living and well. But, here, I acknowledge the contribution of some that have come and gone before me on this same journey, which we call mortal life. It is my personal blessing to seem to intimately experience the sweetness of their presence during the final days and weeks of preparing this work for its publication. As I typed those words just now, in fact, I felt that familiar sense of their unmistakable presence and, I'm so very grateful! I had always wondered, in my younger years, why older people seem to think that they still experienced the deceased, as if they had never died. Now, I know that it's only because they *do* experience the deceased as still here, with us!

Along with these, I here acknowledge the Intelligence—The Force—which produced the "spirit written" messages that, I discuss in this work; for, it is that One Eternalness, who directed the context; or, "the language of *beingness*" of this journal record. I have, from my first blush of pubescence, experienced a favorite Christian hymn as a blend of prayer and praise and, also as an erotic letter to a lover: "*Jesus Lover of My Soul*" has always most fully expressed how I experience my God. To me, it is no longer a blasphemous "unspeakable" idea, to experience the Divine as rapturously erotic, *and* also as the Worthy Recipient of my human worship—The Force behind my experience in the experience.

What has caused me to adopt such a radical comprehension of God is how I now self-identify. Much of what is written herein is on this critical theme of Self-Identity. How I self-identify now, is what enables me—as a mere human—to experience God as I do today in my sixtieth year. I have known my God as a benevolent patriarch and then, later, as a Heavenly Mother. Now, I understand each of the, respective, recorded experiences of Jesus, Buddha and Krishna as being parallel paths—that, they may have all been one being, manifesting in a diversity of contexts.

Finally, acknowledging you—the reader—I say that, my tool for conveying how I have come to this place in my journey from my earliest beginning as a fundamentalist-leaning Mormon are the stories, my telling of how I experienced the experiences. What follows then, are true stories; told here, from a retrospective view as I studied their phenomenology from the present. All of the above is to say that, these stores from my personal journals are my honest acknowledgment that it is my fellow human beings who are Co-Creators of our shared reality.

TO THE CHERISHED MEMORY

OF MY BELOVED

MICHAEL S. MARSHALL "TERRY"
&
JAMES F. KINNEY "JASON" & "JIMM"

"**H**ear this, ye old men, and give ear; all ye inhabitants of the land…Tell your children of it, and let your children tell their children, and their children another generation."

—Joel 1:2-3 (KJV)

TABLE OF CONTENTS

"Humanity is not at the end of history...there is potentially at least one revolution left in human history, involving what might be called the 'spiritualization' of political and social life. This revolution is not fundamentally ideological...it is a revolution of 'consciousness.' It involves not the form of consciousness, but the degree of awareness of our connection with each other, an expansion of human solidarity beyond the family, the clan, the nation and the state to encompass humanity as a whole...it involves universal compassion..."

—Joel S. Federman, PhD.
      The Politics of Compassion, doctoral dissertation
      University of Southern California, August 1999

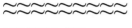

PREFACE

Becoming Open Souls is my healing call to an America that I learned to love as a small child. Much has been written and discussed about "America's healing" in the wake of what we now call the "terrorist attacks of September 11, 2001." In the months after that horror filled date, our global news media reported that we Americans responded to that horror with a "sudden and collective awareness" of our American society as being *one mass soul*. Yet, that response was intermixed with acts of hatred by some of us toward others of us who appear to either be Muslim or Arab. That kind of act has even been directed toward me.

So, *Becoming Open Souls* is about this presently ubiquitous inter-ethnic phenomenon of American fear based responses one to another. This book is published in my awareness that, as is the macrocosm, so is the microcosm. What we collectively experienced, as a healing response immediately after the terrorist attacks of September 11, 2001, is exactly how I've also responded to experiences of my personal journey in recent years—with a renewed awareness of being one *wholeness*.

I herein affirm that all healing dynamics are the same. Thus, the stories told in this book reveal *what I had to do on the personal level* in response to an evolving personal awareness of simply being one more, in a long line of *Californio* Latinos and Indigenous who recall the ethnic violence done to us by an "invasive" Anglo-America. Thus, this book is a discussion of an evolving parallel personal awareness; first, of what I am, as a member of a given cultural/ethnic group and then, of being raised in a seemingly "occupying," usurper culture that remains bent on *consuming* my own family's ethnicity into its less progressive, mainstream make-up.

After the New York World Trade Center, the Washington D.C. and the Pennsylvania tragedies, it became clear. We see that, *this* kind of parallel awareness was at the heart of why those terrorists—not only took their lives but—why they committed an act of barbarous war on us all. Simply put, *they* saw *our American presence* in Saudi Arabia and in other Islamic nation states as *culturally invasive*. In the weeks after September 11, 2001, I realized that this book tells *how I've* responded similarly—as a gay male, who is also a descendant of conquered *Californio*-Latinos—

to being an American in the second half of the 20th century. This book is a phenomenology on my personal love relationship with an evolving American democracy. It now tells how I experienced the experience of being different in a culture bent on the assimilation of my uniqueness into the mainstream, or what I've elsewhere called *"uni-culturalism."* This is my spiritual voice, awakened by the terrorists, who war against political and social pluralism; a war that they each wage by what is part and parcel of fundamentalism's inbred and ugly bent toward violence.

Violence, on any level, is not beautiful. Violence, either from a foreign terrorist, or from within our own *one soul mass,* will not be dealt with effectively by us until we emphasize an internal governance over the external fences that we call our *civil law* and *culture.* It follows that, since we human beings are part of nature, as it is with all of nature, true human beauty is revealed from *within.* Thus: Civility engineered from a source outside of any of us, is impermanent and tenuous, at best. The problem is our own diseased state. Yet, most of us are oblivious to the spiritual factor in *our,* respective, culture's sickness. We need a rebirth.

The spiritual vision, which I offer, is that contrary to the usual political rhetoric more discipline is, definitely, not what society needs. Discipline, like any external government, always involves its masters and *their* disciples, and in a modern, well functioning, ideal electorate of sovereign citizens there are no longer any "masters." *The shameful truth, however, is that America now incarcerates a greater percentage of its populace than any other nation—retaining a quasi-slave class.* We are socially and culturally repressed, like 19th century slaves were, and the message of this book is not about being more repressed through external stuff. My arguments are *not* focused here on our civic policy.

There are many directions one could take in a response to these issues but, the message here is on becoming open souls. My message is about our human collective's healing—our social healing through our individual responsibility—to not be blind to our condition, abdicating our personal sovereignty; for, it is not wise to yield discretion to the powerful whom *we place* over us. Becoming open souls takes us in the opposite direction from the way by which we all got here: Away from all the rules—*Transcending Institutional Seduction and Cultural Rape.*

Thus, this book's purpose is a soulful revolution against what I herein label as Institutional Seduction and Cultural Rape. It promotes a social revolution against how we Americans respond to our inter-ethnic human vulnerabilities: inter-culturally, inter-racially and also between America's diverse sexual orientations. This book opens a gate by its anticipation of inter-ethnic reconciliation. This way envisions the end of our present human condition and, demands a critical mass of opening souls because this end requires massive social change.

But, more important than the apparent politics of my choices that led up to how I perceive the world today, is my conviction that our urgent need is to increase in personal honesty and personal compassion. However, I do not write here about the very politicized 2000 and 2004 Elections' "compassion" that, felt more like only a mere sentimentality but, rather, I write of an *active* compassion, which I define as *empathy rooted in seeing our Others as manifestations of ourselves*. The kind of compassion that I refer to is about *extending one's* individual or, one's own personal *Self-Identity*.

A magnified Self-Identity is that wonderful phenomenon that we all experienced as the global community of nations manifested a universal compassion after those ugly attacks of September 11, 2001. Our National Anthem being played by the official guard of the Queen of England is only one of many examples of *humane acts* that were bred of a truly global empathic response to our terrorist induced distress. It was but, one example among many of non-Americans extending their Self-Identity to also include those beyond their own particular group.

Again, as is the macrocosm, so is the microcosm. If we are to heal from our present condition as a society then, the most critical place to which we must arrive is one where all divergent cultures find ways to be in chordant harmony with one another. The lesson of September 11, 2001 *is* that America *is* an idea, but also that, *America is not an idea about uni-cultural constructs*. My own subsequent experience reveals how I responded also, as an individual. So, in my own microcosm—or, what I herein call "how I experienced the experience"—there is a far healthier place where my personal odyssey has brought me to than, when I walked among the ordained. I now sing out the *beingness* of all whose sacred ways are *not* ways that I hold dear. I have even recently commended the work of some proselytizing elders of my former faith!

Moreover, I no longer feel any of my former religious duty or, compulsion, to change who, how, what or, even *whether* another human being worships. This fact, *itself*, speaks volumes about the difference between how I am today and how I was when I officiated at holy temple altars, which are sacred to my former community. Vested with the most highly revered L.D.S. Sealing Power of Elijiah, the Temple Patriarchal Priesthood, I ministered in my former faith community's holiest and most sacred inner Temple chambers. Yet, having high priestly power that only the President of the entire Mormon Church bestows on any, did not give me the spiritual tools to envision as I can today. In those days, I could not fully respect any non-Mormon truth because—as it is with all closed communities—my programming had me appreciating only L.D.S. Mormon doctrine and policy as *the only* "fullness of truth."

So, I followed another way by abandoning all of my acquired institutional power. In fact, the word "power" since then, became an ugly word to me. Today, I try to value equity with my peers. Globally and inter-personally, I try to value the equality of all who disagree with me either in their religious views or in their ways of inter-relating with Queer people like me. I have come to understand that, *I exist only as I inter-relate honestly with my natural environment, including all others.* Moreover, I know that, as each human soul exists, there is also a unique *mass soul* for every kind of relationship that exists. Through the many stories in this book, I endeavor to show that—in the historical case of an American *mass soul*—our cultural flaw is that today's upwardly-mobile classes link status with having power-over others who are actual *peers.* This is a mark of a classically adolescent behavior, and thus, *Becoming Open Souls* discusses America's presently adolescent, *mass soul.*

For example: The problem of guns in 21st century American society is not the guns themselves. It is that we behave like adolescents. In light of what we understand about the human Mass Mind's part in the creative process in this scientific age, *the key problem about guns is our popular culture of power over peers.* Moreover, foreign terrorist acts are a symptom of this same problem on a global level of inter-cultural domination. In this light, September 11, 2001 was the classic clashing of two incompatible worldviews. Here, again however, *the problem is the same inherited arcane culture of power over actual peers.* On the personal, neighborhood, city, state or global level, the problem is the same inherited cultural bent to seek power over actual peers. Hopefully the stories in this book show how the seeking of power over peers, is an inherited problem of modern civilization and that, all modern terrorism is created by this single, basic social problem.

Thus, this book deals with terrorism. It is about what is rooted in all kinds and types of fundamentalist religious cultures. I frankly tell how I experienced a closed, rigid, religious community that creates its *own* zealots. By using my experiences as an example, I trust that the reader may better appreciate who we each are, individually, in a union of diverse cultures. I also trust that the telling of these stories reveals why, with the advent of today's global communications, we suddenly seem to have now become a violent society. Even before September 11, 2001, how often had we all heard it said, "This isn't the America I knew as a child!" This response is common, and my solution to our present condition is rooted in America's social reaction—in our making of our *One mass soul—by our collective response to the now.*

I affirm that, it is by our individual choices that we make soul as we *live* the journey. I affirm that, the emotional and social soul-place of which I speak, is a deeply personal place; a place somewhere beyond all our, respective, bounded social and/or ethnic groupings. This book is about how one man is approaching the song of light, equality, peace and love: Where emotions sound out peacefully, chordant vibrations of harmony. It tells how I experienced the experiences of the final decade of the last century, in a retrospective mind-set that was impregnated by the ancient tradition of my Indian ancestors, as I researched my 17th and 18th century *Californio* ancestors' lives in the 1990s.

Half of my ancestors on my maternal line are known by most as the ancient *Aztec* people of what is now Mexico. The correct spelling of our ancient name is "*Mexica*;" which is pronounced, "Mae-SHEE-ka." The spelling used in this book is "*Meshica*" because I have found that the "*sh*" best allows most English readers to pronounce it correctly. I prefer to have those who read this book, correctly pronounce the "*x*" in this ancient name of my maternal ancestors rather than, to simply read the correct spelling. I suppose my life-long experience in chronicling oral histories produced in me, a need for the written word to be read, when possible, as it's truly spoken. This personal proclivity is probably rooted in a weighted *Meshica/Toltec* worldview, which thankfully, I gained in 1990 from a small band of six Indian families in Mexico.

Before continuing, I should also explain my use of some of the Mormon references at the end of every chapter. Most readers are only familiar with the Utah based Mormon Church, The Church of Jesus Christ of Latter-day Saints. But, there are many smaller denominations descending from the founder of Mormonism—Joseph Smith, Junior. For example, the second largest group is Community of Christ, which since the 1860s, is headquartered in Independence, MO. So in notes, at the end of each chapter, which reference particular scriptures common to both, or to other religious groups, the Utah-based L.D.S. version is the one usually referenced in the notes. Books and chapters are noted for common biblical references.

It should also be noted that—although, this book is made from many personal stories from my daily journals—each of the chapters is written around or about a specific theme. My purpose is not so much to write an auto-biography or a memoir as, it is to use the stories to try to communicate teachings on becoming open souls, as I received them from a *Meshica/Toltec* wise man in 1990. Yet, as with the stories told in Chapter One, "The Seduction," within each particular chapter, my stories are most often told in chronological order. So, while most stories are related in the true chronological order of how they actually took place, in order to define and affirm key themes about the way of becoming open souls, all stories told herein are not necessarily in chronological order. However, in most cases, I have tried to provide the year in which each story took place.

So, finally, I herein tell how I've experienced the experience of being in America's mainstream in ways that produced an awareness in me of my own personal need for a healing. For, as with many books of other writers, this book began as a therapeutic exercise designed for my own healing. Thus, as a result, I herein tell how my *Meshica,* and the more ancient *Toltec* tradition, both nurtured my own healing because I had experienced America as an invasive experience by an alien people on our ancestral land.

In a humility born of sixty years of life, I acknowledge that the ideas, thoughts and concepts to which I refer in this book are old, and they are not uniquely my own. I am not—nor, in any way, do I claim to be—their author. What I *do* affirm and, do claim to be the sole creator of is the *contexts* of those ideas, thoughts and concepts. For what *is* uniquely mine that *I* bring to the discussion of these notions, is how *I* experienced the experiences that brought them into my life's journey. I take full ownership *of these contexts* of those old points of view—the stories I tell herein—for, *how* I experienced the experiences that taught the teachings to me *were* my own creation. My hope is that, by a telling of these true stories, I open the gate for you to the way I now try to go on. This is the way for us all to transcend our cultural and, ethnic barriers. It is the way leading us toward *Becoming Open Souls*.

> —Antonio A. Feliz
> Summer Solstice, 2004
> *Earth's Cyclical High Point of Natural Light*

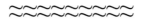

"However, for the purposes of this book, the cosmic body to which I refer is what I am here calling our society. The key is that, as a society—as it is on any level—a spiritual healing is now needed for us to fight off the effects of our vast, institutionalized religious abuse; for, an abuse of religion is the core cause of terrorism. Indeed, it is the cause of Osama bin Laden's terrorism..."

INTRODUCTION

WHAT IS AN OPEN SOUL?

Over the centuries, there have been many that have traveled the path of becoming open souls. Each, in turn, did so because they had also become aware of massive moral problems that confronted their personal integrity. Buddha, Moses, Jesus and Mohammed are the most honored of the ones whose own experiences on this one path evolved into sacred stories. Yet, my premise is that not only were *these* opening souls called to travel this path to respond to humanity's moral problems, but each of us is also called to deal with *our* moral issues. This book is about that universal call to a higher morality.

Our great moral problem today is that our culture is founded in a Christian tradition of religious fundamentalism, which was derived from *purist* ideals. I affirm that religious fundamentalism, *per se,* is America's most urgent moral polemic and that, moral issues do obscure any nation's domestic politics. For example: In its September 20, 2001 edition, the New York Times actually labeled the leaders of America's Religious Right as, "America's Taliban." Specific reference was made in the piece to comments by the Rev. Jerry Falwell—to which Pat Robertson said on national television, "I concur"—in which Falwell had blamed the September 11, 2001 attacks on: "Pagans, Feminists, Lesbians, Gays and the Civil Liberties Union…," among others. These anti-feminists' harsh words exemplify the clouded reasoning into which fundamentalist views will take, otherwise, highly educated and moral Americans. It is the dark mists of reasoning that, I call a purist's cultural *tribalism.* Our social psychologists term this dynamic, "*xenophobia.*"

Our domestic xenophobia stems from our public policy that is impacted by the Religious Right, a public policy, that has not yet caught up with the written vision of our national foundational documents. In spite of those charters of freedom, America remains a classist society, complete with our "aristocratic" elite and those still seen as, "unclean," by some. Our world was created by the ways that we inherited to see our others, and *that* lack of sight obstructs our vision of our peers.

So, I ask: Is this why, in the aftermath of September 11, 2001, a little girl told ABC News' Peter Jennings: "Maybe we're just getting our own medicine?" Perhaps, she was thinking of the fact that, other than poverty dynamics in *foreign* constructs revealed in the reasoning of the September 11, 2001 terrorists, these dynamics equally impact Americans *from within us*. For example: In The Kindness of Strangers, the late Dr. John Boswell informed us that our city streets are as densely populated with the homeless as were the streets of 17th century medieval Europe. As in some nation states in South America, the throw-aways of America now include the teenage classes, many of whom don't go home at night because of a "religiously motivated in-hospitality" stemming from their biological families. Americans seem to behave as if we were blind to the pained condition existing in our adolescent population. So, I ask whether we are, therefore, blind to similar conditions in global populations? *Our ethics—the social truths of our day—are in question.* Is our culture now so ethno-centric that, as a national consciousness, we are blind to the greater reality around us?

The above is not only a secular question. This behavior toward any whose ways are considered unholy by us, are equally significant to all fundamentalists; to all Bible-based Christians, to all Koran-based Moslems, to all ultra-orthodox Jews and to all who follow a literal view of their canon. They are equally important to anyone raised in a home in which a strict religious standard on external purity prevailed, where things sacred are always taught in the most literal interpretations of the collective's laws. Others, who might come from less fundamentalist environments, also find these issues significant. For example, social anthropologists note that our American history of civic polarization has never gone away since the beginning of American slavery. Historically, American social polarization has always remained under the surface, like the iceberg that destroyed the *Titanic*.

While September 11, 2001 did produce a renewed American *soul mass*, the context of the stories in this book is our polarized society. As this book's manuscript began to flow, America felt far more united than at other times in over a half-century of my life, as an American. Yet, it is because I do remember the journey that got us all to this place that, I can affirm that, *historically, we've always been socially polarized as a society*. The historical polarization of our society is like any open wound that needs a healing, and exposure to the light of day is a proven remedy for an infection by promoting a disinfectant process. Like any damaged tissue, all of America must be emotionally cleansed in order for our humanity—our wholeness—to return.

But, most remedies usually bring pain when they are begun and—much like it's already been for us all on a national level in the wake of September 11, 2001—that is why it may be difficult for some to read on. But, know that my purpose is not to be unjust here nor, is it to offend the devout. Simply put, I espouse honesty; thus, here, *I* must be honest. So, if conflict arises out of what is written here then, please consider it a part of my healing process, for, my writing *washes my woundedness*.

The point on which to agree is that, today's human condition is a complex sickness of our collective heart—our soul mass. And, holiness (among other things) to us, is about our concept of "heart" because the heart is culturally seen by most Americans as the vortex of our human soul. The popularization of this affect imagery—of a human heart—in today's America makes the heart symbolize our inner selves to our *mass soul*. The concept of "heart" reminds most of us that, the true nature of each human creature is so intricate and mysterious that the physical body's emotional responses, alone, haven't been exhaustively explored. So, irrespective of one's personal ethnicity, most Americans can agree on this "heart" metaphor.

The metaphor of our individual physical heart is totally clear to our Mass Mind because we all perceive ourselves as highly complex beings. Because like a heart we *are* so complex that we can accept our inward journey toward becoming open souls as one, not to be confined by mere *external* rules. No, the modern notion of "heart" is warmly intuitive, rather than being coldly logical. The hard strictures of any bounded social culture that are external to the human soul have no positive effect on modern Americans because we are much more multi-cultural now; we're far more complex than any bounded culture can contain within its external fences.

To most of us, human holiness does not demand pure *behavior* anymore. To us, behavior is an external phenomenon; it only *partially* reflects inner human reality. Indeed, in many metaphysical systems, the heart is understood as the center of much more—as the *core* of the soul—and as such, it manifests the way in which purity seekers must journey: *Inward*, away from the mere external, and into the soul's *core*. There is a metaphor in the design of the human heart to which I refer here, because this central vital organ is a series of chambers that are, themselves, also within chambers. This complexity in our individual physical body speaks volumes to us about our mental, emotional and spiritual natures, which are much more subtle to many of us than is the physical body. For example:

As an innocent, little, Mormon boy who's worldview had not yet been tarnished by exposure to the culture in which I was developing,

I would hear the charge to approach God with "a broken heart..."[iv] As a result, in those days, I often had a question in my mind that remained unanswered by adults: *Why should approaching the Father in Heaven require a "broken heart?"* As is the case with all true innocence, in my child's way of experiencing the experience of living, my heart was still open. I did not yet need a healing from the separateness of an acquired culture. My soul had not yet been closed off by the blockage of early imprinting. In those early days of innocence, the notion of breaking open the center of my physical being felt anachronistic to me. It did not compute for me because, at that point in my developing life, I had no experience yet to relate with such an idea. Being an innocent, my life journey hadn't exposed me to the conflicts that block us up as we live.

So, I affirm: The truly natural human state is one of a dynamic openness, that our nature is to be open souls, and that one's individual soul may be best described like Gary Zukav describes human beings as "vessels of energy in which transmutation takes place." *We are each, literally, vessels of transmutation because as physicists confirm to us today, everything, all things are in vibration.* Gary Zukav writes that, on the physical plane, the human heart truly is, "The Seat of the Soul." He explains that this is because, on the plane "of more refined light," the "energy vortex" that processes a dynamic flow of "universal energy and intelligence, occupies the same cosmic space" as does the human heart. However, for us to see ourselves in these cosmic terms naturally brings up the problems that are associated with language, itself.

One of the core issues in the polarization of a pluralistic society derives from the cultural roots of language. For example, the language of the ancients who originally wrote of a need to be "broken in heart," was not efficient for universal communication in today's modern world. This phrase, "a broken heart,"[vi] –in my opinion– would better translate into "an *open* heart." When any vessel is broken, it *becomes* opened, and if the seat of the soul is open, it is not limited by culturally rooted illusions of a self-concept. When the soul is open then, it is capable of attunement with the rhythm of All Eternity! All boundaries are gone!

Moreover, for the purpose of relating the stories that I tell in the following pages, the operating definition of the complete human soul is inclusive of the physical body of flesh, bones and blood. Additionally, *the whole of the human soul is energy manifesting in multi-dimensional space.* This is modern physics! The human body, therefore, is only one aspect of what is here called a human soul. In other words, the complete human soul *is our creation.* It's also composed of matter that is the stuff of more than merely our three dimensional plane of awareness. Yet, it is *not* other than the body like the spirit but, rather, the soul *includes* our environment, our individual and inter-relationship memories because, as modern physics teaches today, *all physical matter* is, "in vibration."

Additionally, all our physical bodies are also a part of another living organism and, that other living, intelligent organism is the planet. Our bodies, which are all made of flesh, bones and blood, are to Earth, what all single human cells are to a physical human body. Dr. Michael Guillen, of ABC News, reported on March 8, 2001, "...DNA molecules tend to disassemble relatively soon after death in all animals..." To me, this is clear evidence that, we each *are* the planet—that we are, *literally*, the Earth,—whether we agree to this idea or not. And, if we are to Earth what single human cells are to physical bodies then, like the metabolic processes that these single cells carry on in the human body then, is a metabolic dynamic in operation on the soul mass level of humans also? Affirming this theory, I say it has implications for becoming open souls.

A book on becoming open souls infers that, we—as vessels of transmutation of our planet—are blocked; for, some souls are closed or blocked, in other words, *not open*. This infers they are unhappy and/or without joy. Yet, Tibetan Buddhists understand that our life purpose is to be happy. In like fashion, Mormon history teaches me that the first Mormon prophet wrote that we each exist that we "might have joy."[viii] Indeed, what we commonly label the human spirit is that pure, pulsating energy that is felt by us in this world when we say that, we "...*feel* Love."

But, usually, our spirits *visually* manifest in our common three-dimensional reality as if being only one of several multi-dimensional phenomena, which for the lack of a better term, may also be called a humanoid shaped body of light.[ix] In new age traditions, they are given other names, yet, they are seen as humanoid forms of light. Others say spirits manifest as small lights. The point is that, on this plane, knowing our reality processes through physical senses, retarding the *probability* of seeing our spirits—our humanoid light forms—naturally.

The circumstance of our common condition inhibits the human personality from being aware of the fact that the physical body has its *equivalent* elsewhere. However, this book affirms that we *are* each energy systems—that, everything is in vibration, including us humans. Awareness of the other dimensions of our existence is attained through intuitive, cognitive processes which occur in the profoundest reaches of soul-space. For some blessed souls, this soulful awareness comes most easily during acts of lovemaking because making love is the sharing of human energy.

But, whatever the tool which may be used by us, intuitive and cognitive processes often enable us to be aware of realities not known through only our limited physical senses. As a result, our body of flesh, bones and blood knows its own connection to Eternity best when it gets in sync. with all of the energies and intelligence in all of nature. This is because our physical bodies are also a part of nature; they are each part of the living organism we call Earth. This wisdom of nature-centered peoples adds light to the wisdom most of us inherited from societies from other parts of the planet. For example, in America's Indigenous traditions, *all* earth-forms are as alive as we are! To us, all that is, is spirit—including unacknowledged siblings; whom the ancient people of the Americas know include all vegetation and all non-human animal forms and, *everything else, also.*

Moreover, besides being composed of spirit, humans are also beings of mind. Readers should know that, in this book, Mind-space is not a spirit place, but, it does occupy space. Mind has a location in inner space. But, Mind is probably the least and, likewise, the most discussed of the three dimensions of existence to which I refer in this book. Least discussed, in that when one experiences the experience of life, words become so inefficient that, communication through language is limited. Except for those of the diverse fine arts, Mind is most discussed by us, in that Mind is usually manifest in the dimension of the natural world that is common to all of us through spoken and written *language*. The problem prohibiting our efficient communion mainly through human language is that modern languages are culturally based. But, because all sacred stories are "the mortar" that holds each culture together, the major religions of civilization are the arbiters of conduct and thought.

As a result, in Mind-space, we all each perceive reality through encoded messages that originate external to us. In Mind-space, all the decoding of messages takes place by the use of our inherited imagery. But, all language is a system of symbols, the product of culture and, as such, language also impacts the constant dynamic that any culture is.

The result is that, as a medium of manifesting Mind, language lacks the integrity to fully manifest thought forms –which are original to the world of memory– in our common natural world, where we inter-relate as physical beings. Personality is, therefore, the result of Mind, and Zukav has taught that our purpose in life is to "align the personality to the soul." I'll add that, if alignment with spirit is the goal on the personal level then, alignment is the purpose of societies as well. But, *in the world of Mind, we are no more equal than our earliest imprinting allows.* If we are to align our mass personality with the mass spirit then, all culture must be transcended by each of us before any connection can make an authentic integrated mass being out of us, as a collective.

Thankfully, for us as thinking Earth beings, an awareness of our person's independent nature is the starting point. It is perceived as a need for unification with all that is. Unfortunately, *in Mind-space, all that is, is limited to individual bounded cultural limits.* Like our body of flesh, bones and blood is driven to get "in-sync.-with" all of the energies of all of nature, so also does Mind also seek to be in-sync.-with all that is Mind. Moreover, Mind is another way of understanding others, who are also Mind because the observing human Mind will perceive itself to be a separate and distinct entity. Otherwise, there is no observer to observe that which is other. Naturally, those with whom one is first programmed –our individual family, cultural group, etc.– will allow for a maximum comfort level—emotionally—as we each, individually, experience the universal life experience. In Mind-space, affinity is determined by our early cultural imprinting. In that world, the culture into which we were each born is what rules our reality. It determines all our automatic affinities; it creates default dynamics.

It is no accident that human inter-relating with one another is termed by us as, "*social intercourse.*" Indeed, although language isn't capable of fully expressing thought forms in our common more grossly composed dimension, like fish swimming upstream to spawn, we all engage in efforts to communicate through this medium because of our universal, innate drive to unify with the rhythm of all that is other. On some profound level, we crave identity with all that is. As creatures of Mind-space, we all seek union with our other Mind-space beings, to one degree or another, through what we call, "social intercourse," and this process takes place within a field of consciousness.

In other words, mental processes are in a context. Because of our initial cultural imprinting of how to understand our reality, in the dimension of Mind-space, each of us are, literally, unique worlds of independent truths. Moreover, in that dimension, each of us is actively independent; we are each *active Intelligences.* There, we each act only for *ourselves.* This is the reason why I use the phrase "experiencing the experience" throughout this volume. The universal experience, which is common to us all, is not the same experience in any two of our cases *because we humans are each unique worlds of independent truths who act intelligently, i.e.: we are each, individually active, Intelligences.*

This concept is crucial. We are each like little, single birds flying in formation with our peer life forms. Fortunately, the initial awareness of knowing human separateness –as our very nature– is an initial beginning of the healing process for the human soul because, that is what wounds in need of healing do; they separate what once was whole. America's spirit mass, for example, received such a violent wound on September 11, 2001 that our domestic crime rate thereafter, dramatically dropped. We each got in formation. Our *mass* recoiled in our common, horrific pain. Our national cohesion suddenly became a far tighter fabric than before. For, as it is with any healing, America's healing could begin only when we understood ourselves as wounded.

America began to heal on September 11, 2001 and, this volume is my sacred medicine to our present common wound. As it is with all open wounds, being separate from all that is in order to observe it; our mass personality's nature, as an observing Mind, will eventually reveal a breach in the observing human cosmic body. Likewise, on the level of our national *Mass Mind*, we suddenly became aware of our oneness again and, that holy awareness allowed us to begin to heal our polarized society. For the purposes of this book then, the cosmic body to which I refer is what I am calling our society. The key is that, as a society—as it is on any level—a spiritual healing is now needed for us to fight off the effects of our vast, institutionalized religious abuse; for, religious abuse is the core cause of what today terrorizes America. Indeed, it is the cause of Osama bin Laden's brand of terrorism.

The point is that none of us is born into a vacuum. For each of us, life is designed in such a way that, it insures that we are all born into a religious/philosophical system that interprets who and what we each are. In itself, this is not bad or evil, it is simply the reality of our cultural imprinting during the development stage of our programming for our future adult life. Both our religious, and cultural systems are composed of sacred stories that are the mortar that holds the bricks of our cultural edifices *together*.[xi] All these provide form and texture for the illusion, which we know today as our individual reality. Religious abuse always happens when the individual is not allowed to manifest his or herself, and is also replaced by an imprinted personality exclusively patterned after one's religious or philosophical social culture. This is the stark stuff of an external imprinting—usually in the early part of the journey of one's life—and, it is the common obstacle of all bounded Minds.

This is why most cultural systems are bounded societies. That is to say, they are closed off from their "Other." This is because bounded human societies gain group cohesion and definition by differentiating their group from their "Other." Thus, by definition, bounded societies are exclusive in nature, not inclusive and –because no cultural system is strictly universal– sooner or later, systems must deal with persons who do not fit the norm of the group because, all creation is relative. That is the condition offered to us by our innate human free will. Thankfully, free will allows for personalities to evolve, including a collective one.

Yet, since human beings are all driven to inter-relate and unify with all that is, a cultural system will have not only those who conform to its social rules but, also the non-conformists who endeavor to extend themselves beyond their bounded society. The former; self-identify with only their "first estate" while the latter; self-identify with far more than only their "first estate." Whether the group's non-conformists are considered by its mainstream as being on its fringe, will usually be determined by the degree to which the group celebrates diversity. This dynamic will largely determine how an individual human soul develops within all religious/philosophical systems.

For example, the more closed a society is, the more those living on its defined fringe will be socialized into being closed souls –racked with energy blockage in their finer body of light– filled with the pain and suffering of shame and guilt in their Mind and memory. On the human personal level, finally, the effects of shame and guilt will, in this way, result in a mass decomposition of the individual, fleshy body until, eventually, death overcomes us. Unfortunately, this is how we are.

The problem is our Cartesian Minds. It is a common notion in our civilization to see one's self as *observer and knower* of the world. I am suggesting that the Cartesian reality into which most of us were each, respectively, born in modern society is an acquired illusion to which we must each die in order to allow the body, itself, to more effectively avoid the inevitable onslaught of earthly disease and death discussed above. I also affirm that this rebirth amounts to a new way to envision because being born anew is, actually, the death of reality as one has known it so far. The death of the Cartesian illusion becomes the necessary process for the generation of any new life within the same human soul. This has been, at least, how I experienced the experience.

So I affirm that, this was the call of the biblical Jesus figure of Christian tradition. It is recorded as the conversation between Jesus and the Levite Priest, Nicodemus in the Christian Gospel. At the root of the call to be born of the Spirit, is to be as the "wind" that "goeth where it listeth…" to be the soup, of which –in the non-Cartesian worldview– we each are, collectively. This is in sharp contrast to the Cartesian view that we are all apart and separate, and merely *observing* the soup of life. To become as the "wind," we must first reject notions of reality to which we have all been socialized. The call of Jesus is a challenge to "…be as *little* children," to return to the way that all, yet, un-socialized human beings view the world. *To be reborn is, therefore, to be deprogrammed.*

In the perspective discussed in this book, therefore, the call of Jesus is to eschew our cultural conformity—His call is to transcend our domestication. For example: Elsewhere, Jesus is recorded to have rejected the *cultural* definition of family, which was most *predominant* in his own time and society, and still is in our own.[xiii] This call to non-conformity is, thus, a call to take courage because the opposite of any external conformity, within a cultural system, is a call to courageous action. I am suggesting that the call to be "born again" in the religious tradition of my own cultural upbringing, is a hidden call for us all to be delivered from the *dominant* worldview of our civilization. This is because the ways in which we each picture or, envision our world to be, and our individual and collective relationship to it and to each other, are our worldviews and, as stated above, we are each unique, active and independent worlds. So, significantly, one's personal worldview is one's pattern for living one's life.

This understanding—that, our worldviews *are* our pattern for living life—is crucial for anyone who desires to journey on the way of becoming open souls. I am now convinced that the reason for the call of Jesus, in the above metaphor of Nicodemus to seek a total rebirthing, is because there is a profound relationship between how we each see the world is and, what we do as individuals and societies. Our choices and worldviews seem to be inseparable, as if our inherited worldview is our script for the play of life, assigning each of us our role in it. In theatrical terms then, it directs all the "blocking"—the *business*—which, we, the players do on life's stage.

Ultimately, considering our innate, natural, human drive to commune with all that is –as a body, mind and spirit– our current ways of seeing reality are toxic to one another in that cultural worldviews are tribal in nature. All formative imprinting is about "us and them." Thus, all of our, respective, sacred stories are each culture-centric. Although today's multi-cultural world includes many symbols which can often be found in the vast majority of the diverse societies of the world, all these symbols are seen –are envisioned– by us according to only the cultural light which comes via each culturally programmed pair of human eyes. Yet, *these inherited symbols rule our every choice*. Whether we are aware of it, or not, our inherited affect imagery rules our inter-personal activities. In this awareness, it is no wonder why our common world is filled with such distrust, deception, division and derision. All of our common inherited imagery is violent stuff.

Our sacred stories, like our rituals, are ideas; cosmic concepts which are culturally impregnated and because of that, these stories seen by some as history, are only metaphor. The cutting is precise; it is that the context of a sacred story is a tribal worldview and, sadly, this means that, although the reference of the metaphor is universal, the context —or the external stuff—its interpretation changes from group to group. The photographs at the end of *Becoming Open Souls* are an example of this dynamic. Taking metaphor literally is why we each consider the same canon differently. What I endeavor to demonstrate is the healing balm that truth is not in our inherited imagery; but, rather, *truth is the hidden reference* of sacred stories. Inherited imagery is cultural. Only its *reference* is universal. A universal way of seeing transcends all the boundaries of culture, time and space; it's a key to becoming open souls.

Truth is attainable if one does as Jesus is recorded as saying: "leave father, mother, family..."[xiv] This refers to *culture*! It is *Culture* that must be left in order to go on the journey within; for, all the holy ones of history have counseled that the "kingdom of God is within..." *This* is why mystics of all societies begin their journey by going within, first. In the cases of Moses and Jesus, the metaphor was a desert but, they still left "father, mother, family," etc. *first*. Then, their universal mission was possible because, with a broken heart –with an *opened* soul– they were then, each ready to change their, respective, legendary reality. Thus, the hidden truth –the non-literal reference– is that, it is no different for any of us who today endeavor to journey on the way of becoming open souls. We are each called to "leave father, mother...!"

So, what was the significance of the awesome unity we gained after September 11, 2001? Well, elsewhere I have said that the greatest "...domestic enemies to America's increasingly diverse, democratic society are racism and sexism, including heterosexism. Racism, sexism and heterosexism are, actually, all issues of social classism."[xv] But, in my youth all around me, the symbols of our American society said to me: "Why, this is *America*, where we know that all of us are created equal. This isn't India! We're not a *class* society. Not *here*, this is *America*." My earliest mentors had, dutifully, inculcated me with their own vision of our nation's reality and sadly, as a result, I have since discovered that my envisioning was limited by their denial of truth.

So to me, the fantastic lesson from September 11, 2001 lies in hindsight. It was in my later life, when I came to know that our nation is, after all, a highly stratified society ranked into the exploited and into the exploiting classes. It was decades before I learned that issues of class are factors, which together with a few others, are at the root of all that is keeping the much promised millennium of peace, equity, love and justice from becoming our true, acknowledged, reality. The sad historical fact is that our present has always been true. Historically, Americans have never embraced our civilization's truth in our entire history, except in times of attack from *outside* of us! That truth which we deny is that, America *is not composed of only one culture and, specifically, America never has been a uni-cultural nation state.* No matter how much dominant groups tried to enforce their mainstream worldview onto the rest of us, their actions never changed the truth of America's true multi-cultural, multi-moral and multi-ethnic historical nature. Unicultural is *not* what America is, or was! In America, the Revolutionary War for Independence did not end when the cannons and muskets were silenced.

That 18th century war is still being waged. There have always been Americans who've been forced to make war for an independence. In effect, the 18th century Revolutionary War has continued on from the privileged Anglo-Saxon propertied males through an enslaved African community in our Civil War times and then, later, in the subsequent 20th century civil rights movement. In the current century, other groups are still at war for their own true independence from the tyranny of a non-empathic majority, as Americans "equal under the law." Our voting franchise is no longer the only issue for which we still struggle.

Today, the American Gay, Lesbian, Bi-sexual, Trans-gendered and Inter-sexed community is one of the recent groups in America's War for Independence. These Americans declare their independence from the arcane cultural norms of civil marriage that, even today, have the effect of disenfranchising them, insofar as their human right to have spousal relationships civilly recorded in an equitable system to civil marriage. After all, civil marriage was originally established in ancient times as a simple legal device to govern how real property was to be dispersed on the demise of the landholder. If there was no real estate to consider on the demise of a spouse then, why have any civil marriage? Marriage was then, only for nobility in Europe, from whence America's jurisprudence comes and, there was also a time when race determined whether anyone was granted civil marriage licensure here in America. Thankfully, however, Emancipation eventually did change that one delinquency of our American sense of political pluralism.^{xvi} Yet, many families in society still do not have access to an equivalent system to have their honest familial relationships recorded in our most permanent civil records. So, Revolution remains part of the American experience.

The point is that, as a nation, America is and it always has been multi-ethnic, multi-moral and multi-cultural. But, since beginning this democracy, inherited biases have been dominated by our monolithic hierarchy of cultures. Today's wisdom, however, can no longer afford to point to old monolithic ways of our inter-relating among ourselves. The great lesson from September 11, 2001 is: *America can no longer sustain the illusion of its feigned uni-culturalism.* Just as our citizenry is composed of souls who, respectively, view their other as being in a different class from their own; conversely, each of us is also in a class of society which is seen as alien to the other. In our 21st century global village—to one group, or to another—we are each seen as being the:

Infidel, gentile, sinner, unsaved, wicked, dirty, racially inferior, rag-head, bitch, bastard, faggot, queer or—as a Queer friend of mine sadly refers to mainstream, middle class families—"breeders." Indeed, none of these labels are terms of endearment.

Yet, the horrible truth is that these terms are used by some of us in reference to others of us. When we view ourselves from within the encasement of our various bounded social cultures, we see our equals as if being in another class of what is –for all practical purposes– an ugly American caste system which, is centered more in cultural values than in the pure economics of traditional class divisions. But, America is simply far too culturally diverse today for us to keep up this illusion of *uni-culturalism* by allowing ourselves to be dominated by that old, monolithic, hierarchy of cultures. This book is my contribution against the horrors that result from this ugliness in how we often treat those different from ourselves—horrors such as one briefly described below:

In late 1984, I put a young man on a bus back to Kansas City so he could return to his family. Jerry had insisted on going with me when I'd returned to California. As it turned out, in the few months we lived together, Mom met him and actually approved by saying, "*Mijo*, I can see that you love each other in the same way I have also loved." But, I'd helped him to see that returning to his family was best for him because he'd come home one night from his job covered with blood. He'd just escaped with his life from an attacker who'd decided Jerry merited to be executed. During our last night together, he had written "Jerry Howell, K.C., M.O." in wet concrete that had been freshly set that day outside of the Los Angeles County Courthouse—as if to create a kind of marker to attest to having, actually, been alive. Tragically, two weeks thereafter, his father sent me a copy of the front page of the Kansas City Star. The story reported how my sweet Jerry had been discovered in the bushes of the Kansas City World Wars Memorial—in pieces. His body had been cut into pieces. Jerry was executed by hatred. My sweet Jerry and the victims of September 11, 2001, not only all lost their lives to hatred, but they lost the freedom to be who and what they were meant to become.

Yes, America has a long way to go. Yet, as a citizen of these United States of America, I have claim to a national doctrine and civic mythology that invokes the promised millennium of equality, peace and harmony as our true national domestic dream, and as a global goal. Significantly, "Mark Bingham, of San Francisco…" was one of the heroes on the hijacked jet that passengers kept from our Capitol with Congress in session. Mark was a man who's own gay identity was well known to his San Francisco gay community; yet, the media did not *initially* report that this national hero was a man to whom being gay was extremely important to his own self-identity. It wasn't mentioned when the media first reported that he'd had a major part in saving the lives of Congress assembled in Washington, D.C. Yet, had his sudden tragic and posthumous celebrity been because of an accusation of some sexual impropriety then, the reports would have read: "Mark Bingham, *a Gay man* from San Francisco...!" In this 2001 climate, Utah's Alliance For Unity also got organized to do good but then, it went on to omit inviting any Utah representatives from the state's sexual minority community. Why? Sexual minorities are also a "Utah community." In fact, the Utah GLBT community *has their institutions*, including their own churches!

So, I say: Read the *"language of beingness."* Read what people and institutions *do*. Don't believe the spin put out by public relations spokes people—especially when it contradicts *what is being done*, for what is done speaks in the "language of *beingness*." Don't forget what originally got us to this place of our separateness. Open your evolving vision to all of our past injustices. Start to envision with the perception of more than just the place from where you, historically, reckoned. Then, change any behavior which is seen by your true cultural equals as oppressive to them. My aim is to awaken each reader to see that your *Other* is, actually, *Yourself.*

****

Some may ask: Why should a former Mormon ecclesiast write such a book? Simply put; I understand how a closed community works and, that knowledge is now critical to our common survival of not only foreign terrorists but, of also what I herein call, America's "nice boy massacres." To use the example of guns in our society again, the one common factor involved in every violent terrorist event, which we have all had to experience in recent times, is the "under siege" consciousness of any closed, religiously fundamentalist community. I've known this mind set from within the inner circles of my former faith community as well as from far outside of it. Why is such experience valuable?

Understanding Mormons is important to the rest of us because the Mormon hierarchy works hard at understanding the rest of us. As it is with all seeking to persuade us, Utah based Mormons see the rest of us as their market. But, most observers don't comprehend this about the Mass Mind of this hierarchy, yet, *that* focus is what differentiates this Utah based religious group from even the second largest descendant institution that claims Joseph Smith, Junior as its own first prophet/president. The second largest group is Independence, Missouri based Community of Christ, which, is also led by a prophet/president and his two counselors in what is also called their First Presidency. But, the Community of Christ prophet/president is neither, theologically, nor is he, historically, a member of this group's Council of Twelve Apostles. Conversely, the mentality of the Utah based L.D.S. Church leadership is born out of the reality that this Utah based group is led by what is—for all practical purposes—its *chief corporate sales division.* The Twelve Apostles of this Utah hierarchy is its supreme authority. This Council of The Twelve is a self-perpetuating body which, is the group that oversees all global proselytizing work of their community. Moreover, this Utah based body is headed by its chronologically most senior member, the President of Twelve Apostles—who, theologically and historically, has always become the next President of The Church upon the demise of their prophet/president. Traditionally, their new President of The Church, picks counselors to jointly serve with him as their successor Mormon First Presidency, who then, becomes the top ruling body over the entire religious institution. In this way, *this Utah based organization's chief sales officer is always the new head over all Mormon activities, worldwide while, this has never been the case in the Missouri based denomination, Community of Christ.*

So, as it is with any multi-national corporation –whether it is a political party, commercial enterprise, or a fundamentalist and convert-seeking religion– *What is important to the rest of us, is how to retain our individual sovereignty* in all their spin. When a culturally biased group, such as a Utah based Mormon corporate empire, directly controls large media groups and at least one political party then, *that* is true political power, irrespective of its religious, or its other claimed, "non-political" camouflage. As with any movement marketing their products to our civilization's consumers, whether their orchestrated activity is in sacred Temples or mass media boardrooms, in executive suites or at political party events, public image projection is always part of those equations. Because of their market wise proselytizing efforts to appear to be in the desirable cultural mainstream, to gain future tithing converts; when we come to know the orchestrated experience of experiencing institutional Mormonism then, *we actually, look at the rest of ourselves, reflected in a cultural mirror. Understanding the Mormons, per se, will allow us to understand ourselves, a*nd to my eyes, our current crisis calls us to gain an increased understanding of ourselves. It is our greatest need.

Toward that end then, my personal stories tell how one person has experienced the abusive experience of being subject to strategies of a cultural invasiveness into his sovereign and individual mind. Again, another example of what I mean may aid communication here: What a savvy, public relations corporate officer understands is, irrespective of whether any immorality is assigned to a given behavior, it is the winner who is always celebrated in American society. Mormons know that, in America, what is important –from a practical view– is that the "winner" *did win*. Marketers know that –if the winner cheated– then, they "got away with it!" This paradigm—of valuing the winners the most—is prime cultural middle class *Americana,* and all successful spin-doctors know it. Untold billions are regularly invested by this one Utah based Mormon hierarchy –as is by any other corporate empire– in buying the science to better understand the psychology of all global middle classes because of this Utah based group's chief leaders' strong *sales mentality*.

For example: The Utah based Mormon apostles know that the psychology of America's middle class is about *celebrating competition*. In fact, the middle classes of the entire world are all about an "upward mobility" *because* this dynamic is the *essence* of a competition which, is increasing exponentially today because of the invasion of our own American Pop Culture through the global media. Significantly, what the terrorists of September 11, 2001 saw as evil is that, even when we Americans are aware of the manipulation of our own perceptions, we tend to call it "brilliant" because—in spite of its true Orwelian nature— American media driven Pop Culture consumes other global cultures!

America, is socialized by its commercials. Today's Superbowl commercials are an excellent example. We see them and then, we try to emulate them. American spin-doctors can manipulate our Mass Mind's attention! This truly is a global form of human domination and control that manipulates human perceptions as skillfully as any devoted parent manipulates the perceptions of their innocent pre-school children.

Understanding these dynamics is important to all of us. Being dominated by others in our civilization has always required having the knowledge of the science, and the art of persuasion. This is a tool used by demigods of every stripe, and *this* is why the older societies hate us. Because of global media, religious extremists know that this is true of groups sufficiently savvy about using the mass media to get their own message across in the most persuasive manner. Now, although this is true universally, since my personal experience is within the context of Mormonism, my examples will focus on how *Mormons* do it.

For example: By mirroring our mainstream, Mormons appeal to others by presenting themselves as *the* desirable mainstream cultural group, in which "to be." As it is with a truly good political machine, the Mormon corporate mentality understands that their convert baptisms are linked with their image being projected to the greatest number of shoppers, in the marketplace of souls in search of institutional religion. As it also is with all politicians, all corporate marketing departments and all proselyte-seeking religions; projecting the illusion of being in the status, which a sociological mainstream market admires and seeks to emulate, is the key to all good media marketing, worldwide. Utah based Mormons want to be "on top" as "the market's winners," and if that isn't Americana then, nothing is! As is true of marketers of any American product, Mormons want to be seen as "*America's* religion."

But, as it is with any promotional campaign, some relative data important to contrary prevailing opinions is not offered, "up front." For example, one fact, which is never mentioned at all in Mormon media spots, is that membership in my former community requires a precise level of personal behavioral purity common to fundamentalist religion. Like all fundamentalists, Mormons are behavioral purists, yet, that data is not offered to the prospective proselyte. However, I am now able to see that, a purist is usually blind to the perspectives of those who are not of their particular group. Back when I was a true believer, for example, I had no idea about what I now know as the imperative for us to become open souls. Thus, this book establishes several key factors that I now see clearly but which, I could not see at all when I was in their hierarchy in Utah. So, I raise my voice because I see what causes the horror of violence by terrorists and America's "nice boys." The basic cause of all these is *only one,* yet, to my knowledge no other has chosen to address it. May it be sufficiently addressed here, in *Becoming Open Souls.*

The solution to our American domestic sickness, which I offer here—although our disease is now appropriately dormant in America's present wartime mode—is centered in our becoming sufficiently open to our personal evolving awareness of our species' nature. Much like the individual cells of any living organism that is suddenly attacked from without, we citizens of our multi-cultural society, have naturally become one whole in our defensive purpose. Yet, my warning is that, as it was in the case of the Balkan nations and elsewhere, our polarization is now only dormant. It is not yet healed. Sadly, our social roots still feed off of inter-cultural enmities from an inherited collective "hell."

What I hold out in this book, as our best way out of "hell," will permanently change how we envision "…ourselves, each other and our world." Then, once a critical mass has a clear, balanced and open soul to travel on the way we all go then, we will increase as the dynamics of mass consciousness take their natural course. Those who learn to travel the journey of human life, as open souls *–open to the wisdom of their others–* can self-identify as being greater than the limits established for them by their individual, bounded society. This process allows them to envision in more inclusive ways that will, eventually in turn, broaden our understanding. It is the way out of our commonly inherited "hell."

****

The liberating understanding I offer is that both foreign based terror, and our American "nice boy" terror have the same root cause. What brings peace to me in knowing why American "nice boys" have massacred their peers while in prayer –or, why "nice boys" seek justice by killing– as well as why today's religiously motivated terrorism even exists, is in anticipating where we are collectively headed. Seeing what I now see, takes all uncertainty out of the equation, and my vision shows me that we can still choose a non-violent transition. This, in fact, is why I have written this work. But, we're running out of our collective's time.

In fact, all the mythological calendars with which I'm familiar put the possibility of our Earth's transmutation within our generation's most immediate future. All of the old signs point to the violence in the, "...land where my fathers died...," as only being the last, shaking death rattle of an arcane and dying worldview. They announce the promised mythological time: A glorious New Age, one that will be magnified in empathy, in forgiving, in compassion and in joy—the Sixth Sun of my *Meshica/Toltec* mentors—has now dawned! The worse thing that can happen now is that, all end-time mythologies or, calendars *could* be used by an awesomely intelligent species that is alien to our planet. To me, "end-time" sacred stories can take any one of their multitudinous forms. This event's scenario is, in my view, the only true uncertainty:

If "They" knew about the dark prophecies of the Biblical book of Revelation, "They"—some, galactic aliens—would be able to come, masquerading as the promised "City of God" returning in the "midst of heaven," as "God's angels" sent down to Earth in the fabled "conduits of light." What if the claimed 19th century visits to Joseph Smith, Junior by "resurrected beings appearing in pillars of light" were, in fact, "beam me down, Scotty" ship-to-surface transports of real, "Trekers?" Then, what I call; a *Cortez-Quetzalquatl Syndrome* will have come full circle, and that little girl's words to Peter Jennings about "what goes around, comes around," unfortunately for us, may have become *prophetic*.

I affirm that the fabled "paradise lost" is almost here –that is– if we who can, *choose to agree to its return.* Thus, this book explores the Christian Millennial ideal in the context of how I have experienced the past six decades of American history. Like President George Walker Bush, I have also read the Bible, several times. I've also made the "end time" prophecies of the Torah and the Christian Bible, a major focus of my early seminary training and, later, as a seminary instructor, it was a specialization. But, I have other perspectives of, "end-time" events:

I now also accept the ancient wisdom of my Indian ancestors, whose final date for this present age is December 23, 2012—which, happens to be the birth date of none other than Joseph Smith, Junior, the founder of all of early Mormonism! Then, in the last twenty years—for reasons explained by the stories told in this book—I've come to accept that beings *"not from planet Earth"* may be about to claim planet Earth as "Their" domain. In this, I am also informed by the life experiences of my Spanish ancestors who conquered my own *Meshica* ancestors.

Because of the above awareness, I can imagine that 16th century Spanish *Conquistadores* took advantage of the ancient, Indigenously prophesied, return date of "the benevolent, white bearded *Quetzalquatl* of the ancient *Toltecs."* Thus, I can envision that inter-planetary aliens may also "beam down" from outer space at the precise time when old religious texts say that, a "Savior will come..." to "establish his reign" at "...the end of time." I no longer see with my fundamentalist eyes. So, it would not surprise me if alien beings did to us—who expect a coming "Savior of the world"—exactly as gold hungry Spaniards did to our 16th century Indigenous peoples who, likewise, expected "a deity's return!"

The question I ask, therefore, is: How will I know if the alien being, *beaming down at just the right time*, is the same as "The Savior of the World" or, the true promised "Messiah?" This way of envisioning is uncertain and fluid—open to adjustment by the human *Mass Mind—it is* open to *all* of humanity's sacred wisdom. This way of envisaging is to be guided by openness because it adventurously leads to where the path of becoming open souls leads us. May my telling of how I came to this way of being, promote the healing that most hymns say they seek.

For, hymns are prayers. Older L.D.S. hymns reveal what all Mormons seek. Many lyrics use the ancient Babylonian civilization as a metaphor of a localized, social evil and, the L.D.S. ideal of Zion (not to be confused with modern Zionism) as a metaphor of *social good.* In this example, Zion is not a place, but rather, *Zion is a social condition.* This verse from an old hymn is a good example of an *affect image* that is potent with thought—with what I, herein, call Mind Energy:

> *"Babylon the great is falling!*
> *God shall all her towers or'throw!*
> *Come to ZION! Come to ZION!*
> *ZION's walls shall ring with praise..."*

Babylon, in the above verse's context, is a clear mythological presentation of an archetypal secular civilization which, oppresses the people of "the city of ZION" or, those defined in Mormon scripture as, "THE PURE IN HEART," and "THE PURE IN HEART," are told that the secular "towers" of a future secular civilization, will fall. So, I ask:

Do these lyrics sing out a hymned echo of a prophecy of Nostrodamas that *"the twin brothers of the great city shall fall and, the great city shall be afire?"* I don't know. But, I *do* know that the above is only one of many examples of hymnology that sing out old "end-time" scenarios to the *Mass Mind* of its singers. Yet these meditative humans, all of whom assemble worshipfully in hypnotic-like states—across the globe—in their, respective, local assemblies. In this way, they collectively create a global experience in the dynamics of repetitive musical worship, and thus, they mold the group's *Mass Mind* because all group minds, *create!*

What I am saying is that we need to be extremely aware of the absolute power of the *linked* human mind, when the active principle is the collective agreement of *any* group. It does not matter which group is in question. The infinitely powerful creative dynamic of agreement, *per se,* is this book's theme, and its medicine is *creating by agreement.* I caution, however, on one thing: *All words are encoded energy systems.* Agreement is a vibration or, a word-encrypted energy. Recall that Ilan Ramon—the Israeli astronaut—who'd written in his last e-mail to his family just before the ill-fated Columbia was lost, "…I'm so happy here that, I do not want to go back to Earth…"[xvii] Although, his exuberance in hyperbole was born of his joy of space travel; in retrospect I believe that, because of the powerful nature of his Mind, his words may well have prophetically created his fate, in fact, to *not* "…go back to Earth."

Here then, are my personal stories. They re-present the honest retrospective of this adult man, in the hope that their telling will help others, to avoid what I here call, *institutional seduction.* The seductive aspects of the events related, will not be readily apparent to some. Yet, as it usually is with any seduction, the stories told in the first chapter are laden with the insidious hidden agendas and the occult manipulations by others, of an innocent's perceptions. The seduction may be revealed –depending on the reader's worldview– as either an *agape love dance* rooted in compassion, or as a totally *unwelcome penetration into my psyche.* This perception disparity comes out of each individual reader's earliest programmed envisioning.

Whichever any individual reader's point of view is on how I experienced the experiences, the point is that, I later came to see it as an *uninvited and, an unwelcome penetration* into my second womb which Mom and Grandma Nica had created for me. I have since reasoned that, if a seduction proves in retrospect, to be an "uninvited and unwelcome penetration" of another's mind then, *that* seduction –at *that* moment– is rape. It is as much a violent invasion of another's innermost humanity as if it were, in fact, a sexual assault. It came to me the day I finally saw the magnitude of the invader mind-set's ability to distort the wondrous beauty of my Queer sexuality. The Church had re-created my uniquely personal humanity into a sexual warp—into an imagined, "evil."

Sexual rape is the ugly, violent, penetrative abuse of an unwelcoming sovereign being by they who make love into ugliness. The perpetrator may even consider his or her invasivness of others as, an "understandable passion." However, like it is with any story of classic date rape, once the victim of the abusive act is able to acknowledge the rape for what it is, *in their own mind* (where it counts) then, a new and a clearer vision of what happened causes the victim to re-experience the experience differently. What was once perceived to be only a trusting, nurturing environment of Love is, in the end, understood for what it is: A forced and, therefore, a hostile and abusive attack that objectifies a sacred, sovereign human being as an object of institutional seduction.

When this kind of a seduction is carried out by institutionalized hierarchies, it is in the context of the institution, i.e.: It is *institutional seduction*. It then, follows that, if it is institutional seduction and then, it is later discovered to be an *uninvited and unwelcome penetration* into the sacred mind of an unwilling, and sovereign human being then, it is *cultural rape*. For example, had I had the beautiful clarity of a *Meshica* heritage earlier in life then, I don't believe I would have been so quick to create a reality for myself that mirrored a world empty of that part of what I am. As all rapists violate innocence, the rape of my ancestral, Indigenous culture violated my *natural sense of personal goodness*!

What was created was a cultural rape. I label it cultural rape, because cultures are what all institutions and hierarchies devour. The consumption of other cultures is how all institutions live. In the case of all hierarchies seen as "parental figures," it is more than simply taking something precious away by force, or by threat of force –such as taking away a guiltless way to perceive one's own sexuality without shame– it is, "like unto murder." It is murderous because it kills natural humanity from sincere, devoted, Queer persons of faith who seek to *love honestly*.

So, I consider the first chapter in this book, nothing less than the story of my cultural rape. It tells about being programmed to see the world in only one way when, in reality, my deep, personal experiences consistently revealed that the world has always been quite different. It contains true stories, through which, I tell what processes were engaged that guided me to the transcendent point where my sanity depended on, eventually, becoming aware of the imperative of becoming open souls. When I was able to reflect on how I had experienced the experiences then, I was able to see that public institutions had played the invasive predator with me. My vision of reality was revealed to me as the mere homophobic, *spin of institutions*.

Yet, as I hope the reader will also be able to see, by the time I'd experienced the experiences that are told in the end of this book, I saw a distinct pattern in my personal choices. In the end, I am now able to understand that, our lives are the sum total of our personal and most heart-centered choices. Significantly, we have heard and read much in the past few years about the genetic code. My envisioning today –as I herein reflect on my life journey– speaks about the spiritual equivalent of a genetic code. These are each, therefore, fateful stories that seem to reflect the real existence of the soul's equivalent of the genetic code. For, in retrospect, it is easy for me to see that there is purpose in the path that I have followed over the years. It is when I've felt most aligned with my true *sexual* nature, when life has been most joyous.

On the other hand, it's been when I have *not* been aligned with my true sexuality, when life has been like a hell. This book frankly tells the phenomenology that took me out of that hell. What follows first then, is the story of how all the institutions, which provided me with the current social structure of mainstream America –including the church– had played the role of invasive predator with my innocence. It tells how I experienced the experience of growing up different in a world bent on *uni-culturalism,* molding me into a closed and blocked off soul.

Finally and significant to our present, particular, political time; it reveals the frustrations in my earlier life that are astonishingly similar to what I see taking place on a global scale. While, in absolutely no way do I agree with, nor do I condone violent behavior, I admit that I identify with those who have also felt the effects of "Americanizing" our planet. This comment is in reference to Pop. Culture. It has nothing to do with our system of government that we all cherish and hold so dear. It has to do with how civilization has, historically, behaved *whenever we have encountered other equally unique, and aware civilizations.* There are many examples of this, including America's 19th century expansion that was labeled by the politicians of that century as a, "Manifest Destiny."

Naturally, in *Becoming Open Souls,* my family's *Californio* history of being conquered by an American society obsessed with its 19th century Manifest Destiny is a context for the teaching of important ideas. In this, I give voice to frustrations claimed by today's enemies of our beloved America. By openly telling my personal story then, I hope to answer a question asked so often in the aftermath of September 11, 2001: "Why do they hate us so much?" In the process, I try to reveal the role played by *uni-culturalism* in the answer I give to this question, for, I affirm: Hatred is not natural to us humans, but rather, love is our species' soul nature; a nature that includes all of what we each are—our spirit, our mind and our body, including the physical world we know.

So, in an awareness of all the above and related issues, what follows, is the story of my own institutional seduction that I, later, came to understand as the cultural rape of my ancestral ethnicity. Eventually, I would come to feel that the behavior of my earliest religious mentors —although, intended as a pure expression of Christian tender care on their part—had actually, worked toward the creation of a personal "hell on Earth." My hope is that my own transcendence of their institutional seduction and cultural rape of my "second womb" nativity may serve as an example for others, in the words of the late Joseph Campbell, "to experience the experience of eternity; right here and, now...!"[xviii]

NOTES TO INTRODUCTION

---

[i] New York Times, September 30, 2001

[ii] The Kindness of Strangers, Dr. John Boswell, (Yale University Press)

[iii] Children of The Night, 2000 Annual Report, Los Angeles, California 90027

[iv] Book of Mormon (LDS) Moroni, 6:2

[v] The Seat of The Soul, Gary Zukav (Simon & Schuster, Inc. New York, New York, 1990)

[vi] Holy Bible, Isaiah, 61:1

[vii] The Power of Compassion, His Holiness, The Dalai Lama (HarperCollins Publishers, London, England 1995) page 2

[viii] Op.Cit. II Nephi, 2:25

[ix] Hands of Light, *A Guide to Healing Through the Human Energy Field*, Barbara Ann Brennan (Batam Books, New York, New York 1987) pages 28-29

[x] Op.Cit.

[xi] The Power of Myth, Joseph Campbell

[xii] Op.Cit. John 3:1-12 (italics added)

[xiii] Ibid. Matthew 12:47-50

[xiv] Ibid. Luke 9:59-60 see also Matthew, 8:21-22

[xv] Christianity, Social Tolerance and Homosexuality, Dr. John Boswell (Yale University Press) see also Same-Sex Unions In Pre-Modern Europe, Dr. John Boswell (Villard Books, New York, New York 1994) and The Issue Is Pluralism *An Urgent Call To Greater Pluralism In Civil Marriage Law*, Antonio A. Feliz (Editorial Los Feliz, Los Feliz Village, Los Angeles, California 2000)

[xvi] The Autobiography of Malcolm X *As Told To Alex Haley*

[xvii] ABC News, February 3, 2003; quoted by his father to Charles Gibson KCET Los Angeles, California PBS Special, "The Power of Myth" With Bill Moyers and Joseph Campbell, aired December 29, 2003.

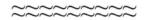

"Had my former mentors been able to provide the data, which I now see I lacked then, choices would have been extremely different. As difficult as what I write here may be to some, *all story-telling is about identity, and I tell these stories because they reveal what mine actually is. What is, is revealed by what is done. Truly, in the final analysis, after all is said and done; doctrine, theology and culture mean nothing. It is in truth telling -in telling what is- that our behavior speaks out clearly to anyone seeking... understanding...*"

CHAPTER ONE

THE SEDUCTION

The following reveals how I experienced the experiences. The reason for this telling is my hope that my stories may help open the souls of others. These connected stories are, "a phenomenology guided by a compassionate Universe"—it may be called, "*a science of beingness*"—from which anyone may also learn. In a sentence, this book examines one human being's life, *intensely lived*. It is my honest, intimate retrospective study of how I personally experienced the experiences of the second half of the last century. These are all true stories. Each is told here in the context of a now, increasingly maturing life, revealing early, innermost, spiritual awarenesses and synchronicities—if you will—which, in this frank telling, reveal a natural sense of knowing my world through the dynamic of truth telling. So, I guess, I've always been a journalist at heart...

****

Even as a small child, even then, I was aware. Dad was the man of the house, and when Dad wasn't there, he still dominated what took place in our home. After all, we are all *his* family—we are all called by *his* last name. In fact, I have his full name as my own, Antonio A. Feliz. It's after Dad, and his dad who, I'm told had died just minutes before my birth on June 26, 1943. So, I'm the fourth Antonio. Each of us was named after the first Antonio Feliz, my murdered great-grandfather; who was also killed, like his own Feliz grandfather, *Don* Francisco Feliz was previously also murdered, by the ones Dad calls the, "*Gringos salados...*!"

Sunday mornings are my most favorite of all times. Every Sunday, the intoxicating aroma of the freshly made tortillas and the refried beans that, Mom had spiced-up for Dad, would awaken me. While I was still in bed but, not yet totally awake, Mom would come in and let me eat some of the burritos she had fixed for Dad. The warmth, the texture and the flavor of the refried pinto beans wrapped inside the open-flame-heated tortillas, immediately upon waking up, was always pure ecstasy to me. Nothing; before or since, has ever tasted quite as good to me in the morning. My idea of heaven, in those days, was eating those hot, tasty, bacon flavored, refried bean burritos in the cuddled comfort of my own warm bed.

Going to mass came after finishing my yummy burritos and a hot, morning bath. Later, Mom held tightly onto my hand as we crossed busy Center Street in Anaheim, California. She always had big sister, Maria, by her other hand because we always had to cross Center Street, in order to get to old St. Boniface. It was the oldest church in Anaheim and, the older part of town had grown up around it and the St. Boniface Catholic School. That's where my big sister went to school on weekdays.

Mom's little Sunday morning lecture was the same one as always. So, crossing Center Street on this Sunday was no different than on any other. "Always look both ways when you start to cross any street," she'd say. "Remember, the big trucks can't see small people, even if they're right in front of them."

We were still only half-way across the street. Usually, by this point in Mom's street crossing lecture, we had already made it across. Maria kept on interrupting, holding us up, "...Where are we going to eat after mass?" We always went out to eat at a restaurant after going to mass.

I could see a real big car. It was two blocks away, coming toward us. Maria was still slowing us down too much with all her questions...

"We'll talk about that after mass." Speeding up our pace, Mom seemed to tug a lot harder on my hand and kept pulling as she continued her usual Sunday lecture, "you never knew her but, your grandmother..."

Years later, I have internalized that old family story about *Mama Cande*. Eventually, I would come to know *Mama Cande* as, "Grandma Candelaria Gonzales," through my personal research of our family's genealogy. *Mama Cande* had been a devout Roman Catholic. In fact, it was during the last Mexican Revolution that—it is said—she'd cared for the town parish's holy Eucharist. This was because the parish priests had all been put in jail when the church had been outlawed in old Mexico.

Mom jumped up onto the curb saying, "*Mama Cande*... was...run over...by a truck," It was on this street, right here. It happened right after she received Holy Communion. Your *Mama Cande* was a very good woman. It was a day just like this one..."

Whew! We were all finally across the street. I looked over my shoulder as I stepped onto the curb and...

The car I had seen approaching us roared right through the intersection. It was the first time I realized how fast cars can go...

Usually, Mom picked me up in her arms about then, high enough so I could dip my finger in the holy water and cross myself, just like Maria did. Then, for a moment, Mom would stand there before we'd all walk to our seats. This time was no different, and I always enjoyed this part because this is when I was high enough to look all around us. I *loved* that moment every Sunday!

Mass was always like we had all come into another world. Mass had its very own sounds, its own smells and colors of light. We always did exactly the same things—every time! When we would pray at home, my knees would hurt, but here, at Saint Boniface we had soft things to kneel on. The neighborhood boys who got to help at mass must have been especially good boys to get to wear long robes like the priests. What I call the *upside down pyramids* in the ceiling, all seemed to be singing all the time. Mom calls the upside down pyramids in the ceiling, "ceiling arches."

Anyway, for a long time I had wondered where the pretty voices came from because the pretty sounds just bounced off one upside down pyramid, onto another. Then once, I finally saw that the beautiful voices came from real people who were all dressed in those robes too. Mom had only chuckled because she said that she now knew that I was getting taller because, if I was already able to see the big choir then, I must have grown some more!

I remember that day really well. It was the day that, I saw something that I had never seen before, or since. Like any other Sunday at mass, the smells of the incense, the beautiful voices and the loud music of the organ –the robes, colors and the kneeling– were all exactly the same as at any other mass. But, on *that* Sunday, well, it had happened so fast...

I had to blink my eyes to be sure my eyes were okay. Right after the point when the bells were ringing and everyone was still kneeling, I looked up. That's when I saw that all those pictures in all the colored windows, suddenly, came all alive! In total surprise, I nudged at Mom, but she just kept her head bowed and wouldn't look up at me to see what I had wanted. The glass stories were moving, becoming real! That's the day I realized that there was some kind of magic at mass. But, since Mom didn't look up, I kept it secret just in case it wasn't real, like "Let's Pretend" on the radio on Saturday mornings. I decided to wait to see if it happened again another day.

Most Sundays, after mass and after eating at a restaurant, we'd walk home to Grandma's house. We'd get close to her house, and I'd hear the sounds of squawking chickens, and loud thuds from the back yard. Those noises only meant one thing: Grandma Nica was in the back yard preparing her chickens for supper. With a look up at Mom, I would make my face into a plea for her to let go of my hand so, I could go watch Grandma Nica working in her back yard.

Mom would always let me go, "*Mijo*," she would then call out, as she'd let go of my hand, "don't get your clothes dirty!"

Anticipation would always build inside of me as I'd then run down the long, narrow, concrete walk on the north side of Grandma's old gray and white house on Clementine Street in Anaheim. To my little boy's eyes, Grandma Nica was really huge! She seemed to be built like a massive fortress. I could never get past her!

Maria Nicasia Tafolla de Acosta, I had learned years later, was a woman who had experienced eighteen, single child births, one of which, was delivered while she fled her war-torn family hacienda as a refugee from the last Mexican revolution. With her husband far away, fighting with General Pancho Villa, she had raised a family of fourteen children to adulthood. She'd, eventually, live long enough to know some of her second-great-grandchildren, living to be only two weeks shy of 100 years of age. Years after that period of my life, my Mormon influenced genealogical research would teach me that five generations of living mothers and their daughters was not a common circumstance.

Even later, when Grandma Nica eventually lived with my own immediate family, I would discover that she had been known as a healer, serving others as a midwife most of her life. It was in those later years, that she would admit to me that she had used peyote and marijuana for divination since her days in her native, Guanajuato. This newfound awareness is only one of many factors that glared their contradiction out at me in those days when both my Grandma Nica and Mom had lived under my roof in a suburb of Salt Lake City, Utah, where I was the bishop of the local Mormon ward. Knowing her admitted bent as a jokester, I doubted her story. But I'm getting ahead of my story…

In her back yard, with her strong legs spread apart to give her balance, she was wielding her axe down on the big chopping block on the neck of a chicken.

I ran up to her, from behind her.

"*Cuidate, nino!*" (Look out, little one!) Grandma Nica never spoke in English in front of any of us. But, somehow, she did seem to laugh along with the rest of the family when someone said some funny stuff in English. She was swinging the axe in the way she'd always done. First, she made the sign of the cross, and, then...

I covered my eyes with my hands, just as I had always done, when the axe came down hard making a swooshing noise in the air. Just like always, I held my breath.

Thud. The bright red blood squirted out toward the left side of Grandma Nica's towering legs.

I was always completely entranced by this one sight. Of all the women I that knew then, this one was such a great mystery to my developing soul. But, today for some reason, I had enough nerve to ask her a question I'd wanted to ask for a very long time. "Grandma Nica," I began, tugging at her long skirt, "why do you always make the sign of the cross above the chopping block before you chop the chicken's head off with the axe?"

"*Mira lo que pasa,*" (Watch what happens,) she answered back to me, simply.

I came around to the opposite side of the chopping block so that I'd have a clear view. There were already two headless chickens on the ground to one side of her right leg. Both of them had their feet untied. What I then saw, will never leave my little boy's memory...

Grandma Nica picked up the next chicken from the opposite side of the chopping block. This is when she had normally made the sign of the cross and untied the legs of the chicken. But this time, she didn't make the sign of the cross. She just untied the legs as she'd always done and then, she came down hard with the axe like always.

Thud. Suddenly, the bright red wetness was all over me, and the Sunday clothes that I'd promised Mom I wouldn't get dirty. Horror shot through me! Shivering, in shock, I couldn't move.

The blood squirting, and headless body of that poor, white chicken went wild! I had never seen anything like it in my life. This had never happened to any other chicken before. It was all so awful! The headless, bleeding creature was jumping and running aimlessly all over the back yard, getting blood all over the dry ground, on the narrow concrete walk, on the guava trees, and on Grandma Nica!

It was too much for little me. I had to do something. But all I said is, "Grandma Nica, do something!" I yelled it in Spanish.

But, she just stood there, with one hand on the axe and the other, open and held out –as if to say, "Do you seen now?"

The terrorizing scene went on , and on for–I don't remember how long...

"Stop it, stop it Grandma Nica, please" I pleaded, "make it stop, please!"

"*Nada se puede hacer, Mijo. Esto es lo que pasa cuando uno no bendice ni agradese por el uso del pollo.*" (Nothing can be done, my son. This is what happens when one does not bless the chicken or give thanks for its use.)

Instinctively, I ran after it, trying unsuccessfully to hold it, to comfort it. I felt responsible for all that was happening. I felt the tears wetting my clothes, and all I heard was the flapping of its wings and my own loud crying.

That's when she said back to me, "*Mijo, algunos hechos no pueden ser cambiados despues del escojer hacerlos.*" (My son, some deeds cannot be changed after one chooses to act.) Finally, though, she grabbed the poor little bleeding thing and held it close to her, as it kept on trembling and shivering. I'd never seen so much blood on her before. It was all over her usually bright white apron, all over her dress, on her flesh-colored cloth nylons and, it even got on her shoes. As I looked up, I saw she had blood on her face too...

"Oh, Grandma..." I heard my voice trail off into silence as the chicken kept shaking in her big arms. The muffled noise of its attempt at fluttering with its imprisoned wings was all I heard, now.

Blood covered her apron, and I couldn't see that any of it had been white. In Spanish, Grandma kept saying something over, and over again. But I couldn't hear all the words because of the loudness of those trapped, feathered limbs. Finally, she got down on the stool just behind her, and with that, I understood her softly spoken words, "*Que dices?*" (What did you say?) She was talking to the chicken!

That was the first time that I realized that Grandma Nica did know the chickens just like she also knew me too. I have always remembered that she talked to the little, headless, feathered one .

"Why does the sign of the cross have so much power?"

Then, with a huge sigh she said, "*Tantas preguntas.*" (So many questions.) As she gently put the still quivering body down with all of the others, Grandma Nica turned on the garden hose and washed down her arms and the entire back yard.

As she did this, all her Spanish words seemed to echo inside of me, "*Algunos hechos no pueden ser cambiados despues que uno escoje hacerlos.*" (Some deeds cannot be changed after one chooses to act.)

"*Mijo*," she answered, "*No es la senal de la cruz*," (It's not the sign of the cross.) She continued hosing down everything. The dust on the top of the ground seemed to jump when the water hit it. "*Ni tampoco es el percinarse que contiene el poder, Mijo. Sino, el percinarse solo es la via que da vida al poder de Dios que ya esta en cada uno...aqui, en tu Grandma Nica.*" (Neither is it in crossing one's self that holds the power, my son. But, crossing one's self is only the channel that gives life to the power of God in each person... here, in your Grandma Nica.)

What magic this is, I thought to myself, what a wonderful mystery! In that brief moment, I knew that there was something –some unseen stuff– which, actually, connected everything and everyone. She had not said it. I knew it somehow, and that sense of knowing caused me to, literally, run inside the house.

Several months passed.

There was a really hard knock at the front door. As usual, I ran over to answer it. That's when Mom seemed to fly out in front of me, from nowhere.

I stepped aside. It was clear to me that she meant business.

Mom always means business when she speaks back to me in Spanish, and by calling me by my given name, "Antonio! *Salgate de alli.*" (Antonio! Get out of there.) But this time, she was kind of, whispering. She was whispering in a loud voice. *Why?*

Why was she whispering loudly? I thought to myself, Mom had never done *that* before. And, when she wasn't at work, she was always too busy in the kitchen or, in some other place in the house to answer the front door. And, if Mom wasn't home then, Grandma Nica didn't speak enough English to get it, and Maria was away at school most of the day. So, it had always been my job to answer the front door when everyone else was busy. This time though, I knew to get out of her way, and I just stood way back. Her whispering so loudly, as she stepped closer to where I'd been playing, there on the living room floor, somehow, made everything different this time.

The knocking just kept on.

But, she just stood there, looking at the front door.

Grandma Nica came out of her room, and she began saying loudly, "*Que diablos pasa?*" (What in the Devil is going on?)

"Shhh…" Mom's face told the whole story. She didn't want to answer the front door. But, as long as I could remember, Mom had never hidden from anyone. She had always taught me to be open, honest and unashamed. So, that isn't it, I thought to myself. No, something must be, really wrong. But, what was it?

I just stood there, feeling all tied up inside. Was Mom really scared?

Then, Grandma Nica and Mom whispered something to each other, quietly.

But, the knocking went on for a long time.

A long while passed with us just standing there: Silent.

I grabbed Mom's skirt. I looked up at Mom. Then, I looked up at Grandma Nica. That's when both their faces let me know that it was definitely not shame they felt. That wasn't what was wrong. No, they *were afraid...*of...something. That's when I began to get scared too. But, *why?* What were we all so scared about?

Exactly when I'd asked myself that last question was when the knocking suddenly stopped. Then, I heard the sound of footsteps begining to walk away from the door; down the big concrete steps, down the front concrete walk, and finally, I heard the loud squeak of the front gate. That said they'd gone away through the front gate.

So, I looked up at Mom again. Her face was different than it had ever been before. Mom *was* afraid! With that in my mind, I knew for sure that I was afraid too. I had never before seen that look of fear on her face. She had been afraid of whoever it had been, but Mom had never been afraid of anything before. *Never.*

I turned to see Grandma's face, and fear was still in her face too. Who was so bad, so awful that, Grandma Nica was scared?

That was the very first time that I knew that bad feeling that, I've since come to know, was pure *terror*.

The knocking at the front door came every day at about the same time for over a week. At the same time, every day, the hard knocking was always followed by the softer sound of two pair of feet walking away. The dark fear of what was on the other side of our front door was overwhelming to me. If Mom was in the room, she'd grab me clinging me tightly to her thighs. One time, Grandma Nica picked me up in her big arms and held me so close, I thought she'd hurt me. By the time the last day of that terrorizing knocking had passed, I noticed that both Mom and Grandma Nica were really trembling when they'd pick me up and hold me in their arms.

Who could it have been? Or, I wondered, what was it? It had to be something ugly, like the old "*boogy man*" my cousins had always talked about or, maybe like "*La Llorona*" that my cousins Gracie and Manuel had whispered about to me one night as we lay in bed before going to sleep. The shadows of the big trees against the window that night took scary forms, and I knew that someone was after all of us. Maybe, it was something just like that scary night? Then, when it stopped, all I could think of was to ask; when would it come back? And, then when it did, all those scary thoughts came flashing back into my little boy's mind.

Then, one night after Dad had been away for a long time, we all had a big supper. Everything was there! *Frijoles refritos, aroz, salsa, carne asada, elote*, all the stuff for *tostadas and enchiladas, tameles, chiles rellenos, sopa de fideo, mole con pollo*, lots and lots of tortillas, and even *arroz con leche*! It was fun because the whole family was over to visit us all for a big supper at Grandma's house.

This was the day when Maria, my big sister, taught me the word *assume*. It happened later that night, after everything had happened, while we were getting ready for bed. I had been telling her how I'd felt about the knocking and the evening's get-together. She said, "Tony, you are *assuming* what was taking place tonight." But, I did not understand what *assuming* was. It was a word I didn't know. Then, she said that I had not yet experienced life enough to understand the experience. That's the first time that I knew that I'm really lucky to have a big sister that always knew more than I did.

That was when I discovered that, sometimes, I do not have enough *data* to understand situations that; I didn't know enough. Eventually, I learned that Maria was right.

Like she'd said, "There's nothing wrong with not having all the information. It means you have to be patient 'til you learn more by getting more *data*." But, again, I'm getting ahead of the story...

Some grown-ups had been crying in the dinning room. I was in the kitchen with the other smaller kids and, I got down from my chair. I wanted to know what was going on...

Dad was saying something to everybody.

My aunts, uncles, Mom, Grandma Nica, Maria and all of my big, older cousins seemed to get it but, whatever it was that he was talking about, I couldn't understand it.

I knew that it must have been something important because almost everyone was crying and, even looking down at their food. That never happened to big people before. Had someone died? This is what it was like when Uncle Art passed away. But then, when the woman down the block had died a few weeks ago, this stuff didn't happen. So, why is everyone crying?

Suddenly, Grandma Nica got up, and went into the kitchen. When I saw her face, it was almost pure red, like the *chile salsa*.

Just then, everybody got up and started hugging Mom and Dad. But, I still didn't know why, though. But, when Mom and Dad kissed and Mom picked me up onto her lap, I got the same old warm feeling inside me that I always did when she did that. Cuddled up in Mom's lap, leaning against her softness, I knew that whatever was going on, it was okay.

I felt her arm resting on my shoulder. That's when I could see big tears were falling down her face –wetting her dress.

Then, looking at Dad, trying to understand why Mom was crying, I saw that even Dad's eyes were filled with tears.

I wondered to myself, why was *he* crying? What was so wrong that even *Dad* was crying?

Several days passed.

Then, at the same time as before, the knocking returned. But this time, Dad was home too. I looked up at him from the floor where I was playing with my new logging truck. What would he do? He and I were the only ones in the living room.

He just got up, and answered the front door. It was two men. Dad went out on the front porch and began talking with them. He wasn't afraid at all. "*Quedate adentro,*" (Stay inside), he said to me, as he closed the big door.

I wanted to go out with him. I wanted to understand better. So, I jumped up on the seat of the old blue sofa that was against the front window. Leaning against the back of it, my eyes could see over the window sill behind the sofa.

One of the two men looked a lot like Dad. He had a black mustache and dark, wavy, short black hair. The other man was very tall, with short blond hair –and, his eyes– his eyes were the bluest eyes that I had ever seen! The blond man smiled a lot. Both of them were dressed in black suites, with white shirts and colored ties. I could easily see that they both had a book with them. I wondered if they were selling books.

Just then, Grandma Nica's voice bellowed out from behind me, "*!Mijo! quitate de alli!*" (My son! Get away from there!)

Jumping down from the sofa, I went into the kitchen where Mom was fixing supper, "Mom," I started, "who's that with Dad?"

"*Ya veras,*" (You'll see), she answered, "they're going to stay for supper and you will behave, no?"

I nodded in agreement and then I looked back through the kitchen doorway. That's when I felt myself say to myself, What wonder! And, who is that blond man? Years later, I would come to remember this particular day and moment in my life as the earliest memory of being aware of experiencing an extremely fascinating curiosity. I'd seen blond people before at mass but, never a man so tall and beautiful, in a business suite. His smile was calling a feeling from deep within my body. The sensation was different from any other I'd ever felt before. Little did I know...

Grandma Nica was still listening through the crack of the open door. Then, as if she somehow knew that I had been watching too, she suddenly turned around and began walking back toward the kitchen where Mom was, "*Mija,*" (My daughter) Grandma Nica said to Mom, "*acuerdate lo que te dije.*" (remember what I said to you.)

Mom didn't look up then, at Grandma Nica. She just kept on kneeding the tortilla dough on the kitchen counter.

Grandma Nica didn't eat supper with the rest of us that night.

Elder Swensen was the really, really blond man with clear, deep blue eyes. He and Elder Gomez are missionaries from the Mormons. They're fun –lots of fun– for me! They both played with me on the living room floor after we ate. When they had to leave, Elder Gomez asked if they could, "leave a blessing on" our "home."

Right at that moment, Grandma Nica quickly opened the door of her bedroom. She stared directly at Mom and Dad...

Mom and Dad looked at each other.

That's when Grandma Nica walked real fast through the room where we all were, faster than I'd ever seen, and she sped right by all of us without saying anything, and went on into her kitchen.

Nobody said anything. It's why I could tell that something was wrong –really wrong. I asked, "What's wrong with Grandma Nica?" I looked up at Mom, but when I couldn't get a clue, I looked over at Dad.

Elder Gomez didn't wait for an answer, and he got down on his knees. Then...

Elder Swensen got down on his knees too.

Dad said, "Thank you, Elder Gomez," and then, Dad got down on his knees.

Then, almost like we'd planned it, Maria and I got down on our knees, at the exact moment. I looked up at Mom and then...

Mom just bowed her head and she stayed sitting in the big blue chair.

Elder Gomez said the prayer. His voice was so low that, to me, it sounded more like a whisper than like a prayer said out loud.

The Mormon missionaries came over every week after that first visit. They lived in Los Angeles, and they would travel all that distance down to us in Anaheim [this was years before the Santa Ana Freeway even existed] in Orange County. Elder Gomez and Elder Swensen were more fun than my older cousins were because they would bring filmstrips to show us on the wall [although we'd been the first on our street to get one, we hadn't yet bought a TV]. We'd turn out the lights, and it was like a movie show—right in our living room! They'd tell us about their families in Utah and Idaho. Elder Swensen's home had a lot of snow on the ground in Idaho, and since I had never seen snow in person, his stories about playing in it made it sound like a lot of fun. I especially liked his stories about Joseph Smith, Junior. I remember saying that I thought that, I must be like Joseph Smith, Junior because I was a Junior too!

I said, "Dad and I not only have the same name, but his dad and his grandfather were both called by the same name too! I am the fouth Antonio Feliz and, I wonder if Joseph Smith, Junior had ever felt like I sometimes do about being a Junior. I mean—how did he feel about others calling me 'Junior?'" I really wanted to know a lot more about him, and, one day I asked Elder Swensen, "Was he like the saints?"

"Saints?"

Just then, Elder Gomez stopped what he was doing and then, instead of Elder Swensen answering my question, Elder Gomez asked me his own question back: "Tony, do you mean like the Catholic saints?"

"Yeah," I said, "was Joseph like, uh…uh…San Antonio de Padua? I mean, you're Letter-day Saints. Are all Mormons saints too? Is that why your church is called Letter-day Saints?"

The missionaries both looked at each other. Neither one said a word. Then, Elder Swensen laughed and Elder Gomez said, "It's Latter-day Saints, Tony. Not,' Letter-day Saints.'"

Everybody laughed, like I'd made a joke.

"Son," Dad said, "Joseph Smith saw a vision when he was a young man and…"

"Like little Diegito saw our Holy Lady in Mexico?" I asked. "Don Diegito was visited by La Virgen de Guadeloupe so, Dad, was Joseph Smith like a saint, like little Diegito was?"

"What do you think?" Dad asked back.

"I think he must have been a great saint," I answered in the most certain voice I could, "because he talked with God and with the angels. I know that much. That's what all the saints do. Saints can talk with God. They have visions, and stuff like that."

I didn't know why but, within just weeks, we had moved out of Grandma Nica's house on old Clementine Street.

Dad's work was supervising harvesting crews in the orange groves in Orange County. As the years went on, Dad's job required that he go northward, into the San Juaquin Valley for his work. An agricultural cooperative had invited him to manage their labor force. These were temporary laborers who the government had brought to California from Mexico. They were called *Braceros*. Because she still had her job at the fruit packing business in Orange County, Mom stayed with Maria and me in a house in Anaheim, on Paulina Street.

When Dad had left us to work "up North," he and Mom had already been missionaries for the Mormon Church. They worked in teaching, or converting as many family members and friends as they could. Since Dad had gone away, Mom continued her missionary work gaining converts with Sister Elsie Frayer, her new missionary companion. So, Maria and I got to go with Mom and Sister Frayer on their visits to people who were thinking of joining our new church too! I loved to visit new people with Mom and Sister Frayer! That's when I learned new things about Joseph Smith, Junior. It was fun to hear the stories Mom would tell –just like Elder Gomez and Elder Swensen had taught them to us all, when I was an even smaller boy.

But, less than a year after Dad went away to a new job, we all followed him to live in the San Juaquin Valley. I was in fourth grade, and that's when I learned about our family's role in California history from books! I liked my fourth grade teacher. In fact, her real name was actually Miss Morman!

"Today…" Miss Morman said, "today, boys and girls, we're going to start our projects on the California Missions." She showed us pictures of how other children had made paper mache replicas of the old California Missions.

When I told my family about the class projects, Dad just kept on eating without saying anything.

"What mission should I make?" I asked, "Miss Morman says that I can make any of the missions I want."

"Well, why don't you make a replica of old Mission San Juan Capistrano?" Mom answered. "Antonio, that's where all of your own great-grandparents were baptized, as little children. Some of your Feliz people are buried in the old mission cemetery there."

"Were they all Mormons too, Mom? Was the baptism I had last year, like the baptisms they had there?"

"No," Mom answered, "they were all Roman Catholic, and in the Catholic Church, little ones get baptized when they're new babies."

Dad still wasn't saying anything. He just kept on eating.

Now, our family in early California was mostly from Dad's side of the family. I knew *that* much.

"But, I thought Dad's family was from Los Angeles, not from Orange County," Maria said, "didn't we once even own an old Spanish rancho in Los Angeles?"

"Wow," I shouted, "a rancho! Really? Miss Morman told us a lot about the old *Californio Dons* and the old Spanish ranchos back then in old California."

Mom got up and went into the kitchen to get desert for us, "Your Father's family, not only owned that rancho in Los Angeles, but they were also part owners of the old Rancho Santiago de Santa Ana. It was down in East Orange and East Anaheim, and it included Yorba Linda, Placentia and all the area we call the Anaheim hills. It was east of the old houses where you were both born."

I turned to Dad, "Did they, Dad?"

He started getting up, "Si, Antonio, that was the Feliz, and the Peralta/Yorba side of my family."

"Antonio, aren't you going to have any desert?" Mom had asked, "It's your favorite."

But by then, though, Dad had already gone out through the back doorway, "No," he answered, slamming the back door.

"What's with Dad?" Maria asked.

"Nothing," Mom answered, as she came back to the table. "I think the San Juan Capistrano Mission would be a good choice," she said turning to me. "Now, eat."

Two weeks passed.

I had the best mission replica of the whole class! I'd even put white paper *mache* swallows on top of it. That was the first time that I remember studying any kind of history in school. But, in the

Mormon Sunday school classes, we always seemed to be studying some kind of history—Mormon history, or Book of Mormon stories.

I didn't know my new Mormon Sunday school teacher's name. I just called him the Science Man because he'd visit our home and he'd always teach me new things about science. He'd teach me astronomy through his big telescope and we'd both do experiments with my chemistry kit that Mom and Dad had got me for Christmas.

"What's your favorite subject at school, Tony?" he asked while we worked with sulfuric acid from the chemistry kit.

"That's easy," I answered, "California History."

"Why, California History?"

"Because, that's all about my family. Dad's family had all these old Spanish land grants during the early days when the old California Missions were the center of everything and my ancestors got baptized and buried in them."

"But, Tony," he said with a big frown, "don't forget that your people go way back to the ancient Book of Mormon times, not just to the Spanish Catholic colonists of California."

"But, I like to study about those old missions," I said, "it was Father Serra that founded them. He was a good Franciscan priest. I think he must have been like Brigham Young, or even maybe, like Joseph Smith, Junior."

"Why do you say that?"

"Because Father Serra was the priest in charge of all those old mission colonies, and he was a man like the Presidents of our church: Father Serra listened to God."

"Oh no, Tony," he said quickly, "there is a lot that those Catholic priests did to the American Indians here in California that was very bad –very evil."

Now, *that* was the first time that I ever truly doubted one of my teachers. To myself, I wondered why my fourth-grade teacher, Miss Morman, had never taught us anything about the bad stuff that Father Serra had done. Looking up at the Science Man's face, I asked, "Really?"

"Yes," he answered, in a stern voice, "the first thing that they did, when they arrived from New Spain, was to keep the Indians they found from using their original language so that they couldn't tell their own old stories. Then, they replaced the old Indian legends about God and their past history with the Catholic stories that had lies and false stories about old Virgin Mary appearing to them."

By now, I had been taught in the Mormon Sunday school class that the stories, that my Grandma Nica had told me about the

Mexican Virgin of Guadeloupe, were really, "old women's tales." I remembered when my Mormon Primary teacher had said that those old stories my Grandma Nica had told me were not true stories, but that, they were like the story about Santa Claus, and Goldilocks and the Three Bears. So, by now, I knew the difference between the truth that Mormons know, and the false stuff "that other churches teach."

With that thought, I dropped what I was holding in my hand, and while we both wiped it up, I asked the Science Man, "Why did the Catholic priests replace the older Indian stories with their lies?"

For the rest of his visit, he taught me about many of the mean things that the Catholic priests had done. He told me about how the original California Indians had all been killed off when the Spanish gave the unsuspecting Indians some blankets that had been infected with a smallpox virus. He told me about how the priests replaced the stories that the Indians had used to remember their knowledge of the Book of Mormon stories, with fake stories about Catholic saints. He told me this was why none of the Indians in America can recognize the Book of Mormon now, as their true "ancestral history."

"That's bad! That's terrible!" "But," again I wondered why Miss Morman hadn't said anything at all about the bad stuff that the Catholics had done to the Indians, and I asked him, "why didn't my own teacher at school tell us about all that stuff?"

"Maybe she simply doesn't know," he answered in a matter-of-fact kind of way.

"Or…!" Then, without saying a word, I thought to myself, maybe she's a Catholic, herself!

"Or, what?"

"Well, I already know that she isn't a Mormon. She told me so herself, when I first met her because of her last name's spelling." I thought about it silently for a moment more then, I added, "boy, I'm glad that I'm a Mormon boy because –if I was still a Catholic like my cousins– then…!" My thoughts ran faster than my voiced words.

"Then?"

"You know? I have to help all my cousins see what really happened back then. I have to teach them so, they'll all know too!"

"Now, that's a good Mormon boy," he responded firmly. Then, he continued to wipe up the sulfuric acid I'd spilled and added, "let's you and me study more next week about what happened to the Indians when the Catholic Spaniards came and brought the Church of The Devil to the people that, we Mormons know, descended from the Book of Mormon peoples."

The next day was going to be Saturday. It was the day when I got to go to the Mormon Primary school. So, after supper, I went to my room so that I could read more in the Book of Mormon. I wanted to be ready for the lesson in Primary, and Sister Howell had told us last week that it was going to be about "Book of Mormon stories."

My favorite Mormon Primary teacher was Sister Howell, and today was no different than other Primary Saturdays. When she first saw me coming up the walkway, she held her arms out wide for me with that big smile. Now, she was standing up in front of all us kids, welcoming everyone to another Mormon Primary. She was tall and wore rimless glasses. I always wondered why she was so white, and I had guessed it was because she never wore any make-up, like Mom did. But, the things I liked the most about her were her hugs and her smile. "Today's lesson," she began, "is from the Book of Mormon!" Then, she went on with other stuff...

I sat there, not listening too well either, because I tried to remember the stories that I'd read the night before.

Then, Sister Ingolsby got up, and she began to lead all of us in a new song, "Book of Mormon Stories." It was a fun song.

After the singing time, Sister Howell started to talk to all of us, saying: "Children, we have a real Lamanite with us, right here in our own little class..."

Everyone else looked at me. I wondered to myself, Why are they all staring at me? I turned to Sister Howell.

Her smile got so big right then. I'd never seen her shine so. "Tony is very special to us because he comes from Father Lehi, the first Book of Mormon prophet..."

That was something I'd never heard before. Mom and Dad had never told me that our family had come from the first prophet written about in the Book of Mormon. But, I'd learned that, because a part of us was Indian, we were from some, "*La-man-ite*" ancestors.

"Now, Father Lehi...," Sister Howell went on, "...brought his little colony from ancient Israel at about 600 years b.c...."

Then, one of the older boys in Primary raised his hand, "the Book of Mormon says that the Lamanites were cursed with a brown skin because they were *wicked*. So, is Tony *wicked*?"

Everybody giggled and laughed.

At least, every one—except me. That's when I felt a feeling that I'd never felt at the Mormon Primary before. It was the same feeling that I remember having when Jimmy Campbell called me a "dirty Mexican" at school the other day.

One of the girls on the other side of the room raised her hand and asked, "Wicked? What's wicked?"

"Oh, no!" Sister Howell started to come down the aisle toward me. She got me by the hand and she took me up to the front of the room. "Get up on the piano bench, Tony," she said quietly to me, with her usual smile.

With that, I was suddenly taller than everybody! I was even taller than Sister Howell!

Some of the older boys laughed real loud.

This time, I laughed hard too.

"Some of Tony's ancestors were both Lamanite and also Nephite and…" she went on telling the story about how Father Lehi had had two sons, Laman and Nephi. "Laman was their bad boy and Nephi was their good boy. Their families were called after each of them: The Lamanites and the Nephites..."

"I know! I know!" Jimmy Howell had his hand raised way up high.

Everybody looked toward Jimmy.

"Alright, Jimmy," Sister Howell said.

"Remember? The Book of Mormon tells about how both of the races here in America before Christopher Columbus, came from Father Lehi's boys. All the Nephites and the Lamanites were the children, grand-children and, so on, of Nephi and Laman."

"Good," Sister Howell said quickly, "and, that makes our Tony a real *Lehite*! Tony isn't just a Lamanite; he's a *Lehite*!" she said with excitement. Then she went on talking about the only Book of Mormon prophet—that, Mom and Dad had ever talked to me about—who was a Lamanite, Samuel. "Okay Tony, you can get down now."

As I got down and started walking down the aisle, I could feel everybody looking at me. But, this time, it felt good –real good.

Sister Howell kept on saying, "The day will come when the Lamanites will come into our church in very large numbers and our Tony will play a big role in that work."

As I walked and sat down, her words seemed to be like sharp arrows –the kind my cousin Albert plays with– piercing my chest. It felt like something had hit my center. It was a feeling that I had never felt before, like a huge change had come into me –deep inside me. I guess I was happy to see that I was a *Lehite*. The Science Man had been right, I thought to myself, it was only because of our new church that I was able to know how good it really is to, not only be part Indian, but to also be a Mormon! As the class went on, I sat there feeling glad that I wasn't like my cousins in southern California because they were all Catholics, and because of that, they didn't have the Book of Mormon stories like I did. I had to do something to help them understand the truth too.

The next day was the first Sunday of the month. The first Sunday is Fast and Testimony Meeting at our church. That's when anyone in church can stand up at the pulpit, or just where they're sitting, and speak to everybody else about whatever they're feeling at the moment. Sometimes, we had been told, the person at the pulpit will even speak in words, *right from God*! This was my favorite of all the Mormon meetings because you never knew what the people were going to do. One time, when we'd moved to another ward, a sister didn't say one word; she had tears coming down her face and just went up to the big organ and played it. It made everyone cry.

I don't know what made me do it. But, when it was quiet for a long time, and nobody had gotten up to say their testimony, I got up and walked up to the front of the room. All the way I wondered to myself, what's happening?

I could feel Mom's eyes follow me right up to the front of the whole church.

I was even shaking a little and, I even wondered to myself, what am I going to say?

Sister Howell's husband was one of the Elders who sat up at the front, behind the pulpit, facing the rest of us. With a big smile, he pulled out the step behind the pulpit so that I could be high enough to speak right into the microphone.

There was this really exciting feeling inside of me. I took in a deep breath and began, "I love my Mom, my Dad and Maria. I love the Lord and Joseph Smith, Junior. I'm thankful for all the stuff that our modern prophet does for us." Then, something began to happen. It was like a different person was inside of me, growing and pushing outward. The feeling came from so deep that I wondered if it was going to come out of my little boy's chest. I noticed that I was crying because my tears were getting the pulpit all wet, and whatever it was growing inside of me, it made big pulling feelings that kept on...and on. I tried to stop crying, but I couldn't stop.

Brother Howell handed me a handkerchief from behind me.

Everything was getting wet, my tie and shirt...then, I said, "I know this is the only true church." I said a lot of other stuff but, I can't remember what it was I'd said. All I knew was, my heart was pounding so hard inside of me that I thought it would come up, on its own. Anyway, because I had heard so many others give us their own testimonies, I already knew the words to use to end it. So, I just said, "In the Name of Jesus Christ, amen," and I got down, and then, I just walked back to my seat.

When I got back to where Mom and Maria were sitting, they were both crying too. Mom gave me a big hug and Maria patted my lap. I also felt the touch of somebody behind me on my shoulder, but I didn't look back to see who it was.

"Mom," I whispered, "I felt the Spirit! I really did!"

"I know, *Mijo*," she said through her tears, "I know you felt it. I know."

Several years passed.

Mrs. White had just called me to her home classroom. Our high school's journalism club used her homeroom for work on *The Pleiades,* our yearbook, and for our work on the *Spartan News,* the school paper. Meeting with her was, in itself, a common thing for me. Her reason for me to see her after school today, however, was a change in the exceptional teacher/student relationship, which we'd worked to develop. She'd always carefully avoided confronting me on religious concepts. Mrs. White was a devout, Irish born Roman Catholic, and as a result of my recent trip to my first Mormon Church General World Conference in Salt Lake City, Utah, I was determined to become a Mormon missionary someday.

It's my junior year of high school. For me, this is the period of greatest impact in my life, that I write about in the first part of an essay [which was, eventually, published under the title, "Personal Dichotomies" in a 1999 anthology, edited by Katherine Kurs, titled, Searching For Your Soul]. I'd played the role of Pater in *The Diary of Ann Frank* and, we had won the Best Dramatic Production of The Year Award at the Barn Theatre, a local community theatre. Besides being a yell leader, on our yearbook staff and a writer for our high school newspaper, life was good for me; I was dating. But, in other ways, it was far more complex than life had ever been before. My inner conflict was apparent when a cast member, Gretta Stewart, spoke to *"The Diary of Ann Frank"* cast about her ordeal surviving The Holocaust. I'd responded with uncontrollable weeping.

Only last month, I had totaled Dad's new car. I had begged the police officer at the crash site to run strong interference with Dad for me. A memory was still fresh in my mind of how Dad had hit my sister (for an infraction I couldn't understand) when she was roughly sixteen. In school, I'd recently bungled some stuff working on the yearbook, and my counselor thought that it was because of some "emotional conflict." When the car crash took place, the officer found me crying like a baby, with my head slumped on the steering wheel. Even though it had been raining, and I couldn't see, I knew that I had failed to turn on my headlights when I'd left *Terry's* house.

What is it? Was my up-tight high school counselor right? Was something else that I wasn't consciously aware of, *the problem*? And now, Mrs. White called me to see her after school? What else had I done wrong? Would whatever it is, come between us?

The loud period bell rang and I nervously joined the rest of the students in the hallway rush. I tried to maintain my usual facial demeanor, as some of my friends flew by in the opposite direction, asking where I was going, "Uh, going to Mrs. White's homeroom. You know how ol' Mrs. White is..."

There she was, sitting at her little desk. White hair, like her last name, all primed and properly set up, and away from her face, although it was full and healthy. Her thin glasses lightly lay across the bridge of her nose, low enough for the usual twinkle in her eyes above the blue rimed lenses to reveal her fantastic joy for living. Her trademark gray sweater, buttoned at the top, was a constant message to me that her physical frailty was a disguise that covered her street-wise, New York life experience prior to coming to our town. In fact, we'd all often wondered why a woman of her high caliber and power would want to teach in our small out-of-the-way high school.

I took in a deep breath and then, let it out as I strolled into her room, "Okay, here I am. What's up Teach?"

Her big smile was always so disarming to me. "Tony," she began, "please. Over here, sit next to my desk." Mrs. White would always have me sit there whenever she wanted one of her heart-to-heart chats with me.

Like always, I went to her desk and sat next to it. But, this time, I'm all too aware of the sting of perspiration in my armpits. Of all the people in my life, I did not want *her* to be disappointed in me. Too many others in my life had been disappointed by my behavior, and my foolish choices, lately. "Okay, Teach," I said sitting down, "what's wrong?"

"Why, Tony," she said back, looking up at me over her blue glasses. That look was the same look that was later made so famous by the late Princes Diana of England. "Nothing's wrong," she went on, "at least, not that I know of yet." Finding out what stuff was going on in my life "away from the classroom" had always seemed interesting to her.

"But, your note said we needed 'to talk even after all we've said about politics and religion.' Is this about my editorial column in the Spartan News last week on the JFK presidential campaign? Did some board member, or the principal…"

Interrupting, she said, "Yes and no, Tony. Yes, it is about your editorial, and no, no one has complained about it to me."

"Well that's good, 'cause some old G.O.P., republican types among my friends have given me 'H' about it."

"Members of your church, you mean?" Mrs. White's fingers played with a number two pencil, waiting for my answer…

Although I shouldn't have been, like always, I was shocked at her insight. "How did you know that? Did Alice or David –or, maybe someone from the campus Bible study group– tell you that they didn't like…"

"Calm down, my good Friend," she interrupted. That word, *Friend*, was our agreed upon code word that meant I was being too excited and that I needed to calm down and just listen.

So, I took in another deep breath, and let it out, real slowly, like she'd taught me at the beginning of the year. I automatically folded my arms across my chest and my legs flew straight out; knees locked and feet out, with my heels, the only part of my feet touching the floor. "Okay," I said, "go ahead..."

"Tony," she said in a much more serious tone, "have you seen today's Los Angeles Times?" With that she picked up the folded newspaper on her little desk and opened it, holding it up to my face, adding: "I think it would be a good idea for you to read it here and then, let's break our rule for one hour. After you read it, say anything to me *immediately* about it that you feel and, what you say to me will be strictly confidential…" Then, she waited for me to read it…

The absolutely shocking headline staring back at me was: "MORMON LEADER BACKS NIXON." Suddenly, my full body went totally numb. I just sat there for, don't know how long. Then, I realized I was reading the headline—over and over again—without going on into the body of the shocking story, and I think that's when I got it. This is a life-changing moment for me. This is big!

What had been my biggest surprise because of all the talk after my editorial about Kennedy's campaign for President was that, it was the very people whom I loved, as Mormons, who were all against JFK *solely because he was a Catholic*. Our family had one of the first TV sets in all our neighborhoods and, over the years, I'd watched Nixon very carefully. As a teenager, I could see that he'd cause our nation some ugly problems if he were, actually, elected President. So, I decided to carefully look into his opponents. That was when I had discovered JFK. Nixon seemed too much like the bigots that Dad had talked so much about at the dinner table. But all the people who'd been my mentors, those I'd respected most in life it seemed, were adamantly for Nixon! I loved the devout members of my Mormon ward almost more than I loved my family. But, since my last editorial, these "saints" were laughing openly at what I knew was my rather serious observations on then, Candidate Nixon.

Mrs. White put down the crisp newspaper, and reached out a hand, and gently touched mine. Without a word, she smiled, and she left her hand on mine for a moment.

Finally, still silent, with my pained heart stuck in my throat, I picked up the paper myself, and slowly, I read the buy-line: "'We hope you win,' says Mormon Prophet, David McKay to Richard Nixon in Salt Lake City, Utah..." I felt betrayed, and also totally *mortified*. I could feel the well of tears building in both my eyes, and I said, almost inaudibly, "You saw this coming, didn't you."

She simply nodded her head, still being tender with me.

"Ahhhh..." The unexpected weird sound that was coming out of my mouth was like an animal's howl! Heat had mounted in my abdomen and it felt like it was now about to burst my head open. "But, he's The Prophet of God!" I knew the high tone in my voice was that of horrified confusion. "How can the Lord's Mouthpiece take the side of a radical, ultra-right-winged bigot like, Nixon?" I found myself re-reading the first sentence over, and over again, until my disbelief found an unfathomable profoundness—deep inside my soul's core. Then, after a lot of rambling and confusion-making with my words...

Mrs. White asked quietly, "What would you like to do, Tony? People who have read your words on Kennedy probably know of your profound religious conviction about your spiritual leader, and you know that they'll read this week's Spartan News to see how you deal with the fact that he has now come out openly for the Republican."

I knew she was referring to the Members of the high school Bible Club with whom I'd had an open, and on-going debate on the quad about scriptural interpretations. I had been trying to be a good Mormon priest, looking for ways to get our unique message out to people within my own influence. I had been tested several times by our open dialogue there because most of them were fundamentalist Christians, and they did not consider us Mormons to be Christian, in their way of interpreting the term. Mrs. White, I'd thought to myself, had obviously understood my predicament. Looking at her, I said, "In my heart," I began, "I want to follow the man I know as God's Prophet to the entire world. I've already told you about the epiphany I experienced a few months ago, when I got to meet him when I went to Utah for the L.D.S. General Conference."

She nodded, "ah –the light you saw and the voice you felt. Yes, I recall, Tony."

Then, getting up from my chair, and going over to the big windows overlooking the entire campus, I added, "but, –in my core in my soul's core– I know that I'm right to argue against Nixon and to argue for Jack Kennedy. I *know* I'm right on this one!"

"Tony," she said getting up and walking over to where I stood, "I am your English Literature teacher. I've talked much in our class about England's Sir Thomas Moore. Do you remember that particular section in your text?"

"The section on Becket," I answered.

"Yes," she said firmly. "Now, while it's not precisely the same kind of circumstance, you and Sir Thomas Moore have similar dilemmas –don't you think?" Mrs. White and I spent the rest of that hour talking about the similarities of my own dilemma, and the one that confronted Sir Thomas Moore centuries earlier. Both situations involved "politics" and, in both cases, there were "efforts to entrap" by persons of less integrity than Sir Thomas Moore, and also of far less than the personal integrity to which I'd aspired. Her answer that day in her home-room was that it was still possible to win the little social battle going on, if I had the presence of mind to, "...use... words well...What counts, is where *you* are; exploring your own life, irrespective of what anyone other than you thinks you *should* be..."

Kept within me, however, unrevealed even to ol' Mrs. White was, my sexual attraction to Terry. I admitted it to myself, and now, it was as if all Creation was conspiring against my desire to commit myself to the faith of my church, *The* Church. Only last Fall, I was in the old Mormon Tabernacle on Temple Square in Salt Lake City. Only last Fall, I sat at the feet of modern-day apostles and prophets, making my personal commitment to keep the faith, and to become a

Mormon missionary to the Spanish-speaking people of the world. The man who had declared for a candidate, whom I was convinced through my research was a bigoted man, was the very prophet whom I expected would write to me to officially extend the call to me to my expected ministry, like the prophet would do with any good Mormon boy. So, after our chat, my mind wandered...the rest of the day...

The other day in the rest room at the Mormon chapel, after early morning seminary, but before school, Terry came out of a stall behind me, as I finished at the urinal. When I had turned around, he exposed his semi-erect penis to me and asked if I'd help him tuck in his shirt! Too shocked, I hadn't told anyone of what had taken place.

I had kept the entire experience a secret. Nobody else knew that the powerful urge from within my body had been a spontaneous impulse to reach out and touch those forbidden parts of Terry's body. But, I had made a personal covenant with God when I'd met the Prophet at the conference in Salt Lake City, and like the poetry we'd studied in our lit class, "...*I had promises to keep*..." Like Joseph in the Bible, when he was confronted in a similar way by the Egyptian ruler's wife, *I feared for my* eternal welfare more than for my present curiosity and obvious physical drives. Like that ancient son of Israel did, when I was offered the sweetness of my most private desire, I also *ran* out of that rest room with, "fear and trembling"—*literally*!

It had been Terry, with whom I had been, on the night when I'd wrecked Dad's new Chevy car. It was anguish over my struggle to still be chaste, when Terry's overtures were so open, so honestly offered, that had caused all of my tears that fateful night, when the woman had run the stop sign because she hadn't seen my car coming. The tears that had half blinded my sight that night had been because of Terry's efforts that night in his bedroom to seduce me while we studied together on a seminary project. They were not because of piety, but they flowed out of me because I wanted to still be back there, on his bed, and as naked as he'd invited me to be with him! I knew, deep down, that the *real* reason I had forgotten to turn on the headlights that night, was because I was so dissected –cut-off from my true self– because of my need to be true to my understanding of right and wrong, as we'd been taught in *The* Church.

I knew that I was the true guilty party in our accident. I knew that it had been the combination of the rain outside *and the emotionally-charged shower pouring out of my eyes inside the car,* that had kept me from being able to see the woman's car to my left, as I had approached that intersection. Now, the shameful horror faced me squarely and conclusively. Even the Lord's own prophet seemed to be saying in the newspaper quote that my political choices were also suspect, exactly like my unrevealed, innermost and undeniable sexual longing for Terry! Beginning to feel turned upside down, it almost felt like I was going dizzy. I thought to myself, over and over, my emotional pain is a kind of wrenching...and it's reaching its limit.

However, Mrs. White had helped me to see now that –like Sir Thomas Moore in old England– I also still had options *with my words*. I might still retain my dignity and my integrity through all of this mess if I remained focused on my own inner awarenesses of all things political being completely separate from all the ecclesiastical stuff. She had also quoted Jesus, advising me to, "Be '…wise as a serpent…' with *words*, Tony" in my responses to those who were trying to set their silly little theological traps because of my personal convictions. I spent many soulful hours on my knees in prayer that night, and silently, in the days following. Although Mrs. White did not know the whole story, her wisdom had prepared me for what was to come; not only in my political talk, but in my sexual choices also...

Going to Mutual, the Mormon weekly youth activity night, was difficult for me. I'd always loved Mutual –it was where my need for friendship and my religious proclivities interfaced– but now it had been soured by the ugly politics of the election. The people at church events before the election had acted like loving brothers and sisters. But then, after I got involved in the public dialogue over the televised Nixon/Kennedy Debate, these people acted as enemies.

I often found myself even wondering within: *Why can't my Mormon brothers and sisters be like my Roman Catholic teacher, why can't they separate our religion from their politics, like she can?*

I didn't attend Mutual, or even early morning seminary for two weeks, and that, was unusual for me. When I did make the leap of faith to start attending Mutual activities again, it was Mrs. White's quotation that helped to keep me from loosing my sense of my own, personal dignity—to stay focused on what was important to *me*. In my mind, her last advice would calm my responses to the ugly jokes of others, "'*be wise as a serpent*' with *words, Tony*" I kept thinking her words to myself.

In spite of all the difficulty I'd had among those who claimed to be my spiritual brothers and sisters, I still would not change to the view they espoused. In the final analysis, however, John F. Kennedy won the election that year, and rather suddenly, my fellow Mormons stopped saying anything controversial to me about my own political choices. Although I'd worked in the local, "Youth for JFK" when I wasn't even voting age yet, I had learned some good lessons about integrity, and about the separation of church and state. Most of all, I'd learned what a strong-willed person I am. In fact, this was the first time I'd known my inner personal strength of will.

After President Kennedy took office, the issues that I'd been plagued with over the past months took on a theological dimension. Mrs. White and I had become a lot closer because of my ordeal, and the Wednesday morning after the voting, I found myself running to her home-room a half hour before the first period bell. A seriously adolescent question plagued me: How is it that; the Lord's Prophet apparently voted for *the wrong man*? I had to resolve it in my mind, or where would it all lead? This pondering brought me, the first time that I recall when *I, actually, overtly chose to simply overlook what seemed to clearly be an illogical, and an unsupportable theological contradiction.* I had to choose between my understanding of official Mormon doctrine about personal freedom of choice, as a private, sovereign citizen, and a public statement on the "political wisdom" of men whom I'd learned to call, "The Brethren" –the inspired seers and revelators– the Apostles and Prophets of The Church.

It had been Mrs. White who'd helped me travel through this dark night of my soul. With her help in our private sessions, I had chosen my future way to go, as I go on living. That was when, using personal intelligence instead of only loyalty to the men whom I still believed spoke for God on earth, I'd learned that *social survival is often about playing a role.* Retaining my sense of personal dignity was the best growth of those days, because I chose my inner voice over the words of another person, in spite of his rank in the Kingdom of God. Out of her own Catholic awareness, Mrs. White had taught that, my obedience to spiritual leaders is not good, if it contradicts my inner voice. Her words had agreed with what I'd learned about free will in The Church. A *non*-Mormon had taught me how to still remain a Mormon! That fact, would stay with me for decades.

So, it was because of Mrs. White's insight that I went on, and served a full-time mission for the Mormon Church because I could still believe our message was, "the only true message." But at the same time, by choosing my inner awareness, *and* living externally as I choose to live; living my personal life with a dignity derived of my now growing sense of personal integrity became my life's prime objective. Yet, I was not prepared for what this kind of honorable path would bring. I hadn't yet wrapped my mind around the idea of the cost of maintaining personal integrity in a world of total justice.

Indeed, the clarity of my inner processing didn't change my, increasingly, powerful contradiction of being attracted to Terry in ways that were incongruent with the Mormon way of heterosexual chastity. I wanted to be, "a good Mormon boy." In my freshman year at Brigham Young University I majored in theatre arts, and my extra-curricular activities had me playing in a lot of college stage and television productions. I was busy because I *had* to stay busy. I knew that, if I didn't, I might do something against my strong desire to stay "a chaste man." So in retrospect, it isn't surprising that I was awarded the "Most Promising Actor" award that year at B.Y.U. To others, my life was successful, filled with obvious accomplishment. But, mine was a deeply personal, *inner* conflict. It would, fatefully, engage me during my 1960s L.D.S. mission experience in Peru, in the company of my equally virile missionary companions. We were young healthy men, all from age nineteen to twenty-five—a prime time for major conflict and massive contradiction in my case...

All during my missionary experience, I would often ponder on this experience in high school. More than anything else Dad taught me as a child, foremost was the need for a guy to retain his personal dignity by strengthening his personal integrity. With my male companions in my mission experience, I would be tested over and over again on this single point, but I'd find a way around the demons that seemed to appear from behind the beautiful theological path I had come to know and cherish. The Church had become my pseudo-family, and forgetting the past, I trusted my church family would "be there for me" on the important stuff—especially, if I fell. However, more experience would teach me in unforeseen ways...

Two years passed.

I dated girls in high school. I dated a lot in college. But, I never found fulfillment in the dating game. I never approached the same level of intoxication with sex that I had been faced with in my high school seminary classmate and in Terry's bedroom the night I totaled my Dad's new car. I never had to struggle about sex in the way that my buddies on our high school football teams did. With females, I discovered that sex was an easy thing for me to avoid. So, when the official letter from the Prophet came calling me as a full-time missionary to South America, I easily qualified. I was a virgin.

When the letter finally came, I had taken a year off after my first year at BYU, and I had been working in Orange County, trying to save enough money for my missionary expenses. So, when the day came for us to have the customary farewell service at our church in Porterville, California, I had been away from that area for almost two full years. My biggest test of personal integrity relative to my recent commitment to Mormon sexual chastity hit me like a train the last Sunday before leaving for Peru. It was at the farewell service. In those days, Mormons *really sent off* their new missionaries!

It had taken me about fifteen minutes to walk from the car to the back row on the north side of the chapel. The ward members all seemed to go out of their way to greet me. Me! It felt great to be so warmly encountered by all of them. The conflicting issues that I had experienced growing up seemed like only a distant drum to me, now. Those issues, which I'd encountered during the presidential election, were like a far away reality compared to the reality, which I now had.

Renee was a young Mormon girl with whom I'd been good friends since sixth grade, and it was great to see her that day. Though her long bright red hair had now been cut short, it was like old times to have her presence in my world again –like one Sunday morning after I had been chosen as a part of our high school's cheerleading squad. Renee yelled out the same words on this day, that she'd called out that Sunday years before, as I had walked up those concrete steps to the church building, "Hail the conquering hero! See how he now mounts the steps, returning!"

Climbing up those old concrete steps, I thought to myself, what a tremendous greeting! Immediately, I was in that same old really good emotional place, all over again. Renee's greeting had filled my soul with an awesome confidence and sheer joy!

As I sat on that last row in the chapel, I thought to myself, we Mormons sure seem to make a big thing out of a guy going on his mission. Nevertheless, this thought didn't keep me from knowing that "I had arrived," into my planned dreams for my life to this point. I'd been ordained to our church's higher priesthood the previous evening by a member of our high council. This was my time now. I had come home.

Then, suddenly, my balanced sense of confidence began to swirl around me like a vanishing cloud. To me, it was as if he had brought an energy with him—as if a force field had radiated from him—causing everything to go into slow motion. So, I knew without looking behind me, that Terry had come in to the room...!

He came right to where I sat and he sat down right next to me on my right side.

Without looking at him, I went completely numb. That's when I first knew that, no matter how much I tried to be chaste, life for me, would always be a battle. But, today, I *had* to be strong.

The voice of the elder, standing up at the pulpit making the weekly announcements, became a distant noise. The swirling I'd felt an instant earlier, now, became a whirlwind.

Terry suddenly extended his left arm to hug me, squeezing my right shoulder with his body, while he extended his right arm to shake my right hand. There was Terry's big smile, right in my face. I had forgotten that his smile seemed more like a happy frown than, anything else and...oh, he looked so fresh...in his military uniform!

What should I do? Then, with that single question, I found myself embracing Terry as openly, and as completely as our seating would allow. The brush of our two thighs sent an electrifying rush though my whole body. Feeling that excitement, I nervously patted his back. But, it felt so good to just touch him! My blood became a boiling pot within me. I was torn asunder because I knew that the past two years had not dimmed my desire to be with this man.

"God, Tony!" he said, "it's great to see you again!" He then, placed his hand lightly on my right thigh, and squeezed it slightly.

That did it. I knew what was happening here. Now what? Arousal had usually been somewhat easy for me to control—but not, with *him*. "It's so wonderful to hug you too!" I said spontaneously.

In the distance the elder, standing up in the front, was still not finished with his announcements. Everyone else was focused on him, unaware of what was happening between Terry and me.

All I *really* knew at that moment was the aroma of Terry's breath. I had forgotten how absolutely intoxicating his warm breath was to me. His whispering in my ear was what I heard most clearly. The sound of his voiced words were so fulfilling to me, it felt as if I actually hungered for the sound of his voice!

I really have to keep my emotions together now, I thought to myself. I pulled away from him, "Wow! Look at you," I whispered, "you're a military man now!" I felt my whole being. I felt so alive! My entire body began to rattle, to shake—to literally, convulse—with fantastic, physical, sexual tension for the first time in my life!

"Yeah," he whispered back to me, still keeping his hand on my thigh, "when you went to BYU, I joined the army."

"Oh, Terry—you haven't been to Vietnam, have you?"

"No, but that might happen. I'm just back for a two-week stay and…"

That's when it happened. Again, I –he and I– were all that I was aware of. It was as if, in that instant, we had been relocated to an entirely different environment. In fact, I can honestly say that I had no clue about where we, actually, were in that moment. "Terry," I said, "I'd forgotten how good your breath smells." Those words came out of my mouth, so naturally that, I didn't hold them back.

Then, as if in response to my openness, Terry gave out an exhale that was long and slow, breathing his longing into my face, "Tony, in the past year, I've…uh…I've tried every kind of sex I can imagine…" His breath was so clean, fresh and sweet…!

Chills enflamed me; all over, I felt chilled *and* hot.

"Tony, I've done everything! So, now, I know what I want."

My vision was transfixed on his face. Everything else was a big blur. In that brief moment, to me, there was nothing else but his luminous face. He'd never looked so absolutely beautiful.

Then, with the last breath of air that he was breathing out slowly, he pleaded, "Come on. Let's get out of here. Let's drive up the canyon into the mountains east of here and let's do it up there, Tony. I *want* you. After all these years, Tony, I've tried it all, and I know now that you and I really are meant for each other. You and I are the same." He inhaled deeply, and let it out with, "Come on, let's you and me finally do it! Let's start a new life together. Let's be one. You want it too. I *know* you do. We're not like other people," he said emphatically.

That's when the elder's voice at the pulpit broke the wonder of that moment for me.

In my ears, Terry's honest passion was suddenly replaced by, "…and last but not least, tonight's service will be a farewell for Elder Antonio A. Feliz, Jr., who has been called to serve the Lord in the Andes Mission of The Church down in Peru in…" I could hear all the people turning their heads and looking toward us…

Terry's face went solid, like a stone. What had before been his flushed, glowing countenance, suddenly went rock hard. It went white. The weight of his hand lifted off of my thigh. "God Tony," he said turning his head down, as if to look at the floor between his two feet, "I didn't know…"

I struggled to maintain a smile because I knew that everyone else in the room was looking right at *me*.

"…forgive me, Tony," he said, still looking down at his two feet, "I'll never bring it up again, I promise."

At that instant, I knew I'd learned a valuable lesson for one who travels through socially threatening terrain. I realized that, if I don't actually choose, if I allow another to act while I merely react, then I am totally vulnerable to their choices. *As long as I am in the company of my church group*, that supports the goals I have made to conform to the way I had been taught to live, *then I don't have to make choices that conflict with my mind's values.* In that moment with Terry, I had also discovered how totally vulnerable I am to my physical passions. My libidinous limit had been revealed to me...

Three months passed.

Mormon missionaries usually labor in pairs. I had been a junior companion—our training status—for one month. My senior companion was easy to learn from. The rules said that we must pray "side by side, at one, or at the other's bedside every morning upon waking up," and I soon became accustomed to the forced intimacy.

We had been taught at the orientation in Salt Lake City prior to our missions that; we all needed to express love to our companion daily. Two times every day of our two and one-half year mission, we missionaries each had to verbally say to whomever our companion was at the time, "I love you Elder," either right before, or right after one, or the other voices the prayer, to which the other companion responds "amen." This rite was like a virtual *commandment* to us.

The big personal lesson I had discovered with Terry before my mission served me well in these moments of powerful intimacy. Nothing else frightened me more than these highly charged times of this daily regimen. At those early morning times, the sheer, one-piece under-garment (all us missionaries wore in those days) could not hide the raging hardness that is any nineteen-year-old, young man's early morning experience. Often, my embracing companion and I seemed to be more conscious of our mutual awkwardness in this daily/nightly obligation, than the mandatory, "companionship" ritual was probably, originally, meant to cause.

Once, my companion had such a huge one that, the tip of it got lodged in the material that makes up the fly of the under-garment we all wore to bed. So, trying to avoid getting into what became an inadvertent penile sword fight, he slipped, and began to fall on the floor! In trying to break his fall, my hands pushed away at either side of his torso, causing his huge and un-sheathed fleshy dagger to come out of his fly, gently tapping down on my own erect phallus!

Our mutual and instinctively loud laughter was the only honest, or even natural, response that could have been marginally acceptable to our strict mission rules. Even though we were each supposed to report any homo-erotic behavior that "might flare up" in our missions, we decided that this wasn't worth writing about in our weekly letter to the mission president. Later, I would think to myself of this incident far more constantly than I thought would be the case.

Mormon missionaries get transferred regularly for a good reason. I wondered if the mission president had heard of our fleshy sword and dagger incident when my first transfer came in a sudden way. Being suddenly transferred away was not my greatest moment of fear and insecurity, however, in those first months of missionary service. No, that fateful day came one full month after my transfer.

My mail had been kept in Lima, Peru because—supposedly—the office staff knew that I would be going away to another city to the south. Whatever the reason, it was after a full month of being newly assigned to supervise the missionary work in the city of Ica that I finally received mail that had been held up at the headquarters in the capital city of Lima. I had no idea of what was coming; I had thoroughly immersed myself in the work of my mission's call from a man whom I'd accepted as a prophet of God.

The previous two months had been my first as a missionary, and to my surprise, I'd ranked higher than most of the missionaries in the "numbers of new converts" who had come into The Church by my work. As a result—I'd assumed then—the mission president had called me to, additionally, minister as the branch president of local members of The Church in Ica, Peru, where we missionaries were stationed. I was to be a local spiritual leader of the local branch, at nineteen years of age, until a Peruvian was assigned.

It was after another month of being a new presiding elder of one of The Church's congregational units, when I finally received my personal mail. In the package, there was a letter that would force me to become aware of the impact of another person's choices. It was the dawning of a keen awareness within me of how significant each of our choices are, in a intricate way, intertwined with one another's. This was the letter that broke my wild inner being-like a wild horse is broken into submission to his human rider. It was in this way that, the external circumstances provided by my evolving life's journey, now, made my domestication by others complete.

"Dear *Mijo*," Mom had written, "Today, we laid one of your good young friends to rest in the old Porterville cemetery. Terry was buried…"

Suddenly, I was only aware of a horrifying echo in my room. It was a loud wail of pain. It was the terrorizing sound of a scream, bouncing off the stone-like walls of that Peruvian concrete room.

I was alone. That horrific scream had to have been my own. Later, I couldn't recall how long it was before I finally came to sense the anguishing pain in my solar plexus that had now firmly lodged itself into my core. But that's when I first saw the gushing wetness pouring out of my eyes in the reddened face, reflected in the mirror on the wall. Then, I began to feel the sensation of the mucous, freely flowing down from my nostrils. The terribly hurtful pain I felt cover me had overwhelmed even my, now, numbing senses. Oh, God! I thought, is this what it's like to loose a loved one?

Mom's letter went on: "It seems, his car went over a cliff on a mountain road east of where the church is, in Porterville…"

With those hand-written words, my mind's eye was open to the last time I'd felt Terry's warmth next to me in that chapel. He had talked about that green mountain place to me. The drops had now thoroughly wet the large envelope Mom's letter had come in, as well as the little desk at which I sat alone. Then, I felt nothing. I had now gone all numb, totally numb. I'd never felt this sense of non-feeling.

"[T]he note he left on his bed, told his mother that Terry had committed suicide because he had felt that he didn't 'fit in anywhere.' *Mijo*, she told me you would want to know. Be strong, *Mijo*. I know he was a good, sweet, young man because you were always so happy in his company. At least, he did not have to die in battle in Vietnam, but he left this world for a better place where he would 'fit in,' *Mijo*. My Blessing for you is that his spirit may now be allowed to be your guide as you labor in the Lords work. *Mijo*, the way that people pass on, is not for any of us to judge. The way some go, is not important. It is possible that, because he and you were close, his reason for his passing on was so that you could have his sweetness by your side, as you continue to serve God in all the rest of your life. Just remember the friendship you had with him, and use that memory for good in your own life. My prayers are with you. Be strong, *Mijo*."

When I finally got myself together, I tried to go on with all my duties as normal, but it was to no avail. I needed more. I terribly needed to find comfort in the words of my seniors in the ranks of the priesthood. So, I wrote a letter to my mission president about the sad news. So, until I heard back from him, I read Mom's letter over and over again, but I wasn't open to her wisdom and compassion. I was far too guilt ridden to be as charitable. I felt responsible somehow because of my choice to be a chaste missionary, instead of being who I knew I was, deep inside of me. Terry at least, had been honest with himself, and with me. I had been neither. The personal integrity, for which I had worked so long to attain, was open to my view now as nothing more than, a hidden sham. All of my efforts to hide myself from myself, and from others, was becoming unbearable.

A week passed with no response from the President.

A second week passed…

The Mission President finally sent a short note to me. He said, "Ugly ways of dying always await the unchaste and sinful. God's judgments take many forms, and suicide is one of them."

He'd written what I had felt, deep inside myself, would be the only way a priesthood leader in The Church *could* respond. The naked terror that I knew the horrible night when his response arrived was unlike any that I'd ever known. I, finally, understood. It was all horrifying, and clear to me. God only knows what else awaits those who remain unrepentant, with unclean bodies, when they die. The unspeakable fear of the damned was taking its unrelenting hold of me. *Would I also end up like Terry?* That ugly night, my sleepless body lay on my lonely bed—mentally traveling in my dark night of despair. The mission president's words had not brought me solace. His note had brought the vision of damnation and judgment, and his note had the authority of my file leader—heavy with the full weight of our belief in "inspired" leadership—for, he was my Moses figure.

I knew in my heart that I was, actually, no different than Terry. I knew that I had only repressed and controlled my own drive to express my love for him. I knew that I had been acting; playing the role of a truly chaste missionary, but Terry had been the truly honest, integrated personality in God's eyes. As a result, that awful night was filled with images of my relationship with Terry over the years of our youth in Porterville. On one dark, four hour long road trip with all the priests of our old ward, one that had begun at three o'clock in the morning, I had put my head on his lap, in the back seat of the car. I couldn't get *that* memory out of my mind. I could no longer deny *my primal lust for him*, which had begun in my earlier teen years. I finally understood that I was no different than Terry after all my efforts to obediently repress my true inner *queer* nature. God forbid, I thought, that anyone else becomes aware of this!

That night, for the first time, I became terrified of my own self. That was the first time when I, finally, understood the ancient advice from our holy scriptures; that we must all, eventually, "work out [our] own salvation in fear and trembling…"[iii] I, now, had begun my way on the path that forces any of us to live out of *fear*. At this stage of my life, I was definitely no longer on the way traveled by those becoming open souls. I had become domesticated. I'd been domesticated, like any of the weakest of us.

****

In his great book, The Sanctity of Dissent, Paul Toscano defined the phenomenon typified in my old mission president's written response –in contrast to my mother's far more open response to the same issue– as "Patriolotry, the worship of a *false* father-god."[iv] After reflecting on the stories, which I've related in this opening chapter, my sense now is that Toscano's idea perfectly fits our present civilization. Thankfully, I've now come to see that, whether we realize it or not, the globally common sacred stories actually give many messages to us, on various levels. One message is the vengeful and violent nature of our civilization's idea of an Almighty Father-God. Whether we realize it or not, sacred stories speak out loud, sub-conscious messages, given in ways in which most of us are not aware of having received them —*unconsciously*. Science terms this *subliminal communication*.

The level, on which this book will now focus, hopefully, is one that responds to some of those messages. We must not ignore these subliminal messages. One message in sacred stories is saying: *It is the externals, the penetrative rather than the receptive, which have ruled our behavior for over six millennia.* As we often hear, "the Devil is in the details." *It is the details which tell what has been done,* in contrast to what has been said and what *is,* or *what is done*, now, is the focus of this book. May my stories lead some to see that, in order to understand, instead of only reading the story line, we need to see *what happens* to comprehend the message of the sacred story.

In this way of focusing on our sacred stories –in what has taken place– we find a key that is far more important than what was said or taught by the ancients. The stories in this book tell how I've personally experienced the experiences, and because the telling of what has taken place is a clue to the dynamics which are engaged, the dynamics inform the whole. While engaged, not only on a personal level, this telling reveals that it is no different on the societal level.

The microcosm reflects the macrocosm and visa versa: I am saying that, it is no wonder "nice boys" in America massacre their bullies in Christian places such as, Peduckah, Kentucky; in Santee, California and in Littleton, Colorado. In middle America, this kind of violent behavior is what "nice boys" all had modeled to them. For, on the surface society deplores violence, yet, social behavior speaks the louder truth of a denied, but ubiquitous, violent American culture.

The one, common factor in all of the "nice boy" massacres and killings in the schools of our nation, and in workplaces where guns and bombs have taken the lives of innocent people, is the mind-set of a bounded, tribal worldview. In all of these ugly massacres, including the September 11, 2001 attacks, the terrorist was only reflecting the culture in which the terrorist was programmed as a developing child. This is not a condemnation of any religion, and this does not excuse the perpetrator, but it does point to a root cause of his evil act. When we consider *what kind* of sacred stories were recited, and *where* they were recited to each perpetrator in all these cases, we can see that the perpetrator sees his others as meriting capital punishment. This is because *that*, is the kind of response to their ugliness that had been previously modeled to the terrorist. As demonstrated in many following stories, the killer of his peers *is only a mimic of celebrated role models in sacred stories* heard in the sacred places of hypnotic, group recitation during his developing years—the biblical Samson, being the avenging killer's archetype.

In our 21st century, common, inherited cultural environment —in modern civilization—an unbalanced aggression, violent rage, and a justice which is based solely on retribution, are the driving dynamics of how we have historically evolved. The problem is that Toscano's patriolotry is about tribal, male-centric loyalty and values, which flourish in a social context like ours, which is today heavily weighted in the extremes of older fundamentalist ideas from another age. This inherited false extreme view of "goodness" is then fed by our human nature to mimic what we are modeled by others, for that is how humans evolve. For, before all else, we are *mimics*. We're all like the monkeys in the Hundredth Monkey 1940s experiment!

This is the great global problem: We humans each evolve by our mimicking of modeled patterns of behavior, and our Western cultural patriolotry is patterned after an image of an "almighty," "vengeful" deity of ancient, marauding, patriarchal, tribal societies. The United States Secret Service recently released a related study aired, October 14, 2000: According to their findings, the common factors in all the shootings and bombings by "nice boys" against their peers, and in some cases, against their teachers –in each case over twenty years– all had to do with their "response to being" previously "bullied." As in the Santee, California case, all of these "nice boy" massacres—as I call them—were actually retaliations for the wrongs of others. This is because the deity that we have mimicked –all we, who come from the three religions that descend from Father Abraham– we call the Almighty Father, but to me, this deity seems –in retrospect, at least– like he is neither "Almighty," or fatherly, in the loving sense of that word.

There are many examples of what I mean by those words. But, the one in the biblical Book of Numbers, Chapter 31 is typical. Here in this example, this god sounds more like a puny man, than like an actual deity worthy of the worship of any who value peace, love, harmony and innocent children. Or, I ask: What do we –in our modern era– understand, when it is written there that, this ancient god commanded religious patriarchs to:

"Kill every male among the little ones and every woman who hath known man by lying with him, but all the women children that have not known a man by lying with him, keep alive for yourselves"[v]

This is the father-god of our Western spiritual ancestors. But as for myself, I will not and I cannot respect a god whom we claim behaves in an absolute awareness –for, an "omniscient" god would be absolutely aware– of his abusiveness. Abuse is not any evidence of love. So, because I don't worship a god who knowingly behaves in this way, who also knows full well that we humans will mimic his behavior as if we were literally his children, I do not, and I will not worship a god who models abuse in his "omniscience."

My point is a simple, basic one: In light of the reality that it is a natural universal trait of human beings to mimic what is modeled to us, in retrospect, I can clearly see what the ancient record reports. These documents, which are usually read and recited in our most holy days and at times of reflection –these sacred stories– teach an ugly, pseudo-morality in which the will of a ruthless "father-god" is revealed to actually be a manipulative device for covering up the harsh and cruel barbarity of our Western spiritual ancestors.

For centuries now, our Western authors and writers—like most any other human being will do—have mimicked the scribes of those ancient times. Thus, with precious few exceptions, our more modern storytellers give only footnotes on the work of the original Hebrew storytellers of Eden. Our civilization only produces writers who offer us more of the same arcane story line. Even the great Star Wars epics—and the Matrix movies—are about good verses evil, as if the two were mutually exclusive. Yet, what I have learned in the last part of my life, as will be told herein, is that *there is another way of seeing* the world. Yet, these films do emphasize a key that will be explored in the stories that follow: All these works tell of an actual, *tangible* Force—a vibrational *Energy*. The existence of this *Energy* reveals a certain interconnectedness in, among and through all that is, including all of us human beings.

Understanding this single idea has been an essential factor to my personal healing. This interconnectedness of all things—of us—is a key of knowledge that our human Mass Mind now, *today*, critically, urgently needs to comprehend. For, the alternative to such awareness is ignorance of truth, and ignorance of this truth is why our species has continued to make the same ugly mistakes from our present civilization's earliest moments. Where "The Force" in Star Wars is central to the theme of all of these films, I will endeavor to show through the true stories in this book that *The Force of Mass Consciousness* uses the chaotic nature of the universe to create our common reality. For, *that* realization has been my experience on the personal level. I am today far more aware than I was as an ecclesiast, of the absolute ability of the human Mass Mind in our molding of, refashioning of, and creating future reality. The film vocabulary of The Matrix calls it "belief"—religious vocabulary terms it, "*faith*."

The personal experiences, which I related in this chapter, took place in the fifth and sixth decades of the last century. They are how I experienced the experiences that I shared with others. Yet, to be totally truthful, these are a re-visitation to those experiences, in the context of today's turbulent political and social times. Those experiences, in this way, expose the terrible mistakes I made. They especially expose my personally vulnerable periods.

However, my sense is that the mistakes were made because of my lack of relevant data. Had my former mentors been able to provide the data, which I now see I lacked then, my choices would have been extremely different. As difficult as what I write may be to some, *all storytelling is about identity, and I tell the stories because they reveal what actually is. What is, is revealed by what is done.* So truly, in the final analysis, after all is said and done, all doctrine and theology and all culture mean nothing. It is in truth telling –in telling what is– that our behavior speaks clearly to anyone seeking greater understanding. This is because *experience is the master teacher.*

Yet, we must not be too harsh on ourselves because –as it was with me on the personal level– all our cultures are inherited. Moreover, the common stories that I speak of are far more than mere cultural traditions. These stories are our *sacred* stories, and I do not write on these ideas without considerable personal concern. I value the sanctity of all myth, and history is replete with many examples of martyrs who challenged their own culture's sacred stories, and *that*, is not something I seek. However, it has now become far too clear to me that much of our current civic and social disintegration comes directly from the old sacred stories, *themselves*! They are repeated aloud to us in our most sacred places, and at our times of holiest reflection. These are always times and places where our human sub-conscious mind is vulnerable to the awesome power of suggestion.

Consider how seriously child developmental psychologists view the new experiences of a child's first three to five years of life. The music and aromas—the affect images—are all the same as when we first experienced them in religious services; first, as evolving infants, then as toddlers, and then finally, as pre-pubescent children. For many of us, a nearly hypnotic state is achieved by this kind of mass ritualized social experience. If I am correct on this observation then, particularly that specific repetitive environment –public places of weekly worship– makes us all vulnerable to a systematic, psychic suggestion technology known to ecclesiasts. In retrospect, I find that I now discern what I could then, only sense; back then, when I was being subversively influenced by the mentors of my youth. I see that their behavioral contradictions did not compute with what they had presented publicly in their role of "tellers of wisdom."

However, back then, I was not yet experienced enough in life's journey to be aware of the fact that my own personal beingness is not about *what should be,* but it is about *exploring what is*. This notion of "should" will be further discussed in subsequent stories. For now, let me say that I now see that –even in those adolescent years– I was a truth teller; a truth teller relating within a culture of *untruth*. Even in high school I was one who said what I saw, because by that age of my life, I already knew that telling what had happened was the only way I could discern deceptive defensive dynamics in others from the more honest and authentic ones. That is when I first saw how they abuse scripture.

Yet, I wanted to believe the sacred stories. I wanted to fit in, and well, everyone else—all around me—seemed to really believe in them! The primal social urge to be *in-sinc.-with*—to be accepted by the others within my "second womb"—had overwhelmed me. It was easy for me to develop faith in my mentors, *if I could hide from everyone, that which they would all condemn.* Although, this was decades before our military community adopted the policy of "don't ask, don't tell," I began to live my life *hoping* that no one would "ask", and by finding ways to never "tell" any others anything about what I knew then, that I was. I had known shame in my life up to that point, but now, I worked hard at building illusions of denial about my sexual attraction to other men, and it was all based in shame.

I had gone into my homosexual, queer closet—my *faggot's* closet—by classic institutional seduction because of an institution's expertise in systematic institutionalization of myth *as history*. As in date rape, it was seduction until I'd gotten more sight, by experience in the experience, to be aware of my true, personally *violated* state. Unfortunately, *that* enlightenment would take many years to bless my—by *then*—extremely complicated emotional life. Until I went through those years, I would not transcend what I had become...

NOTES TO CHAPTER ONE

[i] Out of The Bishop's Closet, *A Call To Heal Ourselves, Each Other and Our World* by Antonio A. Feliz (Alamo Square Press, San Francisco, Calfironia, 1992).

[ii] "Personal Dichotomies" in Searching For Your Soul, *Writers of Many Faiths Share Their Personal Stories of Spiritual Discovery,* edited by Katherine Kurs (Schoken Books, A Division of Random House, Inc., New York, NY. 1999) pages 64-75. This piece was also published earlier in the 1996 Lambda Rising Book of The Year Award For Religion anthology edited by Brian Bouldrey, Wrestling With The Angel, *Faith And Religion in The Lives of Gay Men* (Villard Books, New York, NY. 1996).

[iii] Mormon, Chapter 9: verse 27.

[iv] The Sanctity of Dissent, by Paul James Toscano (Signature Books, Salt Lake City, Utah 1994).

[v] Book of Numbers, Chapter 31, verses17-18. Also note especially verses 25-41:   "And the Lord spake unto Moses saying, Take the sum of the prey that was taken, both of man and of beast, thou, and Eleazar the priest, and the chief fathers of the congregation: And divide the prey into two parts; between them that took the war upon them, who went out to battle, and between all the congregation: And levy a tribute unto the Lord of the men of war which went out to battle; one soul of five hundred, both of the persons, and of the beeves, and of the asses, and of the sheep: Take it of their half, and give it unto Eleazar the priest, for an heave offering of the Lord, And of the children of Israel" half, thou shalt take one portion of fifty, of the persons, of the beeves, of the asses, and of the flocks, of all manner of beasts, and give them unto the Levites, which keep the charge of the tabernacle of the Lord. And Moses and Eleazar the priest did as the Lord commanded Moses. And the booty, being the rest of the prey which the men of war had caught, was six hundred thousand and seventy thousand and five thousand sheep, And threescore and twelve thousand beeves, And threescore and one thousand asses, And thirty and two thousand persons in all, of women that had not known man by lying with him. And the half, which was the portion of them that went out to war, was in number three hundred thousand and seven and thirty thousand and five hundred sheep; And the Lord's tribute of the sheep was six hundred and three-score and fifteen. And the beeves were thirty and six thousand; for which the Lord's tribute was threescore and twelve. And the asses were thirty thousand and five hundred; of which the Lord's tribute was threescore and one. And the persons were sixteen thousand; of which the Lord's tribute was thirty and two persons. And Moses gave the tribute, which was the Lord's heave offering, unto Eleazar the priest, as the Lord commanded Moses."

"Words carry vibrational keys that engage the creation of our future reality in our common world because words re-present thoughts. This truth - that our words are merely symbols of our own thoughts - is a key to changing our future because our thoughts are the vibrational keys that engage the creation of future reality in our common world... "

CHAPTER TWO

EXPERIENCING LIFE AS IF UNDER SIEGE

Eventually, my life journey brought me to an emotional place where it became obvious to me that, the Universe had repeated a similar phenomenology, over and over. *How* I had experienced the universal experience had become so repetitive that I had to stop and examine what I'd been creating in my world, over and over, again. That process, took a few months, and it brought me back to the decade of the sixties in the 20th century, and I was forced to face some extremely painful realities.

As was the case with Osama bin Laden's Afgani Taliban society in the early 21st century, the exploding American social awareness of the sixties was *not* experienced by some of us Americans who were then, in America's sheltered, ethno-centric, patriarchal, rigid, closed communities of faith. This was especially true for the religious Utah based Mormon community. I personally know this is the case because I lived within that religiously rigid Utah Mormon community of faith in the 1960s. For BYU students, the sixties of the last century were not the social, political epiphany which, *that* decade was, for the mainstream of my generation.

Decades later, a long talk with a new friend from Kashmir would teach me that, experiencing life as if under siege for *us* was, no different from what had clearly motivated the September 11, 2001 terrorists. That old sting of perspiration then, came—as if on cue—and I had to ask myself: Are *we*, those of us who come from *America's* Religious Right, an American equivalent of Afganistan's Taliban?—are we, *really*? But more importantly, if that *is* so, then *how* can I change, after all—if this *is* my original programming—I *can* change, can't I? I saw that on the way of becoming open souls, I must now dare to ask what, were *unthinkable* questions in my former contexts. It was time to transcend my religious abuse...

That kind of openness is what had initially begun a nine month-long, intense introspection of what I can now understand as a personal phenomenology. I began to explore how I had experienced all the social experiences of my past. The surprising part of it was that, the process took me back to a dramatic series of experiences I'd had when I was about to finish my missionary experience, living high in the wondrously quaint and small Andes mountain villages of *Ancash*, in the Peruvian Switzerland, as a youthful Mormon missionary back in 1965…

****

I'm nearing the end of my time as a missionary. I have often opened my journal to that date; nearly three years ago, when high in a jet that was circling around Cuba because of the Cuban Missile Crisis of 1962, we six new Mormon elders had met *that* American couple. I've noted how I'd been struck then, by their sense of the mystical, and how I'd been so relieved at having known the ritual of the Mormon Temple because—other than healings—I hadn't seen any mysticism The Church I've known out of the Temple. Before my Temple initiation, at nineteen years of age, I often privately longed for some equivalent in my Mormon experience of my holy experiences in Roman Catholic liturgical affect imagery. Mormon meetinghouses have no altars. Mormon services are *meetings*. We Mormons use altars only in dedicated *holy* places: *In our Temples*.

So, in that moment in the jet flying toward a land I was to live in for almost three years—away from a Mormon Temple—I was happy I'd experienced the Mormon Temple Endowment Ceremony. Also, because of a special ritualized commissioning blessing by an apostle, as part of my missionary orientation experience, I knew that a "fated encounter" in "a village, high in the Andes" was in store for me. That sensation in the core region of my solar plexus had confirmed it back in 1962, precisely as *that* couple had spoken in that jet of things mystical existing here.

Looking out on the puffed softness of the clouds below us then, in that environment—where only that certain undercurrent of noise made by the jet is audible—I mentally reviewed the words of the apostle who'd laid his hands on my head in Salt Lake City. As an apostle, he had been commissioning me for this assignment. In those days, he was a member of the Council of The Twelve Apostles of The Church, and eventually, he became President Howard W. Hunter. One of the few ordained prophets of The Church had then solemnly spoken that prophetic promise to me:

Suddenly, that early morning sun's bright, yellow rays had flashed in, from outside of the coach window, with fierce intensity, blinding my vision. It had been as if pondering my journal entry with the sun glaring so, had been a phenomenological punctuation. I re-read his 1962 prophecy...

"...*and before the end of your mission, you will be called to preside in the work in a small village high in the Andes Mountains. When this happens, be faithful and fearless and obey the direction of your mission president...*" I'd often gone back to that journal entry. The words had been electrifying, an adventuresome foretelling—in tones, ominous—warning me, counseling me about some yet future event in which I should be "faithful and fearless" "...*before the end of* [my] *mission...*"

Then, we'd all arrived in Lima, Peru, my first mission field city in the Andes Mission of our church:

The first day, as we arrived in Lima, the older elders had told us "greenies" that they were taking all of us to visit 'the city's gold museum.' But their bad denominational sense of humor felt like an attack to me when we arrived at the place they had *condescendingly* called the 'gold museum.' It was on the second day:

As we entered the massive, colonial, wooden doors of that large, Roman Catholic Cathedral near Lima's touristy, *Giron de la Union*, the darkness of the inside was intensified by the brightness of the overcast Lima sky. I couldn't focus my vision...I couldn't see...I couldn't walk.

Then...the aroma. The flickering colors. The glittering candles. The, oh so angelic distant echo of a woman's voice practicing a rendition of *Ave Maria*–

Suddenly...everything...went into...slow motion... What had happened? I'm on my knees! Have I fallen? My fellow elders are all helping me get up from the dusty, cold concrete floor. I look around me, and I see that we're in a dark alcove of that old Lima church. Evidently, I fell—for some reason. How awful! Did I pass out? I felt mortified!

A distant sounding voice asked, "Elder Feliz, are you...are you, okay?"

I think it had been his question that had helped my mind to focus. The first awareness I'd had was that we'd all walked into the church. I kept looking up, and around me. The uh, aromas...the real smoky incense, the mysterious, dark shadows, and all the glittering, candle-lit, bright side altars! Stained glass filtered the sunlight from above me...and the echoes! Oh, the echoes—I'd forgotten about the *echoes*! The sound of a fallen kneeler land hard, on the stone floor, and it echoed throughout the darkness.

One of the elders gave me some water from the little canteen he always carried with him, "Here, drink all you need, Elder," he had said with compassion.

As I drank that water, I was able to go inward. There, in open company with my fellow Mormon missionaries, I was able to see my response for what it was—The problem was that; I couldn't share my newfound awareness of how my stumble, was probably an emotionally programmed response, one that had been imprinted onto my mind when I was a child who was frequently at mass inside a Roman Catholic church. I would not be able to freely talk with any of them how I could see it as a dynamic that was built into who and what I still am; that, *it* decides *how I am in such a place.* I couldn't reveal what I felt to my fellow Mormon elders here, on my knees, *still*. It hit me after drinking some water in that huge cathedral. I had realized that I'd felt that old urge from my early childhood to cross myself! No, none of these seven elders—now, my fellow Mormon missionaries—would understand. Not, *that*! Not, *crossing* myself!

Although every bit the Mormon, as any of the young men who'd stood by me at that moment; I'd known that there had been a profound automatic response built into me. That, deep within me, it had energized an inner urge to cross myself by making the Roman Catholic sign of the cross as I'd been taught as a small child. But, this was *not Mormon* behavior. I'd felt an overwhelming spontaneous urge to cross myself there on that cold concrete floor in old Lima, Peru, and *I was terrified* because I'm a *Mormon* now! Even more distressing, I'm a Mormon *missionary* now!

Eventually, nearly three years passed.

The small village of *Yungay* was my final assignment before my release as a full-time missionary for The Church. This village is a post-card, picture, perfect place huddled against emerald green foothills below a huge mountain locals call, *El Huascaran*. It is due east, and there is an awesome turquoise colored lake at its top; *La Laguna Yanganuco* is one of the area's most sacred places. The people known in the villages of *El Cayejon de Huaylas* as the "Highland" people—because they live on the *altiplano*—consider the lake to be a residence of their ancient pre-Colombian ancestors. Below the four little mountain villages –due west and away from *El*

Huascaran and its wondrous turquoise lake– is the fast-paced, red-brown and turbulent *El Rio Santa* (The Holy River). It winds its way in and out of the checkered verdant fields of crops on either side.

In my mind, I often remember that this is the mystical place those two American tourists had talked so much about on our flight to South America over two years ago. That man had called this, "...a place where mystical/paranormal phenomena are pretty common," and the woman on that 1962 flight had added, "...it's because of the meshing of pre-Columbian perceptions with those imposed by the dominant Roman Catholic tradition there." This was the way that the couple on that flight had used to describe this place. It could not have been better phrased to intrigue the mind of a new Mormon missionary in Peru who, at the time, believed the stories in the Book of Mormon are a valid historical record of pre-Columbian peoples, and I think *this* village is *the one prophesied of...*

"What is it about these people? Why are they afraid of us?" These were my constant two questions, lately. My new companion, Elder Harmsen, was probably beginning to wonder about me because of my verbalized questions. Our mission president had directed us to open our proselytizing labor in a mountain canyon called *El Cayejon de Huaylas*.

My companion's response was, "Yeah Elder Feliz, in this little town, the small kids run in their homes and close up their shutters when we walk by. You said 'it's the kids who first get friendly with us, Gringo' missionaries.' That surely isn't the case here, Elder."

He was right. We were now walking down a street, by the many concrete colonial doorways and wood shuttered windows in the massive adobe outer wall, against which the stone sidewalks were constructed on either side. We'd been walking down the center of the old cobble stone street—that people back home would call 'quaint'—and I realized that, very uncharacteristically, as we'd all approach a doorway or a window, on either side, it would slam shut. The more I thought about what was happening here, as we both walked by, the more the slamming sounds were like firecrackers going off as we walked down that old narrow cobble stone village street. I thought to myself, these little children are actually afraid of us. So, turning to Elder Harmsen, I said, "you know, Elder; this isn't normal, and I bet it has something to do with what that little boy said to us at that café where we've started to eat breakfast every day."

"You mean what he said about the village priest getting back from Lima last night?"

"Yeah, I mean, what else is different? Yesterday, the little kid in that house we just passed was super friendly to us." With that, I got a vivid picture in my mind of where we had to go to confirm —or to, at least, eliminate our suspicion. "Let's go back to the house where the two sisters said they'd gotten permission to…"

"Elder," he interrupted, "remember, we're not supposed to teach them unless we have written permission from their head of household. You know the rules."

"Well," I said, "if those two *women,* finally, have their dad's permission then, let's ask them what they know about what's being said about us that makes the children run off as if we're the boogy man, or something."

Fortunately, they'd both gotten written permission for us to be allowed to teach them the sacred stories of our proselytizing gospel. So, after setting up a date to actually present our lessons to them, we were able to learn from them that, indeed, Father Gomez had returned to *Yungay,* the village where Elder Harmsen and I had been assigned.

Yungay was, up to that ill-fated day, a serene environment during weekdays. But, because of its location in *El Cayejon de Huaylas,* when the sun sets every Saturday afternoon, the locals are no longer the only residents in *Yungay.* As if on cue from out of the wings of a staged pageant, the highland Native people come down into *Yungay* from the *altiplano.* Sunday is market day, the day when the "meshing of pre-Columbian perceptions" that I'd heard of years ago are visible to us all.

All the aromas changed. Gunny pig is the favorite meal being bar-b-qued on open flames a block from the old Catholic Church. Even the colors, which everybody wears in public, all changed. Vestments become brighter and more traditional than during the week. Instead of the infrequent group of children playing along the narrow cobble stone streets—on weekends—the local Roman Catholics proudly process their shoulder-born images of their dead saints, venerating them, as they are reverently paraded by the townspeople. The constant sounds of, even nature, dramatically changed. The wind bellowing through eucalyptus groves and the distant roar of The Holy River changes into thousands of human voices chanting out their Christianity as local musicians play their old instruments of the sacred religion of their ancient Inca ancestors.

But, this weekend, I should have sensed a major problem could be brewing for us *NorteAmericano* Mormons. When I saw the distant, tweaked look of cocaine addiction in the dull, glassy eyes of the highland people, I should've known better *sooner.* Usually, they would all sit along the main road that goes in and out of *Yungay* all night on weekends. I should have put it all together, then. Our little group of foreign missionaries, who had come into *Yungay* to take converts away from the local priest's parish, was in mortal danger, now that the priest had returned from Lima. Much like today's proselytizing American Evangelical Christians seem unaware of how their form of proselytizing and their Bible distributions must appear to mainland communist Chinese Government officials, we Mormon elders saw ourselves as spiritual liberators of the villages. But then, I was seeing only from within the encasement of my own second womb.

It had not occurred to me that it might be significant that on the earlier weekends –when the priest had been away in Lima– the highland people, who sat along the main road in and out of town all night long, did not have that tweeked look of cocaine addiction! That look had appeared in the eyes of these people from the *altiplano* after the priest had returned from his two months of being away from *his* parish—the same parish that the two families, who had already joined our church, had left. We had built a concrete baptismal font into the ground floor of the place we had rented and there, they had all received *our* baptism rite. We'd been extremely successful at also acquiring several more prospective members…

After leaving the home of the two sisters who confirmed to us that the local priest had returned from his two-month time away, we decided to officially ask the local police to be aware of our concerns for our safety. The *Yungay* Police Station was located on the northwest corner of the town plaza. Along the main plaza's entire eastside, the Catholic Church reigned over the scene from a higher elevation than the rest of the plaza because of the slant of the mountainside on which the village was built. The tallest objects facing the plaza were four tall palm trees that were a bit higher than the church's bell tower. By this time, it was nearly noon and that meant that the station would soon close its doors for three hours for the afternoon siesta. As we approached the big front door, I could see that the mayor of *Yungay* was talking with one of the police officers in the doorway. The mayor liked us. We missionaries spent dollars here.

It was *Yungay's* village mayor, a successful businessman who owned the only hardware/general store, who'd introduced us to a full city council at a banquet only weeks earlier. We missionaries had seen that event as a part of our call to introduce this village to our unique Mormon brand of Christianity. To us, there was no problem with a businessman's ulterior motive in the mayor's exuberance;

exuberance, which became all too visible to us when he'd introduced us to his other guests at an event:

"Y *Estos dos Senores*," (And these two gentlemen) are the two North-American missionaries. They have purchased three of those porcelain toilet bowls that I've told you all about," he had begun, and eventually, he'd ended with, "They got three for three rooms in their new places." It was like a television commercial.

It was his blatant sales pitch that did it. His transparent use of us importing the town's first porcelain toilet bowls through his hardware business as a *gringo* endorsement of his product; had generated a totally unexpected response within me. It was free enterprise at its finest! But, an unfamiliar sensation, deep in my center had become engaged, and I asked myself what it was? I'd say, "We're very pleased with them." We were all heard to say that, in response to every query at the banquet about the good mayor's toilet bowls. I felt used, yet, I thought it wise for us to play along with the manipulated endorsement from us that, the mayor had staged.

That was the event after which I first wrote in my journal on our implied endorsement, and how it may impact future events to our benefit. "After all," I'd noted in that night's crisp spring air, "it's not a bad thing to have the mayor in our social dept." Then, "in light of how the town's children were now reacting to us," I noted in my journal today, "who knows?—we may need to 'call in' the mayor's indebtedness to us."

I wanted to be a truly good leader here. When the mission president had assigned me to labor in *El Cayejon de Hualas*, I read and re-read the words that I'd recorded years ago when [the now late] President, Howard W. Hunter, had commissioned me nearly three years earlier: "*...before the end of your mission you will be called to preside in a small village high in the Andes Mountains...*" I'd prepared for this, or so I thought...

Over the previous two months, all of our major efforts were focused on informing the village leaders–the mayor and his town council–how our being in their town is a positive advantage to them as men. Elder Harmsen and I visited each of the men individually, and asked them to respond to our genuine friendship as part of their Andean economy. We not only let them know about the average amount of American Dollars each of us would spend at any their business, but we also spoke to them about the many other pairs of Mormon missionaries who would visit. We told how all our fellow *NorteAmericanos* planed to reside on the road connecting all the small villages along the full length of *El Cayejon de Huaylas*. I knew that these men ruled the civic establishment in *Yungay*. They had each been made aware by us all, how supporting our presence in *Yungay*, was good business sense in their favor.

All of our reaching out to the city fathers paid off one night as we were in our weekly Mutual Activity, The Church's auxiliary for teenagers. The two sisters, who now were receiving lessons from us, were both present. The two families who'd first joined our growing branch of The Church were in attendance. Half a dozen boys were part of the Mutual Activity group that night also. My companion and I had alerted our district leaders in the village of *Huaraz* about our sense of being under siege, and they [our mission district supervising elder, together with his companion] had also come to *Yungay* for the weekend. They had all stayed into the week because of what had happened the previous Sunday down at the plaza at the *Yungay* Police Station to all four of us...

We'd finished our after Sunday services business, and all of us were on our walk toward one of the two cafes where we usually had our late Sunday lunch meal. As we approached the last block of the cobble stone street before the town plaza, we all heard the raspy voice from loudspeakers on top of the Catholic Church. The man's loud voice was piercing me to my core.

His words yelled out the ugliness of hate and of the vilest of intentions. Among the more tame of his ugly, verbal insults from loudspeakers on top of that domineering village church building, Father Gomez had had the inhumanity to lie, saying that our prophet, the president of the Mormon Church, David O. McKay, was "...a practicing polygamist."

Okay, that did it! Now, his lies were attacking our Prophet! Stopping in my tracks, I turned to my companion, and then to our district leader, Elder Zabriski, and then, finally, to his companion. I didn't have to say anything. Immediately, we all began to run down that hard, cold cobble stone way. Each leap forward quickly became a leap for safety, a leap toward the *Yungay* Police Station, due west of the old church, where the sound was blaring from. We had not panicked. Our only rational choice was to make a fast dash for the one place in town that the mayor had promised would never betray our trust.

Suddenly, as we all entered the intersection at the village plaza, in my right periphery vision –eastward, toward the Catholic church– there were a lot of angry looking people, easily over a couple hundred Highland people. They were coming toward where we were, and they were now, at the point of entering the plaza itself.

"Faster, Elders," I yelled back, "Look! There's a real angry mob coming from the right." Like a track and field day event, the four of us went into a fast sprint, as in the final meters before the line. Then, after about half a dozen running leaps across the town's main plaza, to me, it all went into slow motion...

To my right, the mass of hatred seemed to be far larger than I'd originally guessed; the men were brandishing thick sticks and the women were all carrying rocks, by holding tightly to their folded aprons. They now seemed more than double the number that I had calculated earlier. The air felt cold and crisp, penetrating my inner sleeves, coat lapels and even forcing itself through my shirt at the openings between the buttons. The chill thrust itself up my pant legs so forcefully, that it shot right into both of the loose, knee-length legs of the sacred traditional undergarment, which all of us Mormon missionaries wore in those days. Ohhh, I thought to myself; that must be how cold air makes skirted women feel all the time! With that sensation, for an instant, everything seemed to stop.

"Start yelling for help, Elder," breathed out one of the elder's voices from behind me.

"*Socorro!*" (Help!), I yelled out as I kept on running. Then, suddenly, it seemed like I was watching myself. It was as if I was not in my body, but up and ahead of it. "*Asilo!*" (Asylum!), I saw myself yell out within a few meters of the station door.

The human figure in the tiny window in the massive wood door appeared as frightened as I looked. Then, I heard sounds from behind the door that meant they were beginning to open it.

I saw myself yell out, "They're opening the front door, Elders. Just run on, inside!" With everything still in slow motion below me, I heard my own heavy breathing just slightly louder than that of the elders running behind me. It was uncanny.

To our right, I saw that the swelling mob was closing in on us. With that awareness, I was again in my body. I saw a face in the front of the crowd that was so distorted with hatred that it was difficult for me to see it as fully human. Highland people...and some of them –I thought to myself– might be strung out on coca!

That instant, I flashed the loss of emotional equilibrium that I had known over two years earlier when I had arrived as a new Mormon missionary in Lima. But, I made it inside first, so while the others ran in from behind, I tried to catch my breath. Again, I flashed the experience that had taken place on my first full day as a newly arrived Mormon missionary in the Roman Catholic Cathedral in Lima, Peru two years earlier.

"Close the door! Close it!" Elder Harmsen's energized voice brought me back to the present.

I immediately asked for a meeting with the *comandante,* but I was quickly informed that he was on vacation. The only official in government who could intervene on our behalf was the prefect in the *Ancash* Department capitol city, *Huaraz.* It's the larger village to the south, where our supervising elder –Elder Zabriski– and his recent new companion now lived. I turned to Elder Zabriski, "Elder," I said through my still strained breathing, "you and I should go down to *Huaraz* and talk face to face with the prefect. Your companion can stay here with Elder Harmsen to maintain a stronghold in the two-story place we've rented for our services. They don't have to stay in the little cottage we normally sleep in because it would be safer on the second floor than down on that ground floor."

"Good thinking, Elder," he responded. With that, he looked out of the small window and said, "Elders, look at this."

When I rushed back toward the window along with the others, I saw that the people outside had begun to migrate away from where we were. It looked like they were gathering at the Catholic church's front door, to the left of where we looked out.

The officer had said that they could do nothing for us unless someone did something illegal to us, first. That was their law. I asked if they could at least guard all of us back to the safety of our two-story meetinghouse. They responded that their orders in this kind of situation were to keep the Highland people out of the government facilities, at all costs. Evidently, fifty years earlier some had stormed the same *Yungay* Police Station. The Highland people were then, trying to kill Evangelical Christian missionaries, and the local police authorities didn't get the use of their police facility back for several years thereafter. These men had their orders to not allow the same mistake to be made again.

Somehow, we sneaked around the blocks that touched on the plaza and we got back into the safety of our rented facility. I was at a desk, which we had set up in an office-like room on the second floor. This particular upper room had a connecting door with our landlord's home balcony looking over his private inner patio. The knocking on the door startled me. It was our landlord. He had a small black gun in his hand and he was trying to hand it to me, "*Tenga usted, senor,*" (Here, sir), he said, "it's my pistol. You need it to ward off all those Highland folks. They'll kill you all, as easily as not. They're not like us, who live in the village. No, sir, you take this gun for your protection. I don't want you to get hurt here on my property. So, here," he said thrusting it out to me.

All I could do was grasp the cold, black, heavy metal in my right hand. I looked at it, there, in my hand. I'd never held a gun.

The landlord walked back into the darkened thick adobe hallway that connected our two places and closed the connecting door behind him at the other end. Thud. Click.

I just stood there, completely stunned—staring down at the black gun in my hand. I didn't know guns were so heavy…

Hearing the noise upstairs—I guess—Elder Zabriski came up the inside staircase and saw me standing there with that little black pistol in my hand and yelled, "Elder Feliz! What's that about?"

Instinctively, I put it down softly, on top of the desk. "Our fine friend, the landlord, is concerned for the safety of his tenants."

"Concerned about loosing his steady income from our rent, you mean," he responded.

"Maybe so," I said, "but, it seems that he also knows about those Evangelical missionaries that we heard about, for the first time, down at the police station."

"Yeah," he answered, "did you ask if he can he find us a cab that will take us to *Huaraz*?"

Eventually, our landlord was able to get a cousin, who drove one of the three taxis that served *El Cayejon de Huaylas*, to take two of us down into *Huaraz*. When the cab arrived and Elder Zabriski and I had begun the harrowing ride through the main street out of town that was lined on both sides with Highland people high on cocoa leaf, it became clear that all, us missionaries, could be in real danger. We had to be able to find the prefect of *Ancash* in *Huaraz*. That was our only open hope.

It was the longest night taxi ride I'd ever taken in my life. I tried to call our mission president in Lima from the single telephone office on the town plaza. But, all I got was his office assistant. He only informed us that the President already knew about our situation in *Yungay* because the Roman Catholic Cardinal in Lima had called him and told him about the Indian types trying to kill us elders, like they'd killed the Evangelical missionaries fifty years earlier. The Elder seemed a little flippant to me, "Some news travels fast in the Andes," he'd joked.

"Well," I impatiently asked, "where is the President? I need to reach him and explain that our lives are in danger here. Look, Elder, it's as if you don't grasp the seriousness of what I'm saying…"

The voice on the other end interrupted. He reiterated that there was no way to reach our mission president because he'd flown to La Paz, Bolivia "to open up the work" to that nation state.

That prophetic Apostolic warning, that commissioned me for my mission over two years earlier, was all I heard: *When this happens, be faithful and fearless and obey the direction of your mission president…"*

Behind my private thoughts, the voice on the telephone just went on. Evidently, one of our church's General Authorities Elder A. Theodore Tuttle, of the Council of The Seventy was in the area, traveling with our mission president, and according to his office assistant, "Elder Tuttle assured the President that nothing will hurt [us] missionaries in *Yungay*."

But, I thought to myself, we're *here,* and they're *not…*!

Finally, the Prefect of *Ancash* allowed the two of us an audience. After some initial pleasantries, and some very welcome hot cocoa, we all took seats in his office. We took great pains to let him know that we had dutifully called our mission president in Lima to report the happenings to him about the mob back in *Yungay*. Afterward, we must have sat there–in our two chairs in front of his old, large, dark, wooden desk–silent for several minutes. For the first time in my life, I'd run out of words. The more we talked, it seemed, the colder the room temperature got.

So, when we had finished stating our case, we just sat, and looked back for some kind of response from the Prefect. But only silence came back. Only silence came from that man, as he stared at both of us –first one, and then the other.

Out of the silence, the balding and mustached, large man behind the massive dark desk slowly said in a low but, calm voice: "You know you will die if you return and stay in *Yungay*."

Again, the words I'd memorized, from over two years ago, came forcefully into my mind: *"When this happens, be faithful and fearless and obey the direction of your mission president…"* So, I pleaded again, "But, don't you see? We can't leave! We can only take orders from our mission president, and he's traveling in a different country! We cannot reach him until he returns and until then, we have no choice but to obey his last word—his last direction to us."

"You mean that you will go back to *Yungay*?" he asked.

"That is our right place until we receive some other order from our president," I said calmly, "I must 'obey [my] president.'"

"But," he said, "Senor Elder, you will die!" He stared at me, and then, he stared at Elder Zabriski. Then, without a word, he looked down at some papers on his desk in front of him for what felt like minutes. He simply sat, and stared downward. Finally, he slowly looked back up at me, took in a deep breath and he said, "I can sense your faith. I can feel your faith. Our combined faith will get you out of this."

After that, the meeting ended abruptly. We reviewed what had been accomplished by us. We had failed at reaching our mission president, but we'd met with the Prefect of *Ancash*. On the long, two hour drive back up the *callejon's* winding mountain road to our two companions in *Yungay*, we had both felt that we had done all that we could do. As we approached the village outskirts, both sides of the road were lined with many Highland people, crouched down on the sidewalk and covered in their ponchos and hats. We could only hope that they were all asleep, unaware of who was riding in this taxi.

When we got back, Elder Harmsen let us know what had taken place: He told how a small group of the mob had huddled in front of our place earlier that day. Evidently, he'd leaned out over the people from a second floor window and preached the gospel of Love and peace, trying to let them know that we weren't bad people, that we meant no harm. Evidently, he'd been so good convincing them that we were good people that, the smaller group that had gathered around stayed—while all the other *Altiplanos* had left hours earlier.

The following Tuesday evening was a weekly Mutual meet for the teenagers who'd become accustomed to coming by. They had news about the Catholic priest. As they told it, the priest was also the head of the local school and he'd threatened all six of the boys saying that they'd all get excommunicated if they persisted in visiting any of the Mormons in the village. Naturally that was a challenge to our teenage friends. As a result, the boys had come by to visit the four Mormon elders, of course.

"Aren't you afraid of getting kicked out of your church?" I asked them.

"We don't believe in them anymore," one of them quickly said in response. "Anyway, all of our fathers are on the city council with the mayor, and they tell us we don't have to stay away from you."

That's when a hard, fast knocking came to the big doors that we used as a main entrance. Opening the small peek window to be sure it wasn't something dangerous to us, we saw it was some of the members of the town council.

"Open up, Elder," the male voice said through the little opened window, "we have something to show you." Then, he held up a piece of paper—a printed document—to the little window.

After we let them in, four members of the town council showed us a document, which had been signed by the entire town council and the mayor. It was their official proclamation about what the priest had said about us and how they stood by us, and of our right "to stay in *Yungay* to practice [our] religion." Even though the Highland people had all stayed over on Monday night, most of them were gone now and had vacated the streets of the village. The worst had come and gone.

With the end of Spring, the horror of the past weeks seems long ago. It's much warmer now, and as a final outing before my release as a missionary for The Church in Peru, I want to visit the fantastic turquoise lake. *La Laguna Yanganuco* is set in a massive ring of long, tall, grey granite rocks, up near the top of mighty, *El Huascaran*. So, after the taxi took us part of the way up, we all got out and hiked up to the lake in the fresh, moist air. The depth of color in that place was totally uncommon. The land surrounding the turquoise water was cut away from the sky by those tall, jagged, circled granite peaks that walled-in that entire green *shangrila*-like pristine beauty of this Andean scene. This was a scene I knew I'd never forget! The fresh aroma of tiny fragrant flowers and the clean crispness of that *altiplano* air made this, one of the most naturally remarkable places I have ever visited. Even the green moss on the trees seemed a deeper emerald color than any moss I'd seen. It was a place of high energy—sacred. We all had our cameras out...

Awed at the absolute otherworldly serenity of the place, I took out my eight millimeter and played photographer along with the others. As I enjoyed taking footage of the deep turquoise lake and its awesomely verdant boarders, it happened. If I hadn't been listening intently, I think I would have missed hearing it. But, I had heard it, all right. I turned to see who'd also heard...

Elder Harmsen was standing there, his legs spread out at military ease, looking west toward the other side of *El Cayejon de Huaylas* at *El Rio Santa*. In the far, clouded distance –through the narrow divide in the massively tall granite rocks that seemed to have been pushed up from the mountain base– the incessant river looked like a swift red snake. "This mountain…" his quiet voice began, "…is going to come down on top of *Yungay* because of what those people tried to do to us." His voice was uncannily sure, "the mud from this high and hidden place will cover the town and only *a testament to us* will be left above the mud."

I kept turning to see if the others had heard what he'd said in such a calm voice. They hadn't. They were too busy taking photos.

But, I'd heard his words. "Is that a prophecy, Elder?"

"No, of course not, Elder" he answered simply. But, his stance didn't change. There was an essence about him that I'll never forget.

"So, Elder," I went on, trying to get him to say it again, to be sure I'd heard right, "...what do you think about what they did?"

"I don't," he said simply, as he continued taking pictures.

Another five years passed.

I worked out of the Washington, D.C. area corporate offices of the Marriott Corporation, and I was sitting one day in one of our hotels in Chicago, Illinois. As I calmly sat there, after ordering my meal, I noticed a used, folded newspaper in a neighboring booth, next to the booth where I sat. Chills shot throughout my body. Numbed at the headline and the page-wide photograph on the front page, I gingerly reached over to pick it up.

The photograph was of a dark gray, massive mudslide of an, obviously, Peruvian mountainous area. The stark headline read: "MOUNTAIN FALLS ON ANDEAN VILLAGE." The dateline; "*Huaraz*, Department of *Ancash*, Peru." Both of my hands began to shake. As I held the paper closer, I saw it said, "The small Andean village of *Yungay* is no more..."

Days later, I found myself reading the list of survivors that had been published by the Lima newspapers. The names of the only thirty-four survivors from the village of *Yungay* were names that I recognized. Every member of the town council, and their families, had survived with the mayor and his family. Through friends from Peru, I was also able to discover that the people who had joined our newly established branch of The Church had all been away at a church outing in a neighboring village when *El Huascaran* came with its boulders and deadly mud down onto the little town.

Later, a California friend shared a front page newspaper picture of the former town plaza with me. Only the top palms of four palm trees in front of the old Catholic church could be seen above the rocky ground. None of the building, itself, was at all visible. In the distance, beyond the four tree stumps, sticking up from the hardened mud, there was only the white statue of the Christ that had stood on top of a hill overlooking the village cemetery—before the disaster. It was the only visible human structure that stood higher than the mud and boulders that had covered the entire village of *Yungay*.

That lone statue of the Christ, and the four palm tree-tops' that stuck out of the brown, hard blanket of dried mud and boulders, had indeed, now become "…a testament to us."

****

Long before September 11, 2001, America's mainstream was—like I then was also—unaware of the real danger posed by America's religious, ethno-centric, patriarchal communities to America's homeland security. Like me, middle class America back then, couldn't have cared less over the lack of political pluralism that would set the world on fire for some of us in these United States. Then, September 11, 2001 forced our mainstream 21st century American society to become aware of—and to acknowledge—that, experiencing life as if under siege, is also the case with all groups typified to us in the 21st century by Aftanistan's Taliban.

Precisely as I had to first, become aware of and then, be able to acknowledge and face my own out-of-sync. attitudes—on the personal level—so, also, the force of terror has now opened us all to the same basic social issues. As a person, as a human being; I had to squarely face the truly "*out–of–sync. nature*" *of any closed society*, like The Church wherein I had learned to envision. Likewise, *The Force* of our human Mass Mind is now forced to, "face the '*out–of–sync. nature*' *of any closed society.*" Initial global events of this new century have, so far, proven to open up the eyes of our civilization's Mass Mind. So also, were the 1970s through the 1990s for me on the personal level, as the following story will reveal. But, recall that; as is the macrocosm, so is the microcosm…

****

It is the end of the sixth decade in the 20th century, my new wife and I are both employed in the center core of the American conservative political circle. She's one of a very abundant other Utah based Mormons traditionally employed in the United States Department of Agriculture in Washington, D.C., since the day Ezra Taft Benson—who eventually then became the President of the Mormon Church—had served as Secretary of Agriculture under Eisenhower. I'm employed out of another place with a historically strong Mormon presence in Washington, D.C., the corporate offices of the Marriott Corporation in the suburb of Bethesda, Maryland. Being dutiful, obedient Mormons, we are both "good" employees.

In our religious life, we've become friends of people who work in vague, bureaucratic, federal government assignments. As a result of the way both of us have experienced life up to this point, in time we're both registered as two of Northern Virginia's newest Republicans. Our closest, and seemingly mild-mannered, friends are among the notoriously large number of us Washington, D.C. area Utah based Mormons who work at the Central Intelligence Agency, the Federal Bureau of Investigation and at the United States State Department.[ii] At this time, neither of us; have a clue that our equally devoutly religious friends all, actually, live double lives of intrigue. The newspaper headlines of the day are all about the aftermath of the race riots in the City of Los Angeles, California…

During the burning of Los Angeles, and immediately after those horrible times, my ex-wife and I had lived in the socially conservative and largely Republican Provo, Utah, and then, on the somewhat upscale Northern Virginia side of the Patomac River. In those polite, middle class circles, the ugly Los Angeles Riots of a few years ago were all in a very distant place, they were a mere story on the evening news to us. In those *first job out of college* days, I knew more about the Bible *as God's law* than about civil rights law.

When it all came down, I had not yet come to understand that the horror of those tragic weeks had happened because of our sad choices to ignore our long American history of ethnic strife. So, because of my family's distinguished heritage in Los Angeles' city history, I am sorely pained. Slowly, I'm becoming aware of how that city experienced the experience of this mid. 20th Century time. But, when it had actually taken place, I'd been too sheltered in my old faith community by the imprinting we'd all been given, to always trust anyone put in authority over us.

Our programmed bent toward ignorance by a Mormon brand of mental manipulation, intended to maintain obedience to authority figures, had shielded us from knowing the true stench of the abuse of power over others. Such is the end result of human beings being reared in any kind of a bounded, closed society. We are not aware of the realities all around us. So now, driving the Los Angeles freeways in early 1970, because of my new job here in the City of angels, I still feel as if have no clue…

The enlightenment came when I, finally, understood that I had no clue! It was at that precise point when I could finally comprehend that, now, I actually had an option to choose how I self-identified from that moment onward…

So, what is *Self-Identity*, anyway? Among other things, to me, Self-Identity especially defines *how* we each are, how we *behave* within our respective environments. Our behavior manifests *how* we perceive or *how* we envision, because the working idea here is as it is in anything; *we exist only in what is manifest as we inter-relate*, even if it's only in one's inter-relating with one-self. Truly, none of us exists within a vacuum, and as a result, with *whom* or with *what* we each personally self-identify determines our individual *beingness*; it forms a unique *inner* being. That inner Character is playing her or his role on the stage of life's play.

One's Self-Identity is the Character who is manifesting on that cosmic stage, which William Shakespear called our mortal life, playing roles in whatever mortal life phenomenology that we each personally experience. If, as Shakespeare is credited to once have written, "all the world's a stage" then I say that, *that* Character *–that* Self-Identity– is manifest to us all in the dynamics of individual life experience. *That* is the One character who determines how we each experience the experience of the play of life.

Self-Identity, among other factors therefore, will determine how we individually respond to life's inevitable eventualities. It has a particular psychic place of reckoning, one *from where* we each, respectfully, perceive and decide between envisioning one's life as if being under siege; verses envisioning one-self –simultaneously– as being both, the One who is the attacker, *and the One who is being attacked.* The first way is to envision from only our tribal –or a xenophobic– place, and the second comes from a way of being that –at the same time– includes both of the warring classes as equals in *empathy*, or in other words, as being two aspects of the *same* Being.

This more open way to inter-relate in our common natural world –by experiencing experiences as being more than only one-self– manifests empathy because of how we all magnify ourselves through our Self-identity. Without Self-Identity, none of us would experience what we call the universal experience, each in our own, individual, uniquely personal way. The *empathic* way to becoming open souls *is to increase beyond our native culture in how we each personally envision what and who we each are in life's experience.* As for myself, my individual Self-identity in the 1960s and the 1970s is not one that I am proud of in the 21st century...

As I said, it's 1970. In the wake of the Los Angeles Race Riots, the local President of the Los Angeles Stake of The Church has called me to serve on the Los Angeles Stake (diocese) High Council. Mormon stake high councils are all composed of twelve high priests who "sit in council" with the three high priests who are a stake presidency, the actual presiding authorities in a Mormon stake. In an early 20th century book, Priesthood and Church Government, a late L.D.S. apostle, John A. Widstoe, teaches Mormons:

Whenever their "stake president is given the authority to preside by a visiting" authority, he is then ordained, *literally,* as "the president of The Church" in that geographic area called a "stake." His, is a social position of immense power over all the lives of all the members of the various Mormon wards (parishes) in a given L.D.S. stake. He is not merely a ministerial figure, nor a regional officer of an ecclesiastical group—Utah based Mormons do not even use the term, "minister." *Mormon stake presidents are all Moses figures—in every sense of that metaphor—to the mass mind of the Utah based Mormon people.* [Although organizational mechanics (regions etc.) have slightly changed, I'm sure the unspoken attitude is still that, a stake president is the *local* Mormon prophet figure to their faithful.]

This is not an insignificant fact, because to the Mormon mass psyche, their prophets are understood to be no different in spiritual giftedness than the biblical canon reports of the ancient Hebrew prophets. In every respect, in 1970 I, therefore, believe that I've been called by the gift of revelation through our stake president as a member of our new stake's high council. To what purpose God called me at a relatively young age? I don't know, but because of my family history in California, I have the sense that the experience will turn out to be a fated destiny.

In each high council body in which I've previously served, I was the youngest. In Los Angeles, I was twenty-seven years of age when I was called to this auspicious work. I've already served as a stake high councilor in the Arlington, Virginia Stake of The Church before moving back to California—the church unit where feminist, Sonia Johnson, was excommunicated. Over the years, I have begun to see a pattern in how the high councils in the Mormon Church conduct their business. I, more often than not, am in awe at the obvious reverence that each of my fellow high councilors brings to our ecclesiastical deliberations.

In the first months of my service on the Los Angeles Stake High Council, I have become friends with another high councilor. He is of a Jewish ancestry, and often says, "You know, Tony, we're both minorities on this high council. You know that I'm Jewish, don't you?" he says in an awkward way. Meeting after meeting, he often says that, as he gets in his car, after our weekly high council meetings in the old Wilshire Ward meetinghouse.

I always know that it isn't a question he asked but, rather, it is "a statement." But, my unspoken question is: Is he driven to try to get me to relate with him more than with the other men because he also sees himself as a racial minority, or is there something else I'm missing? Unfortunately, at the present time, as I have just begun to ask myself this question, I still don't have access to all the relevant data. I have not yet observed the whole context in which we make our decisions on the high council. Because I've only recently returned to reside in the Los Angeles area from the East Coast, I am clueless—I sense—to the cultural stresses around us in my new Los Angeles environment. I guess that he is trying to help me through the seeming difficulties of our deliberations.

But, he doesn't need to worry about me—not *me*—he has no idea how clueless I am about what we've all been doing! I can tell that we've been in a heated debate in our high council meetings about the recent closure of two of our chapels: Both, the Adams, Los Angeles meetinghouse, and the Arlington meetinghouse, are south of Los Angeles' downtown urban center. Both of these areas of Los Angeles—only a few years ago—had been heavily populated by many loyal *Anglo* members of The Church. But now, in early 1970s Los Angeles, *because our leaders have not yet opened priesthood ordination to men of African descent*, our present dwindling urban Los Angeles membership has very few African-Americans.

In the aftermath of the 1960s riots near those specific areas of the city, all of the Mormons have, literally, relocated—moved. In fact, all the Mormons from those wards have moved away *en mass*. As directed by the top hierarchy of The Church from Salt Lake City, Utah, these two local buildings are being closed now. So our local members emigrated; to The Church's lands being developed by a corps of professional city planners and land developers, who all "*just happened to be*" Mormons. We, the Los Angeles Stake High Councilors, have just finalized the move of the entire membership in more than two wards of our urban stake, eastward and northward —and ours isn't the only L.D.S. stake involved.

When my wife and I had moved into the Los Angeles Stake, the centrally orchestrated L.A. Mormon exodus inland into San Bernardino County and north into what has become Simi Valley, California had been going on for years. This massive 1960's L.D.S. migration of all Mormon residents out of areas in and around south-central Los Angeles into the more upscale and white Anglo-Saxon suburbs has been totally designed, orchestrated and executed as if by an army under siege. To me, it truly is an "army" of loyal rank and file Mormon *Anglo-Saxons*.

What can any, that try to understand these key decisions of our Mormon leaders on such matters, think? I know, intellectually, that this massive removal of an entire populace is a real historic behavioral pattern of Mormonism. Emigration is part of Mormon history. But, I have had no idea how large a part of the Mormon psyche this response still controlled.

I had not yet been exposed to enough data to even ask the critical questions! Because of a truly compassionate Universe, however, I would learn years later, as I did some research in the L.D.S. Church Archives in Salt Lake City, Utah, that –*to us*, in the 1970's– we Angelino Mormons *were* "under siege." Moreover, little did I know that these observations would, eventually, bring me to divorce and excommunication as revealed in my first book, *Out of The Bishop's Closet*. And, I'd later discover in my initial assignment at the LDS Church Offices that, The Church *had* had a program to improve on its, "disaster," and on its, "emergency preparedness."

My assignments would let me see the paper trail that told how The Church 1970s "exodus committee" had been the same organizational structure; made up of all the same men with whom I would later work in Salt Lake City, Utah during the Teton Dam disaster of 1975. Because of the pre-1978 official policy of The Church prohibiting any priesthood ordination to a man of African descent; the hierarchy, evidently, felt that the membership, who lived in the urban areas of Los Angeles at the time, were all in mortal danger. And, this was not to speak of the danger that *even we* had envisioned to all property owned by us, i.e.: Local Mormon ward meetinghouses and our holiest place, The Temple in west Los Angeles on Santa Monica Boulevard—three blocks from our home.

Much like a more recent example in the town of Gilbert, Arizona related in another chapter, as the police officer observed in that case, this behavior of an entire group soul was patterned after the old model of "the circling of the wagons" type of mentality. It is the classic Mormon way to react to social difficulties outside of their community. The reason for the similarity in the responses is that, Utah Mormons had learned a long time before the Race Riots in Los Angeles that, their practices toward racial minorities are not in political sync. with the evolving mainstream culture of the rest of our nation. But, in those days of our legal work as a stake high council of The Church in finalizing the mass exodus of the members of our stake from older parts of Los Angeles, it didn't occur to me that my Jewish fellow high councilor was exploring my loyalty. I had no idea what a 'cloak and dagger' period it was for the other members of that high council. I had no clue at all! I was a mere dutiful and obedient young Latino man, one who *never* consciously questioned church authorities.

It had never struck me that, what we had been discussing in our council meetings about the mass relocation of our entire Anglo-Saxon membership to cities outside of Los Angeles, may be of any sensitivity. I had not yet become aware of the reality of our sad condition as a mass mind. I was totally unaware politically; I knew nothing of our Utah hierarchy's favorable position toward what was then known as the racial apartheid government of the nation of South Africa. It wasn't until I came out as a Queer Man, that I discovered how ultra-conservative the politics of my spiritual leaders were in the 1970s. Again, I had no clue!

I thought to myself years later, "My Jewish high councilor friend was probably assigned to monitor me, by our cautious stake president." *Maybe*, I later reasoned to myself, they thought that because I was new, they had to test my loyalties. In retrospect, I can honestly say that if I am correct on what was happening back then —then, my immediate leaders simply didn't know my sense of loyal consecration. They had no need to worry about me! I had no clue of the social implications of the decisions we were making during those months as Mormon high councilors. I was too blindly obedient in those days. *I did not question authority back then.* I didn't know questioning authority was even in me!

But, the Universe compassionately provides us all with whatever we need to know as soon as we're ready to receive it. As for me, I would not learn until my 1990's research in the old archives of *El Pueblo de La Reina de Los Angeles* Historical Monument that there was something disturbing to me about that 1960s to 1970s mass migration. It was a total exodus of Anglo-Saxon Mormons from two entire southern California Mormon Stakes (diocese)! I'd learned, through my 1970's experience on the Los Angeles Stake high council, that we had relocated an entire population eastward, into Rancho Cucamonga, northward to Simi Valley and into other middle class, predominantly Anglo-Saxon Los Angeles suburbs.

However, what I did not know until 1998, was that our massive, hierarchically orchestrated, late 1960's Mormon exodus was onto lands that had been acquired by the Mormon Battalion during their 19th century take-over of the *Californio Ranchos*. These lands had once been owned by my Feliz paternal grandfathers and by their *Californio* cousins! The Church had arranged the purchase of large tracts of land from 1895 and into the early 20th century. Those large land purchases had mostly been carried out in the 1930s, through individual members of The Church who'd been sent on "real estate missions." They had all acted as legal "agents" of Zion's Securities Corporation, a holding subsidiary group of The Corporation of The President, the Utah legal entity that is the Mormon Church.

These massive tracts of real estate were then, all sold in the fear-laden aftermath of the Los Angeles Race Riots as new, small, residential plots in, "single family," planned neighborhoods to those 1960s to 1970s Mormon *emigres* from the more urban Arlington and Adams areas of south Los Angeles. As a result of conversations with my Jewish friend on the high council, I'd understood that ours had truly been "a veritable exodus." In his eyes, it was, yet another historical removal of our faith community from one place to another because of our "peculiar beliefs"—the one in question being, our belief that Father-God prohibited the ordaining of any African descendant man to our priesthood. He had made a strong argument about us as "the victims of an intolerant society" –one that is unable to let us practice our religious truth, as we understand it– "abused and misunderstood until, as in the past, we have to move on." He'd said, "It is like when we left Illinois for the Great Basin—for our own safety."

I had not yet explored the glaring social implications of the hard theological juxtapositions of those days. Specifically, I hadn't yet considered the cold truth that *this*, our exclusionary theology on priesthood ordination, in effect, kept our fellow Mormons—who all happened to be Black—locked out of the holiest *and also, the most required* Temple rituals for the Mormon Afterlife! I hadn't yet seen that, in this theological way, we Mormons had kept our very devout Black members from being married in the same ceremony used by the rest of us! I hadn't yet seen the parallels between South Africa's Apartheid policy and that of my own community of faith. I hadn't yet acknowledged our group soul's bent toward seeing humanity in classifications of varied –and thus, *lesser*– degrees of humanness. I hadn't yet asked how a loving priesthood could bar an entire race from our practice of sealing Mormon family relationships *by simply omitting the names of their men from the master list of the ordained.*

Hindsight now lets me clearly see that this was experiencing the experience, as if we Mormons had been "under siege." The increasing number of African-Americans then, moving into the old neighborhoods, we had thought, "might react to news in the media that their Black Mormon brothers were being bared from priesthood ordination in local Mormon churches." We'd feared that, some might even do to Mormon buildings what had been done by others, for generations, to Black churches in the South. All the other high councilors, with whom I'd served on that high council, understood our actions as being a reaction to the "evil" going on all around our local neighborhood facilities. But, I had no experience to relate with how my fellow councilors were relating with the ugly social realities around us in those last days of finalizing legal documents of our abandoned church buildings. I'd just transferred into Los Angeles from Marriott's headquarters on the East Coast—I had no clue!

Finally, however, the realization hit me. I was troubled by the realization that I had been a silent witness to the mass migration of many thousands of our members of The Church. But, more especially, that I hadn't understood any of the implications that now screamed out to me from the very reasoning that created that mass movement of our people *to begin with*. Eventually, this recently acquired awareness ate at me to the degree that, I had to try to understand all of the factors that had led our leaders to treat our members in urban Los Angeles as veritable *refugees*.

Did it *have* to happen in *that* way? What choices were made in previous years that had caused the need for our mass exodus? Why had it been carried out so quietly, hidden from any media awareness? The problem was that I'd had no conscious awareness that these issues had been festering within me. Consciously, I was still in major denial of how I then, sub-consciously judged our own ecclesiastical acts.

In fact, it was long after I had been excommunicated from The Church when I'd mentally returned to these puzzling questions. Later, a psychologist, whom I would see professionally said, "You have always experienced life as if under siege—haven't you? I mean, it's part of your heritage—from both your Mormon and your *Californio* roots." Then, more recently, in one of my discussions since September 11, 2001 about that day I said, "We all live in a world today wherein all of us can, now, experience the experience of being under siege."

But, I'd never before envisioned myself as behaving as if I made choices out of an awareness of experiencing life as if I was *under siege*. Yet I knew that, as a communal social being, I thought to myself; I have lived in Mormon communities that actually have a long history of being under siege. Then, as a direct descendant of a long line of men who still remember how our Los Feliz estates were taken from us by the 19th century land-lusting army recruits—who happened to be Mormons—my views had to have been influenced by all their collective experiences of being under siege. Moreover, later on in my life's journey as a more politically aware, out Queer man, again, I have personally known life in a community of sexual minorities that, in critical ways, is still under siege. Eventually, I would see that I'd probably been programmed to see myself as if under siege on several levels of inter-relating with others.

****

The ultimate conclusion I came to is: We missionaries *had* been under siege. Writing this chapter has brought back a flood of memories about that period we now call the, Cuban Missile Crisis. I distinctly now recall how uncertain those times were for us all. We did not know if any of us would live through the unknown events yet to come. When I and my parents made a pact to seek each other out —at Grandma Nica's old Anaheim street address—in the event of an all out nuclear war over the Cuban missiles, our family was experiencing life as if under siege. Moreover, since September 11, 2001, we all know what it is like to, literally, be "under siege." America's naïve adolescence has been attacked.

Yet, the above-related personal experience reveals that, I'd also known years ago—not because of Fidel Castro—but, because of tribal worldviews in Peru's department of *Ancash*, that we all can, and we all often do, find ourselves in conditions that qualify as being under siege. At least, in those moments when my companions and I were, literally, running away from the angry mob, we all *were* under siege. However, to Father Gomez, our presence in his village had placed *him* under siege too! He was under siege in the same way that Osama bin Laden's terrorists must have also seen themselves as if "under siege" by us, non-Muslim, Americans; and none of the above says a thing about how the Indigenous felt about what had happened!

The fact is: From the solitary perspective of our own tribe-like second womb societies, in the modern globalized world we are all under siege, to one degree or another. Since September 11, 2001, we all know what it is to recoil for protection—because being under siege causes that reaction in us all. It's part of being human and living in a cultural group.

If the leaders of the Los Angeles Stake saw the Race Riots of the 1960s as a threat to the life and property of all their non-Black membership in that area then *to them* they *were* also under siege. It was the same, "circling of the wagons" response that—as will be told—a police officer in Gilbert, Arizona had seen in his largely Mormon community. This is what *any* people do whenever they experience life as if under siege; we remove ourselves into ghettos –separate and apart– in segregated parts of our cities within which we each, respectively, feel safer than we would feel in our Others' neighborhoods. Feeling this, is part of how we are.

In the following chapters, I describe how it is that we all create closed societies. These are the second wombs that continue to produce people who are much like the trench-coated high school teenagers who'd been bullied by others in Littleton, Colorado. In all of our societies, all the people experience life as if under siege. The obvious idea that stems from *that* fact is that, what got us all to this point were *former ways* of understanding *that we've collectively inherited from former generations*!

The most recent example to me of this phenomenon came as our Commander In Chief traveled in Europe in May of 2003. The media was ablaze about the fact that weapons of mass destruction had not been discovered in Iraq, although *that* was the reason for —the Whitehouse spin—why the then, sitting American President had "pre-empted"[iv] the 2003-2004 war against the Saddam Houssein regime. That was when I started "connecting the dots" that I had observed over the previous twenty-five years:

A television news item in early May had reported that, we had begun to pull our military installations out of Saudi Arabia. Yet no one, reading the news copy in any of the televised reports I saw, had recalled that, *that* had been exactly what Osama bin Laden had declared was *his* goal. Our leaving Saudi Arabia was his exact reason for the September 11, 2001 terror! That was when I realized that, America had *capitulated*.

Then later, as I'd read about our relatively quiet exodus from his homeland, I saw how "the dots connected." I had observed: In 1979, a few Saudi princes had visited my superiors in Salt Lake City, Utah, and a colleague of mine had then, told me our Mormon First Presidency was trying to get them to invest in the rebuilding of a down-town area of Salt Lake City to prepare for that city's bid on the 2002 Winter Olympics. I had asked why the old six-pointed star [Israel's Star of David] windows had all been quietly removed from the Temple Square Assembly Hall, where Brigham Young had originally put them. He responded to me: "They're being removed so as not to offend the Saudi Princes!" Then, years later, the Star of David windows were all put back in—again, without fanfare.

Moreover, as an employee of L.D.S. Welfare Services, my work was in overseeing and training what were then called Welfare

Services Missionaries[v] in South America. In that work, I'd learned that we L.D.S. often used conflicted ways to find inroads for our proselytizing activities in the nations that do not allow us to overtly convert their people. Then later, in July of 2003, media revelations told how the C.I.A. was responsible for George W. Bush's "false statement," and also about a "forged C.I.A. document" on Saddam Houssein's efforts to get "weapons grade uranium from an African nation." Significantly, in Mormon circles, it is common knowledge that our State Department and our Department of Defense are filled with devout Latter-day Saints whose first loyalty is *to their Utah Mormon President.* Since most of the 2001 terrorists had been Saudis, I *naturally,* wondered: Had *Mormon* C.I.A. officers been motivated to do something imprudent because of a devout L.D.S. need to cover-up their unavoidably intrusive proselytizing of Saudi-Arabian Muslims? Was there a Mormon factor in the war?

By 1983, Utah based Mormons were the "only recognized legal non-Muslim religion in Saudi-Arabia."[vii] But, I naïvely wondered: Why had secrecy accompanied their creation of their "Saudi-Arabia Peninsula Stake" (diocese)? Then, five weeks after September 11, 2001—October 9, 2001, to be exact, I was doing a book-signing event at a Borders in a downtown Salt Lake City mall and I had heard Gordon Hinkley's World Conference speech, days earlier. I'd been shocked because his voice had had a *fearful* tone, and this Mormon President had done something I had never heard a Mormon President do in public before. He'd prayed at the pulpit, "Father, forgive our arrogance!" *That,* was far too anachronistic. Public contriteness by an L.D.S. President was not a part of my old Utah Mormon experience, and thus, I knew *there was something* —something none of us knew—behind his *fearful* words. From personal experience, I knew how the same Gordon Hinkley had acted in previous scandals The Church had endured. So, I mentally re-examined what had taken place:

a) The reason for the secrecy behind the establishment of the Saudi-Arabia Peninsula Stake of The Church of Jesus Christ of Latter-day Saints was probably Muslim extremists, like Osama bin Laden. b) Utah based Mormons abound in our armed forces there, and in ex-patriot positions in oil companies there. c) Allowing Mormons to be recognized *legally* there, would be a motive for Osama bin Laden's fight against the Saudi Monarchy. d) Mormon C.I.A. employees would be there in large numbers. e) In 2000, the Palestinian suicide bombings had mushroomed in Israel, and peace could not exist between Israel and the Palestinians until suicide bombers were stopped. f) But Saddam Houssein bankrolled a quasi-life insurance coverage of the bombers'—benefiting the families of the bombers. Thus *removing Saddam Houssein was a logistical prerequisite for our military to leave Saudi Arabian holy lands—to eliminate what is angering global Islam about us*—because *Without us in Saudi-Arabia, Saddam Houssein would dominate the region*! What was my key clue?

I knew when I'd personally heard *how frightened Gordon Hinkeley had seemed to be as he apologized in that globally telecast speech in 2001*—a speech that would be seen in the entire Middle East! If anyone knew the details, Hinkley did. If bin Laden held any one person responsible for the invasion he perceived of his Muslim "holy *land*" then, it would easily be the head of the only non-Muslim religion *legalized* by the Saudi Monarchy!

In 1990, I was taught Earth's ways to envision; so now, I can see *land* as Utah based Mormons see their *Temples*. Both groups protect their sacred spaces so, old *Utah based Mormon proselytizing ways may have drawn Osama bin Laden's terrorism to us—forcing us to leave his Saudi-Arabian holy lands*. Likewise, evangelicals sneak Bibles into China and then, complain to our State Department about Chinese abuses of Christians. But, *who is under siege* there? Experiencing life as if under siege is a universal phenomenon; it's a multi-generational legacy. The problem is not religious intolerance.

Rather, experiencing life as if under siege is a worldview that we all need to change into a new envisioning. *All of us create problems by pushing our ways onto others. So, now, we all need to change our place of reckoning to outside of our closed societies.* In America, police often behave more like occupying armies than they behave like officers of the peace. Our hero firemen still hiss and boo their woman Senator because she's a strong woman, and men like me still get verbal epithets in public. So, we all need to see that, often, *we inadvertently choose to do harm to another* because *we don't yet see them as, actually, being us*!

Finally I invite you to re-examine the stories related within the pages of this chapter. One is a story that, on the surface, may be seen by some only as evidence of prophetic ability. The man who'd commissioned me as a missionary prophesied that at "the end" of my mission I would be assigned to "a small village high in the Andes." My companion made a statement that some might see as a curse while others see his comment as "prophecy." How the statement is *envisioned by anyone* is, in large measure, determined by one's own worldview. In fact, years later, I'd ask Elder Harmsen if he would comment on his words, and he did not even recall them. But, the reality of my journal entry, its date and the papers that reported its outcome five years later, are things that I can't deny. But, prophecy is not the point.

The point is that, whether we acknowledge it –or not– our words are a power because each one carries an energy. In the *Huna* tradition of ancient Hawaiian Kahunas, all words are a psychic force.[x] Words carry vibrational keys that engage the creation of future reality in our common world because all words re-present thoughts. This truth—that our words are merely symbols of our thoughts—is a key to our future because thoughts are the vibrational keys that engage the creation of future reality in our common world. As was masterfully illustrated for our Mass Mind in The Matrix film trilogy, *what we believe* is what we use—through thoughts—to engage the creation of our future reality in our common world.

The obstacle to evolving toward a place called a, "Zion," as described in all of The Matrix films—where freedom is—is how we "*believe!*" The obstacle is our insistence in believing that it cannot and, thus, will not be attained. And, *this lack of belief in what is the obvious to me*, stems from our belief in our separateness. Yet, even the Star Wars trilogy teaches that the opposite is the truth—that, we are all One! Again, the problem is how we self-identify. The above story from my Mormon missionary time is a personal testimony, which is offered here, as an evidence of the interconnectedness of us all. My personal witness is that, *words are how we reshape and reconstruct our world*. If we were of a mind to do so then, my inner sense is that we are capable of, collectively, using words to bring about the transmutation of our world.

As will be shown through the remaining stories in this book, the major obstacle to this is that most of us still swim in the common illusion of our separateness. We don't yet, "see as we are seen." I reiterate: Our problem is in how we self-identify! We do not focus clearly because we still use the old lenses of our inherited, external, hierarchical ways of envisaging. We need to, collectively, leave all of our cultural stratifications and classifications, and embrace our mutual equality by fostering equity in how we inter-relate. We need new ways to be Another Yourself to our others.

NOTES TO CHAPTER TWO

[i] See Washington Post, March 21, 1970.

[ii] Since the Eisenhower/Nixon Republican Administration, it has been a matter of record that the F.B.I., the C.I.A., the Department of Defense and the State Department of the United States of America employ a disproportionately large number of Mormons because of two reasons: First, most Mormon men usually serve a two to three year mission for their church and, as a result, they often speak multiple languages; Second, Mormons are inculcated from their earliest years as the stories in this book attest with a strict ethic of obedience to any authority figure without asking questions on why a given order is given to them. These two factors are both seen as valuable assets to offer these three agencies of our Federal government. However, in my personal observation, the 1990s reported fiascoes of the F.B.I. may also be attributed to these same factors.

[iii] See Los Angeles Stake High Council Meeting Minutes for 1970 through 1973, The Church of Jesus Christ of Latter-day Saints, Los Angeles, California Stake. Although, I wasn't present then, I'm sure earlier minutes would reveal far more.

[iv] The name of the War Department was changed to the Department of Defense to establish American foreign policy as "defensive." So, with his "first attack" against Iraq, George W. Bush was the first American President to claim the right of "pre-emption" instead of "defensive response." "Pre-emptive War" is called the "Bush Doctrine" because taking a first offensive against a sovereign state with no "first attack" by them was not established foreign policy before Bush.

[v] Today, the L.D.S. Church calls these, "Humanitarian Missionaries."

[vi] L.D.S. meetinghouses were bombed in several South American nations in the 1980s. Those responsible let it be known through local media outlets that it had been in retaliation for "C.I.A. operatives" living in their country "as employees of the Mormon Church." When the socialist President of Chile [Allende] was assassinated, the Chilean media had reported that the C.I.A. was involved. Later, I confirmed the Chilean media reports in a conversation on C.I.A. involvement in the Iran-Contra Affair with the then, L.D.S. Central America Area President, William R. Bradford (who was then, serving as Mission President in Chile) as he and I traveled in a jet between Santiago and Arica, Chile in 1979.

[vii] The Mormon Corporate Empire, by John Heinerman and Anson Shupe (Beacon Press, Boston, MA, 1985) page 233; organized in April of 1983 "...the church has...missionary inroads in the local population..." and it is "attributed to a crucial link...between the highest LDS...and a family...investing heavily." That "family" was the Saudi royals

[viii] This is the same Gordon B. Hinkley of whom I wrote in my first book as the point man over the Utah based Mormon fight against the E.R.A. in the 1970s.

[ix] Salt Lake Tribune 1985 articles & The Mormon Murders published that year.

[x] The Secret Science Behind Miracles, Unveiling the Huna Tradition of the Ancient Polynesians, by Max Freedom Long (De Vorss & Company, Marina Del Rey, CA., 1976).

"No amount of income, real property, or any earthly material possessions can compare with the joy, sweetness and awesome love that we can receive in life when a child joins us on life's journey so, I still see that this ideal is true. But, hetersexual coupling was *the only option* that I was then, taught to envision..."

CHAPTER THREE

WE ARE THE SUM OF OUR CHOICES

I had chosen the path that I was on, and my wife had chosen her own path. We are all the sum of our choices because we each exist only as we relate with our environment—especially with other humans. For some, their choices will coincide, letting part of the journey to be shared. That's how life is set up, and yet, the journey is experienced uniquely by each individual. Free will decides how the experience is experienced, and because of this, choice is a personal dynamic. As *Meshica* Indians would teach me later in 1990: "*Cada cabeza es un mundo*" ("Each mind is a world").[i]

****

I'd received the notification letter from the Superior Court judge the day before. It informed me that, our civil divorce was now official, and Jimm was especially happy so, we had both decided to celebrate my new freedom to live with him as "spouses" although no government recognized our spousal relationship.[ii] As the Director of Human Resources Management of a Hughes Aircraft Company division, I had hired Jimm to work in our El Segundo, California mail-room, so our life together was beginning to take on trappings of familial bliss. It was early in 1982 now, and Jimm and I had moved in together, in a hillside Hollywood apartment in a large Beachwood Canyon home, just below the famous "Hollywood" sign.

When I'd met Jimm in 1980, he'd encouraged me to become a political activist for same-sex spousal civil rights, so I soon became an active member of the Los Angeles Chapter of Affirmation, Gay and Lesbian Mormons, and often spoke out on the issue of same-sex spousal relationships. In 1984, speaking at the annual conference of Affirmation, Gay and Lesbian Mormons in Phoenix Arizona, I'd say that; "...'same-sex marriage' is about to become one of the most important political issues in America...!" Even back then, I could clearly envision what the next couple of decades would bring to our disenfranchised community of sexual minorities.

But, my prophecy on the progress of political pluralism fell on incredulous ears. My fellow disenfranchised Utah based Mormon Queers in attendance mostly responded by saying, "That won't happen for at least another hundred years or more!" With that, I knew they didn't have my vision, and I lessened my activism in that group thereafter. I would not raise my voice again regarding this issue until well after Jimm's passing from AIDS in 1990. But, I'm getting ahead of my story here...

It had taken me decades to come out to myself but, when I first met him, Jimm was the key person who had helped me to enjoy my new life as an openly Gay man. His joy for living had helped me open myself up to the possibility of finding an *honest happiness* in living honestly! Honesty breeds happiness, and happiness was now how I most often experience the experience of my journey, instead of the constant dread of "being *outed*" by someone. All of my anxiety, and familial discomfort, now, felt as if it had been washed away by my simple choice to, finally, stop living my heterosexual marriage lie. *Finally*, life *had* become an adventure for me! It seemed like, every day, some new joyful experience encountered me...

Because I'd been raised to avoid all kinds of alcohol, I'd never let myself drink wine or spirits. So, since Jimm had asked me to pick up some "wine and cheese" at the local liquor store on Sunset Boulevard on my way home, I bought my first bottles of wine—two of cabernet and one champagne—along with fresh cheese and veggie dips to celebrate our future together. I thought, as I parked the car at the liquor store, what the hell! So, although still a Mormon, I bought my first bottles of wine.

Coincidentally, that 1982 March night happened to be our first anniversary anyway! In my thirty-ninth year, I'd chosen to experience new things, and in that process, my new life became a constant stream of tasting new flavors and experiencing exciting new things that I had avoided before, I'd been purely plucked out of my ultra-religious upbringing! Barbara Streisand's vocal rendition of a Broadway musical hit, "Memory" was playing on my old eight-track throughout the entire night—over and over—as Jimm and I drank the champagne, while we enjoyed the cheese, the dip and veggies; as we both prepared the romantic steak dinner on the deck. Overlooking an awesome Los Angeles panorama, as the sun had just set, we freely danced, cuddled passionately on the chase lounge and made-out like the lovers in love that we were. Needless to say, that was one of the most memorable nights of passionate, godly, lovemaking in my life!

When the sun's first rays burst on us, as we lay in bed, I noticed that I'd forgotten to turn off the music before we'd both fallen asleep. Barbara Streisand's voice was still singing out from the stereo speakers, "*Memoreee...!*" Waking up to her awesome voice in that rendition, I looked over and saw my sweet Jimm, innocent and asleep in our bed and then, I saw the letter on our night-stand from the judge that had arrived the day before. Jimm's beautiful nude body moved slightly as I then, carefully got up to go out onto the deck to enjoy the new day's sunrise.

That early morning sky—from east to west—was covered with brightly painted clouds in the orange, yellow and golden hues common to my beloved California's already warm Southland. I stood there for a moment, gazing through the wall of windows, and I was mesmerized by the contrast of the deeper heavenly background of blue and purple shades against which the mass of clouds and dark silhouetted vegetation below seemed to be painted. One by one, the downtown towers seemed to be moving as the sun's orb came up over them. I thought to myself, it's a totally new day! The world had never before looked so beautiful to me!

On the deck, with the last bottle of cabernet in my left hand, and with my right, I chose the largest bit of cheese that was still left on one of the plates we'd used the night before. As I picked up the remains of our anniversary celebration, I thought of Terry. Would Terry approve of my sweet Jimm? Yeah, he would, I answered myself. Then, walking closer to the deck's wood railing—I *knew*. The house was situated on a hillside facing a small canyon in the foreground, and with a glittering panorama of the still lit downtown towers in the distance, *I felt Terry's presence.* So, instinctively, I lifted my arms high up in jubilation, and spread eagle, I yelled out in utter bliss to the Universe: "*Wine and cheeeeezzzzzzzz!*"

With that, I heard a distant, slow applause from way down in the canyon below me. I had not expected applause and...

Suddenly, I felt the coolness of the morning breeze waft up from beneath me, between my bare upper legs, I discovered as I then, looked down toward the direction of the applause to see what it was. That's when all of me went suddenly chill...

At the bottom of that canyon, I saw two people who were still applauding and looking up, right at me! A man and a woman waved as if to signal me down...

Realizing that I was totally nude out there in open view of some neighbors that were living below us, I scuffled back into the house as fast as I could! Jimm was awake now, so I quickly forgot our neighbors, and we continued to celebrate our loving relationship. But, that is not where this little story ends...

Two weeks later, we were both at a neighbor's house party, up the same street that we lived on. Mingling with our new friends and neighbors, a beautiful blond woman approached me. A blond version of Cher, I thought. I was so struck by her waist long, straight, perfectly platinum blond hair.

"Nice to see you again," she initially said to me.

"Well, you've got one over me," I responded, "sorry if I don't remember; have we already met? I mean, I don't remember having met you. I'm Tony, and...."

Smiling widely now, she interrupted, "Why, yes! Of course, we've met—in a way. Don't you recall?—'*Wine and cheezzzzz*!' she said, as she began lifting both her arms." Then, she mimicked with both her arms open wide, as she fought back her laughter.

****

I was mortified, but the point is that, *we all choose out of our perceptions* –the individual view– that each person has at every point on their unique journey. My wife and I were different worlds. At any point on this time-incased journey, we are the sum of only *our* past personal choices, and if we examine them, where we've each come from informs us each on the personal direction to take at any point. This is the way to be delivered from our second wombs. I suggest that it is the reference of how to meet the call to be "*born again*" in the biblical Nicodemus story.

Seeing life as a journey is a crucial key of understanding for any person that endeavors to travel on the path of becoming open souls. At first glance, this idea may appear obvious to most of us. Sadly however, the truth is that this idea is not stressed for those of us raised in a closed community. For us *in closed societies, life is not seen as a journey*.

For example, although their Utah based Temple Endowment ritual teaches that life is a journey,[vi] the Mormon community does not envision life as a journey but, rather, as a *school*.[vii] Yet, in schools, what is right and what is wrong is set and taught by those defined as the *teachers*. But, in real life, teachers are all also our student peers. The problem is that a school teaches only what its teachers know how to teach. The curricula is set by those defined as the "educators;" not by those defined as mere "students." So, the school metaphor doesn't work—when we apply real life experience into the equation.

As I found with the Utah based Mormons, envisioning life as a school usually causes us to envision only in broad, general terms, and to see ourselves only as "children" learning what *others* teach. From our pre-school experiences, we are all socialized to accept that teachers know what we need to learn. Yet, if we envision life more as a journey than as a mere school then, the curriculum based lessons of our second womb's teachers [our group authority figures] no longer are, the important guide in our personal evolution. The great teacher, *then*, becomes *how we each experience the experience* of a common journey, as we go. In this way, life becomes a phenomenology or, the science of what *is*—that is—*if we truly examine our past choices*.

This is why, all of our individual experiences—our personal choices— truly are, meant to be examined. We learn by our personal experience. In this way then—by experiencing life as a journey—following a set of commandments, or an ideological scheme, or some theological strictures are no longer as important *as, knowing who and what we are, as we experience the experience*. This is because self-awareness is always a by-product of all kinds of journeying. In this way, religious laws become mute in light of the truth of what *is*. This way is to be "added upon," it is being spiritual, instead of "religious." Significantly, the Latin *religio,* literally, means "to bind again;" in Spanish, *re-ligar* means "to *re*-bind"to a thing or person *in the past*. In this linguistic light, my call is not to any religion.

My call is to be a more open soul; for, I believe this is life's goal. This key for understanding why we are here in this life was profoundly impressed upon me in a series of circumstances. These circumstances forced me to see that *living life as a journey to be experienced* is what enabled me to become free of the judgement of, and of the stereotyping of the behavior, of others. Judgement always accompanies closed and bounded groups, and my excommunication freed me from judging others.

I had learned that being an intolerant *true believer* did not work for me anymore. The old rules had proven to be incongruent with my reality. They didn't compute with the truth of *what is*—with what I'd learned was my true nature. Self-awareness became more important to me than institutional strictures. Self-awareness became more important than my not tolerating another's ways. I'd learned from Dad that *the most important thing in living is to discover who I am*—that, "personal integrity is life's goal" that, "knowing who I am allows me to be integrated as a being of mind, spirit and body." Now, I understood *why* he said it! Life is not about us conforming to a system. But, life is all about self-awareness because only by self-awareness is personal integrity possible. This knowledge, gained by frequent examination of my past choices, lets me see where, what or how it is that I need to improve. For example, in 1997...

****

I was visiting my friend, Phyllis, in Salt Lake City, Utah. The downtown area had gone through huge transformations since I had last been there. Modern, tall towers now lined the area between State and Main Streets. I was in awe of how a downtown area can so quickly be transformed from what it had once been. Change was in the air, and as we drove in her car away from the train station, all I could do is silently scan the scenery on either side. Everything spoke *change*. I assumed that, "*the Saudi princes*" had invested, as hoped...

The following day, we decided to browse the booths in the new square between State and Main Streets where artists were selling their wonderful wares. I stopped at a booth where a woman from Tibet was selling jewelry, while Phyllis walked on.

The woman radiated an air of mysticism. I recognized that she was dressed in the colorful vestments of ancient Tibet. She also seemed to be watching me carefully.

I wondered, as I looked at her jewelry, if these beautiful things were made in Tibet? I asked, "Where were these made?" I had also wanted to get a clue as to why she'd been eyeing me so intently.

"In India," she answered, "that snake you wear is also from India, but it is of Tibet—like I am." Then, she reached down into a small bag underneath her table, and with a smile, she held up a silver snake bracelet *exactly* like mine. "You like?"

"Oh, my!" The synchronicity of it all took me back to a sweet experience in 1988. David, was a man that I'd met in San Francisco. He'd been raised as a Roman Catholic, but his interests at that time were more along the Buddhist tradition...

David had bought me a silver snake bracelet from a small shop on Larkin where a gentle, sweet man had told us that it was from India. "It's a symbol of purity," he'd said, " so, wear it on your left wrist to receive positive energy from others, or on your right wrist, to give out your own positive energy to others."

Holding my left hand straight out, I had said to my friend David, "here, help me put it on this one then."

"Always remember," he had answered, putting it on me, "I only give you my positive energy with this." We'd been spending our last day together, shopping. He then went on, "Tony, let this silver symbolize the purity of my feelings—of our being with each other." He'd decided to move back to the East Coast. "Someday, you'll be guided to another one. Then, put that one on too."

I didn't think much of his comment back at *that* time, but young David was a deeply spiritual being, and his ability to voice what would always, eventually, take place was my way to experience him. Along that part of my journey, his sharing had been a powerful prophetic voice to me.

"Yes, I like," I said to her, holding out my right wrist to let her put it on me.

"It is meant for you," she said, "look, do you see how the big clasp is made to be like a snake's open mouth that is, eating itself?" With that, she finished putting it on my right wrist. "When we eat, we all eating ourselves." With that, the woman simply smiled and then nodded to me saying, "all is impermanent—everything passes."

I was struck with the sense of a sacred moment. I stood there for a minute, remembering the *Meshica* mother in Mexico who had first taught me about the symbol of the snake eating itself. "It's the eternal round," I responded, "eating is a sharing of ourselves, isn't it."

She simply nodded back to me.

Thrilled with my new purchase, I hurried around the people in the area. I was looking for Phyllis. After finding her, I showed her my new piece and we started for her car.

As we began to walk she said simply, "Nice. So, now you have two silver serpents, one for each wrist."

"Yeah," I said back, and I related the story of young David in San Francisco. But, as we walked, I sensed a totally new energy that seemed to radiate from one of the booths to our right. Yet, there were only T-shirts hanging there. So, since I didn't need one, I didn't stop. But then, after we got into the car, I couldn't shrug off that energy that I kept feeling. "Phyllis, could you wait here for a minute. I think, yes, I do have to go and get one of those T-shirts. You know, I really don't need one but..." Then, sensing awkwardness in my feelings, I went on, "...just, wait for a minute, okay?"

Phyllis just smiled and nodded in her knowing way.

When I got to the booth, I noticed that they were all T-shirts with hand painted replicas of *Anasazi* pictographs! They all seemed to have been tie-died, and then overlaid with pictographs. At first, none of them seemed like something I'd want to put on. Then, suddenly, one of them seemed to stand out from all of the rest. As I picked it out, I asked the woman selling them, "Do you know what this symbol means?"

"Oh, I doubt anyone really knows. They're from an *Anasazi* site. It's pretty ancient though—that's all we know."

Looking at it carefully, I recalled how my *Meshica* friends in Mexico had taught me that they believe that their own ancestors had once lived in the American mountain-west. I had been taught by them that, when their ancestors had emigrated to what are now the ruins of the more ancient *Toltecs* in what is now Mexico, they had come from a place that had earlier been called, *Aztlan*. Examining the pictograph on the T-shirt, it seemed like a spiral that is either; going inward, or expanding outward; and the spiral seemed to be superimposed over the sun because the outer edge of the image was like light rays going outward from a center covered by the spiral. The sun's rays *curved* so as to denote movement. I thought to myself, it's a spiral in front of a sun; it eclipses the sun but, I wondered, what does it mean? And why am I so attracted to it?

Suddenly, she interrupted my thoughts, "I like to wear things that feel good to me when I put them on." Putting the shirt up against my chest, she asked, "Does it feel good to you?"

I thought to myself, yes!

That was enough. "Yes," I answered, holding out a handful of dollars, "thanks for helping me to focus with my heart rather than to try to analyze the meaning of this."

Like the woman from Tibet, she also simply smiled, and then she folded the T-shirt for me.

When I got back to the car, I showed Phyllis my find saying, "You know, Phyllis, it was the strangest thing. I don't know why, but I know that I have to wear this thing a lot. Like it's supposed to say—to speak to me—*something* to me. It is meant to teach me something."

Two years passed.

Although the T-shirt was getting frayed because of all the use I'd put it though, I still didn't know what the symbol on it meant.

More especially, I had no clue as to why I had felt so strongly that it really was important for me to wear it for some yet unknown, but significant reason. It was so frayed, that I now rarely ever put it on.

A friend once told me that he thought it was an expanding heart because it was over my heart. But I knew that wasn't what it meant, at least, not to me. Another friend suggested that maybe because of the spiral it's a symbol that signified the tunnel that a shaman takes, as the shaman goes into the underworld. Another said it means, "whirlwind." But, that didn't feel right to me either. In the two years of wearing it, more and more, it felt good to have it on –like it was meant for me after all. There was definitely purpose in it. But what purpose?

Another year passed.

Not wanting to wear it out, now, I avoided using it. But, after another half year passed, I discovered in a meditation session that I was still focused on it. So, I put in on for three consecutive days. On the last day, I was out of clean clothes and I had to wash it. As I picked it up to wash it by hand, a thought came into me:

Stop now. Go to the grocery store.

But, I don't need any groceries!

Go to the grocery store, the thought commanded.

So, I hesitatingly put on the unlaundered shirt and went out to the grocery store—hoping that its unwashed sweaty musk odor wouldn't offend anyone. After getting some ice cream –I can always make room for ice cream– I went and got in the shortest line at a check stand. My mind wandered...

All around me, there was only the "busyness" of a large modern supermarket...

There was one man in the line next to mine. He kept staring at me. He appeared Latino, but not Gay so, I knew it wasn't a come-on.

I thought to myself, why is he staring at me? I hope that he can't smell this shirt. I wondered, do we know each other?

Suddenly, he yelled out to me, "Do you know the meaning of that symbol on your T-shirt?"

Shocked at his absolutely timely question, I got a bit tongue-tied and answered, "Uh, no. Do you?"

"Yeah. My half-brother is Native-American. He says that it's kind of like a charge, a challenge, or how to live a noble life in the crazy world that we live in."

"Really?"

"Yeah, it tells us to 'Follow the sun.'"

"'Follow the sun?'"

"Yeah, it's a prayer. It prays that, you will 'Follow the sun.'"

I looked down at it, "Yeah," I said, "that makes sense…" At that point, I had to deal with the checker. And when I was done, I couldn't see the man anywhere and I guessed that he'd left the store. I never saw him again.

Walking back home, I was hearing his interpretation in my mind, "Follow the sun." It rang true. Like the clear sound of a bell, it felt sure to me, and with every step that I took, I felt an increased sense of peace about the entire thing.

After getting home, I took off the shirt in order to wash it. While it soaked, I picked up my journal from the year that I'd first met my old *Meshica* friends in Mexico in 1990. That's when the entire journey of the discovery finally made sense to me. They had taught me about their concept of living life as if it were a journey. But, since that day on the beach when I'd taken my walk to think about that first sharing of sexual energies with a *Meshica* Indian friend, I hadn't thought of these ideas. Then, it hit me—Why, this symbol is the Four Directions, as *they* know them! They didn't use the four directions of the compass for *that* reason!

He had told me that, I should honor the Four Directions as they understood them to be –not the directions of a modern compass– but the Four Directions known by Father Sun, in His daily journey across the daytime sky: "Above Him; Below Him; The Beginning Place; The Ending Place." The Four Directions, he had then said, are: "Above me, Below me, Where I'm coming from, and to Where I'm going; for *each day is the journey. Every step is the journey.* The journey is over your whole world, Antonio; all day long, each and every day."

Recalling his words, I looked at the T-shirt. The symbol had become absolutely clear to me! Of course, the spiral is *the journey*, and it is superimposed on Father Sun—as if going toward it or, *following Him*! *Follow the sun*! I thought –knowing that each of us *is a unique world*– live life like the sun: As a daily journey over my whole world! To the *Meshica*, our reality is a collective dream in which we all journey.

****

It took years, but I had diligently tried to see where I have come from, because that revealed the direction toward which I was going. This knowledge is important, because knowing the direction of any path that a person may take, is the best way to be aware of whether that particular path is a good one for her or him to take. Since, all of our past choices determine our present direction for each of us then, it's logical to assume that, an examination of one's past personal choices can be a critical key to allow anyone to focus clearly on their present life direction.

This awareness is crucial to how we all make choices in the present. It is truthfully said that, "an examined life is the only life worth living."[ix] And, as I examined my life's choices, I consistently came back to how it was that I had now become estranged from all of my children. In the process, I saw several significant situations –all of which, involved choices–choices which, had all contributed to my personal phenomenology, as it relates to my children. My choices were *default dynamics* or, what Lewiki called "post-decisional."

I had been raised to understand that –after one's marriage has become one's reality– our children are our true treasures in life. No amount of income, real property, or earthly material possessions can compare with the joy, sweetness and awesome love that we receive in life when a child joins us on life's journey. I still see that this is true. But, heterosexual coupling was *the only option* that I was then, taught to envision. In the Mormon cosmology, the ideal Afterlife is about sexual reproduction. Heterosexual marriage is *absolutely necessary* in order for any to be in the highest heavenly Afterlife with Heavenly Father. In the Utah based Mormon future Celestial Afterlife, if a guy is not married heterosexually then, he will experience "all eternity" without his family, without his loved ones, without friends, "worlds without end." For a young man who served as a missionary for The Church such as I, a wife and as many children as God blessed us with was merely part of life's true equation—a part of the Lord's "plan of salvation." I did not want to experience eternity as I had been taught would be the lot of anyone not married heterosexually, *and* with their civil marriage solemnized by a sealing ceremony in a temple. I did not want to live "separately and singly, worlds without end." Thus, as Lewiki wrote, my "choice" was made *well after I'd decided what marriage was. My decision* only considered "heterosexual" options.

Moreover, getting children in one's home usually engenders compassion. Although, I think our world's greatest global problem is over-population, I cannot deny this truth. So, to me, my friends who see breeding with a bit of disdain are at a disadvantage because they do not know what I have known about the absolute treasure that one's children truly are. I know it because I have four. But tragically, mine didn't know me for eighteen, long years. It was the mid. 1990s…

****

It was painful and destructively angering for me to realize what had happened. The anguish of that day in the early 1980s was more than I'd ever known. Since that day, my mother, father and two life partners have passed on, but for me, even the death of family members through the years up to the new millenium was not as filled with the unspeakable despair as what had taken place back then, in the early 1980s.

My choices had cast me out of The Church's community. My wife's choices had, predictably I guess, been influenced by my choices because, in the context of our community at the time, I was the family patriarch. I was the steer to all the choices that were made in our home. She was the anchor. That is the way of patriarchally-centered homes.

Back in the early 1980s, as I had opened the four letters, one by one, I'd recalled a conversation she and I'd had when we had been sealed as a Mormon couple for only one year. For that anniversary, in our bleak economic restraints, I'd translated a verse into English for her from the 1930s torch-song French singer, Edit Piaf "*Hymne d' Amour.*" I had verbally counseled her, "Laura, if I ever do the unthinkable, and I leave the Church for whatever unknown then, please, Laura, you follow God. Don't go the way that I choose, if that ever happens."

At first, she had responded with surprise and then, as if to reflect on her wisdom, she answered, "Tony, you won't ever do that —not *you*—you're good as gold!" She'd used that phrase every time that I would need reinforcement in whatever endeavor we'd tried to accomplish, as a family. Her trust of her husband was beyond my own self-trust.

A Mormon man is raised to choose a wife who is totally capable of being the best mother to his children as possible, and I had made my own choice accordingly. I knew that, when we'd have children in our family, she would be the best of all mothers! So, I'd insisted, "Laura, for the sake of our future children, please, promise that if that ever happens then, you will choose to follow God instead of me." She'd promised to do as I had asked, and now, these years later, as I read each of these four letters, I know that they were the awful result of that fateful covenant. As good Mormons, we knew the meaning of covenants. Laura had kept her promise.

The letters had all been dated the same date. Only one was from my ex-wife. Another was from a former stake president of ours, who was now a General Authority of The Church as one of the Quorum of The Seventy—a part of the church hierarchy that is second only to The Twelve Apostles and First Presidency, who together, preside over The Church. A third letter was from my ex-wife's then, local ward bishop—a man who years later, was fated to also come out, as a Gay man after notorious service as a prominent Mission President, and respected church leader. The final letter was from one of the lawyers in the Salt Lake City law firm that was (and remains as) The Church Legal Counsel. Each of the four letters were written on the, respective, official stationery of each party; evidence, to me, of the secretly organized response—a clear message to me that they'd all acted in unison, in doing what Mormons call a, "secret combination."

While they did not state that clearly, in my awareness of our church's political dynamics—as one who had been employed at its world headquarters offices—I saw what had happened, clearly. One letter stated that, "the sin" is what was condemned, "not the sinner." Yet, I knew by that point in my life that, *what we do* by our life choices is what, actually, defines who and what we personally are, as sovereign souls. Although the writer probably did not see it as I did, to my new vision, what he condemned was, in fact, *me—because we all exist only as we relate*! Another letter was a threat about what would be done to me, if I endeavored to "contact" my children.

It was an arrogant challenge, in essence, an open admission of their concerted effort because my wife had chosen to disobey the court order of the Los Angeles Superior Court. She had secretly moved out of California to Utah, while the judge had ruled that we'd both have joint custody and that *she must stay in southern California* "within the five counties stipulated." One was a legal device that claimed to inform me of my alleged illegal status in the State of Utah. Evidently, an old "Utah law" officially defined me as a "criminal" because I now acted as an openly "homosexual" man. My ex-wife had done her duty, because as she had also written to me on the same date, saying, I must be "possessed by a demon."

What I had now chosen was unthinkable. To her, it was the behavior of a man, whom she did not know anymore. As a result of both of our choices, she'd chosen to disobey the law of the State in which we had lived. Feeling abandoned, she had sought for refuge among her faith community of Saints in Utah. But their, "secret combination," however, had left me –the *rightful* father– with no opportunity for any visitation with any of my children. In my still evolving worldview, and also in my acquired knowledge of Mormon scripture, I saw what they'd done as, an ugly, and gross, sinful thing. By their response to my choice, our children grew up with one parent.

The Book of Mormon calls this particular kind of hidden *illegal* agreement a "secret combination." "Secret combinations" in their most benign sense, are at least, "unethical." To *illegally* keep my children's whereabouts a secret to me became *their* "secret combination."[xii] As teenage Mormon seminary students know, such "secret combinations" to go against "the law of the land" are very harshly condemned in their sacred Book of Mormon. All the people who had written these letters knew they were acting *against* their own strictures. I knew it, and they knew that I knew it.

I was a complexity of emotions. I had been convinced that *I* was the massive guilty link in the entire chain of this true, human tragedy. Within two months, my whole world had fallen apart. I'd lost my children, my divorce had been finalized, I'd been forced to resign from my work by a man who'd discovered from his Mormon neighbor that I'd chosen to live as an openly Gay man, and –as a result– Jimm had gone in psychotic shock. Our two gay landlords then, asked me to move out. They saw me as the reason why Jimm had gone into a fetal position on the bed that day. In their eyes, it was when I'd been forced to "resign" that Jimm had totally "lost it." Out of my guilt, I had moved out leaving my sweet Jimm –whom I'd later call Jason in my first book– in their care. I had fallen into agreement with my condemning behavioral judges.

The result was my suicide attempt in April 1982, as I relate in my first book.[xiii] In my horror, I had seen that my choices had ruined everyone's lives, including the life of my children and the man I loved. Yet, I can now see that it was all for a purpose. Thankfully, time is the great healer. Old college friends had helped me—devout Mormon friends—who, surprisingly, still seemed to love me. Then, after more than six years had passed, my first book was published. It's wherein I was able to write of my mind-set in those darkest days of my life. But, the words relating those dark events don't reflect the joy that my choices had taken me to, when that book's second edition came out as a paperback, in 1992. Even so, I had written in 1988:

"I wondered if it wouldn't be better for all of us, especially Laura, to find another man. She needed another man so she could be sealed in the temple to a normal, heterosexual man who could take her with him to the highest glory of the Celestial kingdom of God. She deserved much more than I could offer. My mind accepted the prognostication of doom. My mind told me that all that Dale Hansen, Bill Detton, and those months in the archives had taught me were mere rationalizations. I found myself accepting the idea that rationalization was my effort to cover up my sins. I thought of my

children almost every waking minute of those difficult weeks and months when I expected excommunication from the Church. I often thought to myself that getting out of their lives at this early age would be the best thing that I could do for their spiritual welfare. After all, I had bought into a view of my utter ugliness in God's eyes and I didn't want them to have someone like me around them to influence them for evil."

The irony, as stated earlier, is that after my first book was first published in hardback, my family's own bishop (who had joined in their "secret combination" to keep the whereabouts of my children away from my awareness) has also, since then, come out of his own Gay closet. When I learned about his own coming out, I thought of the old saying: *What goes around, comes around.* It was when I'd lived in San Francisco in 1992, and after my lover, Jimm, had died from AIDS, that he'd acquired after our break-up. One day, a friend happened to talk of his own past sexual intimacies "with an L.D.S. bishop"—and, it turned out, he was *my family's* former bishop...

I hadn't yet totally healed. Filled with the rage of that dark moment, I'd yelled out loudly, "The Bastard! That ass-hole!" Mike's, face had gone totally white. He had never seen me this angry, and he had never heard me talk this way.

"Do you know him?" I was immersed in anger. "Yeah," I yelled out –pacing back and forth– "he's one of the bigots that kept my kids away from me!" The irony of it all was overwhelming me, and I caught myself wondering if *the man* had even seen his duplicity against us all. "Tell me about him! I need to know what that fucker is doing these days. Is the hypocrite still in The Church? The heat within me was intense now, "Well, tell me! Is he?"

"Uh…no," my friend said shyly, "I think that he's since been excommunicated too." Then, after a pause, he said, "like you, Tony."

With those three last words, I stopped dead in my tracks. Suddenly, I felt a palpable energy fill me from head to foot. I felt only sadness at what had happened to him. An *awful* sadness had engorged me. I knew exactly what he was now going through! The pained empathy I felt, the clarity, the compassion—that I was washed in—made tears begin flowing freely. So, taking a seat next to my friend on the sofa, I said simply, "Oh, my God, no! He must be in real horrible anguish! He must be in *agony* over what he did to me!"

Mike held me, as I wept—bitterly—uncontrollably. I really do not remember how long Mike held me there but, I know it was my most personally draining emotional experience in the mid. 1990s. A man who had pointed the accusing finger had proven, again to me, that this world is a world of genuine justice, after all...

Another year or two passed.

The telephone rang...
The familiar voice on the other end was one of a man I hadn't forgotten. He said, "Tony, this is_____. Do you remember me? I was your family's bishop in…"
Interrupting him, I answered, "of course, I recall who you are. Then, after a few pleasantries, we agreed to meet in a restaurant. He needed my forgiveness, and of course, he got it from me.

I've even forgiven the rest of the others who had been party to their "secret combination" because I have examined all my past choices from my own time in their institutional church. I know that, were I in their exact circumstances today in their specific religious institutional context, I would have probably done exactly as they did. If I had been on the same path on the journey of life as they were at that time then, I know that my choices would have been no different than theirs.

This is why I say that, *where we are on the path* of this single minded journey is what determines our direction. But, if we'll look back, and examine our choices; if we'll only see our past life as our individual phenomenology then, we can change, and go forward in wisdom. Envisioning this way is how we know to change from one path to another path, for, indeed, we are all free agents. In this way, Don Miguel Ruiz teaches, "we recover free will."[xv]

Like it is with any path, the path we travel on determines our ability to envision. Even though I was no longer going along his same path, I'd been on the same path as he'd been on. I knew what he probably felt. As a result, I could empathize. The result was that it was easy to forgive him because my children were not taken from me only by his choices nor, even by only my ex-wife's choices. *I had also made choices* toward that end, *myself.* We are each, and all, the sum of individual choices, and by examining *my own choices*, I was able to take responsibility for them.

When our paths had crossed again that day, I had the sense that we both were traveling along parallel paths. While, he had been able to continue his own role as father through the years, I'd had no contact with my own children. Moreover, in retrospect, I see that my choices were compounded by –not only his choices and those of my ex-wife but– also by choices made by that L.D.S. General Authority and that staff guy from the Church's legal counsel.

****

Moreover, as usual, all things worked together. Century old Utah State laws were used by their 1980s "secret combination." I was technically deemed a "criminal" in the State of Utah. As a result, my ex-wife was not legally obligated (in the State of Utah) to get my permission to have the children adopted by another man. The result was that my children are no longer known by my family's surname. Thus, it would be many years later when I'd be able to communicate in any way with my eldest son because he had sought me out on his own. I didn't even know about the adoptions when he had looked me up in San Francisco…

When he was about to marry in the L.D.S. Temple, my eldest son informed me that his legal surname was no longer mine. That is how I first learned that my children's legal adoption had taken place several years earlier in Utah. For only a few minutes, I felt the hot surge of inner rage over the final outcome of all our various choices.

But then, seeking comfort with my sister by telephone, her wise words reminded me: "We're all products of our choices, Tony."

While I had already been exposed to that idea, I needed to be reminded. I'd chosen to sacrifice all of those spiritual relationships, for all Mormon "sealed" familial relationships in Utah Mormonism are first, and foremost, *spiritual*—not biological relationships. In the Mormon Temple sealings tradition, our biological and legal nuclear family relationships are actually secondary. Temple Sealings, in the Mormon community headquartered in Utah, take institutional pre-eminence over all other familial relationship, legal or not.

This is why my reason for marrying a woman had had its root in my nature to obey my spiritual mentors. It is the duty of any faithful Mormon to obey their priestly hierarchy; it is the "First Law of Heaven." Thankfully, however, my experience in the experience had taught me that, it is not the first law, in the sense of the first rung in a ladder, which one may climb. I had long since become aware through my personal journey that, it is "the first law" only in the sense of being *the lowest law*—for all lower laws are all meant to be overridden by "higher law"—in the Mormon cosmology that I had learned in seminary as a teenager.

"Higher law" are two verbal terms that most Utah Mormons understand. Theologically, however, Utah based Mormons cannot obtain "exaltation" in their unique version of an Afterlife without being totally obedient to the leaders, in spite of having "higher law." In their view, when one "disobeys" after being endowed with certain Temple rituals—or "blessings"—disobedience, will put disobedient ones beyond the saving grace of the traditional Christian deity. Thus, one endowed, such as I had been, "worlds without end," would be in a "lesser glory." I would be forever consigned to an Afterlife where my children would *not* be—that is, if my children continued to obey their leaders—for their leaders, are their life *teachers* in the "school of life" metaphor mentioned near the beginning of this chapter.

But, the fact of the matter is: Had the designated *teachers* not taught me that "marrying a woman will heal" me "of the sickness of homosexuality" then, *I would not have chosen to marry.* Had I taken life as a journey in those days, I would have been better off. I knew about my natural bent for other guys as an adolescent! My sexual orientation had been made entirely clear to me that day in the chapel with Terry that I wrote about in Chapter One: Contrary to my teachers' teachings, my life's journey had told me that *my nature was to not marry*—a *woman*. But, because of early imprinting, I had used my personal free will to obey the "counsel" of my "inspired" church leaders because I had been taught to consider them as true guides, or as my *faithful teachers—the* role models, *for me to emulate.*

That was the institutional seduction, however, because they had not provided me with sufficient relevant data. I'd married out of what was pure obedience. If any kind of marriage had been an option for one such as I knew I was then, even back in my teens, I'd have chosen the monogamous and loving union that Terry had offered me so honestly! When I found that *this was an option in the eyes of the 1830s founder of the Mormon Churches*—as I reported in my first book[xvii]—then I came to see my adolescent Mormon experience as a definite, cultural rape. It was religious abuse because some modern Mormon must have hidden all of the documents—later, in late 1970s or early 1980s—that I'd seen in the L.D.S. Archives in the mid 1970s; documents revealing the Utah based *mercurial* marriage theology.

However, this is the stuff of all tragedy. All of these various choices –going back to probable decisions to hide those records– had intermingled to create the texture of our future collective's reality, for that is how our human Mass Mind created our present. Therefore, I am saying that, *what* encounters us on this journey, which we all call our mortal, individual life, is—ultimately—not important. We have no personal control over past mentors and models. We only control *our present choices.* We are only the masters of *our* single direction.

****

As my *Meshica* friend would teach me that night, on that dark, sandy beach, when we first shared our sexual energy: "The past does not exist anymore. The future does not yet exist. All that we have is today, the present." In other words, *how we choose daily* to respond to those encounters that meet us along the journey of life is the all-important factor. This is because we are each the sum of our choices. That fact, alone, impacts us universally. As mentioned in another chapter we, together, create our reality. Although we do it as individuals, the fact that we are all One Whole –like the individual cells of a human body are all One– so also is it with us, as a collective of individuals who have personal free will.

In other words, as it is with us on the personal level, so it also is with us as a society. It bears repeating, we, *together*—all of us choosing, as *individuals*—create the truly common reality. This is because of the dynamic of microcosm and macrocosm. I hope that, all of the stories in this book reflect that, for me—on the personal level—connecting with my own ancestral Indigenous awarenesses has opened a new way for me to envision our common world. Over the years I have thought to myself: It is rational, therefore, that if our society becomes more aware of blessed, nature-centric truth, then *that,* likewise, opens new ways to *collectively envision* the common world, which we all share with each other and with all other species. Then we, as a global, living, human collective soul mass, would be more responsible in our present context, i.e.: In the natural world.

Scientists are believing; that the dynamics of our collective mass consciousness, actually change reality. Recall the examples in this book from history. They demonstrate that, before American Indian societies were confronted with what we call our proprietary worldview and our current drive to dominate—as if we were meant to own all other living beings—*their* Indian societies didn't work out of the creation of conflict. These examples are offered to help us all consider that, the dynamics of mass consciousness are what have made the world into what it now is, today. We are all part of a Greater Whole. Individual choices do impact the future of every other being in the whole world of nature. For example, physicists tell us that a small butterfly in the South Pacific impacts all global climates.

When I became more in touch with my own Indian roots, as anyone that does so, I also became aware of the world of nature in a way that I'd not clearly done before. Where, before 1990, I was only aware of political, socio-economics—in our global world order—as a then, loyal employee in international corporations; today, I am now, increasingly, aware of the consequences that obviously stem from how our industrialized nation states fuel our appetite for energy. We are conspicuous consumers of the planet's toxic energy producing fossil fuels. I now see anew, with eyes of nature-centered peoples. I can now understand! The developing nations of our common planet have, sadly, become our modern civilization's main warning system of problems produced by the phenomenon of global warming.

For example, in a PBS television report aired in the month of June 2001, it was reported that "Western Samoa, the Marshal Islands and other island landmasses" of Earth are where we can now "see the effect of global warming in the water level of the rising oceans." I was not previously open to even acknowledge this kind of scientific data before my recent connection with my cultural roots. However, today, I hear the warning of the scientists who labored both at Rio de Janeiro, Brazil, and at Kioto, Japan. They pleaded intelligently in those two conferences to heal the nations so that some way could be agreed upon to lower the emissions of the gases that result from our burning of fossil fuels for our human energy needs. They warned us all that, "there is a clear connection" with the "warming of the planet, the rising of the waters of the seas and the human burning of fossil fuels." Yet, the United States of America not only declined to sign the treaties but, *we Americans have not yet led toward any solutions.*

We have, instead, retrenched into our gluttony. Scientists tell us that diesel exhaust is now burning the ozone layer. On June 25, 2001, the Los Angeles Times[xviii] reported that:

"In the early 1980s, California accounted for 95% of the world's wind generation, but the state has failed since then; to keep pace with Western Europe. There have been no serious proposals for offshore wind parks...Paul Gipe, a leading American expert on wind power says California gets little more than 1% of its energy from wind power—far more than any other state but paltry compared with Denmark."

According to this report, Denmark "expects to generate enough renewable power to account for 23% of its energy needs within two years and 50% by 2030, mostly from wind." Denmark has led the rest of us, where America has not led in these issues—at all!

According to the article, "Wolfhart Duerrschmidt, head of the Environment Ministry's section that handles renewable resources" for Germany, recently said "If all goes well with next year's pilot projects, such installations could lift the wind-generated share to 20% by 2020 and 50% by 2050." The European Union has taken the moral high ground on the issue of the environment. But what is noteworthy, is that "China," according to the report—even with its billions of people—actually ranks among the top ten nations "per capita" that now lead this environmental move toward wind power. Do they know something we are ignoring?

When the sitting President, George Walker Bush, went to Europe in the same month, he chose to rebuff the scientific warnings saying, "we need more study." At the same time, he proposed American long range energy continue to come from Earth's fossil fuels, "like coal," adding, "the economy will be hurt if we change to alternative energy sources." Then, later in June of 2003, a report was released by ABC News telling that, "...the Administration had 'doctored' the Environmental Protection Agency's report on global warming..." As I sat in my comfortable wing backed chair in my living room—far away from the Islanders who were now making plans to relocate their entire national population—I felt complete shame, disgust at the way our political leaders had, reportedly, acted regarding the scientific data on global warming.

So today, I easily see that *Europe is leading where we have not*: The European Union's change to alternative sources will not "hurt" the global economy, but rather, their change to alternative sources of fuel will probably only redistribute where the economy is centered! The renewable energy produced from wind in Europe, according to this 2003 Los Angeles Times report, "has produced a huge increase in investment in research and development in wind." We all need to look with the view of nature-centric peoples. So, my non-professional advice to profit-savvy stock investors is: If you're shopping for new stocks to buy then, look to alternative technologies.

As I watched the PBS report mentioned above, my sense was that the Native representatives from the island nations to the Kioto conference put it all too clearly. Two of them had said, "the scenario doesn't look very good for us. At least our children will know that we have done what we can" and, also,

"We are the first ones to now have to look at the relocation of our country's populations. But, your time will come also, unless you change. Before it's too late, recognize that, you also have coastline communities."

Where we usually see only our separateness, they all only envision our connectedness. That is their nature-centric heritage. The point is: We are all, individually, part of a web of global inter-relatedness that is part of yet another, Great Whole. But, we are all also the sum of our choices, and thankfully, many of the souls who have met me along my journey have taught me that we are all one, as well. Because of them, I can now see that the path on which we collectively journey may take many of us to our destruction, at or immediately after our entering the new century. Of this, I am all too convinced.

My use of the term, "immediately" is relative, but my sense is that the global human collective desperately needs the wisdom of our human elder cultures, for, we *are* each and all of us, the sum of our choices. And what does the elder wisdom of this planet's older societies consistently say about where we're all headed?

In a recent conversation with descendants of the *Yanya* Indians, a society that California history books say is "extinct," I was poignantly reminded by one of them that, "California was once an island..." Evidently, ancient stories of these Pre-Colombian earliest inhabitants of Los Angeles, California—the place which, the *Yanya* called *Yangna*—the year that we now call 2004, is a time they have anticipated for many generations: "It is about the right time *when the Island is to be, again, recreated by the old cyclical Earth-moving..."* phenomenon..."Remember Antonio, all the most fruitful California low lands were under sea water long ago—as they will soon be, once again....!"[xix]

But, I ask: Will America choose to be open to the wisdom of nature-centric peoples? Isn't it, now, time that we accept that each of us—together with the entire universe—are all part of an intricately connected, intelligent and living web? Whether that old, expected cyclical Earth moving happens in 2004, or 2012, or 2020, the point is, it will happen. It is time, now, for the head to stop saying to the hand and to the foot, "I have no need of thee."

As for me in 2004, I'm finally sure of my own path because I now frequently stop and examine my life. Are you also sure of where you are now headed? Moreover, what path will America now choose to follow—as a human collective—and what will be the rest of the world's response, for that matter? Aren't these the true, all-important questions for each of us to, now, ask because—as I've endeavored to show by telling a few stories from my personal journey—we all are, *together*, the sum of all of our individual choices, after all.

NOTES TO CHAPTER THREE

[i] This was the band of families with whom I briefly lived in Mexico in 1990. None of the others mentioned in this book who call themselves Indian use this terminology with me, as we talk of the common experience we all know as life.

[ii] The complete story of my coming out and my divorce is told in my first book.

[iii] The complete story of this experience is told in a forthcoming book.

[iv] In my second book, The Issue Is Pluralism, *An Urgent Call To Greater Pluralism In Civil Marriage Law* (Editorial Los Feliz, Los Angeles, California, 2000) pages 3-4 I would later write:

"...history has shown that the emergence of the AIDS epidemic at that point, literally, overwhelmed all other issues within the gay community. The political Gay, Lesbian, Bi-sexual and Trans-gendered community became a culture of survival—unable to do anything but survive. First, we had to live. Then, we could seek redress. Nevertheless, less than seven years after I had made that declaration, the political battle over same-sex civil marriage licensure began to surface in Hawaii. Eventually, because of the behind-the-scenes organizing and financial and legal contributions of the Utah based Mormon Church, it mushroomed—in Hawaii...As I had foreseen, it did not die in Hawaii...Then, in 1999 same-sex civil marriage licensure surfaced powerfully in the State of Vermont. The Vermont Supreme Court protected the human right to civil licensure of a same-sex couple..." The rest is also history.

[v] The painful story of the passing of my companion is told in my first book.

[vi] The Endowment ceremony of The Church of Jesus Christ of Latter-day Saints has a statement that says that "Adam" and "Eve" were "to learn by their own experience" to distinguish the "good" from the "evil." Initiates are then, told that they are to each "consider" themselves "as if" they were "each, Adam and Eve." A film dramatizes Adam and Eve on a journey. Then, the initiates are symbolically taken on a journey into various stages of enlightenment. This is to teach life as a journey. In fact, in the older pre-1950s multi-media endowment ceremony, Mormons were made to literally move from room to room during the process of this ritual. This is why all their original, post-Kirtland Temples built before the 1960s were constructed with: Initiatory Rooms; a Creation Room; a Garden Room; a World Room; a Terrestrial Room and a Celestial Room. All of these rooms were used in this one ceremony. This elaborate, congregational liturgy was meant to reinforce to the mind of Temple initiates, the idea that life should be envisioned as a journey. This is only one of many aspects of the LDS Mormon Temple Endowment Ceremony that—in light of the Puritan/Protestant heritage

of Brigham Young, who wrote the ceremony as the Latter-day Saints have it—all seem to have been lifted directly from Native-American Tradition. One must keep in mind that, a key mid. 19th century distinction of Mormonism is the official doctrine that the Indians they encountered in their settling of lands were, literal, descendants of some ancient Israelites whose, religious tradition, it was written, contained "the fullness of the gospel." It is natural to assume that, in his final writing of the L.D.S. Temple Endowment Ceremony, Brigham Young had generously used Native-American sacred terminology and knowledge.

[vii] The metaphor of a school is the usual one applied by the modern Utah based L.D.S. General Authorities in their sermons and writings. See LDS Conference Reports for the actual texts of their sermons on life being "a school."

[viii] The complete story of this experience is told in a later chapter in this volume.

[ix] Most often attributed to Socrates, Plato's mentor.

[x] Organizational Shock, by Lewicki

[xi] These letters are still in my personal files. However, as discussed herein, the identities of those who sent them to me are not relative to my purpose in telling this story. Rather, the important reason for the telling of this story is my truth, or how *I* experienced the experience. Thus, I have purposely not revealed the identities of the parties involved, and where names are used, they are only pseudonyms. Specific details, other than how they are discussed in this book, are private in nature and irrelevant to this work. All the parties involved know that, what I have stated in this book is true and correct. Their identities are not my issue but, *my own experience is*, which impacted us all.

[xii] Prophecy about a "latter-day" in the Book of Mormon; II Nephi; Chapter 26:20-23.

[xiii] Out of The Bishop's Closet, *A Call To Heal Ourselves, Each Other and Our World* by Antonio A. Feliz (2nd ed. Paperback, Alamo Square Press, San Francisco, CA. 1992).

[xiv] Ibid.

[xv] The Four Agreements, by Don Miguel Ruiz (Amber-Allen Publishing).

[xvi] This is parallel to how many polygamist families view their own familial relationships because the concept of sealing in the Mormon churches that still practice polygamy—as well as in The Church of Jesus Christ of Latter-day Saints—is separate from civil unions of any sort. In fact, in some nation states, the Utah based Latter-day Saints must *also* be *civilly* married, in addition to their Temple marriages, because civil marriage definitions and/or authority to marry couples in *civil* marriage does not extend to Utah Mormons from the, particular, government involved. This fact, has highly significant possibilities for America.

It has occurred to me that, whatever the church, synagogue, temple or mosque, its right to continue to celebrate its own sacramental "marriage" as they, respectively, believe is *lawful* to their God must be protected. In this way, "the sanctity of marriage" remains the sole responsibility of those who claim to represent Holiness. But, Jefferson's separation of church and state demands the elimination of any "civil marriage" *per* se. All civil state licenses "to marry" are *legally* defined only as *secular* licenses to establish a "domestic union." Thus, by eliminating "civil marriage" *per se*, and by labeling the two parties to any application for a license as only, "applicant A and applicant B, what kind of "domestic union" it is, could be *legal* under the penumbra of our judicial judgments regarding equal treatment under constitutional law. This equitable language in state civil statutes would eliminate differentiation between those couples currently licensed to "marry," from all others. By differentiating all other tenancy statuses from a spousal cohabitation, with no reference to; the sex, the gender, or the sexual orientation of any of the applicant parties involved, it gives equal treatment to all citizens. In this way, all marriages would truly be religious, or "holy unions", and remain the specific responsibility of only the religious institutions, and state civil statutes regarding joint tenant legal benefits for all spousal domestic partnerships would be kept separate from marriage, *per se.* [In the special case of Utah based Mormon Temple "sealing" traditions, this arrangement would not impact their current temple ceremony at all, since the wording used in their marriage ritual is already about the performance of a "sealing."] This arrangement, thus, allows state governments to enact laws on domestic partnerships however they wish, and to treat all citizens equally "under the law" of our common, secular society. Jefferson's definition on the purpose of our First Amendment (and others that impact human rights) solves the issue.

[xvii] Op.Cit.

[xviii] Column One Article, *"Danes See a Breezy Solution"* Los Angeles Times, Monday, June 25, 2001.

[xix] Leonard K. Hernandez to Antonio A. Feliz, November 30, 2002. (The italicized words are from his family's memorized oral tradition.)

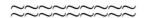

"What didn't compute for me was the stark reality that, present practices of institutions that claim their first authority from Joseph Smith, Junior, did not follow these older principles of church governance either. The "linking of souls" was not as important as the "ranking of souls," in the 20th century church ..."

CHAPTER FOUR

FROM POWER
TO AGREEMENT

There's a profound difference between the terms *acquiesce* and *agree*. To acquiesce is to look up to a superior from below, in a hierarchical way of envisioning. When we acquiesce, we only agree to a particular way to be, or to go with another's perspective. Yet, we do not necessarily agree that what is acquiesced to *is* correct. To acquiesce is, to behave in accord with an illusion that the other party is superior to—or better than, or more desirable than—the one who acquiesces. To follow the temporary whim of popular style is *also* acquiescence. It is mere compliance with an external culture.

Conversely, in all agreement, there is a true coming together of diverse wills, with the energies of the integrated forces that all of them comprise. The Force, or the *energy* created by such a coming together of equally sovereign, individual souls, is what creates. Yet, by its core nature, this "agreement" way to envision is not seen at all as being hierarchical. No, this way of envisioning is egalitarian, it is a free integration of *equals* for, any *"equity,"* or any *cosmic balance* is what allows any true agreement to exist.

When we choose to only acquiesce to another's will, *then,* we are merely confirming a personal agreement with another's self-proclaimed and imagined superior station to our own; when in truth, both they, and we are peers. While, to acquiesce may be practical in present ways of inter-relating, no lasting energy is generated in this way to be, because it is not an honest coming together of free wills. Thus, acquiescence isn't the integrated Force of two or more *equals,* and acquiescence never produces sufficient energy to create any *new* circumstances because *acquiescence is always impotent.*

Acquiescence is not about authentic power; it is not about *your* energy, or *your* vibrations; it is only about status in hierarchies. So, it produces class-centered behavior in those who succumb to the allure of perceived style and status. It is hierarchic in its true nature. Conversely, however, authentic power is born by agreement among sovereign souls, who inter-relate in equity. *Agreement is, therefore, a generative force, which, in itself, is capable of regenerating its own energy.* Agreement is a *natural* dynamic, it is of our world. Like the *literal* agreement between an innately sovereign single sperm and an innately sovereign single egg, it is generative. Agreement is able to generate another innately sovereign soul mass that is composed of all the individual, innately sovereign souls, who are each party to it, by their own free will and choice.

Acquiescing with another, on the other hand, only generates an extension of the one perceived to be superior. This is done through the dynamics of compliance. Acquiescing, itself, does not create new energy. With this dynamic, *only the dominant energy is magnified.* That is why, when we choose to acquiesce, we are merely choosing to maintain the *status quo.* That choice is to keep the present illusion of the conditions. This is true because mere *acquiescence is impotent to impregnate the naturally chaotic nature of the universe with a new way of being.*

This is the reason why I choose agreement as the way of being that I try to be in the world. Experiencing the experience of our common human journey out of the attitude of agreement is to truly maintain one's authentic individual empowerment. Power, in this way of envisioning, is not about *power over others.* True agreement is to magnify one's own self-identity, to be magnetic to all our others, and to *also* be equally open to *their* magnetism. In truth, agreement is about our soul becoming more massive but, in Agreement, we do it *without dominating others.* These ideas became clear to me in the following experiences, as I read of them in my 1979 journal from my second year as an ordained bishop...

****

The telephone call came, as usual, after we had all gone to bed. Whenever a member of my Mormon ward (parish) needed my advice or just my listening ear I as their local ward bishop am seen by them as the "father of the ward"a non-scriptural title. So, culturally, I am their designated minister although, Utah based Mormons avoid using the title of minister. So, when such a call comes, I must respond with complete compassion, as would Father in Heaven, and that's why, after clearing my throat, I sleepily tried to cheerfully say, "Hello, this is the bishop."

"Bishop Feliz," the woman's voice said nervously into my ear, "I'm truly sorry to call at this hour but, something very distressing has just happened over here, across the street…"

By the time I had hung up the telephone, I'd decided to do what had been advised about such circumstances in one of my high council meetings, when I had first served in the Arlington, Virginia Stake High Council. So, before hanging up the receiver, I told the concerned sister who had called that I would investigate the case and then, I thanked her for her conscienciously provided information, about her fellow L.D.S. neighbor's activities.

The following morning, after arriving at my desk at work at the Church Offices, I dialed the work number of a man on whom I knew I could depend to do some "leg work," with no questions asked. After the pleasantries, I began, "Darryl, I have a favor to ask of you."

"What can I do for you bishop?"

"Is there any way that you can identify the owner of a car from your resources at work?"

"Of course there is. I'm always getting information for other bishops in our stake. What's up?"

"Well, I just got a call about a strange car that's always parked overnight these days in front of the house of one of our single mothers in the ward." I listened for any negative response before continuing, "…so, I thought; if I could get the name and address of the registered owner, by giving you the license plate from the…?"

Interrupting, the dutiful member answered back, "Sure, I can take care of that, Bishop. That's an easy one. I'll call you back in a bit with all the identifying information you need."

Within minutes, the telephone rang. It was the police officer, who happened to be a devout member of a neighboring ward of the one over which I presided as the bishop. After he finished giving me the relevant data, he quickly closed the conversation, as if he and I had done nothing untoward.

But, I, on the other hand, sat silently slumped over in my chair. I knew that what we had just done was not only an illegal invasion of privacy, but I also knew that it was a violation of my personal sense of moral behavior. I have far too much power over these people, I thought to myself. No one person should have this kind of awesome power *over the behavior of other individuals*. But, I went on thinking to myself; we can each choose *not* to be the kind of church leader that isn't swayed to do something untoward by the availability of this kind of power. I mean, we bishops *are all* moral, aren't we? The question seemed to hang on…

My mind reviewed over, and over again how it was that I had used my ecclesiastical authority as a default mechanism to illegally gain access to information meant to be kept private, by constitutional interpretations of the law. I reviewed some old memories from all of my former experience, as a member of several high councils of The Church that are located in different parts of the country. I had to admit that this kind of abuse of power had been very common among all my fellows, of all ecclesiastic circles where I had previously served. This review of my choices, as an L.D.S. ecclesiast, included experiences that, years later, I would re-read from the record that I had made that night in my daily journal. So, eventually, by years of retrospective pondering, my ecclesiastic power would become *ugly* to me.

At about that same time period, in our monthly bishops' meeting with the local stake president, I looked around. All around, were other men; men, whom I knew to be honorable, and as just, as they knew how to be. They were also as equally as concerned, as I was, about all the important things in life. Yet, I also knew that each of us had been part of a, literal, underground political force, which had organized to destroy the Equal Rights Amendment. We'd seen it as part of our ecclesiastical duty to rank and file leaders at our Church Headquarters. I knew that we had each engaged in an illegal political activity. I knew that we had collectively acted in secret, in ways that I understood to be *illegal,* in light of federal, and civil tax law.

The political and ethical issues over all the juxtaposition of religious imperatives, tax law and Constitutional rights of privacy caused me to carefully ponder the whole matter in the warmth of my study. There, next to the hot wood stove that, I had designed for the brickwork in that room, I came to decide that, we were being led to be Mormons *first* and *then*, to be "good citizens." With that thought, in the silence of aloneness next to the crackling, burning logs, I felt a nauseous and overwhelming sensation in the deep pit of my stomach. But, there, with the only light I had was coming from the open stove, my nausea was not only about the way that we the ordained had been marshaled to political action.

Weighed down in the depression of my dark memories, I stared into the fire. Over the past few weeks in my work at the Church Offices, I had been researching all the recorded statements of former members of the Quorum of The Twelve Apostles of The Church. I had discovered to my absolute amazement that, in the mid. to late 19th century, members of this highest rank of our sacred ecclesiastical structure had once taught *against* the "amassing of personal property" by any one member of The Church. Since my research had produced four thick, three-ring binders of these quotes, I'd been transferring that philosophy into my other work, like the newly assigned writing of the televised World Conference speeches of the Presiding Bishopric and of the First Presidency of The Church. I believe I did this, because those quoted teachings seemed to be solidly founded in what I then, understood to be the correct principles of egalitarian ways of inter-relating, as taught in our Mormon scriptures, the Standard Works.

In those days, I often found myself asking inwardly: Are we bishops using the awesome power in truly egalitarian ways? I was thinking of what I ultimately admited was an obtuse, and inordinate influence that we, the presiding officers, wielded over good people. I constantly asked myself, Am I behaving like I know how to be? Do we bishops only have a power that is *acquiesced* to us because our members are fundamentalist, or "true believers?" But then, I asked: More importantly, do we bishops [in like ways] acquiesce *our* power over to our own file leaders too, when they also likewise make human mistakes? The fearful question was: Isn't this all like *cult* groups?

This thinking, inevitably, led to comparisons of the religious hierarchy in which I labored, to that of an ethno-centric cult group. The pure agony that I felt inside for those weeks, as I pondered the absolute power, which we as the ordained *pseudo-fathers* held over all faithful church members, was overwhelming to me. My personal experience had clearly taught me that this truly absolute ecclesiastical power *does* "corrupt absolutely." Those times alone were filled with the ugliness of my guilt. I concluded that, my religious duties had interfered with my personal spiritual evolution.

I had to find a way to reconcile what I'd been raised to know as the correct principles, which our church aimed to emulate, with the reality of my experience, as one among the ordained. As a result of that one contradiction, I decided to do a quasi-scientific experiment to work at understanding my condition more thoroughly. I did what any modern, educated, seeker after knowledge does; *I would test this power*, which I'd observed was manifesting the dynamics of how we, the ordained, inter-related with our members, our "laity." I decided that, *if I was right,* then I'd choose a better way to go…

Eventually, I wrote a letter to ten couples in my ward. In the letter, I called on them each to visit my office for what I said in my correspondence (asking them to visit my church office that Sunday afternoon) was to be a "special interview." "Well," I, eventually, said to the first couple, who'd responded and now sat across my desk from me, "what is your first impression of the letter that I've shown to you."

Minutes earlier, I had shown them a copy of the letter, from me, officially "calling them to sign over all of their monetary assets" [their home, cars, etc.]to The Church of Jesus Christ of Latter-day Saints, in fulfillment of their personal covenants, which they'd made in their Temple ceremonies. I had also written in the letter that I'd sent to them, that they "should pray about their choice and be prepared to freely give me their decision in our interview." I had assumed that only, maybe, one couple might be blindly devoted enough to respond.

"Well," the head of the household began, "as the father of my family, I'm prepared to deed over all my possessions to The Church. After all, Bishop, we've all covenanted to do so when we entered the Temple." As he pulled out a pen from his pocket, he began to place documents on the desk, which he was retrieving from his briefcase.

I thought; this guy's actually going to do it! I had to stop him, so interrupting his movements with my hand, I said, "That's enough now, brother."

He looked directly at my eyes; then, he turned to look at his dutiful wife, sitting next to him, and back to me. "What do you mean?"

"This has been a test," I started, "and you have passed the test of faithfulness. You will be blessed for your willingness to follow through with your earthly possessions, as Temple covenants require. But, none of this is necessary at this time."

After sharing lots of tears and hugging because their innocent attitude was so awesome to me, I dismissed them from my office and I was left alone with my thoughts. I had come face to face with new, and unexpected answers to my profoundest questions. The problem came after that first interview...

The child-like faith, of otherwise educated adults, horrified me. One by one, seven of the remaining nine couples had also chosen blind obedience to my invitation, over even asking to know more about what was entailed. The first, however, was the only one that actually brought his official documents with him to sign over their possessions to The Church right there, in the first interview.

I was appalled by their absolutely firm trust in my word, as their bishop. Thankfully, two of the ten couples wanted to take more time to think about it, but unfortunately, only one couple out of the ten, chose to report what was going on to my superior; our local stake president. But by the night that I had let that one couple out of my office, I'd already become horribly disappointed by the results of my little experiment.

Before the end of the week, I sat silent in the stake president's office being severely chastised by him for my "personal conduct" in such a presumptuous experiment. He made me see that I had sought for increased personal awareness, *at the expense of the faithful*. I felt the sting of my guilt; I understood I had been risking a misuse of the trust of the faithful. Mine had been a selfish act, centered more in my selfish need to *understand* than, in any correct sense of the dignity and sanctity of other, faithful, human souls. I'd *used* these devout people to selfishly resolve my personal crisis of faith.

The drive back home after that interview with my local stake president was filled with the wrenching and now growing awareness of my place in society. Much worse, my presiding high priest had agreed with me. My local ecclesiastical leader had also understood what I had come to see about the ordained having far too much power over others than any of us can balance perfectly. He simply trusted himself more than I trusted myself. He'd said that he knew that he'd "never abuse" his "power over the members." But, I kept wondering, how could he be so sure that he'd always act benevolently? I had experienced inter-relating with members of my congregation that could have been tragic, if I had been the kind of person who would actually follow-through on what I'd proposed to the couples. I'd never be able to fully trust another bishop.

Finally, in the quiet of my car parked in our driveway, long after arriving home that night, I pondered on the experiment for well over an hour. Yes, I had done something ugly, and invasive to the sanctity of the commitment of faith of some of my ward members. But, at the expense of that great price, I had also finally discovered, by my experience in the experience, that those of us who preside in the ranks of religion have an awesome and an overwhelming power over true believers. I had seen myself in the clear cultural mirror; I'd been forced to look at what I knew was an honest reflection of *me*. For, I had to admit that I also had been no different than these good and trusting people. *I had blindly obeyed my leaders also.* I had come to understand that ours, was far too much power over others to be safely had by any one man in this cultural world of institutionalized and politicized untruth and, I knew that I wanted none of it. Power *over others* had become the true evil to me.

Six years passed.

Two years after my excommunication from The Church, I had moved back to southern California from Missouri, where I'd moved to after my divorce. A year earlier, I'd gotten active in the local chapter of a support and social group called, Affirmation, Gay & Lesbian Mormons. Although I enjoyed my friendships in the group's Los Angeles Chapter, I had not yet overcome the emptiness that I frequently felt in my soul's core. I'd been removed from my vocation by my search for personal integrity...

I no longer had a ready-made forum to express my views. I'd lost the institutional context for experiencing the joyous, sacred, and emotional sensations I'd become accustomed to, as one vested with the holiest priesthood power of my community. If someone is *not* centered; with their personality, yet, *not aligned with their spirit* then, upon being excommunicated, that person is fated to experience the experience of that loss. In my own case, sadly, I was not yet centered enough when the day came for me to rely on my personal light rather than, on the reflection, which I'd borrowed from my old mentors in the Mormon community. As related in my first book, the 1982 result of that emotionally dissected condition was my attempt at suicide.

One day in 1985, I sat pondering a suicidal memory of that 1982 dark night of the soul. Still vivid to me, I recalled all of its ugly shame, alone there, in my Hollywood apartment. In this deep mental moment, I got a telephone call from another member of the local Los Angeles chapter of Affirmation, LaMar Hamilton. LaMar had long wanted to organize "a new gay and lesbian Mormon-like community church." But, I was still controlled by "in the box" kind of thinking. I did not yet understand how one could organize a new church without any direct intervention for such an act by God, Himself or, by some genuine otherworldly phenomenon.

After all, that was the claim of The Church which, a friend of mine had come to call the "heterosexual Mormon Church" because Mormons did not extend their sacrament of marriage to people like us. In other words, I still envisioned with Mormon-centric eyes. I still needed a revelation, like a new "spirit written" message to even consider being part of LaMar's idea, and none of the past messages had directed me to organize anything.

Then, a week after I spoke with LaMar, I met a man, whom I will, here only call "John," at a Los Angeles meeting of Affirmation. More than anything else about John that was unique to him, was the intensity with which he seemed to go about his life. I was absolutely drawn to him because he seemed so driven by the same profound level of intensity about spiritual stuff as I felt. Our relationship was destined from our first meeting because of our affinity toward one another as we each were in those days. However, as I will now try to tell, before our relationship's purpose had been completed, I had changed. But, on the night we met, I had wanted to get to know John better, so I'd invited him to my home after the Affirmation meeting.

After the usual tour of my private domestic environment, I felt comfortable enough to trust this man with a question I'd had burning within me since May 15, 1983. That was when what I had by then, come to call a "spirit-written" message, had first seemed to flow through me, as I typed the apparently dictated words on the keyboard. I needed to explore in an understanding friend whether I felt those "messages" were a delusion of my inner mind, or whether I believed they were, indeed, *dictated* words or *inspired messages*, from some inner-space dimension other than our common, natural world.

Elsewhere, I have told the seemingly contrary experiences of those times; of being baptized into the Reorganized Church of Jesus Christ of Latter Day Saints only to also then receive the ancient rite of confirmation from the then, Roman Catholic Bishop of Kansas City, Missouri. Few of my RLDS friends, at the time, understood my need to follow the direction that I knew the Universe by means of my daily experience was communicating to me. Truly, my past experience has since turned out to be critical to how I now envision. As a result of being excommunicated from the Utah based Latter-day Saints, it was natural for me to also investigate the claims of the largest rival Saints' community headquartered in Missouri, which since its beginning, had been headed by descendants of the first prophet, Joseph Smith, Junior. This process of hearing another side of the Mormon saga as seen by those who chose not to follow Brigham Young [but to follow Joseph Smith's family] was the process in which I became acquainted with another way to see the gifts of revelation.

It was during this time of new membership in the Missouri-based Latter Day Saint church [now, Community of Christ] that, I had first experienced a phenomenon which a psychologist, who was also then, employed on the same campus as I, had termed "spirit-writing." Other chapters in this book tell how I had, there, first experienced this experience. The experience that, I relate below, is no different:

Naturally, one of my deepest desires was to have another's accepting confirmation from a person whose rationality I respected. I had shown one of the messages to someone months earlier, only to have him laugh out loud at me. However, now, thinking that perhaps my new-found friend John might be able to better handle the bizarre nature of my "spirit-writing" experiences, I decided to share one of those messages with him the next time he came over. *That* proved to be a mistake…

"Wow, Tony," he said as he continued reading from the pages on which I had recorded a message a year earlier, "this is a real revelation."

"You really think so?" I searched his face for some clue as to whether I could trust his affirmation. At least, I thought to myself, he isn't laughing. "What makes you think this is 'revelation.' Tell me."

"First Tony, it speaks to me, to my inner self. But, I have also received such revelation…" He went on to explain that he'd recently also experienced this "spirit-writing" gift, and suggested that we meet with other members of Affirmation, meeting at LaMar's home that night. He, evidently, felt that what LaMar was organizing, indeed, was important for us both.

We went to the meeting, and after all the usual stuff, with which we were all familiar as people who had attended innumerable Mormon meetings, John raised his hand to be acknowledged.

After LaMar had first acknowledged me, John bluntly said, "Tony has revelations. I've seen one of them. It is evidence enough for me that he is the prophet who should lead us in this new church."

I was stunned. I had no idea that he was going to tell anyone about what I'd shared in confidence, much less share it with the entire group assembled in that unfamiliar setting.

Everyone had turned to look at me. Their faces looked so hopeful, so much in need of some clear answer from the God we'd all been raised to believe would not leave us without a prophetic guide. Our inherited need for a prophet, seer and revelator to give the Divine answers overwhelmed our common sense.

A thousand thoughts thrust themselves into my mind… I guess if I'm honest, I have to here add that, I also wanted the Father in Heaven to open the windows of Glory and send us His word so that LaMar's dream could receive His affirming blessing. But, I didn't expect to be part of it. I had already decided for myself that, for now, I needed to stay away from any religious organization especially from all institutional forms of Mormonism. That is why, by now, I had gone out of full activity in the Reorganized L.D.S. community, and it is also why I'd stopped going to Catholic masses by then. In spite of the miraculous nature of my first encounter with the Roman Catholic Bishop of Kansas City, Missouri, I was aware of the bigotry behind the heterosexist policies of the Bishop of Rome to whom my new ecclesiastical friend who headed the Roman Church in Kansas City, Missouri owed his allegiance. I had come to see that, sadly: no *mere* church could be as holy *as I needed a church to be*, if *I* were to become a part of it. I sought spirituality, not religion.

In silence there, I reviewed all of my previous observations: I didn't feel that any institutional religion, of which I was aware, was actually doing the will of the Divine, at least, not relative to my own life. That same Divine Intelligence, Who had made me as I am, had also found it good to continue to be open to my prayers by answering them. In like manner, none of the Mormon churches extended the same sacraments to me as a gay man that I'd come to believe was the practice of their first prophet, Joseph Smith, Junior...

I further quietly reasoned that, since I still received spiritual gifts as before then, The Eternal was, evidently, still open to provide me spiritual guidance for my journey, in spite of being sacramentally ostracized from even my chosen faith community. Both, the Roman Catholic Bishop in Kansas City, Missouri, as also the Reorganized community, had extended a warm welcome to me. But, my soulful allegiance to The Divine had grown beyond any single church, or any group of churches, or even beyond any institutional form of religion. Neither did I, nor did any of my close, Queer friends, have access in any of these faith communities to their, respective, institutionalized marriage ritual. This realization took my mind out, *away from my present,* and into a mythological *wilderness* to seek answers...

So these newfound Gay friends were now my community of faith. At the very least, I had it within my free will to extend the blessings of the sealing power for them to then, marry couples in their Utah based Mormon sacrament of Temple Marriage. I understood the experience of the 19th century Utah based Mormon community when their original view on state civil marriage and religious marriage was declared in response to the United States federal government 1890 law against plural marriage. I knew, because I had read in the original documents in LDS Church Archives, that: Until Mexico's 20th century revolution, Utah based Mormons had vigorously argued for judicial judgments acknowledging a separation of church and state. I knew the theological reasoning behind the behavior of devout and faithful men, who [like I, now, did] had *then*, also held the Latter-day Saint "Sealing Power of Elijiah," but *then, personally chose* to act as, "free agents," in spite of federal laws against the marriages they performed.

Moreover, for same-sex L.D.S. couples to have the L.D.S. Temple sealing marriage ceremony, *itself,* would contain a universe of psychological and theological meaning to all estranged Mormons. In a psychological way, the ability to gain access to this particular marriage ceremony, *a Temple Sealing* by someone who was already authoritatively endowed with the Mormon Sealing Power of Elijiah, [as I'd been] by a late President of the entire Mormon Church may even become a catalyst for the healing of our group soul! President Harold B. Lee had, in fact, laid his hands on my head and vested me with that Sealing Power in their Temple in West Los Angeles in 1973. According to historic Mormon tradition, from that moment onward, I had the "power to bind couples in marriage," not only for time but also, for "all eternity." All we needed was a Temple. But, state civil law in the State of California required an incorporation of a "religious organization" in order to own a property on which to have a *Temple*!

But, where would this choice to participate in this particular group, in this organization, take me? Indeed, where would it take us all? The fact is: Many Mormon Temples have statues of an angel on them for a reason; L.D.S. Mormons accept theology that predicts the extension of their Temple ceremonies throughout the planet "...unto every nation, kindred, tongue and *people*..." Aware of the implied theology, I reasoned that: Helping this Gay group extend "...unto every...*people*..." the blessings of the Mormon Temples, as they are known in the Utah based faith, would provide tremendous meaning to the course that my journey had now taken. Did we dare do what we'd all sacredly vowed *not* to do when we were devout L.D.S., ourselves?

I looked up at everyone in that room, realizing that I'd had my head bowed, immersed in my thoughts. With those thoughts fresh in my mind, I began, "I don't want to be involved in this organization to any great degree, you guys." Again, I looked around the small room, "this new church is LaMar's idea. My purpose here is only as a consultant, of sorts. I'm happy to assist LaMar with stuff but, I am not a prophet."

"But, Tony," John said quickly, "if God has spoken to you like I saw in that revelation at your place then, you are God's choice to lead this movement..." He turned and looked at all the others in the room and added, "I think you should go and ask for guidance from God. Ask for direction for us, Tony." When he turned back to me, his face was lit up. His question had engaged a kind of light energy to us, it was an actual, palpable vibration. We all felt it. It was one of *those* moments. We felt someone, without any of us knowing who it was, was with us, yet, unseen by us.

"I think we should all seek direction," I responded.

A female voice in the group, one I recognized then, said out loud, "I move that we all go to our homes, and seek divine revelation, and I also move that Tony especially seek for the guidance of Divine revelation on behalf of us all, as a group."

Before anything else could be said, LaMar quickly agreed to what had been suggested, and after calling for a vote, he just closed the meeting. The rest of the story is history among those who keep records of such happenings:

I was installed as the first general spiritual leader of the entire church. Our legal incorporation made me the first President, and as such, it was my duty to seek guidance from the Divine Source on all matters relative to how our newly formed group should proceed now to organize. Events progressed, and several messages directed our setting up of a Temple liturgy and rubric so that the affect imagery of our marriage ritual was [except for a word or two] exactly like the Temple ceremonies, as they were celebrated at that time, of the Utah based Mormon Church's Temples, worldwide.

The high point of how I experienced the experience of the new church, personally, was the one posthumous vicarious sealing ceremony I was able to celebrate; with myself as one of the two grooms. In the L.D.S. tradition, marriage is not only for our Earth, or for mortal existence. All Temple Sealing rituals are enacted for "all eternity,"and Mormons practice a vicarious temple marriage, where one of the parties is already deceased. So, it was natural for me; with another man acting as proxy for the man I herein call Terry, to kneel at our Temple Enclosure altar and to then, be sealed "for all eternity…!" Thus, the man I call "Terry" in Chapter One and I, were sealed. We did this, under the specific direction in one of the messages that had directed all our efforts to duplicate "all Mormon sealing rituals" in our new church. To me, if not "the most" then, it was definitely "one of the most" emotional and soul-satisfying experiences of my entire life!

Nevertheless, what ensued a year later is something that has since produced divergent interpretations. However, the way that I see what then happened, is simple: The problem was that I was not only the Prophet, Seer and Revelator to these people who believed in the gifts I had experienced but, I was also "my own person." I was not yet satisfied that I had been shown the way that *I should follow,* as a sovereign human being, in search of *my* further light and knowledge. Yes, I could not deny the fact of the messages in my life. However, on some levels, I was terribly confused by the way some of the messages seemed to contradict themselves.

For example, one message would warn against any more organizing of, "branches" and against any other hierarchical ranks of priestly authority, only to then, also give detailed instruction for the organizing of branches and ranked priesthood councils! Within the same document, several of the verses would speak beautifully to my own personal issues; while, others would speak to the needs of the organization that had called me as *their* Revelator. This kind of utter confusion came through me in the "spirit written" messages for two years, until finally, I came across an article written by an Elder Paul Edwards, of the Reorganized (R.L.D.S.) community. He'd entitled it, "The Ethics of Prophecy" and, in it, he'd argued brilliantly for the separation of the offices of President and the Prophet/Seer/Revelator to the ecclesiastical institution, which, we had called, the church.

He'd brilliantly argued, in his article, how the ethics of all prophecy demand Revelators be unencumbered by the administrative needs of the institution. However, these same ethics also require that the institution's President be unencumbered by the inspired prophetic counsel. The work of either then, was [in the eyes of this author] antithetical to the other. The work of a President is to serve the needs of the institutionalized group, the *externals*; while, the work of any Revelator/Prophet/Seer is the *inner*, or the spiritual evolution of the collective of those hoping to evolve into Latter Day saints. As a result of that article, I spoke to his idea of separating those two offices at our group's next semi-annual general conference that was held in Los Angeles, California in March of 1987. I'd even titled my remarks officially as, "The Ethics of Prophecy" because I saw *our* institutional dilemma as the ethics of the prophetic office, which I held.

Yet, the conference was too imbedded in the old Utah based ways of doing things, which they had all learned in our common, former community. The conference rejected my motion to have the two offices separated. "Because it had never been done," I was left still burdened by the real contradictions that both forces; my own needs and those voiced by the still growing church had produced in messages that I had received, seemingly, as if from two guides; one answering *me*, the other answering the *church*. And, because of my understanding of the difference between the two ideas discussed at the beginning of this chapter about "agreement" and what I refer to as "mere" acquiescence, I could not take any action on my own without the sustaining vote of the various councils, quorums and of the entire membership. There could be only one way to reconcile this:

As will be said again in this book, hindsight is easy, and at the time, I did not have any idea what would take place as a result of my growing dilemma. The parts of the messages, which spoke loudly to my soul were the many parts that warned us all "against organizing" *ad infinitum*. But our quick growth into a little hierarchy created a demand to know more about how to go about the organizing of branches because of our tremendous growth. After just two years, we had units in most major cities in America and some in the nations of Europe. I suppose that, in retrospect, it is easy to see now that *by asking the questions* we were insuring that we would get answers to questions on our organizational structure, *in spite of all the previous warnings to avoid such stuff.*

In hindsight, it is now easy to see that, whatever the Source of those messages, that Source was also not going to stop providing us guidance to a particular point of view on an entirely new worldview, that to me; was one, from which I still sought more knowledge. Now, it does not surprise me that some messages carried contradicting answers to the questions I had asked, compared with the questions the collective group had asked me to ask.

Finally, by the time of our priesthood conference in July of 1987 in Sacramento, California in our new church's third year, I knew that ominous events were about to take place. This was the same conference, to which two of us were both traveling when I first heard Plato's Cave myth in 1987. Weeks earlier, I'd received six messages that were not in-sync.-with the popular attitudes among some of the ordained of our group. Most did not think that these messages were as inspired as the ones that they'd accepted before. Perhaps, it was because these last six messages chastised the entire group for its "disobedience" to the counsel "against organizing *ad infinitum.*" One message had actually prophesied that failure to accept its counsel as binding would result in the complete dissolution of their priesthood church hierarchy, taking away the sacred "sealing keys" that *only I* had brought into it, along with the "loss of numbers of members."

So, in complete awareness of what might happen, I spoke to the priesthood conference on the need to accept the six messages as being as valid, as any of the other documents that I'd submitted to them for their acceptance. I quoted from the message, which had flatly warned of the impending *inadvertent,* dissolution of the group's "sealers" by any dissolution of their priesthood hierarchy, should the conference fail to heed the warning of the last messages.

Then, finally, the time came for the entire conference to vote. To my personal astonishment the conference voted "to reject the six" messages which I had submitted. I could not understand their vote because I knew that the messages spoke peace to my own soul about the issues I had personally been troubled about for three full years. I was no longer envisioning from within the bounded limitation of a Utah based Mormon vision, from where most of our new members had come. These last six messages had, finally, given me peace because their counsel had, actually, reconciled the dilemma I had of having come from Mormonism, but they had also quickly expanded my way of envisioning toward other spiritual ways. So as a result of those messages and newer experiences related in this book, I now envision far beyond the Mormon cosmology.

Nevertheless, after their final vote there to reject the new six messages, I was totally stunned. I only watched in utter amazement at the way in which the prophesied warning, was literally, played out before me there, by the conference on that day. I had witnessed the rejection of honest counsel to the conference. I silently observed the priesthood body's total rejection of messages that were no different than any of the other messages that I had submitted on previous occasions for adoption by the conference. I knew that they had all come in the same way, yet here, I was seeing a different response from our burgeoning ranks. Confused and numbed, several of us in the leadership left the conference never to return again.

It wouldn't be until seven years later, almost to the day, when Paul Toscano's The Sanctity of Dissent had, finally, helped me to understand: Much like Paul Toscano's presentations to his Mormon audiences at the Sunstone Theological symposia, I was now inter-relating with members of this burgeoning new church as one who is a truth teller. Naturally, like him, I would also have to experience similar consequences, for Paul Toscano is a truth teller! Before his excommunication he had written:

"One of the recurring mistakes of my life has been my silly belief that I would somehow endear myself to others by telling them what I believe to be the truth. Jesus, however, did not say that the truth would make us well-liked. He said that 'the truth shall make you free' (John 8:32) What he did not say was that it would first make everybody madder than hell."

I laughed loudly, reading his awesome humor for the first time! Being alone when I first read his words, I was instantly healed of my depression! But, I didn't have the benefit of his humor in that Priesthood conference. So as I'd sat there watching, I thought of the first day of my involvement with the organization of our group. As I sat there, before the assembled priesthood conference in 1987, I flashed the scene in 1985 when I'd accepted the call of the group to "only lend my experience as a guide for the organization." I'd known in the beginning that my purpose with this group was merely auxiliary to my ultimate call in life. I seemed to see myself in that scene say, "otherwise, I will not join at all." As I flashed back to my actual environment, I felt that the only honorable thing to do in light of my clear inability to lead, for whatever reason, would be to retire from my work with the, now, growing organization.

Among other things, I recorded later in my journal that I then stood and said, "I became a part of this church so that you could reap the benefit of my experience in the L.D.S. Church. With the votes we've had today, you have chosen to reject messages, which have all come through me in the same manner as all the others that were accepted by this church as Divinely inspired. Since, I'm no longer sustained as your Revelator, then, my call has now come to an end in this aspect of this movement." At that point, I felt the sting of perspiration do its usual mischief. My abdomen was hit with a pain, as if it had pierced my flesh from beside me, "…and, since I am not accepted as such any more by this conference resolution, then my work is finished with any aspect of the work in this organization. So, I hereby resign as the President and as a member of the Board of Directors, as well as a member of this Church."

With that done, I had then, watched in awe as the conference proceeded to dissolve all the very priesthood bodies, which one of the messages had warned would all be "dissolved" if the church did "not listen." The chain reaction that ensued from that point on completely dissolved the entire general priesthood hierarchy. Even though this was difficult for me to watch, the original purpose of the "continued guidance" through me was dependant "on the Church's acceptance of the messages" through me. We'd been warned that "the priesthood" would "be dissolved" and that its original "sealing mission," which my personal involvement had imposed, would expire in the eyes of Whomever or Whatever it was, who had provided the growing church its "spirit-writing" guidance through me. Silently, I thought to myself sitting there: Our process had literally, fulfilled the warning in one of the messages. I was in shock. I was in total shock…

As of this writing, I've never returned to "full activity" in any of the churches that derive from Joseph Smith, Junior. From time to time, I will go to a mass but, mainly, I will do so when I need to give thanks for my fortunate place in the world. It feels appropriate to do this in the holy places of the largest mass consciousness from which I derive my soul-making experiences. I will attend a service in a religious edifice often because of the pleasure of the sacred music I encounter there. Choral music has always been a great joy to me. But, my profoundest spiritual experiences are no longer limited to any edifice or community of faith, although I still retain my membership in Community of Christ.

The reason why I had gotten such divergent instructions through the channeled messages, from the beginning of our initial organizing, was because the messages were not only directed to the Church *through me*, but, they were each also given *to me, for my own personal guidance.* Whatever the Source of those messages, it was clear that the goal was for me to go in a different way than, the newly institutionalized group was willing to go, *as a collective body.* When confronted by the choice for me to follow the Spirit Guide or the institutional agreements, I chose the Source of the messages, as will be seen in the chapters that follow.

Yet, in the entire experience, a highly intelligent Source had directed the words in each of the various messages; otherwise, the two threads of firm direction could not have been communicated clearly enough to cause me to see them. But the new church, which I'd had a brief part in organizing, *had retained its institutionalized form by the group's use of a political dynamic.* Similarly, as a result of my past experience in the headquarters archives of the majority of our group's "mother church" in Salt Lake City, Utah, I now believed that the highest councils of that institution had also behaved in similar ways as our little church had also behaved.

In hindsight, I eventually came to envision all of these church experiences from a philosophical perspective. I had been true to my purpose in the work of that growing group. I had lent my experience as their guide in their organizing of an alternative faith community to the original group that had excommunicated most of us. Their Salt Lake City congregation still exists but, all others disbanded in other states of this nation, as well as, all those elsewhere. But in the entire process, my personal mission was eventually confirmed as being one that is not only founded in any single institutional form. One of those rejected messages had called me to, personally, "...go south, where the Spanish language is spoken..." But, at that time, little did I know then, who I'd meet when I finally obeyed it!

****

All three experiences, described above, were *political* in nature because they were acts following a group's strictures. What happened in the experiences was not about Love nor, were any of these experiences truly about empathic compassion, either in the first church, or in the later one. I was merely trying to be true to my inner guidance, while it seemed to me that the others followed rules. So, all of the above experiences were revealed as political power struggles.

In the first case, I was doing my duty as the "father of the ward" in trying to preserve the integrity of the institution's rules. This was an ugly abuse of power. In the second, I mistakenly used my position as a bishop to experiment on what kind of power over others we bishops had. This was a dangerous abuse of power. Although it was, for me, an educational experience, as well as one that provided me with a perceived need [the experienced data], it was an obtuse intrusion into the holy relationship ten couples had with their God. This was political, in that it did the work of opinion polls. It was also political because things personal (property deeds, titles, etc.) can in this way, be controlled by insidious external policies. In our country, this could go directly to our individual rights as citizens. In the last case, the illusion that hierarchical power actually is, was literally manifest when the group ended up by dissolving all of the previous agreements of the church's conference resolutions that, had created it; agreements, which had previously been freely made among all the various parties involved.

This final experience, related above, was revealed for what all ecclesiastical activity sadly is, in truth: *It had highly competitive undercurrents and the ruling tone in the entire experience was not one of, Love but rather, combative and soulless in its core.* In spite of the highest sweet moments of ecstatic union with the worlds of light, which we had all experienced, from time to time, in our little church's Temple Enclosure, the organizational behavior of some in our highly stratified hierarchy felt more like the politics of board rooms than the councils of the godly. The deeply rooted cultural ideas on perceived needs for a Mormon-like hierarchy in our group, had prevailed. This choice was taken, over all of the profoundly spiritual challenges in the messages about becoming *a laity of revelators*, and of *less priesthood structure*. Sadly, the secret agreements, that some in the group had made, had revealed the pride of themselves to me far more than, their humility in the call to become revelatory prophets*, themselves.*

The group, collectively, was not yet ready to receive a new way of envisioning that was being given in the messages. I, on the other hand, had already anticipated that my personal work with any institutional religion would soon cease to be a part of my mission, or purpose in life. It is, in fact, why I'd proposed months earlier that one of my two responsibilities be given to another. One of the messages had firmly instructed me to relocate "…southward where the Spanish language is spoken…" But, the 1987 conference could not see any purpose in it, and they rejected the call. What they did not understand was that it was my call; it was not at all dependant on the resolutions of any conference. So, I had no negative judgment on what had happened. My priestly call was, simply, no longer within the bounds of this or *any* church. It was now in a totally new direction.

Whether anyone else chose to do so or not, I was going to follow the instruction given to me in all the channeled messages. My call was to go, "*southward*,"away from all the competitive natures of hierarchies and institutions. My call was toward other ways of inter-relating. Although, I did not know it at the time, my life would now focus differently. My own life would now become completely about becoming an open soul...

Moreover, this spirit of competition that I experienced above, is a fact of our civilization that I have not agreed with since my youth. I've always had issues with our highly competitive society, as far back as my days as a cheerleader in our high school. The issue that I always raised regarding competition *per se,* since my first days as a young ordained priest, is what I was years later enabled to, actually, label because of my exposure to Riane Eisler's The Chalice & The Blade. In this 1987 work, Eisler discussed the major difference between what she termed the "two contrasting ways of structuring the relations between the female and male halves of humanity that profoundly affect the totality of a social system..." Eisler had defined "patriarchy" as "a social system ruled through force or the threat of force by men..." and then, coined a new term for patriarchy, i.e. "*androcracy*...from the Greek root words, *andros* or 'man', and, *kratos* (as in demo-cratic), or 'ruled.'

"To describe the real alternative to a system based on the ranking of half of humanity over the other..." Eisler had proposed her new term, "*gylany*," which she coined with "'gy'...from the Greek root word gyne, or 'woman'..." with "An," deriving from "*andros,* or 'man'" with the "letter l between the two...In English...for the *linking* of both halves of humanity, rather than, as in *androcacy*, their ranking." This notion of "linking" in contrast to "ranking" was what rang true to my soul because this was the thread that was woven into the messages I'd received up to that point in my life. They were all about linking, rather than, ranking.

Joseph Smith, Junior, had been the only mystic I knew who had used the same term "link" as a critical, and pivotal theological or philosophical need, in order to "restore all things" as they had all been "in the beginning." Additionally, it fit the hundreds of quotes on living in egalitarian ways, which I had compiled in the four three-ring binders, many years earlier as part of my work in the L.D.S. Church Archives in Salt Lake City, Utah in the 1970's. What didn't compute for me was the stark reality that, present practices of institutions that claim their first authority from Joseph Smith Junior, did not follow these older principles of church governance either. "Linking" was not as important as the "ranking" of souls in the 20th century church. It was clear to me that an institution that has a "sealing power" that can reach beyond time and space would practice the *linking* of, rather than, the *ranking* of human souls.

I had become completely entranced by Eisler's book. She discussed in it how it is that the Jesus figure of the Christian scripture repudiated the then prevalent system of rule "through force or the threat of force by men." She had, then, continued discussing in a subsequent chapter how "Socrates' challenge to a system of force-based rankings is powerfully expressed in Plato's Republic," writing on his ideas about "educational equality for women." This view from Eisler, opened my vision to a clearer way of seeing because I'd been prepared for it through the way I'd experienced the experiences of power in the above closed societies.

I knew from my upbringing that Jesus was revolutionary in his approach to inter-relating. Sacred stories tell of how the Jesus figure freely associated with women, which was itself a form of heresy in his time and society. Through the example written about in the Christian canon, Jesus proclaimed through his own example the spiritual equality of all people. When we closely examine not only what this one biblical figure taught, but also at how he went about disseminating his message, we see that what he was preaching was the gospel of an *egalitarian* society. Time and time again, this figure had rejected the dogma that the high-ranking men in his day, the priests, nobles, rich men and kings who were the favorites of The Divine in sharp contrast to the views of relatively later Christian figures who, actually debated, whether woman has an immortal soul. Jesus is recorded to specifically not preach the ultimate dominator message that parts of humanity are inferior to the powerful patriarchs. These things I knew from my upbringing among Mormons.

When I first read Eisler's words, I knew that our civilization's sacred stories spoke of a Jesus who's teachings have, in effect, all been stunted by how we structure our world. I already knew that the sacred stories told of how he had envisioned a different way of structuring human inter-relations. I knew, when I read Eisler that what the Jesus figure is recorded to have taught would have, indeed, transformed civilization's violence-based rankings into what she called, "gylanic" or, "partnership" ways of inter-relating. Competition, which we in society see as winning verses losing, wasn't part of the teachings of the Lord of Compassion. I was sure of these ideas, even as a teen.

By then, I'd even come to see that our American culture sees competition as more about one's domination of others than, it is about anything else. Competition, as I'd come to know it, had no place in an opening soul. An open soul only competes against their own personal prior performance while, always keeping present the sovereign dignity of others because, while an open soul endeavors to achieve excellence, the essence of becoming an open soul is openness to the *beingness* of others, as well as to one's own. Yet, my experience has bitterly taught me that, America values winning *way more* than, other attributes, irrespective of any claimed ethical competitive standards. We see "loss" in a most limited of perspectives.

I knew *religious* competition among differing theological perspectives is not about achieving excellence when it is only about winning. When a group of us once visited the remains of the ancient *Anasazi* civilization and heard the sacred stories from their self-professed 21st century descendants, I was told that the precise reason the *Anasazi* came to their end was about this emphasis in competition on winning and losing. Indeed, there is some evidence to argue for the view that the early olympic-like athletic events of the *Anasazi* were all about games among equals that, when they changed into winning verses losing, the ancients lost their way and became extinct.

It was this insight that drew me, back in the day when I was still in high school, to the Mormon ways of envisioning the Early Christian community. Mormons claim that their existence centers in the notion that the first Christian community was overtaken by the domination of their patriarchal leaders, the Church Fathers and the earliest bishops. Thus, the Mormons claim the necessity of there being a "restoration" of a new way of our inter-relating in the church and the greater world community. But, my experience had taught me that there was no difference in how we Mormons had also behaved in our modern hierarchies, from how the earliest Christian Fathers and bishops had also treated their suppliants. Mormon *words* had taught me what I had perceived as correct principles, but Mormon *behavior* had spoken in louder ways to my inner understanding...

Our Mormon behavior said that, our group was no different than any other fundamentalist, religiously invasive society. In fact, that lack of ethics that, I encountered among the Mormons, is not a behavior unique to only them. It's endemic to all institutional forms, especially religious ones. At least, in spite of pockets of truly devout practitioners, it's been part and parcel of all the institutions that I've known in my spiritual life.

What Eisler did for me, however, was teach me that I was on the right path. She demonstrated to me that, from a purely academic perspective the "Jesus revolution of nonviolence, in the course of which he died on the cross, was then, converted into rule by force and terror." Rather than, any longer remaining a threat to the established order, Eisler clarified for me how Christianity eventually became what practically all of Earth's global religions launched in the name of spiritual enlightenment and freedom have each done. Ironically, while we, in our little new church, aimed to challenge this politicized way of being, our need to mimic the awesome hierarchy of our big, former mother church made us into, yet, another force for the unholy perpetuation of the order Jesus sought to overcome.

What was absolutely clear to me from reading Eisler's work now was that, while the Jesus figure rebelled against it, the surviving way of inter-relating, which endured even among the small churches claiming Joseph Smith as their founder, was the very "hell" against which Jesus is reported to have taught against. In short, Eisler's work confirmed for me that every institutional form of religion in which I had participated, because it was an institution, was patterned after the rule of force, or the threat of force. Politicking, after all, is the rule of the *force* of spin.

In high school I'd learned that this is the exact *force*, which is played out by all that involve themselves in what we term "contact team sports." Because of this, it has never been any wonder to me that so many of our society's violent criminals, who do damage in domestic environments, come from the ranks of men who are now, and have been professional football players, and the like. It must be horrifically frustrating for all line backer types. Having been trained from youth to respond with brute force when a challenge is made, to morph from being pure antagonists, only to then, be charged with a crime, if programed behavior spills into their domestic environment.

I am saying that there is a behavioral link to how we socialize our men and, unfortunately, how we now also socialize our women, as well. Seemingly automatic rage-filled responses are all probably natural to many frustrating situations, which confront professional athletes. This link, I believe, strongly bares-out that institutionalized competitive training in force and in the threat of force is dangerous to all domestic environments, and my inner sense is that this dynamic is also linked to our common inherited culture. Team contact sports are a rite of passage in our culture, and I am saying that they are simply a manifestation of the violent nature of our entire social culture.

Again, from my high school days as a yell leader, I easily saw that our tendency to violence is magnified in team contact sports. But, our civilization's passion for team contact sports is good in that it can be used to sublimate violent tribal conflicts. This is the great idea behind our worldwide Olympic Games. Yet, even in that wholesome arena, the competition to which I refer is more dangerous to our social fabric than our most honored ethicists are aware. After all, what came out of "good Mormon folk" in late 1990's in Salt Lake City, Utah, in how the city had "unethically won their venue" for the 2002 Winter Olympics, overwhelmed the highest ethical spirit which, the Olympic Games mean to engage. And, this does not even speak of the later scandals involving the ice-skating judges!

The first 2002 Olympics ethics scandal was the ugly result. The second scandal involving a French judge arose from a similar lack of ethics. The Salt Lake City problem as I see it was the need to be on top, or the winner, as a city. As of the date when this book went to press, several men had been publicly disgraced. However, the sad thing is that they were disgraced *only because they got caught.* What mattered most in the litigation, and more importantly, in the court of public opinion is that, in spite of the whole ethical fiasco, Salt Lake City had *won.* Our culture celebrates winning above all of its ethical values but, we value not getting caught a lot more, and this flies in the face of our much touted ethic on personal honesty.

This is exactly what I mean here about "tribalism", and I even reiterate: According to ancient Native tradition, this was the probable cause for the extinction of the *Anasazi.* How often have we had to witness violent behavior by those involved in some way with national team sports? I do not refer to the sense of national pride and genuine personal excellence, which are correctly meant to be part of the Olympiads. No, I refer to the tribalistic notions of nationalism that, how I experienced the experiences, taught me are anachronistic to healthy ways of inter-relating. In recent years, this has not only been demonstrated by the players on the playing field but, unfortunately, it has also been re-enacted over and over again by little league parents who can not control themselves when push comes to shove. How many more violent deaths and injuries do we have to see, as television viewers of public sports activities, before we acknowledge that, when competition is carried out under the traditional worldview we've all inherited from more arcane times, the result will be as it also was in centuries gone past? Our national team sports events on some levels are a good context but, how long will it be before we abandon the brutal notion of power over others in favor of egalitarian agreement?

My sense is that it will take as long as we all take to abandon our personal dishonesty because a control, or a domination of our equals uses dishonesty as a tool. The reason why the holy ones of our planet from throughout our human history have urged us to be clear, transparent and honest is because honesty insures our letting go of our imagined need to control our others and our circumstances through our hiding of what is: Truth. But, conversely, our lack of openness in how we inter-relate exists because in some way we are, likewise, each trying to control someone, or something.

This is manifest, to its greatest degree, in our old American cultural propensity toward the kind of base competition, which was discussed earlier. For example, how often does a team player, on a sports field or court, use deceptive gestures to fool their opponent into thinking the player is going in another way, when in actuality, she or he is thinking of going in, yet, another? I am not here saying that all competition is bad or wrong, in and of itself. In a game, it is assumed that there will be some brilliant trickery. What I am saying, however, is that "one-ups-manship," being *numero uno*, being on top, being the "king of the hill" is not congruent with the imperative of becoming open souls. I've been taught that open souls are open, which is among other things, a way to say, "honest," for honesty reflects externally, what exists inside. In this way, life is congruent.

And, an open soul is, first, and foremost, congruent. How one is on the inside is then, open to the view of others. The healing work of becoming an open soul is the *opposite* of retaining rigid control. The healing work of becoming an open soul is letting go of one's imagined control, for truly, none of us is in control. As a result of letting go of the need to control, an opening soul is not competitive in the sense discussed earlier. This is the singular defining difference between competition, as we understand it in modern society, and competition, as Indian tradition informs us was anciently understood on this land by the *Anasazi* prior to their cultural/social degeneration into power, as meaning power over equals.

To be open is to be in our inter-relating with one another as we actually are, in truth: As equals. However, this is not an invitation to ever be hurtful, or obnoxious or holier-than-thou toward others. These are behaviors that, themselves, are tools like dishonesty is also a tool. They are tools, which work toward the domination of persons and situations. From the view that I'm espousing, striving for the domination of persons and situations is, actually, no different than manifesting the imagined status of being above another, or depending on the role being played, the truly imagined status of being less than another. Neither, by the way, is valid in the view I am endeavoring to express through these stories, for, in this way of envisioning, the domination of persons and/or situations, is not found in nature, except in only one circumstance. Most practitioners of traditional Indigenous ways know what that one circumstance is all about.

That circumstance, that mortal condition, is when one species devours another for its nutrition; for, when one of us consumes one of our siblings in the Indian worldview, that is taking what one needs for food, and it is part of the natural order. Any who practice the Indian tradition in her or his eating habits will thank the being whose life was given so that she or he may eat because the food is one's equal.

In truth, all Earth life is totally inter-dependent on a constant consummation of one life form, by another. This is true equality. This is mutuality. *This is eating our food in complete awareness that one day another species will in turn, also consume us for food.* There is no domination when one is totally aware that they also will, literally, be consumed for food as well.

This is the circle of life; it is the meaning of the symbol of the serpent eating itself. I was first exposed to that mystical symbol in Mexico, in 1990 by a young *Meshica* mother of two boys. She was explaining her attitudes about eating her brother and sister animals for food. Her wise words asked me, "If you agree that we are what we eat, then why do you not understand that what we eat is us, ourselves? If I eat the breast of my sister chicken, then, am I not nourishing myself with Another Myself?" She is one who excelled in parenting because her tradition had taught her of the dignity of all souls, including those not yet adult. On one occasion, her manner of discipline taught me that she saw her boys as meriting respect, even if they did not yet know that they were beings of dignity:

One of her two sons who was then, only nine had disobeyed instructions for him to help his younger brother care for domestic chores. It was easy for me to observe that this, particular boy, would probably grow up being a trickster. In *that*, characteristic, his rascally manner reminded me of my own, rather, precocious childhood ...

When his mother discovered that he had chosen to take his brother playing in the sand, she did not spank them. She didn't scold them. All their mother said was, "Oh, no," with a sad face, showing her sorrowful disappointment...and I wrote a rhymed note to myself:

The boy became ashamed, head down.
With that, his Mom just turned around
And, sadly walked a bit away
Knowing he would from then, obey.

From where I watched the entire inter-change, I saw that she had not talked in a way that denied or diminished his equal place in their relationship. She had demonstrated to him, even in disciplining him that she was aware of his equal human dignity and she was merely sad at discovering that evidently he was not as aware of his own dignity as was his mother. This, to me, was a highly consistent way for her to manifest their maternal/child relationship as one of mutuality and inter-dependence, centered in their equality, while also letting her son know how she felt. Their bond of love sustained her method.

Living with those gentle, loving people, I learned that nature is a world of complete mutuality and inter-dependence. In the natural world, when it is time to die, the normal dynamic is one wherein death is not resisted. The next time that the reader has an opportunity to be with a dying pet, notice if the animal does what most of us do. Does the animal struggle? Does the animal desperately try to avoid death? Or, does the animal appear to relinquish all its efforts to the process itself? Does the animal let go when the time to die comes? From the *Meshica* tradition, which I was taught, it is no different with us human beings when we allow ourselves to live in balance with nature. Yet, I know from my observations that most of us [because of our inherited cultural bent to control our condition] will do everything imaginable to stay-off the dying process as long as is humanly possible. This is because we are plagued with illusions that we are not a part of nature. We are infected with the idea that the natural process we call death is, in fact, not natural. Now, that's an illusion if I ever knew of one!

As if to deny our equality with one another in the natural world, we try to rise above, to transcend the dynamic of life, which we call death. But, I am saying that we are no better than our equals in nature. Yes, in some ways from our perspective we may be *better off* than other creatures on this planet but, we are not any different than others in the world of nature. In the common natural world, death is the basic, equalizing fact. All we, who live, also die. In this respect, no human being is any greater nor, any *better or worse off,* for that matter than, the lowly, small, slimy snail.

Egalitarian ideals support the understanding of humanity as only one element in a wise, intricate web of relationships that make up all of nature. Contrary to the dominant view of our civilization, I affirm that, humanity is not meant to dominate nature, or each other. Success is not about domination by a few. No, all of humanity's destiny is to, again, be fully engaged in rhythmic attunement in a balance with all the energies of all of nature. Humanity's final, ecstatic destiny is to vibrate the chordant harmony of life, which is pulsating renewal and regeneration, as it was in the legendary Garden that our civilization calls Eden. Our fate is to bring in a renewal of the paradisiacal ways of our inter-relating.

However, I did not always envision reality in this way. It was when I was blessed to live with a small band of *Meshica* in Mexico that my own view of our relationship with the world around us drastically changed. When I lived among them, they taught me that, if I was to live in harmony with nature then first, I had to forgive the church. I learned with them that it is, institutionalized forms of religion that have acted in ways contrary to their own rhetoric. Like the legends about Jesus, the Indian families with whom I lived and loved taught me that my place was to avoid judging, especially the church. They had said that, "you must forgive them if you are to be healed, yourself."

That is when they spoke much to me about what the rest of us call Love. I learned through observing the loving ways in which they inter-related, that *Love is not a reactive dynamic,* but rather; *Love is an active interest in the beingness of one's beloved.* This is the example personified by that *Meshica* mother I mentioned above. Her Love was not at all about disregarding, what was defined by her disobedient son as, evil. She acted but, she did it, fully open to her son's personal dignity.

Her love was about not judging his act of disobedience, all while, at the same time, demonstrating to him that she thought better of him than his behavior showed at the time. Her Love was not about putting her son down nor, was it about taking away his human dignity. Her Love was about showing her son her honest, personal sense of disappointment in his honest choice. With her, there was no hint of manipulation or external control in how she had disciplined her son. There was never a single spanking of any kind by that mother. It was her Love that sustained her son, and he was able to know it because she saw him enough as her equal to then, be open with him about her disappointment in him.

In one of the following chapters, the story of how I came to experience the experience of my *Meshica* friends is told for the first time. I tell about the dancer, who introduced himself to me, saying, I am Another Yourself." I also tell about the *Toltec* wise man who, likewise, greeted me in the same way, and changed my life forever. It was these happy people who exemplified a way of inter-relating that manifested the principle of agreement among equals.

They are the ones who first demonstrated to me how it is that my health is best served by envisioning myself as a mass whole of individual Intelligences. Today, whenever a doctor tells me that there is some kind of "condition" in my physical body, I take that to mean that there is an imbalance of the individual Intelligences making up what and who I am. My experience is that, this is an awareness that has served me in recouping balance in my physical body, time, and time again. This is because the *Meshica* taught me how it is that all of us are each to our living planet, Earth, what a single cell is to our personal physical body.

As a single human cell has its outer membrane, a wall that allows for the interchange of nutrients so, also is the outer atmosphere of the planet, as well as the skin of our own physical bodies. While the planet's atmosphere protects from the harm of rogue meteors by burning them before they can destroy, it allows the life-giving light of Father sun to penetrate and generate life. Our skin performs the same function for our own physical bodies. But, an individual body's skin and the planet's atmosphere do not separate. Their function is *to protect, while allowing nutrients to penetrate* for the wellness of the whole. Is this not like osmosis in all single cells that appear similar to their environment under a powerful microscope with only their outer membrane keeping in what is in?

I invite the reader to fill a balloon with water and then place it in a clear glass bowl that is also filled with water. Isn't that what we are like also? Isn't that balloon, actually, water encased in an outer layer that provides the perception that it is separate and apart from the rest of the water in the glass bowl; when in reality there is no difference in what is inside from what is outside of it?

My *Meshica/Toltec* mentors have taught me that, since we are collectively the living planet, we all need to return to ways of envisioning ourselves as also being no different from one another because we are all One, after all. I am convinced that my health has returned because I am now aware that we, humans are, *together with all else,* Planet Earth. Thankfully, I can also conceive that Earth is part of, yet, another Great Whole, also. This additional knowing is an understanding from my Indian friends in Mexico. I believe it is a key to our very survival as a society, as well. May my telling of their far healthier way of experiencing the experience of living also serve to enrich the soul of the reader.

NOTES TO CHAPTER FOUR

[i] Out of The Bishop's Closet, *A Call to Heal Ourselves, Each Other and Our World,* by Antonio A. Feliz (Alamo Square Press, San Francisco, CA. 1992) Chapter Four.

[ii] These include a book of revelations called, Doctrine and Covenants. This is in reference to Doctrine and Covenants; Section 82: Verses 17-20 & Acts; Chapter 2: Verse 44.

[iii] The story of how I was trained in opening myself up to what some call "spirit writing" while I attended a workshop at Park College [now, Park University] in Missouri is told in my first book, Out of The Bishop's Closet.

[iv] Ibid.

[v] Ibid., Chapter Six.

[vi] KJV, Revelation; Chapter 14: verse 6. This verse is the reference of the statue of the "Angel Moroni" on top of several Mormon Temples. The Book of Mormon is not the reference, but the "everlasting gospel" in the Book of Revelation is the reference: "And I saw another angel fly in the midst of heaven, *having the everlasting gospel to preach unto them that dwell on the earth,* and *to every nation, and kindred, and tongue, and people.*" (Italics added)

The "another angel" claimed by Mormon theologians to be Moroni, a Book of Mormon prophet who, lived on the American continent in pre-Columbian times is declared to have the authoritative mission to "preach" to "every [state], and [ethnic / racial family group], and [language group], and [all other human groups]. A Mormon theological device is their sacred stories, which have "angelic beings returning" to the planet in order to "restore all things…" –including the sealing power to celebrate marriage "…for all eternity"– "relates to the Temples [of The Church of Jesus Christ of Latter-day Saints]." To all Utah based Mormons [the L.D.S.] these are the holiest places on the planet, and are considered to be cosmic energy vortexes that open pathways between our plane of existence and the worlds of light. Thus, a statue of their Angel Moroni on the highest point of a Mormon Temple is the Mormon effort to create affect imagery, which depicts their Temples as *the only* places where "the everlasting gospel" is "preached."

However, Utah based Mormons still excommunicated any in open same-sex monogamous familial relationships who refuse to leave their spouses and live singly. So, the next logical theological step, for same-sex couples of a Mormon Temple marriage tradition, is to extend the call to "preach" their "everlasting gospel" from their Mormon Temples to "every people," including the same-sex "people" on the planet. This end link in the reasoning chain, I determined, was—in itself—a good thing. I reasoned: a) the Sealing Power of Elijiah is, theologically, not bound by any mere legal institution recognized by a given nation state. b) I had been vested with the Sealing Power of Elijiah, by Harold B. Lee; one of the late presidents of the Mormon Church, in his capacity as the "presiding high priest of the high priesthood" that administers Temple ceremonies. c) Excommunication from the institutional church does not take away this investiture; it only keeps me from celebrating Temple rituals within the Latter-day Saint community. d) So, why not choose to be the catalyst that, literally, extends the Sealing Power to a "people" that the theology defines as including even those who (as also Blacks had been prior to June of 1978) are currently excluded by a view that devalues their Love as coupled monogamous relationships?

[vii] Hidden Treasures and Promises; Sections received through Antonio A. Feliz, The Restoration Church of Jesus Christ, headquartered in Salt Lake City, Utah.

[viii] Audio Record of the 1987 Semi-Annual Priesthood Conference of The Restoration Church of Jesus Christ. Specifically, see the minutes of the June semi-annual priesthood conference, held that year in Sacramento, California.

[ix] The Sanctity of Dissent, by Paul James Toscano (Signature Books, Salt Lake City, Utah,1994).

[x] Community of Christ (headquartered in Independence, Missouri and formerly, Reorganized Church of Jesus Christ of Latter Day Saints) is the church that sponsored the 1983 workshop at what was then, Park College (now, Park University) where I was first introduced to training in receiving what some call "spirit writing" for my personal guidance.

[xi] The Chalice & The Blade, *Our History Our Future*, by Riane Eisler (Harper & Row Publishers, San Francisco, California 1987), page 105.

[xii] Ibid., page 117.

[xiii] American Holocaust, *The Conquest of the New World*, by David E. Stannard (Oxford University Press, New York, NY, 1992) pages 24-25.

[xiv] Ibid., lpage 133.

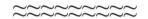

"The lesson I learned on the personal level is, if you want to change the world then, *change yourself.* Cancel out the evil that is within you, *first.* Then, once *you* have been transformed, the rest is relatively easy...I affirm that the key of transformation exists in the power of One. I am saying that, if the reader wants to change the world then, the ability to actually do so -to truly change the world- indeed, already exists within the reader. Awareness is but the first step on the way of becoming open souls... *"*

CHAPTER FIVE

BECOMING AWARE OF OUR CONDITION

I did find a way out of "hell," and many others have also discovered the same way out. However, now, in order for our entire society to get out of the "hell" in which we find ourselves –like any *individual* must– we, *as a society*, also need to be aware of our true condition. Yet, it is very hard for some to see that—for all practical purposes—we *are* in a truly collective, "hell." This is because our religions imagine us in quite another place. For example, Mormon Temple theology puts us in their lowest Afterlife of "glory."[i]

Thankfully, however, Plato's Cave Story, from The Republic, speaks to this question, on the true nature of our reality, and most of us first read it in high school literature classes. But, the following personal experience reveals that I did not learn that great literary story when I was meant to because, as a sadly mistaken adolescent, I had a friend write my world literature book report for me that year. This mortifying fact about my own adolescent life is not something, of which, I am at all proud.

So, the following personal experience from my adult life is told here only because Plato's myth is a perfect metaphor for the way I have come to experience the experience of life. Much like any other, who has learned to see reality differently than the majority of us, all the parties in Plato's Cave myth each have a worldview that is unique to their personal experience. My undergraduate education in Greek Theatre at Brigham Young University notwithstanding, the year when I first learned this theme from Plato's old Cave Story was 1987—it was in my forty-fourth year…

****

Five years had now passed since my excommunication from the religious institution, which, so far, had been my vehicle for experiencing the Divine. From time to time, over that past four years, I had written words in my daily journal that I knew were not from me, nor, from my conscious awareness. My writing has always been something that I've had to work at, but when these words had come, they seemed to flow out of me as if I had been taking dictation from another. Whenever this happened, I would go back to the words on the pages in awe at what had happened because I knew that, it was not my own normally halting way of writing. The interesting thing was, the language was in a *"thee"* and *"thou"* vocabulary of the King James Version of the Bible.

I decided that, I truly needed a professional's advice. So, after showing the seemingly "dictated" words to a psychologist friend, he had called it, "spirit writing" because it came out like a stream of the kind of language, which I used in my prayers. He had said, "It is logical that it would come in your prayer vocabulary, Tony."

But, when I later had, finally, left any "full activity" in all the Utah Mormon communities, I stopped using that vocabulary in my daily devotions. After that change, the messages (as I eventually called them) have flowed out of me without a stream of the old *"thee"* and *"thou"* prayer verbiage of my Mormon past. So, by the time of the paperback publication of my first book, this spirit writing no longer used that kind of language, but it still comes in a tone and a syntax that remains a great comfort to me. Each message brings me hope, courage and inner strength that –in hindsight– has proven to manifest its otherworldly author to be a faithful Guide. And, although to date, I don't know the identity of that Guide, one message, in particular, had never made sense to me, but when it came, I intuitively knew that I had written it exactly as it was meant by my loving Guide to be written by me.

It was a comforting message to me that came in response to my profound sense of loss because my excommunication had ruled out any opportunities for me to speak out publicly in any L.D.S. Church religious services. Prophetically, in 1963, as a young, nineteen year old Mormon missionary in Peru, I'd had a recurring horror-filled nightmare in which my voice had been suddenly taken away. Each time this sense of loss had taken place in my dream world, I awoke feeling that, loosing my ability to speak would be a fate worse than death; for, by then, I already understood that my future life would –somehow– involve my voice as a future vocation.

So, in light of having lost my public forum, it shouldn't have been surprising that this particular spirit-written message would, like my recurring nightmare, prove to be prophetic. It had said: *"You will yet stand and testify before throngs of cave dwellers…"* Yet, when this message came through me in my forty-fourth year, I couldn't understand the use of the arcane words, *"cave dwellers."* So, I tried to edit those words into something else –only to then, be overwhelmed by a powerful intuitive feeling to the point that I sensed a chiding from some unseen Guide, and I changed the words back to the original, *"cave dwellers."*

Sandra McDonald was the good friend who'd introduced me to Marilyn French's masterpiece, Beyond Power (Summit Books, New York, 1985). That book had confirmed my genuine esteem for Sandra because it, literally, changed my life forever. In other words, since having been excommunicated, she had not only proven to be a trusted friend, but also, a mentor, as well. She, eventually, joined me in my new ministry so, as we both traveled one night across a hot Nevada desert in her car to a church conference, I asked her what she thought those words *"cave dwellers"* might refer to in the "spirit written" message that I'd received…

I said to her, "I don't know why the message uses those specific words. I thought that maybe the words actually meant people who live in apartment buildings or condominiums or..."

Laughing, Sandra interrupted, "Oh, you silly. That's easy!"

"Do you have an idea what they mean?" I asked.

"Of course, Tony," she began, "it's from the famous myth of Plato's Cave."

"Plato's Cave?"

"Tony, don't tell me that you know nothing about those old stories from Greek mythology!"

After telling Sandra about my high school mischief, I asked, "Ok, so come on Sandra –can you give me some idea what the *'cave dwellers'* could be?"

"Yes, Tony. If you want, I can actually quote part of the myth from memory," she answered through her laughter, "Tony, it's a classic that you should have read decades ago too! You were a rascal in high school, weren..."

Getting a little impatient, I interrupted, "So come on now, tell me what you know."

"Okay but, these are only parts of it, Tony. I memorized them for a lit class years ago, Tony, like you should have," she said looking at me like a mother would look at her errant child. "Give me a moment," she said, and with that, Sandra tried to focus by taking in a huge breath. Finally, after exhaling very slowly, she began, "Okay, Tony, 'Imagine mankind…'"

I noticed that her voice had changed. Her mellow, lower tone convinced me that she was reciting from memory. She wasn't joking.

"…as dwelling in an underground cave with a long entrance open to the light across the whole width of the cave; in this they have been from childhood, with necks and legs fettered, so they have to stay where they are. They cannot move their heads round because of the fetters, and they can only look forward, but light comes to them from a fire burning behind them higher up at a distance. Between the fire and the prisoners is a road above their level, and along it imagine a low wall has been built, as puppet showmen have screens in front of their people over which they work their puppets."

Listening to her memorized words, I nodded to show that I was listening. The solitary darkness around us on the highway that night seemed to lend itself well to her telling of this famous story.

"…then, bearers carrying along this wall all sorts of articles which they hold projecting above the wall, statues of men and other living things, made of stone or wood and all kinds of stuff, some of the bearers speaking and some silent, as you might expect…" Then, looking into my eyes, she went on, "first of all, tell me this: What do you think such people would have seen of themselves and each other except their shadows, which the fire cast on the opposite wall of the cave?"

I silently shook my head to indicate that I couldn't imagine how they could see anything else.

With only the sound of the motor, the whispering of the wind as we drove through the darkness, and her practiced voice in my ears, she went on with, "…what of the things being carried along? Would not this be the same?"

Again, I simply nodded in agreement.

"Suppose the prisoners were able to talk together, don't you think that when they named the shadows which they saw passing they would believe they were naming things?"

"Aha," I answered quietly.

"Then, if their [dark] prison had an echo from the opposite wall, whenever one of the passing bearers uttered a sound, would they not suppose that the passing shadow must be making the sound? Don't you think so?…"

"Yeah," I said.

"…[S]uch persons would certainly believe that there were no realities except those shadows of handmade things…Now consider… what their release would be like, and their cure from their fetters and their folly: let us imagine whether it might naturally be something like this.   One might be released, and compelled suddenly to stand up and turn his neck round, and to walk and look towards the firelight; all this would hurt him, and he would be too much dazzled to see distinctly those things whose shadows he had seen before…"

In that darkened car speeding on the freeway in the night, I was amazed at the myth's clarity. I was in awe of how obvious its message seemed to be about me. Guilt for my high school mischief filled me.

"…What do you think he would say, if someone told him that what he saw before was foolery, but now he saw more rightly, being a bit nearer reality and turned towards what was a little more real? What if he were shown each of the passing things, and [then] compelled by questions, to answer what each one was? Don't you think he would be puzzled, and believe what he saw before was more true than what was shown to him now?"

The darkness surrounding the two bright beams of the car's main headlights became a part of the metaphor, as her deeply spoken words lodged in my soul. "Logical," I answered, "it all fits."

"Then," Sandra went on, "suppose he were compelled to look towards the real light, it would hurt his eyes, and he would escape by turning them away to the things which he was able to look at, and these he would believe to be clearer than what, was being shown to him."

Suddenly, Sandra turned and looked right at me, "Suppose now", she went on slowly turning her gaze back to the highway, "that someone should drag him thence by force up the rough ascent, the steep way up, and never stop until he could drag him out into the light of the sun. Would he not be distressed and furious at being dragged; and when he came into the light, the brilliance would fill his eyes and he would not be able to see even one of the things now called real?"

"Not suddenly, Sandra, of course not."

"He would have to get used to it, surely, I think," she went on saying, "if he is to see the things above. First he would most easily look at shadows, after that images of mankind and the rest in water, lastly the things themselves. After this he would find it easier to survey by night the heavens themselves and all that is in them, ... at the light of the stars and moon, rather than by day the sun and the sun's light."

In my mind's eye, I continued to liken what she recited to the light and dark environments changing, as we traveled. I nodded.

"Last of all I suppose, the sun; he could look on the sun itself by itself in its own place, and see what it is like, not reflections of it in a body of water or as it appears in some alien setting…Then again… consider; if such a one should go down again and sit on his old seat, would he not get his eyes full of darkness coming in suddenly out of the sun?"

"Uh, he'd be blinded," I responded automatically.

"And if he should have to compete with those who had been always prisoners. By laying down the law about those shadows, while he was blinking before his eyes were settled down—wouldn't they all laugh at him, and say he had spoiled his eyesight by going up there, and it was not worth-while so much as to try to go up? And would they not kill anyone who tried to release them and take them up, if they could somehow lay hands on him and kill him?"

With that last question, I got chills throughout my body.

"The world of our sight is like the habitation in prison, with the firelight there to the sunlight here, the ascent and the view of the upper world is the rising of the soul into the world of mind; put it so and you will not be far from my own surmise, since that is what you want to hear, but God knows if it is really true. At least, what appears to me is, that in the world of the known, last of all, is the idea of the good, and with what toil to be seen! And seen, this must be inferred to be the cause of all right and beautiful things for all, which gives birth to light and the king of light in the world of sight, and in the world of mind, herself the queen produces truth and reason; and she must be seen by one who is to act with reason publicly or privately… and do not be surprised, that those who come thither are not willing to have part in the affairs of men, but their souls ever strive to remain above; for that surely may be expected if our parable fits the case."

Although the language felt somewhat arcane to me, through its awkwardness, the perfection of Plato's words hit me to the core. All I could do was nod in agreement again.

Sandra's voice was still sounding mellow, "…Do you think it surprising if one leaving divine contemplations and passing to the evils of men is awkward and appears to be a great fool while he is still blinking—not yet accustomed to the darkness around him, but compelled to struggle in law courts or elsewhere about shadows of justice, or the images which make the shadows, and to quarrel about notions of justice in those who have never seen justice itself?"'" With that, she stopped speaking. She simply looked at me directly again and then, waited for me to respond as she silently kept on driving.

For the longest time, there was only silence inside that car. The incessant sounds of the motor, the air as we drove through it and the tires on the road were all my ears knew. I didn't know what she was thinking. I was overcome with the majesty –by the clarity– of Plato's words that Sandra had memorized so many years earlier, and I kept silent for what seemed like several minutes. *Notions of justice...* I needed to ponder the words.

Finally, she said, "There's more, Tony." Then again, taking in a deep breath, she went on reciting; "...the law is not concerned how any one class in a city is to prosper above the rest; [the law] tries to contrive prosperity in the city as a whole, [it is] fitting the citizens into a pattern by persuasion and compulsion, [it is] making them give of their help to one another wherever each class is able to help the community. The law itself creates men like this in the city, not in order to allow each one to turn by any way he likes, but in order to use them itself to the full for binding the city together."

With that, I had regained my sense of normalcy and I asked her, "Sandra, are you quoting this now to help me see that even in the days of Plato, democracy was merely the illusion of a democracy? Or, are you underscoring the fact that our civilization's concepts of law and justice do not address the war of the classes?"

"Don't miss the point, Tony," she chided, "But, if the shoe fits... Oh, remember; Tony, you're the one who wanted me to quote the myth of Plato's Cave from memory. Actually, I think you know deep down that the message you received was a revelation given to you about your life's work about your ministry."

"Well, you know me better than most. After all, you were a member of our L.D.S. ward back when I was the bishop. You know where my heart has always been, in spite of what others try to say about me."

"Ok," she responded, "since you seem to accept my advice, let me finish the parts I memorized because I think this is your call. In fact, I know that in some respects, I have the same call. Plato understood that, what our civilization perpetuates is, actually, only a masquerade of what truly can be. Remember that Plato was taught by Socrates, and that Socrates probably had access to all of the most ancient writings, that some good soul must have had the common sense to save from the lost civilization that existed long before our current world began."

Again, I just nodded.

"...Down you must go then, in turn, to the habitation of [all] the others, and accustom [all] yourselves to [all of] their darkness; for when you [all] have grown accustomed you will [all then] see a thousand times better than those who live there, and you will know what the images are and what they are images of, because you have seen the realities behind just and beautiful and good things."

****

How I experienced the experience made the message totally clear to me. As with Plato's cave dweller, awareness of a condition is our first step to genuine wellness. So, if the reader experiences emotional pain because of what I now write in this chapter, it is only because you –like I do– relate with these stories in some way. As it is with most physical wounds or most illnesses, pain is one of the first ways in which humans experience awareness of engaging a healing process. As with the cave dwellers in Plato's cave, the kind of pain to which I refer, is sometimes manifest in us as anger. However, as is beautifully discussed by Gary Zukov in The Seat of The Soul, anger is a "shadow emotion" reflecting an inner pain. So, what now comes in this chapter, may be difficult for "true believers," who understand sacred stories as only being a historical narrative instead of seeing the sacred story as a way for an inner message to communicate universally, *beyond* the context of its original time and culture.

For example, if the reader views the story told of Eden as history then, you are now where I once was. If that is truly the place from which you reckon, then, I understand your hesitance to open yourself to these ideas. However, my plea is that you allow love and genuine openness to Another Yourself to cover fear. The following is out of my profound love of sacred stories and their, respective, inner meanings. I also grew up with the telling of sacred stories and I still hold them sacred. In fact, were I to have children again in my home, I would tell the stories still. However, I would not teach them the sacred stories as history.

How I have experienced the experiences, has always taught me that, there is a far better way to envision. I've learned that the opportunity that is, now ripe, for an impregnation by the intent of our mass consciousness, comes to us all on the vehicle of our nation's, increasingly diverse, disparate and densely populated society. If we all continue to take our plethora of ethnic sacred stories as being actual history then, we –as an increasingly diverse society– will only continue to increase in tribal-like group hatreds. This kind of social behavior will only continue to tear us apart.

But, conversely, any healing is about *changing* a torn-apart condition. Because of September 11, 2001, we all learned that, our faith communities are not where Americans are One. Because of war, we came to see that we have precious little civic culture, but that, the civic awareness that we do have, can become the mortar, which cements the bricks of our diverse American populace into the city on the hill. However, it will only happen if we all open up new ways of envisioning and this, demands new interpretations.

We need a new way of knowing our old myths. We need to interpret them in new ways, for none of us can any longer afford to maintain the illusion of separateness now, which we in the 21st century inherited from former times. The old way of envisioning provided us with the fantastic legend of Eden for our mainstream culture and society. The singular message of all the stories told in this book is that, I, as others, have found a way out of this place –out of our self-imposed "hell." This clear way out has to do with how we envision our, respective, sacred stories.

There are ways of telling sacred stories by which, we may open ourselves to the hidden, yet, universal references in the sacred mythologies. Understanding the hidden and symbolic wisdom of our sacred stories is crucial to our wellbeing because, as has already been stated, myth is the social mortar which keeps the bricks of our civilization in place. Knowing the inner power—the energy—that myth engages, is the business of any that seek to journey on the way of becoming open souls, thus, unless a critical mass can have the integrity that this knowledge engages, we risk being caught in the whirlwind of craziness that results by taking these stories as factual history. This was the problem with Afganistan's Taliban.

It is the same problem that also incited America's Religious Right against people like me and my beloved because we seek the freedom to love the person with whom Love—*Itself*—has caused us to feel eternally linked. It is the universal issue of trusting humans; our becoming aware of how the world actually is. How we tell our sacred stories, impacts our culture so much that, we have all become disoriented from all the realities around us. We're like the way that the person in Plato's Cave suffered traumatically when he learned that the fuzzy shadows were not real after all; we also, as a collective society, will continue to become disoriented by our continuing to stay within our own modern cave of illusory thinking. This is the difference between religious fundamentalists and those who try to follow the higher law of Love—or, the way of becoming open souls. This truth was powerfully brought home to me recently as I swam some laps...

****

Because I now relate with Plato's Cave myth, I'm often seen as a prophet of doom. After being accused by a man who told me that he sees me in this light, I sensed the need to work off the inner tension of his personal attack by doing laps in my pool. But, after a few laps, I stopped to rest briefly, and I noticed the setting sun being reflected on the clear, bluish water. I looked up and saw the orange, red and yellow hues in the clouds above me. Then, looking back down at the bright glittering platinum path on the water's surface, my mind wandered... Slowly, I began to see the experience of seeing the glittering sunlight as metaphor because its reflection focused my views on the man, who had called my words in a paper I'd presented "dooms day" verbiage. Although I was totally alone there, in the glimmering pool, I laughed out loud at my thoughts.

After composing myself, I began to do laps again and didn't get further than about nine meters because the scene being reflected on the surface of the water was too relevant. I was struck by my mind's way of seeing a sacred story from my youth reflected there on the pool's water. So, walking back slowly in the water to the place where I had been only seconds before, I said out loud to myself as I spread out my arms: "This is 'He, who is *Walking On Water*.'" It was a way for me to affirm the sacred story of the Jesus figure, in the Christian bible, in the new way of seeing that I'd first learned from my *Meshica* friends in Mexico in 1990.

I stood there in the blue water, watching the bright sunlight reflecting in the pool. Struck with the sense of a sacred moment, I recalled how they had explained that, "walking on water," was the way the ancient wisdom of the Indigenous of this land saw Father Sun. As Father Sun sets, at every dusk, to their Indian way of inter-relating with the natural world, the sun is manifest as if, "...*Walking On Water*" at the end of His daily journey. When the *Meshica* had given me this new way of envisioning, I had already known, because of my former old L.D.S. ecclesiastical seminary training, that the proselyte-minded Christian Fathers of the first century, c.e. –the Early Christian Fathers– had appropriated the earlier pagan religious symbols of what had been former cultural realities. They had taken the older symbol of the sun in order for them to more, effectively convert, their fellow Roman citizens. It had been no accident that Christianity ended up using the Roman feast day of the Roman sun deity, Sunday, to celebrate its collective's weekly worship tradition.

I felt contentment within, as the smile I realized had formed on my face began to grow, and I continued swimming. As I did so –with the warm water swooshing over my body– I was mentally focused on how today's fundamentalist traditions take the view that the sacred story of Jesus walking on water is a historical event. Still stroking and kicking, I thought of my Mormon Primary and Sunday School teachers, and how much they thought the old story of the Garden of Eden was history. I thought of the Mormon "science man" who had dutifully and diligently drummed the dogma of the institutional L.D.S. Church into my mind. I thought of my devout high school L.D.S. seminary teacher; how, she had unquestioningly believed that this old story was historical and factual. I thought of my BYU religion professors, who had thoroughly convinced me –through all their practiced expertise in appealing to institutionally engineered sentimentality– that our Mormon priesthood leaders had a monopoly on the highest human spiritual path; that we were "the only true church."

With those memories in my mind, I came up for more air again. The sun was now finally setting, and Walking On Water was leaving. When the final slit of the brilliant red-orange orb began turning into the shadow of the horizon, I thought that, I can now easily see why the Jesus figure was originally put into a myth in the Gospels, as a man who was seen "walking on water." I felt total contentment about how this sacred story from my domestication had been transformed in my mind. Drying off, I looked at my copy of John Edward's, first book, What If God Were The Sun? and, then, I laughed loudly—raucously!

****

My detractor had responded to comments I'd made about the Columbine Massacre. Even though we have seen bloodshed in our urban center high schools in our mass media, the massacre at Columbine High School in the quiet, suburban town of Littleton, Colorado, is what got our entire nation's attention in the 1990s. This evidences that, while we have come to expect violent behavior in mega-urban centers, this particular horror violated our imagined sense of peace. Was that because, those involved were considered the "nice boys?" Was it that, those in the majority at Columbine

High School are Anglo-Saxon and are of the middle to upper-middle economic classes, while its other urban high school populations come largely from the working poor? Is it because, this kind of terror wasn't supposed to happen in places where the typical family is "God-fearing" and provides only the best possible educational opportunities for their children, yet, it *did* happen there? And, if the above is true, then, what does all this have to do with America's mainstream's religious mythologies?

From where I have now come to see things, when it comes to understanding our present social reality, it is as if all our "best thinkers" have their heads in the proverbial sand—at least, prior to September 11, 2001. My point of reference informs me that they can't see the forest for the trees. Unless our "best thinkers" open themselves up to the wisdom of others –who aren't perceived to be in the mainstream of modern society– they won't comprehend what has been perfectly clear to us, those of us out in the tributaries of modern America. Remember: The people in the mythological raft, who are unknowingly heading toward the waterfall downstream, symbolize all of *us*, as a society. The message is that the ability to see what we can not see *is in the tributaries* of the raging river of life.

It's always been so. This is why I'm woefully disappointed in the opinions that were initially offered up by noted "experts," in response to our nation's ugly adolescent "nice boy" bloodletting in the 1990s. I have, elsewhere, referred to our modern American society as being in a diseased condition, and in subsequent chapters, I tell how I came to see that, the actual disease from which we suffer is *not* how we treat one another. My hope is that, by now, the reader is aware that my belief is that, our ways of inter-relating are only *symptoms* of something that is truly endemic to all that is modern America.

Yes, it is abundantly clear, to me, that our present condition manifests itself as our behavioral social disorder. But the revealing question is: *What is it? As was the tragic case in: Peduckah, Kentucky; in Littleton, Colorado; in Santee, California and in other towns, what causes the most conforming of teens to consistently mimic violent behavioral patterns? And, does it have significant parallels with today's Islamic terrorists?* Even those extremists involved in the September 11, 2001 terrorist acts were the "nice boys" of *their* respective, society. After reflection on how I've experienced the experience, now, it seems to me that if we, actually, understood the root sources of our distress in terrorist events then, we would know what to do about our sickness. I am saying that, we need to look with eyes, which envision in ways that the mainstream has not yet learned from their proverbial raft.

Because of how I experienced the experience, I suggest that the ugly horror of the perpetrators' behavior at Columbine High and elsewhere, including September 11, 2001, is the behavior of *abused* souls. Exactly as I'd learned to do with myself—when dissecting specimens in our high school biology labs—*we, all mentally dissect ourselves into pieces.* We do this as a survival technique in painful circumstances. And, yet, we choose to call it "being in control," as if, the fracturing of the soul were rooted in good health! This is the exact process, which I endeavored to relate in my past choices to agree with the worldview of my former religious mentors, as I told in Chapter One. In those adolescent days, I was emotionally dissected.

I was forced to dissect my emotional self from the rest of myself. The result of efforts by well-intentioned believers to rescue me for their unique version of the Afterlife was the fracturing of my natural essence, as a sovereign soul. I've also seen this dissection of emotional responses from observing the behavior of others in my adult life, first as a post-graduate student of Marriage and Family Counseling and then later, as an ordained L.D.S. bishop in Utah when I had counseled devout couples. Indeed, this unhealthy soul fracturing is common behavior among adult victims of child abuse whom I've known. So, in my sense, all terrorists are emotionally dissected souls. I've discovered that it is no different for any of us when early life is about abuse. It's a collective inherited problem.

I first became all too aware of the fact that the root of our ills today comes from inherited worldviews of less enlightened times, when I worked as an employee of the L.D.S. Church Offices. That was when I realized that, as already stated above, no matter how evolved we perceive ourselves to be, *our dissected ways of inter-relating are encoded by the envisioning of the former generations of our past.* This was the same period of my life when I was also discovering some very disturbing things in the old documents, I was researching in the L.D.S. Church Archives, at the L.D.S. Church Offices in Salt Lake City, Utah. As the new field coordinator of economic services for The Church to five West Coast nations in South America, I was on assignment there in 1977. This was when I was first confronted with the result of myopic ways to envision...

****

The brother standing at the pulpit was introducing me to the congregation. The chapel was filled with bishops, stake presidents and other local leaders of the Peruvian church. "Elder Feliz," he said, "has come from Salt Lake City to train us in these regions of The Church in the appropriate ways of using the offerings of the monthly fasts of our members."

Utah Mormons, worldwide, abstain from two meals on the first Sunday of every month and contribute what would have been spent on food for the feeding of their poor. The first part of the meeting had been taken up by the representative from the Church Building Committee, who was also down there visiting the same South American nations where I had also been traveling on official business from the Church Offices. My own assignment was to instruct the lay ecclesiastical leadership in their duties of managing the free-will offerings of their faithful.

After gingerly approaching the pulpit myself, I began with *"Queridos Hermanos y Hermanas,"* (Beloved Brothers and Sisters) since all of you have had some limited experience in the operation of the fast offering funds, I would like to simply respond to questions which you may have."

There were no questions for a long, long time. Then, out of the silence, one small man stood up in the rear. His clothing seemed less tailored than the rest of the men in the audience, and he was obviously of mostly an Indian heritage. "Elder Feliz," he asked in a quietly spoken and thickly accented Spanish –which told me that Spanish was not his original language– "can you explain why we need to raise over $24,000 for only the tower for our new church building, when according to what we heard in the last session, the tower has no real purpose?"

A hushed murmur swelled the chapel's entire air space.

I was taken by surprise. I hadn't expected any question on a matter of church construction policy. That was not my work. My only function on this trip was to represent Church Welfare Services to these local leaders. "Perhaps," I began, "that is a question you can ask the representative of the Church Building Committee when we adjourn this session. I am happy to respond to matters dealing with the care of the poor and the needy of The Church."

"But, don't you see," the little man persisted, "we are the poor of The Church."

With that, suddenly, the whole room became a rumble of a mass diversity of voices. I had done my homework prior to this assignment. Indeed, all the statistical information seemed to say exactly that. These good people were what I had also called "the Lord's poor" in the twenty-fourth floor training rooms of the Church Offices back home in Salt Lake City.

I turned quickly to see what the other visitor from Salt Lake City wanted to do. As I looked behind me at Brother Schaefer sitting with the other dignitaries, he got up and came to the pulpit, and putting his hand over the microphone, he whispered in my ear, "Tony, why don't you just translate for me and I'll answer his question."

I'd done simultaneous interpretation for many dignitaries before. That, wasn't my concern. I was at issue about the way I would be seen by these people if I functioned here only as a mere translator –with no, actual, authority from the Presiding Bishopric of The Church. So, I said into the microphone, "Brother Schaefer, from the Church Building Committee, will respond first and then, I'll respond from the view of Church Welfare Services."

The little brother at the rear of the chapel had been waiting patiently. Suddenly, he began, "I'll start at the beginning…"

I also then began the translation into English for Brother Schaefer, who had gotten up and was also standing at the pulpit.

The man went on, "…what is the purpose of the tower in the design of our new house of prayer?"

Another murmur swept throughout the chapel.

"Tell them I don't know. But, Tony," he said to me, "there's one on every L.D.S. chapel throughout the entire world. It's a trademark. It's very recognizable. It wouldn't be immediately obvious as a Mormon chapel without the tower like it's designed."

I translated his words and waited a moment for a question.

Again, the audience began to whisper and talk in a more vocal manner, something that doesn't happen in such meetings.

Another man who, was dressed in much the same way as the first man, then stood up also.

The room fell silent.

This man calmly walked out into the center aisle and came down toward the front of the chapel. When he was close enough for me to see his eyes clearly, he said, "Is this not," he paused and turned back toward the other local leaders behind him and then, back to me, "is this not going to be our house of prayer?" Tears seemed to now be welling up in his eyes. "Is this not to be our house of the worship of God? And, my brother, if this is so then, do we not want our non-Mormon neighbors and friends to know that it is a house of prayer and worship?"

The silence was deafening to me.

Nevertheless, I dutifully translated as best as I could for my Church Offices colleague. However, my eyes were glued to the eyes of the man standing just below us. Seeing the potent dignity of his manner, I thought to myself, there is such an overwhelming honesty presenting itself here...here, in the form of this devoted man of faith.

Brother Schaefer's words interrupted my thoughts, "Yes, of course," he answered.

The little man, standing in unspeakable strength of spirit then said, "Then, allow us to put a great bell in the tower." Suddenly, he threw his hands way up, and holding his arms up, wide open, "Please understand brethren, to us, a bell on a building tells the whole town that God is in the building. A great bell speaks without words to all of the people! It says, 'This is a house of prayer' to all who see the bell, or hear the wonderful sound of the ringing of it!"

With that, the entire chapel was filled with a loud whisper of voices. The people, in their seats, were nodding back and forth to each other.

As if emboldened by the crowd behind him, the man in front of me, stepped forward one step, "I work at the foundry here in the capital city," he said with dignity, "and I can arrange for a bell to be donated to The Church! Brethren," he went on with light in his eyes, "such a bell would, indeed, make it a house of prayer, a house of true worship to all of the people of the town –not only to us."

Suddenly, the human sea of mostly men seemed to become a waving motion, as everyone began nodding their heads to each other in ardent agreement.

As I translated into English...

Brother Schaefer quickly whispered back to me, loudly, "absolutely not!" Then, looking at me directly, he went on, "tell them, 'No,' Tony. None of our chapels in the whole world has a bell, and this will not be the first. Not under my watch."

Incredulous, I whispered back, "Do you, actually, want me to translate what you just said?" I was in shock no, I was extremely disappointed and mortified by his lack of cultural sensitivity. His insensitivity to the culture of these good people became an appalling revelation to me. The least he could do is use more gentle words to respond to their honest articulation of *their* cultural awareness. After all, they collectively knew the importance of presenting the spiritual side of our community to the world. *That*, was obvious to me, because of their questions!

"Tony," he said responding to my astounded countenance, I'm sure, "you say it just as I said it." He radiated a stern quality, one unbecoming of a servant of The Lord on official assignment.

I translated his words, and I did so, precisely. But, now, my personal emotions were engaged. I felt myself getting warm with indignation. We are all servants here, I thought to myself. What a way to talk to those who preside over our Lord's work in this part of The Lord's Church? These good people, my mind went on, deserve respect. We should, at least, give them the courtesy of taking their point of view back to our own, respective, supervisor in Salt Lake City, Utah. With all of these thoughts racing in my mind, I finished translating Brother Schaefer's response and then...

I added, "and, I say that, as the Church Welfare Services official representative of the Presiding Bishop at this meeting, I promise you that upon my return, I will be sure to give the Presiding Bishop a report of your concerns."

"*Hermano* Feliz," another voice came from the rear again, "and, would you please be sure to also tell the Presiding Bishopric how much we each make in terms of North-American dollars? Will you please let them know that $24,000 is far more than all of us together in one of our branches make in one year's time?"

I could only nod my head in agreement.

With that, applause burst on the entire assembly. My shock at applause in a Mormon business meeting in a Mormon chapel froze me in my shoes. The sting of perspiration in my armpits made me aware of my automatic emotional response. Applause is not at all a common practice in L.D.S. services. But, here, in this meeting, the approving sound of a thunderous applause was totally engulfing us. It was amazing to me!

In my peripheral vision, Brother Schaefer took his seat. He was asking another brother on the stand what had been said by me.

I continued to answer questions. As the discussion went on, I knew –as I had never before known– that poverty truly is a relative status. I already knew that poverty usually exists because of the disconnection of the lower classes from all of the other classes. I absolutely knew, at that precise moment, that these members of The Church were not only poor by the standards in the United States. Yet, I was now also aware that this group, actually, made up the more well-to-do members in this region of our church's population. That is what the statistics had told me.

This is the precise moment in time when I first began to question why God was, evidently, not aware of our Utah biases and prejudices, as His "agents" in The Work. Was Father not aware how our, respective, cultural views contained perceptions of exclusive otherness about the rest of The Church? Suddenly, it was as if it had been the first time for me: In an instant, there, I saw both sides of the dialogue we had all been party to that day. In that singular moment, I began to be aware of my Other –especially, those less fortunate than I– because, in *that* instant, I experienced the experience not just in a middle-class assimilated American mainstream mind-set but, in Another's way of envisioning as well. It was, for me, an experience in experiencing true empathy as I'd never before experienced.

Five days later, another defining moment happened in my life. It was the second time that I wondered if God was, in truth, the ruling force behind our policies at the world headquarters of The Church. I was unpacking my suitcase in another city on the same trip, which had taken me to visit several nations of South America. My new boss at the Church Offices had been re-hired after having served The Church as a Mission President, presiding over all of the conversions of Native-Americans on the reservations in the United States. He had never traveled out of the country before and, he had told me that it would be good for us to travel together on his first trip to South America in order for him "to learn" from my "expertise."

Brother Bishop was there, standing on the balcony, over-looking the city's main plaza, twenty-two stories below. "Hey, Tony," he called out, "come out here."

I stopped what I was doing and went to see what was going on. The sounds of the distant cars and horns filled the air. As if from the far side of a very large mountain lake, the street noise had a clear crispness, yet, it remained far away in how it sounded to me.

He was simply staring out into the empty Santiago air, out into the nothingness of the smog-filled currents of rising hot air.

"What is it?"

"It's too bad, you know," he said softly. He'd said it with such ethos. His graying hair was waving in the wind, as the currents rose up the side of our hotel.

"What's too bad?" I wondered why he seemed to use an almost affected manner in his question.

No response came from the, rather, ponderous six foot, plus man standing on that wind-swept balcony.

Again, I asked, "what is it?" I looked down to see if I could find what it was that he was talking about. The cars and busses looked like ants in a wild, circular and unending path beneath us. For a moment, I pondered how much like ants we human beings are –insignificant– going about our daily tasks. My silent thought was, we humans are infesting the planet; we're no different to the planet than are the tiny ants in my back yard back home. Then, all of a sudden, the air felt warm, as it pushed up ward from below –as if in response to my thoughts.

"It's too bad," he finally responded, "that you will never become a member of the Twelve Apostles of The Church. Too bad, too bad," he repeated several times, shaking his head, as if it was something that he'd been pondering for a long time.

What an off-the-wall comment, I thought to myself and said, "what kind of talk is that?" I then heard myself laugh nervously.

With his person still facing out over the circular plaza below, and with a rather serious look on his face, he said calmly, "Oh, I was just thinking about you and another man. I guess I'm thinking about another who also has a Native heritage among the thousands of us white folk who work at the Church Offices in Salt Lake City."

What is he talking about, I thought to myself, "do you want to explain?" I wanted a response.

My new boss just stood there though. It was as if he wanted me to work at getting him to start talking about what it was that he was thinking about. "I mean, I've never been a mind reader."

The noise of the horns and the cars below seemed to get a lot louder. The late afternoon breeze on that high, twenty-second floor balcony suddenly went chill.

At that moment, I knew in my inner being whom it was that he was speaking about to me. I asked, "what do Elder George P. Lee of the ordained Seventy and I have in common –he's a priesthood authority, a General Authority, while I'm just an employee– so, other than the fact that we're both Lamanites, what are you talking about?"

Brother Bishop simply maintained his stoic stance.

The wind was now bellowing up harder than it had earlier. The wind currents were pushing upward because of the day's heat reflecting from the concrete below us. It felt like the balcony had become an oven. As I looked up at him, I saw beyond his darkening silhouette, that the sun was setting. Shadows from other buildings had already crept up against the tall building, from which we were looking out.

His hair was glistening, being blown by the hot air.

This is weird, I thought to myself. Why does he talk in such strange ways, here, where nobody else can hear his words except me? I had to understand what he was about. I responded again, "Elder Lee is a file leader to the ranks of the church's priesthood, he's a general authority, for God's sake! I, on the other hand, am just a wage earner. I'm a mere employee like a secretary or a janitor," I said. "Anyway, Brother Bishop, the vision of my becoming a high officer in the Kingdom, like an Apostle of The Lord or, as one of the Lord's Seventy is one of those occupational hazards of being a Mormon bureaucrat and an ordained ecclesiast that I got over a long, long time ago. In case you don't know it, understand that I'm not about climbing our hierarchical ranks, like some of the others who work at the Church Offices."

Evidently, *that* did it. Finally, he suddenly turned back around and looked squarely into my eyes. Without blinking, his eyes focused, as if to go inside of me. The intensity of his meaning shot right through my core, as he yelled out, "Are you dense? Don't you know that you'll never become one of the ordained Apostles because of the same reason that your Navajo brother, George P. Lee will never become one? Don't you know?"

All I could do is stare blankly.

"Aren't you aware of the hidden doctrine? Don't you know what members of The Family teach?"

Instinctively, I turned around and tried to look away from him –downward toward all the ant-like figures below– and, in seconds, I had a quick conversation with myself. Hidden doctrine? The Family? What *Family?* Family: That was the term that took me to another place and another time...

In the course of my work in recent weeks at the L.D.S. Church Offices, an assignment from my previous supervisor at our church's headquarters had had me doing research in the Church Archives and I had come across some arcane theology, arcane, at least, to me.

This was the late 1970s. The Twelve Apostles, under the then, leadership of Elder Gordon B. Hinkeley,[ii] were leading the lay members of The Church in political efforts to fight against the Equal Rights Amendment. As a loyal bishop, I had been ordered to read a letter in public to my ward membership, which actually denied what another letter from the same member of The Twelve Apostles had instructed all us bishops to do—in private. We were being told that we were "in a, literal, war" against "all those who would change the standing of all women" in our democracy. Our religious duty was to fight against the E.R.A. because "women would be tempted into lesbianism."

It had been in that context—in which I had seen some old letters in the L.D.S. Archives—that, I'd recently been pained to my core. The comments in the archived documents from the first three decades of the twentieth century, to me, seemed to reveal a different consciousness than I'd been exposed to in the Mormon community. Yet, the *attitudes* revealed by them, did provide a certain rational *connectedness* to arcane and divergent issues, which I had noticed in many other hidden documents in the L.D.S. Church Archives, and throughout my earlier life's previous experience.

I could not deny that, although they did seem to add some historical clarity to many other old, confusing, written statements, those archived documents had filled me with a tremendous rage. I had agonized over their content because they had used a language that seemed to indicate a hidden admiration –by men whom I had been raised to see as being holy prophets– of the Nazi doctrine of Arian, racial supremacy.[iii] Needless to say, the language used in them was completely unfamiliar to my Latino way to perceive, from an old *Californio* heritage. The written words of these older men –especially those from the 1930s– were clearly manifesting the ugly consciousness of racism. In the context of the times in which I first read them, in the 1970s when the Quorum of The Twelve Apostles led most of the Christian church in America against the E.R.A., I thought of how my daughters would be impacted. My sensibilities of equity and human rights were being powerfully challenged.

In those few seconds, as I stared down from that twenty-second floor balcony, I became aware of a very old sensation. It was the same feeling that I had known when—as a mere fifteen year old—I had first experienced a conflict between what had been said on a political issue by a man whom I believed was a holy prophet. It was that same familiar emotional sensation that Mrs. White, my high school journalism teacher, had patiently guided me through decades earlier. Suddenly, all I could feel was the hot, blasting air, slapping my face and then, I turned back toward Brother Bishop.

By now, he was a darkened silhouette of the tall figure of a man with a mane of wind-swept hair, that stared at me. Pointing to one of the chairs on the balcony, he said, "pull up a chair, Tony."

As I sat down...

He also took a seat facing me. "Tony, it's time you learned one of the deep secrets of Mormonism." That is when Brother Bishop related a story that was extremely difficult for me to believe.

But, as he spoke, I kept reminding myself that the history of The Church had been clouded many times in the past with doctrines and theologies deemed too sacred for us to reveal them to any prospective converts or, even to some new members. I kept saying to myself that, what Brother Bishop was explaining could easily be one of those secret Mormon teachings.

Maybe, I thought to myself, what he's talking about is like the difference between the Mormon doctrine of a Heavenly Father and a Heavenly Mother and the false ideas about godhood we'd been taught that, the mainstream Christian churches espouse. Or, maybe, this stuff was like the hidden knowledge that, we Mormons had that, The Lord is a *heterosexually active* and "exalted, immortal man," who lives in outer space, near to a planet that, our scriptures call "Kolob." Or, like the truth that, the Heavenly Father—like Jesus— also, has a resurrected body of flesh and bones. I kept reminding myself that, what once seemed bizarre in Mormon Doctrine was, actually, Mormonism's true *genius*.

As he laid it out for me, some of the many bits and pieces of the teachings of the earliest apostles of the Quorum of The Twelve of the Mormon Church became clear. Some of the earlier Utah leaders had said things in their sermons and writings that openly spoke of a "chosen" or, a select genealogical line—a "*royal*" line." Evidently, it had sometimes been referred to as the, "sealing line" in 19th century records. Many archived comments that had before seemed utterly ridiculous to me, when I had first encountered them in researching other things in the L.D.S. Church Archives, were now making sense.

Where I had before seen only innuendo, Brother Bishop was now filling in what had been previously only hollow spaces. On this Santiago balcony, he was fleshing-out an arcane apostolic rhetoric that, I had been discovering over the past few years in the L.D.S. Church Archives in Salt Lake City. The earliest apostles of The Church had spoken passionately about their belief that each of them had all descended from a single, common ancestor. Brother Bishop was laying out the entire story of the famous John Lathrop family for me. I was to learn another of my faith's, *inner fold's* "secret" tales...

He told of old Mary and Martha of Jesus' day, in the first century, c.e. According to the old story, these two women were, actually, two of the plural wives of Jesus. I'd later read how Brigham Young and others had taught this story as gospel truth. Now, Brother Bishop rehearsed it all out for me. Evidently, all the families related to the modern Twelve Apostles, still hold a belief in this story, as a true doctrine that must not be openly taught, except to their family —to *The Family*.

He went on relating to me that according to the legend: Mary, Martha and other women bore children fathered by Jesus, Himself. That, a pure-bred genealogy of the direct descendants of Heavenly Father, through the Firstborn Son –Jesus– exists now through an Anglo-Saxon tribe native to the British Isles, and they had immigrated to the United States as converts to Mormonism in the 19th century. He continued saying that: all the children, were raised by the two women with the help of Joseph of Aramethea (whom some had taught was the same character known to us as Merlin, a magician of Arthurian legends). Supposedly, he had helped them—the family of Jesus—to escape the persecutions from men seeking to take dominance over the growing early Christian Church after the demise of Jesus' first Twelve Apostles. It seems that: Living among the rest of the early Christians had become too dangerous, for those in whose veins flows the blood of the God of Eternity. They had become refugees in a distant land purely for their safety; because of a power struggle between the hierarchically-oriented bishops and the far more charismatically gifted women of the first Christian community of the first century, c.e.

When I first encountered these strange tales during my research in the archives, I had chosen to see these arcane stories as evidence of a culturally ethno-centric, 19th century social mentality's effort to make sense of the transitional processes that Eisler has, since then, termed a "cultural transformation." I had, before, been in the presence of several of the General Authorities and their families when I was traveling with them, and it was natural for me to hear the family stories some of them will tell. However, I never assigned the meaning of truth to them, because I had never heard them taught by a Church Authority over a pulpit, or in a Temple. Never.

Then, the ugliness of the old legend was revealed in his final comment to me: "Tony," he said, "members of The Quorum of The Twelve Apostles of our church really do believe they are all the, literal, ruling descendants of Jesus. That's why only those who descend from that 'royal' line' can become 'lawful' members of their quorum. It is the Quorum of The Twelve, that rules. This, my friend, provides them with the God-given right to rule the planet. Their's is the 'Divine right of kings,' don't you see!" With that, he waited for some response from me.

Yes, I thought to myself, here is the grand justification. Here is the *earthly* purpose of the coronation rituals I had learned about, when I officiated in ceremonies held only in the Mormon Temples. Here is the purpose of what British subjects would call "commoners" receiving all the washing and anointing rites of a royal coronation. Here was the peculiar belief behind the Mormon Temple Endowment and Sealings, which made common folk into "kings and queens." I'd been a sealer in these most sacred of rites, and finally, I had heard a hidden theology, which could be the real hidden foundation of them all...

Interrupting my thoughts, he began again, "Tony, this is why genealogical research is so important to these men. The reason why our Mormon genealogical research was established, in the first place, was to ensure *a pure royal line* to lead us. Do you see now? Didn't your recent research tell us at the Church Offices that the Utah Genealogical Society didn't even exist as a function of our people until 1895 after they had stopped all that bizarre sealing stuff? They needed the genealogies of the people in order to know who was in which line! How else would they be able to claim to be the future kings of the planet? They had to find a way for them to maintain a pure *royal* bloodline. How else would they be able to keep good men out of their quorum, like George Lee..." With that, his voice cracked. Brother Bishop suddenly turned away and, he looked out.

"This is too weird for words," was all I said. Then, "you mean to tell me, The Church is ruled by uh...an...an oligarchy? You mean to say that there's a privileged part of our faith community who consider themselves genetically 'superior' to all other people on earth?" With those words, the ugly significance of his story hit my deepest core. I felt the inner rush of blood. My heart began beating in hard rhythm with the bellowing wind that encircled us both. I went on, "A...uh...a European family—a tribe, a clan that considers themselves *supreme* over all..." I couldn't finish the sentence. But, mentally, it ended with *..races; for, ultimately, that's what clans are?*

Silent now, Brother Bishop turned back around slowly, and he looked at me with only a slight smile on his face.

I couldn't read him. I couldn't tell what that smile meant. "Why are you telling me this? Why am I hearing about all this now? Why haven't I heard any of it told so clearly before tonight? And, why am I getting so angry about..."

"Alright, Tony," he interrupted, "here it all is now: I am your new supervisor at work. Right?"

I just nodded.

"Tony, I have access to your entire personnel file at the Church Offices."

I began to feel a sickening sensation inside of me, and the sting of perspiration became much sharper, like it always does when my inner emotions are somehow being forced. That was when I wondered to myself, "What's in my file?"

"A file on an employee at Church Offices has everything there is to know about you, and it's kept by Church Security. I've seen your file and, Tony, it's pretty thick. I can only surmise from that fact, that some people have been watching you for a long, long time. I'd say, even from your youth; when you were in high school."

"What's the meaning of that? I mean, what does the fact that we all have personnel profiles and bios written on us by Church Security or, whomever, have to do with what you just talked to me about?"

"Oh, come on, Tony," he responded, "I know that you've been employed in the personnel function, and human resources management–*you* tell me."

Putting it that way, this information could only mean one thing. "Someone's been grooming me?" I flashed a score of the experiences in my life that were probably in my file, and then I added, "okay, so what? Why are you telling me this now; and why here, where nobody related to any of this can hear us?"

"Oh, it's all just on my mind. That's all," he said as he got up from his chair. "George Lee is really out of his element. You understand."

"No," I said quickly, "I don't understand. What do you mean?"

"Come on, Tony," he snapped, walking back into the hotel room, "what does ol' George Lee –an Indian guy who was born on a Navajo reservation– have in common with any of the other General Authorities of the priesthood of The Church? All other G.A.s came out of higher education and business. All the others had life careers, in which they learned how to function within an institutional setting like we have at the Church Offices in Salt Lake City. How does a Navajo man relate with all those corporate-wise academics in the highest councils of The Church? How does a *red man* relate with the 'royal descendants of the King of Ki…'" His voice seemed to choke and then, he quickened his step as he went into the bathroom, closing the door behind him.

So, I was left alone in the darkened night. Even though I had followed him back into the hotel room, when he went into the bathroom, I returned to the balcony. I had to think more on what he had said to me. I sat out alone on that balcony several hours after that experience. It bothered me to question my spiritual leaders in Salt Lake City. But, that's exactly what I was doing…

Our work schedule the following morning had us going in two different directions. We weren't scheduled to meet up again until the trip back home. So, I was left hanging.

By the time he and I saw each other again, it was late in the evening and we both had to get some needed sleep because of the schedule we had set up for our final meetings the next day. I asked him to explain further a couple of times but, each time, his answers were too vague and too general for me to get any more information out of him.

Even though Brother Bishop never allowed us to talk about the subject again, the entire conversation we'd had that night on that balcony kept repeating itself over and over again in my conscious mind for the next several weeks. The entire Mormon mythological tapestry was now beginning to unravel right before me. I was now wondering if any of it was true. *Any* of it!

A white supremacist oligarchy? That phrase had lodged itself profoundly in my being. I felt the dark and heavy cloak of a thick guilt weighing down on me. This kind of questioning is never tolerated in the institutional church. I knew that, I was experiencing a major—no, it was *huge*—a *mega* personal life change that was more, a metamorphosis, because my sense of guilt made no difference to my usual purist way of seeing reality. I was becoming almost numb to all my usual emotions. I, literally, seemed to watch myself from time to time, as if I were, actually, out of my body. Yet, I kept pulling on the thin theological threads of the tapestry that make up the mythological maze of generally accepted Mormon Doctrine. The more I engaged in observing my own experience of experiencing Mormonism, the more additional threads seemed to hang out of theological tapestries for me to see all too well...

A week after returning home from that fateful 1970s trip to South America, my wife and I decided to shop for a new home in an upscale neighborhood east of downtown Salt Lake City. Our goal was to get a larger place for our now growing family. One of the consequences of my having had that long, eye-opening conversation with Brother Bishop on that balcony in Santiago, Chile, was a scene that I know my wife did not and would not understand. She had not experienced what I had, on that fateful assignment with those good local leaders in Peru...

Our family practice, in house hunting, was to visit the local ward meetinghouse where we would be attending church services, should we decide to get a place in the area. On one occasion, when we were taking a tour of a meetinghouse, we walked into the chapel and, that's when it happened...

Spontaneously, she said, "Oh, my Tony, how beautiful!"

But, I totally lost it. As we walked into the large chapel of that ward meetinghouse, I flashed the regional meeting with the "poorer members of The Church" in Peru from my last visit to South America—their Peruvian chapel had had no carpeting at all! Seeing myself, as if I was still doing that simultaneous translation for that extremely insensitive field representative from the Church Building Committee, I could see him clearly. I also saw the local Indian leader who'd had a noble dialogue with us in such a majestic, though totally unassuming, dignified presence. I suddenly felt dizzy. It felt like it was getting hard to breathe. Then...

Suddenly, out of nowhere, Laura was helping me stand up. I had, evidently, lost my balance and she'd helped me avoid a fall.

Later, in retrospect, she told me that it was probably the thick, sumptuous carpeted floor of that Salt Lake City chapel, with its thick, huge, purple velvet theatre drapes that covered the lavishly decorated stained glass windows.

Evidently, when I'd looked up and seen all the gold leaf in the trimming of that high ceiling, I'd turned to my wife and said, "all I see is obscene vanity; all I see is the obtuse opulence of a people who see themselves as superior to all other saints. This room is disgusting to me. This place is not holy to me." Then, with my arms stretched out wide, I added, "I couldn't *ever* worship in such a costly, corrupting, conspicuous and gaudy place. I know too much about how poorly our fellow saints live in South America. We're becoming like how some Mormons say 'gold-loving Catholics' are! Look!" I commanded, "We also 'adorn' our churches too much!"

Her mouth had now begun to drop open in obvious surprise at how I'd responded.

I quickly took hold of her hand, and after regaining my sense of balance, I rushed us both out into the parking lot without saying another word.

Out in the church parking lot, her only words to me were, "I don't understand you, Tony. Since you've come back from South America, you're so angry. Why are you so angry?"

Once, I tried to explain it to her but, unfortunately, she was too much a product of the society in which we lived. "Oh, is *that* all that's bothering you," she'd responded. "Don't you remember that when we first got married years ago, I showed you my genealogical pedigree chart? Don't you remember that my mother's ancestor, Henrietta Janes Black had been sealed to the Prophet Joseph Smith as one of his plural wives in eternity by Wilford Woodruff who, at the time of the sealing, was the fourth President of The Church?"

"What do you mean?" I then, asked her.

"Well, Tony, if all you're concerned about is that old doctrine about our apostles all being descendants of the Sealing Line that flows directly from Jesus Christ through the women who had His children then, don't worry."

"Don't worry?" My question had been more about her naïve way of understanding an arcane theology than about her logical response. "What do you think that I'm all stressed about here?"

My words had caught her off guard, "Tony, like I've said to you: I don't understand why you're so angry lately. That doctrine about the John Lathrop Family is not a problem for you. Don't you see, Cutie, I descend from that same genealogical line! *You* are a part of The Family too! Tony, you have married into the Royal Line of Jesus' descendants too! Brother Bishop didn't know that my own grandmother was a sealed wife of Joseph Smith, Junior, *himself,* and *that* makes me, you and our children members of that same fami…"

"I want absolutely nothing to do with any of those stupid old stories, Laura!" I'd interrupted. "What's more," I'd gone on, "I don't see how you can be so…so…so unfeeling about what a doctrine like that does to everything that we've been raised to understand as the imperatives of 'being equal in all things.' Don't you see that such ideas are at the root of all the ugliness that's been part of our life since your own parents came after me with a gun when they found out that you'd gotten engaged to a man with a Spanish surname?"[iv] I saw that she could not understand because she'd not seen what I'd seen nor, had she heard the words that I'd heard from Brother Bishop.

When we had first met, as students at BYU, we were both highly committed to the more openly stated (as well as to the other much more privately kept) doctrines and values of our Utah based community. For example: Any new prospective converts to The Church were not taught about our basic cosmology of an Afterlife when they begin to receive the "standardized lessons" from our missionaries. Those "meatier" doctrines are far too different from traditional Christianity for us to teach to newly found prospective members. If we were to do so then, most mainstream Christian people would reject any further teaching by us because those ideas on the Afterlife are not clearly taught in the Bible. But sadly, my work had exposed me to realities, which neither of us were prepared to deal with. The result was that, my personal experience in the experience was causing a major crisis of ideology in me. But, unfortunately, she had not changed as I had now changed, and she would not change.

****

So, which is the *actual* mythology of Mormonism? Had former generations that had believed in their racial supremacy, influenced our present day church policies toward all ethnicities and races that are not of our *"royal"* genealogical line? Those were my constant two questions in following months and then, in the years to come. Ironically, within only a few weeks—in my capacity as an ordained local bishop—I had been thrown into a hot dialogue with my fellow local bishops in our Sandy, Utah stake about the construction of our new ward meetinghouse.

When I saw that the stake president was not open to our chapel having a new pipe organ—when we had been offered full payment for a new one by one of our devout members—I wondered how our church's policies were being managed. For example: Why had our stake chosen our stake president's father's land over another piece for the new chapel? *What other thing* might be mismanaged for *his* personal financial gain? This stake president had recently challenged my personal ethics so, I now mentally challenged his!

As the months turned into the years described in the stories that follow in this book's subsequent chapters, eventually, I was "disfellowshipped" for my "apostasy." After we'd moved I had told the new bishop, when he'd come by, asking why we were "getting a divorce": "That's none of your business. What's more, you are not welcome, and I don't acknowledge your perceived authority to even ask that question of me."

After six months, our new local high council held what is now officially called a disciplinary council, and the decision was to officially excommunicate me from their circles. Over the years, as I've observed the continuing Mormon involvement in American, and in international political arenas, as it is with anyone that has been victimized by a similar institutional seduction, in retrospect, I see that I was actually a victim of cultural rape. I say "cultural," because it was my ethnicity that was taken from me. For, if a thing is ethnic then, it is about one's social culture.

My life began as an ethnic Roman Catholic, and later, in my high school years, I'd later learned, beginning with my wrenching experience with the young man [whom I've herein called Terry] that I am a Queer man. My choice to reject that man, whom, I now know was the first person for whom I had any true sexual attraction, was based solely on my perceived need to comply with what was a culture foreign to my nature. For, as will be told, my true nature was that of a Queer, "two-spirit man."

Yes, it was my choice *at the time that it presented itself.* But, as Lewiki is quoted in another chapter as having written; that choice was "post-decisional." It was not *my* choice, but rather it was a choice that had been previously, *placed* into my psyche through the imprinting, which I had received in the L.D.S. socialization that I had experienced in a highly controlled puritanical setting.

I know now, however, because of the experiences, which I relate in the following chapters, that my true human nature is to love another man. In what we call hindsight, I can see clearly that my love for other men comes naturally to me; while, sexual involvement with women is something at which I have to work hard to attain. My *natural* culture –my unique, Queer nature– was all taken from me through the violation of my intimate essence. And, that penetrative violation of who and what I *intimately* am came about through an institutional seduction, which was perpetrated by a society that was external to my own nativity.

Moreover, the deeply mystical ethnic earth culture of my ancestors was also taken from me; especially that culture which my strong-willed, maternal Grandma Nica had demonstrated, and so majestically, to my child's eyes as a little boy. I've often wondered, what wonderful truths might I have learned from that great woman that I was not open to because I'd been taught by well-intentioned Mormon people –like the man I'd called the Science Man– that her church was "The Church of The Devil." All her keen insight was taken from me because my heart was closed to it by the invasive teaching of men who saw themselves as "supreme" over all.

Signifying the danger in all of this, is how the ordained and the laity have been trained to refer to each other among themselves in the traditionally conservative, "Bible based," institutional church. In the scripture, the laity only merit's the titles of "children of Israel" or the "daughters of Israel" or, on a few times, the "sons of Israel." After the way I had experienced that giant of personal dignity in the person of that humble Indian church leader in Peru, my sense today is that Infinite Divine Intelligence would have translated it in quite a different way. But, as is often stated in this book; hindsight usually is clearer than most present ways of seeing.

Eventually, I realized that in these societies, even today, mere members are always seen as children, and therefore, they are socialized to only be children to "mother" church, which is now dominated by pseudo, "fathers." The creation of a pseudo-parental relationship with individual, sovereign human souls does grant an overwhelming power to all those who stand in the place of Deity, especially in the eyes of all those domesticated as *their* children. However, this categorizing of all women and, others considered "non-men," is not the only danger, which results from seeing the world only from a rigidly patriarchal perspective. There are some critical human dangers, of a more immediate or practical nature.

One such danger was manifest to me in a rather poignant way: There was a time when I highly esteemed patriarchal notions, and it was in those days when I first saw myself as I truly was. Indeed, my highest official position in the L.D.S. community was that of representing the most senior patriarch over that entire church –the Prophet/President– when I stood, officiating at the marriage altars in the holiest chambers of the L.D.S. Temple. There was a day when I was the very epitome of the L.D.S. ideal of their patriarchal priesthood but, because of how I have experienced the experience, today, I can see that there are mortal dangers ahead for anyone, such as I was. Those mortal dangers have their ugly root in our common inherited cultural propensities that are heavily weighted by religious hierarchies on the side of patriarchy...

****

What later came to be called in the 1970's national media news reports, the "Teton flood disaster,"[v] became a case in point in which I was intimately involved. This was my first awareness that our ways are out of balance. It was when I first realized that we Americans are too heavily weighted in our mainstream worldview on the side of the male principle.

It was in 1975, when I was personally confronted with the real dangers of seeing the world only through a myopic male vision. I was then, employed as a headquarters coordinator of economic services at the Church Offices in Salt Lake City, Utah. The Teton flood in Idaho was my first assigned work in disaster response. One of my official duties involved the co-ordination of our institution's communications response in disaster relief operations. (Mormons have always tried to understand how to best deal with massive numbers of people in situations requiring survival in post-disaster conditions.) It is part of their past best work as well as part of their 19th century characteristic of preparedness for the inevitable. Large numbers of people are the life-blood of the organization and, in their early days, Mormons were forced by their neighbors to evacuate entire cities. Its institutional survival depends on The Church's able management of the total relocation of its vast human resources.

When the Teton Dam in the State of Idaho broke and then, flooded an entire geographic area that was populated by members of our church, I was placed in the middle of numerous meetings in what was then called a *Church Situation Room*. At exactly eight o'clock in the morning, I found myself among the generals of our response team. I say, "generals," because –like with any military– we, there, made system wide decisions to respond to an emergency threatening our human resources, and we did it in a military fashion.

It was the term, "situation room" that I was exposed to then for the first time that, seemed to anchor itself deep in the shadows of my potent, subconscious mind. As the experience of providing emergency assistance continued over the period of the next several days and weeks, this use of traditional military language began to burn a fire deep within my soul. I had the definite sense of being part of a staff of general level officers overseeing what was obviously a military-like operation.

It was the third day of hectic and emotionally charged meetings that, our man on the scene had put the key question to us. Significantly, because of our history, our church's disaster relief effort was far more sophisticated than any government responses. Our man on the scene had finally come back to the headquarters staff with feedback on how our disaster relief preparations had proved to function in the highly critical first sixty hours of the disaster.

There were well over thirty of us men crowded in that modest conference room, and *no women*. In fact, our entire team had no women on it. Of course, we regularly met with the women's auxiliary (with the Relief Society General Board) to give them our direction, but they were not involved in our system wide executive sessions during our disaster response. I had already noticed in my brief time employed there that, the women who headed the women's auxiliary were never involved.

Strategy was what we –only men– dealt with in the Church Situation Room. Our discussions in this room were always flavored with a bit of "military flair," and *that* demanded that no women were present. This experience, in fact, was a mere year or two before the American L.D.S. community openly involved itself in the public battle against the Equal Rights Amendment. It was the week when, one day, a member of the First Presidency at the time happened to encounter me in an elevator and inquired about how that entire matter made me feel. I recall having said, "I look at it in a similar way that I consider our work here at the Church Offices; I see us here, in this building, as being the world bureaucratic headquarters of the, eventual, 'Millennial government of God,' when He returns to Earth." These had been very busy, even "heady," days for us.

He stood up in front of this room of excited men who all had contributed in some way to the distribution of relief to the Idaho saints affected in the disaster. "Brethren," he began, "what do you guess were the two items that were most needed by the flood's refugees who had been suddenly driven from their homes in the early pre-dawn hours of the flood?"

Being a relatively, recent hire, I kept quiet in the back of the Situation Room and looked around at the other men. As I observed what was happening, the thought hit me that all but two of us were married with children.

None of the other men seemed to know. They were each looking at each other, as if trying to discern what the others were thinking.

Realizing that I was no different than any of the others in this, I wondered to myself, what it was that they could have forgotten in their preparations for this moment? I knew that the Situation Room was mostly occupied by men who had worked for decades in The Church's global disaster relief operations. My inner curiosity intensified on what items could actually have been overlooked in their much praised management of our disaster preparedness. The provisions warehoused in our vast bishop's storehouses *had* to have been sufficient; yet, this latest report was telling us otherwise.

Silence.

I kept looking around the room. Each of the men at the table still seemed perplexed, simply looking at each other, and openly shrugging their shoulders to each other.

I was surprised at their inability to even guess what, might have, been forgotten. Were they as equally ill prepared as I was? Most of these men were veterans of other earlier disaster response efforts. Surely, I thought, they hadn't forgotten *important* things!

The brother presenting the data stood in front of us all, quietly staring at each one of us.

After what seemed an entire minute of silence, one brother said, "We've all searched in our minds to guess what the two things you say we've forgotten are but, honestly, if these men can't figure it out then, you're going to have to tell us. You know you have in this room, several decades of experience in these matters. So, what are the two items of supplies that were left out? It's time to tell us."

Then, the man standing at the front finally answered his own question, after taking in a deep breath: "Brethren, the only two items that we did not have in any of our huge shipments of relief supplies from our church storehouses right here in Salt Lake and in Ogden," he said very slowly, "were one; disposable diapers, and two; female sanitary napkins."

Some of the men actually laughed out loud. Others just let their mouths fall open.

I thought to myself, they *actually* think it's funny!

The brother continued answering questions.

My own thoughts reverted back to the fact that there were no women in the room. I thought of the sisters I'd met who work at our auxiliary organization for women, the Relief Society. I recalled being impressed with their soulful and heart-centered energy. That's when I thought to myself about what I'd just heard: *Such is the result of an institutional vision that does not include the perspective of its women.*

Afterward, I discussed the surprising answer with several of my co-workers. The old timers reacted with guarded humor. Those who were more my peers in the department –like me– were shocked at the oversight. After lunch that day, I made a mental note to record this scene in my journal when I got home from work.

Hours later, my wife came into my private study where I was recording the events of the day. "How was your day, cutie?"

"Oh, you wouldn't believe it," I responded.

"Try me."

I did, and she didn't seem to understand my concerns at all. She just said, "Oh Tony, don't be so hard on the men…" She went on to say to me, "…you know, Tony, sometimes you seem really critical of people who are just trying to do their best. You need to be more charitable."

With that, I realized how extremely different our views were, in actuality. I decided that night to be more careful about how I spoke—even to her—about the discoveries I was making at work.

****

Over the years, as I've pondered that experience, I've always come to the same, and difficult conclusion: *The personal truly is political* because the political arena is the only place where our current social constructs define humans as being equal, and my personal life journey has consistently reflected current issues in our collective society. For example: I sat waiting for an archivist in 1998 to finish his telephone conversation in his office at, *El Pueblo de La Reina de Los Angeles* Historical Monument. It was one of those moments, when a book *called out* to me. It was Neal Harlow's great work, California Conquered *The Annexation of a Mexican Province 1846-1850.* Since he'd be a minute, I got up and opened up his office copy, because of a sense that I should peruse it. Thumbing through it nonchalantly, my heart skipped a beat because, at the bottom of one page, it read: "Fremont's battalion moved to the Feliz adobe north of..."[vi] This account was *personal*—about my family!

Suddenly, I remembered Dad's final oral history—given to me just days before he had passed on—in which he confirmed old stories about how our Feliz ancestor had been "tricked" into signing away lands we'd owned to the occupying military men, thinking he was signing "receipts for back taxes."[vii] This was only a few years before early 21st century hostilities between Israelis and Palestinians over land that both claim were "God-given" to *their* ancestors. The parallel to our Feliz family's case was striking to me. *Don* Jose Vicente Feliz was granted Rancho Los Feliz by the Spanish monarch under the "divine right of kings", and to Utah based Mormons, God had given America *our* Feliz lands—through America's 19th century "Manifest Destiny." As a result of that reading, I was *driven* to write four essays for the City of Los Angeles, addressing urban violence.

Luckily, America is a complex civilization that includes not only the traits, which contribute to our present illness but, America is slowly beginning to acknowledge those, traits which contribute to our wellness. A full awareness of our present condition is also being aware of healthier ways of being which, are all also our inherited mythological essence. I now see that, because of being dominated by America's religious patriarchs—"America's own Taliban"—our cultural mentors have usually classified feminine ways as: Weak, wasteful, radical, liberal, and if not totally non-productive, counter-productive. Utah based Mormon sacred stories are filled with the, "*one mighty and strong*" or those who, "*wield the sword of justice in defense of truth and virtue.*" But, my call has now evolved into a charge to a higher wisdom; to use all sacred stories *as a context* from which we transcend older interpretations.

Becoming aware of our present condition –at least, if we human sojourners remain on the same way– will result in a sufficient change within all our souls to empower us to impact an increased balancing of truth and, thus, cancel out evil. The lesson I learned on the personal level is, if you want to change the world then, *change yourself*. Cancel out the evil that is within you, *first*. Then, once *you* have been transformed, the rest is relatively easy. But, in order to know how to do this, when we've all inherited other ways of inter-relating; a new way of envisioning needs to be modeled to us. Eventually, I learned that —much like we do harm to one another— conversely, we also often heal each other by how we model behavior to each other. For, in my own personal experience, it has been my blessing to be surrounded by many true saints.

Again, I encourage the reader to hold off judgment until you are able to consider all the relevant data, which I endeavor to offer herein. I affirm that the key of transformation exists in the power of One. I am saying that, if the reader wants to change the world then, the ability to actually do so —to truly change the world— indeed, already exists within the reader. Awareness is but the first step on the way of becoming open souls. The rest of the process involves an entirely different way for us to experience the experience of life because the traditional ways are what brought us all to the ugly condition that created the Columbine High School massacre. For, the undeniable truth is that those trench-coated young men at the ill-fated Columbine High School in Littleton, Colorado, did not live in a vacuum anymore than *Osama bin Laden's* network of terrorists live in a vacuum. None of us do....

NOTES TO CHAPTER FIVE

[i] This is a theological polemic in that, although the Mormon Temple ceremony depicts "..the Telestial World…" as being "…the world in which we now live;" in the official canon of the Mormon Church; L.D.S. Doctrine and Covenants, Section 76; "…the glory of the telestial…" is the final Afterlife of "These…" whom verse 84 says, "…are they who are thrust down to hell."

[ii] When this book went to press, this man was the President of the entire Mormon Church and, as such, presides over all Mormons, worldwide.

[iii] See The Mormon Hierarchy, *Extensions of Power* by D. Michael Quinn (Signature Books, Salt Lake City, UT) Appendix. Some of these letters between President J. Rueben Clarke Jr. and high officers of Nazi Germany's government in the 1930s have since been published and written about in this work by Quinn, the most widely read historian of Utah Mormon history.

[iv] This experience is told in my first book, Out of The Bishop's Closet.

[v] This is in reference to the 1975 flood that was created by the failure of the Teton Dam in southeastern Idaho, which destroyed millions of acres of crops and private dwellings largely owned by members of The Church of Jesus Christ of Latter-day Saints. The November 17th "Special Thanksgiving Issue" of the Salt Lake Tribune reported it as the, "Teton Flood Disaster."

[vi] California Conquered, *The Annexation of a Mexican Province 1846-1850* (University of California Press, Berkeley, California 1982) p. 231.

[vii] "*19th Century American Mormons Verses 19th Century Californios: A Parallel To Current Conflicts Between Israelis And Palestinians*;" A Paper by Antonio A. Feliz; 2002 Peace Colloquy (November 9, 2002, the Temple of Community of Christ; Independence, MO). "I had written for the City of Los Angeles, Department of Recreation & Parks, about the murder of my great-grandfather as well as the murder of his own great-grandfather by the occupying 19th century Protestant and Mormon beneficiaries of the conquest of California. I named the rut of religious resentment that had led to violent retribution for past injustices as, 'the root of urban gang related murders', and as the reason violence would 'rise in Los Angeles.'" Characteristic of my candid manner, answering questions afterward, I had warned 'a rise in urban gang homicides will befall Los Angeles' because causes of the revenge sought 'by youth'who feel they have a just cause are not yet being addressed." [Later, in 2003, the new Los Angeles Police Chief declared Los Angeles is "…now, the murder capital of America…"].

"I knew that this was a moment of destiny. It was one of those times in my life when answers gushed out for me to see like I'd never before been able to distinguish. Mom even let me set up the old reel-to-reel tape recorder so that Dad's old Los Feliz story could be accurately recorded for our little family. If he had taught me anything, it was the importance of truth telling..."

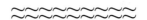

CHAPTER SIX

ACKNOWLEDGING THE RAPE

Let us remember: Modern terrorism hasn't only happened because of "those" terrorists from outside of America's borders. It has also happened in Oklahoma City and in Littleton, Colorado. It hit California's Santana High School much like at Columbine High School in Littleton, Colorado, and school terror visited less diverse towns like Peduckah, Kentucky. Because of mass communications technologies, we all had to bear the ugliness resulting of our hatred in violence, heretofore, not seen in those polite places. The wasteful horror, which we all saw, all around us, is a social polarization of our society. It began prior to September 11, 2001, as if to preface terror: What was, repeatedly, violently manifest to us in our living rooms before Muslim extremists did *their* terror was, in effect, a warning; a cosmic signal to each of us. Sadly, we had expected such violence in our metropolitan areas because of our history of racism. Most of us didn't read the *signals*, most were shocked to hear of the carnage of middle and upper middle class prepubescent and adolescent peers in prayer, by America's "nice boys" in our otherwise quiet, suburbs.

It's time to read the signals! Terror has come from outside of us. We have been told that the usual causes of suburban violence are not the same as what's causing other massacres on American soil. But, my journey's observations had consistently taught me that those less-expected explosions of anger are the last, shaking death rattle of our old, dying paradigms. From where I've been led to see our sick condition; we are today, in one of those pivotal, historical moments in time when, our human Mass Mind is shifting its paradigm at alarming rates! My sense is that, *that shifting* is the common factor in all of these upheavals. A massive shift in human worldviews, in my eyes, is at the heart of relatively recent, "nice boy" acts of terror.

Yet, experts tell us that our urban violence is rooted in a distant past of slavery and class warfare, and we're told that foreign terrorists—conversely—are "religious zealots." The experts tell us that, the violent occurrences of "nice boys" killing their peers in prayer in small towns "have nothing to do with religious training." They say that, "these" acts are about how some youth "fall through the cracks." My experience of the experience, however, has taught me that –while urban violence manifests on-going social struggles of our under-classes for equitable treatment– suburban violence is manifesting, *other*, now unavoidable, pubescent social reactions of our human mass personality. Violence is a natural response of boys, justice-centered boys—*and* of justice-centered religious zealots — who are, more keenly aware than before, of being over-powered by the bullying forces of brutality that they perceive all around them.

In America, our pubescent children are more aware than are many adults. Pubescent boys see far clearer from their natural focus -on-justice place of reckoning than, the rest of us usually do, who are in America's mainstream culture and society—that is, *if those boys have not yet bought into inherited, adult illusions of our mainstream civilization's brand of justice.* This has always been the case. As a result of my past experience in the experience, my sense is that we are in the same place that, Ghandi was when he told the British that the British colonizers had already lost, and that they—the colonizing British—should simply get out of his native India. But, unaware of his awareness, the British prematurely laughed at Ghandi. Clarity on what is the actual reality, as Ghandi knew, is the psychic place from where troubled adolescents, and those who study our collective behavior envision. That view is more objective than, the vision from where they reckon, who impose the bullying on other Ghandi types.

From the Ghandian *open* perspective, any that empathize can also see that we have collectively planned our trip, we have all paid our fare. We have already boarded, and we are on our way now, unable to get off the cosmic train. Now, only our ways of responding to the forces, which we will all encounter, have the power to throw us off the tracks, which now take us to our species' destination. After Ghandi was brutally assassinated, this is unfortunately what also happened to his dream for a united and multi-cultural India. My warning is that, it may so be with us; *unless we become more aware than we are today of the safeguards that are built into the cosmic train* on which, we all now collectively journey. Acknowledging our violated condition contains our hope to now avoid what is ahead, because of the reasons revealed below. It was 1996...

****

Fourteen years had finally passed since my ecclesiastical peers had excommunicated me from the institutional church because I could not acknowledge their authority anymore as, the law of my life. So, traveling on the Amtrak train, between Los Angeles and Salt Lake City, little did I know that I had now arrived at a defining moment in my life. The Universe *punctuated* what had happened...

Naturally, the Universe blessed me by including a man in the synchronicity, a personified omen in my phenomenology. He shared my coach seat today, on the aisle side, this youthful man from Europe. A recently graduated university law student on holiday, touring America after finishing an academic career in Berlin, he had come to tour the United States prior to beginning his employment career as an attorney, somewhere in Germany.

We'd both enjoyed an energetic conversation on differences that appeared to exist between our two nations. Our conversation, had begun somewhere in the vast, inland, dry California/Nevada desert so, our talking on that day, was one of those few, wonderfully soulful, and intensely connected conversations between two total strangers who had just met each other on a train.

I was taking great pleasure in our verbal engagement. It was stimulating to me to honestly express my personal joy over the newly unified Germany to a German national. I was telling him how I had been filled with joyous emotion when I'd seen the Berlin Wall taken down by his compatriots through our television newscasts. "But," I'd added, "my personal experience, here in my own country, is that now we Americans, have become more like the old Nazi Germany was, than we had been here decades earlier in my life."

His mouth began to open.

I went on, "I speak about our repressive ways."

"What do you mean?"

"Well," I said, "there was a time when I never left my home without wearing a business suit and a long tie. Then, with the help of *Meshica* Indians, I discovered the need for me to be more nature-centered in my personal way of experiencing the experience of life. Becoming more nature-centered than I had been, created a transition in my outlook; the kind of attitude change that will impact anyone's personal appearance. It decides how one dresses themselves—what they clothe with—and, or whether one is what others consider fully dressed. Persons, in nature centered societies, clothe their bodies for different reasons than in ours. Assigned meanings *speak out by how*

Indians clothe their physical bodies. For example, in some societies braids may indicate social status.

My companion simply nodded, showing he had followed what I tried to explain.

"Well," I continued, "after changing how I appear on the outside, relative to the rest of the world—because I had learned a different set of values than, mainstream society teaches—strange things began to happen to me that had never happened before."

"What kind of things?"

"When I am a pedestrian—waiting for a traffic signal to change from red to green—and a car comes up to the intersection close to where I stand, the people in it, now, usually lock their doors. I can actually hear the door locks engage. Sometimes, I can even see the little door locks clamp down! They actually fear me! Some motorists fear what I must seem to them to be, and it's too obvious, for me to not be keenly aware of their fear of me."

"What do you think causes such fear?"

"Well, I don't really know for sure," I answered, "but, the only differences about me from before, when this way of being was not my normal experience, are: My facial hair, My hair length, My more casual attire, and the fact that I'm not in a car, myself. So, I can only attribute what has begun to happen to specific appearance factors.

"I understand," he said.

"Since making these few lifestyle changes in my own way of experiencing the experience of living, I have actually been arrested in Los Angeles in the past few years on four separate occasions. In all four cases: I was held overnight, but no charges were made, and *I had done nothing wrong.* I'm convinced that it was just because of my longer hair, my facial hair, and the fact that I no longer conform to mainstream norms of dress. In Los Angeles, this is often called, 'D.W.B.'—'Driving While Black—or, Brown.'

"I've been freed from the consumer's imprisoned ways of being. Our culture is driven by our commercial mass media so much so, that what people wear is determined –not by them– but, by what they are told is good for them by television infomercials and other commercial advertising. I sometimes have the sense that ours is a society of a brainwashed and media-drugged viewing public. We are socialized by advertisements."

"In a way, I'm surprised," my neighbor responded, "it is more like my older conformist East Germany than America, or even like the long-ago days of the fearful Nazi Gestapo. You describe people being fearful of you because of your dress and your ways..."

As we continued our conversation, my friend from Germany told me he had appreciated my sharing in his own society's accomplishments in inclusive politics. What had made my comments so intriguing to him, was the contrast of my personal experience against the much-lauded "freedom" of our 20th century American democracy.

That is the point in our conversation when I, specifically, asked him how he had found my nation to be in comparison to his homeland. But, before he could finish beginning his response, the synchronicity happened...

We had been approaching the half-hour stop-over in Las Vegas in the last part of our talk. While he was responding to my last question, I listened to his evaluation, but my right peripheral vision distracted me away from what he was saying. Off to his right, about two seats forward from where he and I sat, I saw the first of two men in the aisle walking toward us. They had, evidently just boarded the train, and my first thought was that they were two new passengers joining us on our journey northward.

The first man was very attractive to me. He appeared to be in his late twenties, or in his early thirties. He was very blond, had beautiful teeth and a pristine complexion. As he got closer, I saw that his eyes were the bluest ones that I could remember ever having seen in another man. I even wondered to myself if he wore colored contacts. Then, I realized he had stopped and that he was staring directly at me.

I experienced his look as a penetrating scan. My person was actually impaled by a wave of palpable energy. The usual sting hit my armpits. To my left, I became aware of my German friend's open mouth dropping even more. For a split second, the most erotic rush powerfully undulated through the trunk of my body. Was his look, *sexual*?

The blond man put his hairy forearm on the back of the seat in front of us and, as he leaned in toward my face, I could see the muscular cuts of his toned neck. "Do you have baggage up on these racks?" His voice was deep, and his articulation was extremely firm in its tone. Commanding. Gym-pumped, developed biceps and big triceps bulged out of his short sleeves.

Stunned, I answered simply, "uh, yes, I do."

"Are you carrying *contraband*?" Then, very harshly, he commanded; "Open your bags now, and show us your contraband."

I thought to myself, what's *that attitude* about? Through my nervous laughter, I said, "uh, you're not joking. Are you?" Now, I could see the second man more clearly, and suddenly, I felt a burning rage churning deep, inside my gut so, I added, "Why are you asking me this question? Who are you, anyway?" My heat increasing, I added, "why should I show anything?" That's when it happened. The increasing turbulence that was building up inside of me had now created an enraging, disgusting image in my mind...

A totally different scene flashed: I experienced myself as if in a movie about Nazi Germany. For an instant, the two men were dressed in military uniforms the blue-gray uniform of 20th century Nazi soldiers. My traveling companion to my left and I were clothed in 1930s attire. Suddenly, a strong electric bolt surged through me from head to foot. I blinked and then, again the sting in my armpits brought me back to the present.

That's weird, I thought to myself.

Suddenly, those two men were, again, as they were before. With *that* second flash, however, I understood what it was that had caused, whoever these men were, to single me out for investigation. "And," I went on, "why didn't you ask this question of anybody you encountered on this train *before* you came to where *I am* seated?"

The second man had now come directly in front of me by standing in the vacant seat area, directly in front of me. With a dark, rounded face, he seemed to be African-American. Holding out his business card, he said, "Hello, sir. I'm detective..."

Police! Suddenly, my mind became a speedway. These guys are cops! They think I'm some kind of criminal. I knew it was fear that I was feeling. What's happening here? I thought to myself, what's going on? I looked up, directly into both of their eyes...

The first man was speaking, "...and I am a detective also. We're with the Nevada State Police. We have reason to believe that you carry contraband with you into Utah. Our job is to stop it from getting there."

But, I thought to myself, I'm not...carrying anything... *illegal*. What's their reason? With that awareness, I retorted, "What *is it*? Are you following some *profile*? Isn't *that* illegal? I mean, is it my *long hair*? My *facial hair*, maybe? My fury had reached my face, I felt hot.

That's when the second man inserted, "No need to get upset, here." Then, pointing to a medallion I wore hanging from my neck, he asked, "Are you a priest without a collar?"

Instinctively, I reached for the medallion with my right hand and answered back, "yes, I am ordained."

"A priest without a collar," he said with conviction.

With that, the rage within me became an indignant force. I closed my eyes, and taking in a deep breath, I seemed to see the first man clearly. Again, he was dressed in the blue-grey uniform of a Nazi soldier. Opening my eyes, I exhaled out, "it's a violation of my rights as an American citizen for you to single me out only because of how I wear my hair or how I dress, or my skin color..." I took in another deep breath. "Tell me," I demanded, "is *that* the one basis of your decision to ask that invasive question of me without asking it of others seated ahead of me? Well, is it?" I heard a certain, indignant tone in my voice and, I felt my right eyebrow reach upward in a show of personal disgust—wrinkling my right forehead and temple.

The first officer's face had become extremely red, in anger. He leaned away from us now, and then he stepped back into the aisle.

The second man was smiling, "we'll be on our way, now. We're sorry to have bothered you, Sir. You see Sir, there is a lot of smuggling going on in this corridor between Los Angeles and Salt Lake City. Las Vegas is a natural place for us to try to detect anyone who might be transporting fire arms illegally." Putting on the old, familiar, political face of "a person of authority, trying to reassure," he added, "you understand." Then, making a little salute, he ended with, "excuse our interruption, and have a pleasant trip, now."

With that, they both simply walked away with the conductor (whom I hadn't noticed before) following after them.

I felt myself exhaling.

My traveling European friend still had his mouth only half way open. He kept staring at me. In my right periphery vision, the conductor seemed like, a still picture of a man walking away.

That's when I realized that, now, everything seemed to be happening in slow motion. It felt to me like, I simply sat there, silent and staring at my German neighbor's stammered expression.

Seconds seemed to expand into minutes to me. I guess it was the teacher in me that formed the next words I finally spoke out loud, "Well, do you see how much times have changed in our world? Do you see why I've said that we are, now, in a similar circumstance that existed for the Jews and others different from their mainstream society in Nazi Germany? The Holocaust began with us, Queers!"

My neighbor's mouth was wide open.

I felt the energy surge of my awareness confirm the truth of my observation and added, "The tyranny which you just witnessed exists in America today because we have not yet learned the lessons we should have learned from Hitler's old, ugly Germany." Again, the electric rush swept throughout my body.

"My God!" he exclaimed, as even his breathing became more pressed, "it was like out of an old movie about the Nazis, and yet, this is America!"

As the new passengers began to board our train car and searched for their seats, I tried to calm myself down. The other passengers around us, who had also been witnesses to what had taken place, began to hum with their own talk about what had just happened.

The hard throbbing in my chest told me that my heart was pounding, as if I'd just ended thirty minutes on the Lifecycle at the gym. I thought of Maya Angelo's comment on the Oprah Winfrey Show the other day, when she had said, "women" who are going through menopause "should understand" that what they are feeling "…are not hot flashes but, power surges!" With that choice, by me to surrender to the comic irony in my life's realities, I felt the beads of perspiration on my forehead, and I thought quietly to myself—hmm, power surges, huh?—as I laughed out loud!

Unaware of the private comedy that created my laughter, my German friend asked, "are you okay?" "May I get you some water?" Without waiting for my response, he quickly got up and went toward the water dispenser.

Alone now, I stared out the window to my left and breathed deeply. The hot desert in the distance appeared to be so uninviting of our modern human civilization. Massive warehouse facilities in the foreground, just across the tracks, seemed to radiate the heat waves that were visible through the window next to me.

What struck me most about the moment, was the barrenness of everything immediately around the train. Although the concrete and steel buildings, surrounded by stockpiles of wood crates being moved by a man driving a forklift, were loud statements about the healthy life of a vibrant local commerce, my sense was that I was in the midst of a vast wasteland. The only sign of life in my vision lay beyond all the constructed world, far away in nature's desert. Both literally and metaphorically, I became all too aware that I was in the "lone and dreary world" of the murals which I'd been exposed to when I officiated in the Mormon Temple Ceremonies in their temple on Santa Monica Boulevard in West Los Angeles, California.

There was nothing growing on the earth all around us. It seemed that we, who were traversing the hot desert in our train, were the apparent sole reason for this city's existence. The concrete, the asphalt, the bricks and the mortar—all around—seemed to be a non-living penetration of toxicity into an, otherwise, naturally healthy, vibrant ecosystem. But, I must admit that, *that* thought was merely my surface mind exploring the present.

There was a strong undercurrent of thoughts that pulled at me from much deeper, that were questions I've kept secret until now: What was it about that first police officer that engaged such an erotic surge of sexual energy inside of me? I flashed back to his physical beauty. How is it that, that man—who was the very source of my real sense of unjust victimization—was also to me, simultaneously, an equal source of a far deeper awareness of an unexplored sexual fantasy? Why did his mere presence invoke a mental flash, in me, as if I had been instantaneously plugged into a kind of virtual reality? Was it his blond hair? Or, was it his gym-toned body? Maybe, it was his deep blue eyes? Or, maybe, it was that he was an intrusive authority figure? Did the experience give me a glimpse into some sexual kink that was so bizarre to me that, I had never before wanted to even explore it? I would be confronted by this paradox on sex, often, over the ensuing years, but it would be a long time before I'd assign a hard meaning to all these comparable circumstances I have encountered of; young, tall, lean, blond, blue-eyed, hairy *and also* smooth-skinned personifications of virile manhood.

****

In the years since the above definitive moment in my life, I have now come to empathize with us all. I understand that, I've also played the intruder's role. I'm able to see that, actually, we all violate the human dignity of any person that we do not see as conforming to our own customary notions of behavioral purity. It does not matter whether those notions have to do with how we dress, or with how we wear hair, or how much facial hair we grow, or whether we engage sexually with another in ways, still unsanctioned by citizen peers.

I have come to be aware that, the demands by those among us who classify only some of us as being "truly civilized," infect us all with an illness. I now see that, such classifications, *themselves*, are a signal. They all signal a warning of our diseased body politic. Irrespective of how dependent all scientific or, academic research is on classifications and on comparisons, the classifying of souls is objectifying, what *are not objects*. Serious anthropologists work at building boundaries and systems to ensure against their violation of the mass soul of all societies they study. Yet, their *act* of classifying human beings –whether they are individuals, or groups– is, on some primal levels, inhumane because it violates the human dignity of the native self-awareness of the, given, sovereign soul-group. I also see that the 21st century's communications technology has insured that this invasive plague will continue to infect us with pre-programmed responses, unless a critical mass quickly evolves the rest of us into a more open way of inter-relating with one another.

Political campaigns are another manifestation of this same problem, which many see. From my days in college, as campaign manager of a good friend who ran for V.P. of Student Relations, to days in San Francisco, going door to door for favorite candidates, to working precinct polls in southern California, I have seen all these classifications that we use, first-hand. They are constructed on our tribal-like differences. I've often noted that our humanity senses the inhumanity of how our political system is; yet, we remain unaware of a more balanced view because this way of being is so much a part of our inherited civilization. I lost count of the African-Americans who came to vote, only to find they'd been listed on "green sheets" as "convicted felons" when they hadn't ever, even been arrested! Just as we commonly do with our commercial infested mass media, we simply accept the pollsters and the political use of data bases, as if we were totally unaware of the penetrative damage being done to our human dignity by the very, classifications *themselves*.

What my traveling friend and I encountered on that train stop in Las Vegas, Nevada was only a symptom, a manifestation of today's inter-cultural diseases. Before I'd chosen to live much more like my *Meshica* friends, I'd never experienced *open* repression. Through other experiences related herein, I'll try to show that –even though we do not consciously believe in the older ways of thinking, in today's more enlightened age– we are, nonetheless, not immune to all of the social illnesses caused by the older worldviews. These ills have been passed on to all of us by the earlier generations of any of us. It is as if the soul's equivalent of our Mass Mind's "genetic code" passes on a propensity to older, tribal ways to our soulful selves.

I can now, see clearly that, what enables today's mainstream society's incapacity to mask the foul stench of our ugly condition is the contagious agent, which enables the infection of us all, as if with a fatal disease. As it is with any infection, there is an incubation period, in which the sickness is masked by a lack of clear symptoms. However, even when symptoms appear –as in what I perceive is our present, violent condition– we often mistake the symptoms as being indicative of factors that are, *themselves,* only symptomatic. Then, we become aware of a symptom, and thus, diagnose the illness, only to then, merely treat the Mass Mind's symptomatic response to the actual infection. Like Western medicine has traditionally been, on a cultural –and therefore, on a political– level, historically, we treat only what we can see, instead of working on eradicating the, actual, disease, or the root cause of the symptom that is readily apparent.

Eventually, I came to understand that, what I experienced in a handsome man –whose true reason for interrogating me was only about maintaining our orderly society– was a symptom inside of me of a sense of separateness, and in me, it was of endemic proportions. I was far too quick to judge his merely civic purposes. It was only in many years of retrospection that I came to see that my emotional response to him was based in the many years of social domestication experienced by me much earlier in my life's journey.

I was first exposed to male Germanic blond types in life in my hometown of Anaheim, California because, while our family's ancestors owned the territory due east of it,[i] the town of Anaheim, California was established in the 1850s, when the Americans first took over. When our family had moved away from Grandma Nica's home, Mom often told us stories about the cross burning that had taken place in our neighbor's front yard. But then, as a small child, I knew that I could not comprehend the horror of Mom's experience.

Now, I see much clearer. The way in which I'd experienced the 1950's experience of Orange County's Germanic community, had in forgotten ways, programmed my adult responses. A psychologist once suggested to me that, maybe my, usually, "automatic sexual responses to Nordic types' physical features" results from "earliest personal awarenesses of my otherness, relative to them" that, I had "assigned an attitude of mystery to them," because of a "perception of being separate from them." His opinion felt far too Freudian to me; but, I had to admit that my seemingly automatic sexual response was *intense*, an automatic sexual response to men, I perceived as my extreme opposites. I had seen the beautiful blond officer, who only wanted to decipher whether I was doing something illegal or not, as totally *other*. My psychologist said that my reaction was a lot like heterosexual men, who are prone to respond to women whom they see as their opposite. But, *that* was a comment I didn't understand.

Could that have been why I was so taken by Buster Crab as the then, Flash Gordon character in those early days of television? Whatever it was, it was definitely *primal*. I, eventually, concluded that, to one degree or another, we're all in desperate need of a healing from our personal racism, our classism and our sexism, including our heterosexism and yes—for *this* politically active Queer man— my own homosexism. For, the truth is, I found that these prejudices flow both ways. In fact since that realization, I've been somewhat astonished when, in the company of only Queer folk like myself, I've heard their derogatory label for heterosexuals: "*breeders.*"

****

In January of 1978, I'd been informed by the three presiding high priests of our local Mormon stake about my call as the new bishop of our local ward. But, my wife and I had been asked to keep it to ourselves until one of them could officially present my name in our ward Sunday evening service. Mormons prize their adherence to egalitarian ideals of a community voting to accept or reject what is proposed by men whom they believe are prophets endowed with apostolic authority direct from the ancient Peter, James and John. Our modern "peter, james and john" had written our local stake presidency a letter about my call as the spiritual leader of our new neighborhood. I'd been given a premonition about the assignment even before Laura and I had signed our papers with the developer, just a few months ago." I knew that we faced a future of rich inter-relating with the people living in our new neighborhood. With that, we both realized that we'd soon have little time to travel to see my ailing father.

Dad had suffered a heart attack two years earlier, and in recent weeks, his health had been failing rapidly. We'd decided to follow-up our little family's last Christmas holiday visit with an orchestration of field assignments so that –at least– I could be in southern California in the weeks after the 1978 New Year had begun. It was the first of February, and my work schedule for the next week had me busy within two hours of Dad's bedside. On February 6th, I was in Colton, California. Before putting the receiver down in one of my field manager's offices, the woman's voice on the telephone had said to me: "Mr. Feliz, I'm sorry to inform you that your father expired at 9:05 this morning."

After calling my wife and my office in Salt Lake City, Utah, I excused myself from my field visit collogues at our, L.D.S. employment center, east of Los Angeles. So, later, driving north of Bakersfield on California state highway 65, en route to the old town where Terry and I'd both grown up, I had one of those blessed bits of nostalgia that rarely comes along on life's hectic journey. Not only had Terry gone on, but now, Dad had also passed on through his own transition. As I drove on, I wondered; when will that same, terrible pain come? When will the pain that I'd known when I first knew that *Terry* had killed himself come, about *Dad's death*? When will that absolute loss of the part of me that *Terry* occupied invade my soul over *Dad*? That question repeated itself over, and over again, as I drove along that cold, frozen, stretch of black pavement.

Yet, as I looked out at the, brown and barren rolling hills past the Oildale road sign, there was no sensation in my solar plexus.

There was nothing that I'd felt so powerfully when I'd read that letter from Mom about Terry back when I was a, rather naïve, nineteen-year-old Mormon missionary in far away Peru—as I reported in Chapter One. It had rained the night before. Now, the sun was thawing everything. I noticed the wet scenery on both sides of that two-way highway had begun to change from the rolling hills of grapevines into apricot, peach and orange groves, I realized my thoughts had gone to my last day with Dad…

After Mom had helped him with his morning routine, she had told me to go into their bedroom because "he needs to talk with you, *Mijo*." He, indeed, had needed to get some stuff off of his chest. He'd been suffering and he'd had some difficulty breathing, as he spoke…

"This is a picture of my grandmother, *Isabela Guerena, viuda de Feliz.* You already know that she was the wife of the first Antonio Feliz." After coughing, he went on, "as you can see, she was very young when this old picture was taken. My father told me that it was taken in San Diego, California, where her husband had been buried." After drinking some water, he went on, "He was put in the old *Campo Santo* (cemetery) down there because of her great faith in the Catholic Church. All the nuns and priests knew her."

He seemed to speak with such an attitude of openness to our ancestral history in the Catholic tradition. I'd often wondered how he'd really felt about the Mormon Church because I'd often seen him offer a graveside prayer for his Catholic friends in somewhat of a shocking emotional response because he would cross himself in the Catholic way of praying. Did Dad really believe in our church, in the way I'd grown to know about its power and glory? I'd always wanted to ask but, instead, I just listened this time too…

"I want to tell you about the history that you may not know." A cough came, as he held out the old black and white portrait of a white woman in a black dress, with a Spanish mantilla, and long black hair flowing below her waist. "Take it, Antonio. It's yours."

Taking it, I listened carefully. Naturally, I'd had the sense, because of his state of health, that this had to be very important…

"Since I've gotten active in The Church again, I've never told you or your sister a story that I have carried in my heart," he said, with his left forefinger pointing toward his chest. "These are things from our family's past, Antonio. I have not felt that they were important anymore. But, now Antonio…" Coughing interrupted his story. *"Escuchame,"* (Listen to me) he said,.firmly; "You also carry the name of her martyred husband, and you must know how he really died. He was shot –execution style, by a firing squad of vigilantes– executed like common criminals die. It happened at *La Rumurosa*, near the border."

Executed? I asked, "Why?" I was taken by surprise. I had heard something about our lands being taken away from us when the American armies had invaded what was then, *Alta California* right after Mexico gained its initial independence but, now, I was hearing that my great-grandfather—whose namesake, I am—had...had been ...killed by a band of vigilantes? I asked myself, again, *why*?

"Antonio, your mother said she has told you about it. Didn't you know?"

"I knew about the old Los Feliz Rancho down in the old Los Angeles Pueblo being taken from us, and a little about the old Yorba and Peralta lands down in Orange County being taken from us by the Americans but..."

"You need to hear all the truth from me. I am your father. I have carried his name all my life, just as you do. My father told me what happened, and he heard it from his own grandmother, Josefa Peralta. They were both people of high honor and integrity. And, along with *Los Yorba*, Josefa Peralta was an heir to Rancho Santiago de Santa Ana. But, *los gringos* did not allow the women to own land in those days so, the invading army occupied it when they took over California, even with women still living there, because all our men had left the ranchos, and hid in the mountains, fearing for their life."

"But Dad," I asked, "why did those vigilantes kill...execute your grandfather? Tia Teresa told me that he was an 'importer.'"

"They wanted our lands, and our businesses. *La Rumurosa* is by the border, east of San Diego. He was trying to escape them. Some in the family say that he was a scoundrel. But, my father told me that he knew better. Now, although your grandfather did secretly have a second family, it was a different time. He was an honest man of much integrity. He would not lie about *these* things, Antonio." He said, "the man whose first name we all have had, was shot by men who took the law into their hands. They were called 'vigilantes' but, they were..."—his coughing, again, interrupted—"...no more than cutthroat, lawless murderers. The vigilantes hated us, *Californios* because they wanted our Los Feliz properties.

"We, Los Feliz, owned the land that they had invaded so, we were all sought out by them, more than all the others. We were shot whenever they could find us. In those days, *los gringos* hated the Catholic religion, and that was their social excuse to kill us. What they really wanted was to take over lands and enterprises, which we had as a family. It was more about a lust for our possessions than their hatred of anything else, Antonio. Religion was only the social excuse for their murder. That is how your grandfather told of it."

I'd been educated at BYU. I knew the Mormon account of the American invasion of California, in part, by the 1846 to 1850 Mormon Battalion. But, all the things that I'd encountered in the L.D.S. Church Archives at work recently about their belief in the racial supremacy of their ruling family—which I'd first read two years earlier—came rushing into my mind. Because of that personal research, now, I was beginning to believe that the full story had not been told in any of the history books. So I asked, "Did the Mormons in the invading American army have some part in this? Is that what you're getting at, Dad?"

Since his first heart attack, two years ago, Dad had been serving the local ward bishop as his ward clerk—essentially, as a minister's record keeper. He answered, "I have been watching the bishop closely. I have seen that all of the men who lead the ward are good men. They pay much in tithings to God. Antonio, they are not responsible for the ugly past. *Pero Mijo,* (But, my son) you carry his name, and you have the right to know how your people were treated.

"For example: In the 1940s and 1950s, I had to spend a lot of money to prove that I am, Antonio Feliz. Those were the ugly days of the Zoot Suite Riots up in Los Angeles, *Mijo.* The Immigration Department tried to deport me; they deported a lot of us in those days, without even listening to us. All of my cousins, who had also lived here in *Alta* California long before any Americans came, were forced to join the family south of *La Linea.* That's how they ended up in Tijuana, Antonio! But, Mormon missionaries helped me to prove our *Californio* genealogy; first to the federal and then, to the Los Angeles County authorities. That's how you and your sister got to stay in California, while your cousins were raised in Ensenada, in Mexico. With the help from the missionaries, Antonio, your future was secured on this side of *La Linea.* So, don't be angry with the members of The Church. Their ancestors did the wrong, not them."

We took a break at that point because Dad needed to rest. But, after a while, he called me back to his bedside. After spending some time alone in Mom's garden, the heavy portent of that day had sunk itself into my core. I knew that this was a moment of destiny. It was one of those times in my life when answers gushed out for me to see like I'd never before been able to distinguish. Mom even let me set up the old reel-to-reel tape recorder so that Dad's old story could be accurately recorded for our little family. If he had taught me newspaper, and he was a local Spanish radio celebrity. His story *had* to be written, somehow.

This time, however, Dad was cautionary. "These things about our Feliz family are not for your wife's ears, Antonio. She would not be able to understand."

I understood and nodded. Turning off the tape recorder, I said, "Her ancestors could easily have been in the occupying forces that took over our lands. One of her father's ancestors was a member of what was known as the Mormon Battalion."

"Yes, but, you need to know the truth…one day all of this might be important to Joseph, Rafael and their sisters for some, yet, unknown reason. I *do* know that you named your first daughter in honor of Manuel Celestino Feliz, Josefa Peralta's husband. I also know that you named your first born son, Antonio –may his soul be blessed– in honor of the first Antonio Feliz." That's when the only smile came over Dad's face that day. "When you were just a school boy, you already had an interest in your ancestors. We had joined The Church! That's why I did not speak of these things to you when you were growing up. It is a shame that your firstborn died so early! But, now, your family has been replenished, no?" That was the only time Dad had spoken of our deceased firstborn…

Approaching Porterville now, my wandering mind came back to the present, as I drove. I wondered if my memory of Mom and Grandma Nica being filled with fear when the first missionaries came knocking at our front door was because of all the terror that the U.S. Immigration Service had forced on my parents about Dad being deported. It *was* about the time that Dad had said they were trying to erroneously deport him—in the late 1940s. Or, was their fear about those cross burnings? Then, how will Mom be? What will she do *now*? I had to prepare myself for her grief. So, instead of driving right to her little house, I turned the car, and went eastward –toward the Porterville cemetery– to seek some soul strength…

I reverently crouched by Terry's headstone. I thought about the things I had recently experienced in my work. Then, I kneeled down to get more comfortable. The L.D.S. Church Archives had become opened to my view, and now, were proving to be filled with so much verbiage that abound in hatred and in early 20th century white supremacy that, the sweeter tones in the old documents were quickly becoming hidden to me.

On that open, brown, grass-covered foothill of the Sierra Nevada Mountains east of where I'd grown up, I thought of Dad's version of the Mormon involvement in our Feliz family's tragedy with the 19th century Mormon Battalion. I looked up at the large hill east of Terry's grave.

I recalled how it had been covered with bright orange California poppies when we'd gone to that place in our youthful need to get away from our adult church leaders. The entire hillside facing the cemetery that long-ago day, had had a bright orange luminance. Our local church members had been so judgmental about him! Huge tears welled up in my eyes—tears for Terry—then, the bitter floodgates within broke open and on to my cheeks, hands and thighs, and I wailed wildly! Bitterly!

Slowly, I cleaned away the dry brown grass from Terry's granite headstone. Large teardrops fell down, wetting it. That was the first time that I knew that I couldn't deny my powerful, *natural* affection for Terry. I thought of my little family in Utah. The undeniable truth of my sense of loss had overwhelmed me. I don't know how long it was before I stopped weeping alone there, at Terry's grave. All I knew was: I'd lost a man whom I knew, *I still loved in a way that I'd never loved anyone else before*! *Never*!

Eventually, wiping the tears away, I wondered, what else will I discover about our 19th century Los Feliz family's Mormon/ Catholic and about other American/Mexican entanglements? How will I address *that* experience with my children? With those mental questions, my mind flashed back to the ugly scene on that high-rise balcony in Santiago, Chile a year earlier with Brother Bishop, when he had told me that all our Salt Lake City, Utah Mormon Apostles were actually all relatives; *all cousins in a large, extended family*![iii]

That memory was too much. So, getting up, and walking back to my car, I felt myself cringe at the thought of that fateful day in South America. The beginning of my future distresses loomed from out of my past –and out of my future– into that single moment of the juxtaposition of my life's lessons. I had to control myself. Mom was the important person right now...

Difficult days passed, filled with rain, memories, and Mom.

I was giving the main eulogy before hundreds of mourners at one of Dad's two funeral services. We'd, actually, had to organize two separate services, other than at the graveside, because so many wanted to pay their respects; one at the local L.D.S. meetinghouse, and one for the hundreds who went to another service at the funeral home. "Today," I began, "we celebrate the life of Antonio Feliz, who was the son of Antonio Feliz; who was the son of Jose Antonio Feliz; who was shot by vigilantes at *La Rumurosa*; who was, in turn, the male heir of Manuel Celestino Feliz, a *Californio* Judge in 1850 when California became an American State; who was the son of *don* Josef Tomas Feliz, the man who built the adobe that, sheltered the signing of the Treaty *of El Campo de Cahuenga* with the occupying American forces; who was the son of *don* Jose Francisco Feliz—the last recognized heir to *Rancho Los Feliz*—the same Feliz *don* who was also murdered by smallpox infested blankets that were given to him by the occupying army; when he was the surviving son of *don* Jose Vicente Feliz, the first *Comisionado* and founder of *El Pueblo de la Reina de Los Angeles*. We're the generations of Antonio Feliz."

Two weeks later, as we laid Dad's coffin in what had, by then, become a rain-soaked earth—just over the wet scene before my eyes—I saw that we were only yards away from Terry's grave. That's when I noticed that I had not wept a single tear at Dad's passing, and I wondered, *why not?* I wouldn't know the answer to that, until the day when I'd have to say another eulogy.

But, in the years between both of the eulogies, my personal life changes had made themselves undeniably manifest: By then, I had lived and loved with the small band of *Meshica* warrior/priests and their six families on the beach south of Tijuana, Mexico for three amazing months in 1990. Knowing them had changed my way of perceiving myself, in relationship with other people, and with all of the life forms in my world, including the very planet, Herself. Because of how I had experienced the experience of their simple, loving example, my own experience of the experience of life was forever altered. Where before, the contradictory institutionalized mythologies of my world had each produced rational theologies; now, the undeniable truth –what *is* or, the phenomenology of my journey– had nothing to do anymore with doctrine, dogma, tradition or theology. Through my experience of the experiences, I'd *finally* realized before the second eulogy, that I had unwittingly omitted any *women* from my recitation of Dad's genealogy, a few years ago.

As I elsewhere tell it, my move to the San Diego/*Baja* area had largely been so that I could live within a couple hours of Mom's place, northeast of San Diego on the California side of the line. But, a good friend had invited me to San Francisco with the intent of hunting for a flat with him to share in the city. So, I was in the San Francisco Amtrak lobby by the Ferry Building in San Francisco when it hit me. It was one of those *inner* premonitions I had learned to recognize long before that day, by the familiar sensation in my solar plexus…

As I waited in line, to ask a question at the counter, I sensed that familiar feeling in my solar plexus engage a surge of energy in my entire upper body. I had that old familiar sense of a vibrational radiation of energy –a magnetic force– extend itself, and penetrate my person in a palpable way. I don't know how I knew, but *I knew* I had to talk to Mom.

So, I left the line and used a public telephone to call her at her home. After waiting at that public telephone in the lobby for someone to answer, with no success, I called my friend in the city and I canceled my visit in the Bay Area. Knowing that something was wrong, I got back in line at the ticket counter. I got back in line to return back to southern California. Something was not right. Something was not right, at all!

When our train finally arrived at Union Station in Los Angeles the following day, I telephoned Mom's home again. This time, Henry –Mom's friend– was there, and he told me that Mom was in the local hospital. Evidently, she'd been diagnosed with pancreatic cancer and was being kept as comfortable as possible. He was beside himself, and he told me that Mom had been asking for me. The inevitable distress was suddenly horribly obvious to me. No wonder, I thought to myself; that's why I'd had the premonition to get myself back down here! I saw that my best ally in the world was too close for comfort to moving on to another place.

Mom had been in the hospital for three days now. The medical team had been keeping what they called "unavoidable" at bay but, when I arrived, all the people I spoke with "knew" that she was "in her final mortal moments." As I pushed the large corridor doors open, rushing to Mom's bedside, I saw her there surrounded by my sister, Maria, a nurse and Maria's two daughters.

Agitated, Maria said walking up to me, "Tony, where were you? We've all been trying to locate you! Nobody here knew where you were…"

After calming her down a little, I went over to Mom.

Everyone else simply left us alone.

"*Mijo*," she said softly, "you're going to lose me. I'm going on now." She didn't say, "…I'm going on now" first but, "*you're* going to lose me" in absolute conviction. Unlike Mom's usual way, she'd said those words as if there was no other way.

But, I thought to myself, there's *always* another way! Why is she resigned to die? I know she can be healed but… My heart was in confusion because all my experience told me that she could be healed. After all, I'd experienced many miraculous healings in my life. I knew that this sad scene did not have to end with her passing away. Why was she so resigned to have to die? But, because she'd spoken with such finality, I didn't say anything. I knew that she'd be healed only if she was in an emotional place that would let her agree to her healing. But, instead, my greatest ally in the whole world was leaving me!

"I've given everyone else their blessing, *Mijo.* You're the only one who has not yet received my final blessing."

The tears were flowing into my eyes, welling up there, all ready to fall. Three years earlier, I had asked her for a mother's blessing in the same style as Mormon men practiced. By then, I'd come to see that, the women of The Church had every right to bless in this way, as the men bless with their hands. When I'd asked that day for her blessing—by laying her hands on my head in the same way, saying what words came into her mind—I acknowledged to her that –although Mormons did not allow any women this privilege—giving a laying on of hands blessing is her right. "Mom," I said, "don't you remember? You already gave me the best blessing I could ask for when you laid your hands on my head and spoke those words blessing me in your living room years ago." Silently, though, within myself, I knew; if I received her blessing then, she *would* die.

"That is true, *Mijo.* You are the first one who asked me for a mother's blessing, weren't you."

I nodded in silent agreement with her words. Then, after explaining how a sudden premonition had caused me to change my plans and return back to southern California, I asked, "all I need is to know that you will never really leave me alone, Mom."

"*Tu ya lo sabes, Mijo.*" (You already know it, my son).

I could see her resignation. "You're ready, aren't you."

"*Mijo,* my only regret is that my children aren't here to say good-by." Turning her head from one side to the other, as if in pain, she manifested her emotional pain at the absence of her 'children.'

I knew that she was not speaking of either me, or of my sister. She'd always referred to her grandchildren as 'my children.' She was speaking of *my* children, who had all been kept away from her by their mother, who saw both me, *and Mom* as being 'possessed by demons' because we had both rejected the institutional Mormon Church in our later lives.

"But," she went on with a sigh, "I've already received the last rites. What do you think about that, huh?"

Mom's ability to have complete acceptance of what she saw as Divine intent had always moved me. "I'll miss you," I said with a kiss, and that is the last thing I said, before I heard her last words.

Acknowledging The Rape

"Your sister is handling everything, *Mijo*. You won't be alone. You know that, don't you?"

Nodding my head in agreement, I turned and walked out into the hospital lobby, where I met the Catholic priest who had administered the last rites to Mom.

"Your mother," he said, "is a saint. I am blessed to anoint the dying prior to their passing, and I've met many others in your mother's condition. I need to tell you that I am the one who has received from her in that room. I came to bless her, but rather, she is the one who blessed me! You have had a wonderful person as a mother, my son. I will not be the same person from now on because of her example."

"Yes. None of us will be the same anymore because of her," I answered. Of all the people in my family, Mom was the one who was always a model of saintliness to me. During those pain filled days, often, I recalled how—when I was only nine years old—when, we lived in a house that had railroad tracks behind it in Anaheim, California, Mom had, literally, fed countless, "hobos"—homeless men—who roamed those railways. Nobody else in our family had exhibited such charity in my memory.

Two days later, and after a constant river of cousins, uncles and aunts, friends and grandchildren, Mom had mentioned twice again that her "children" were not there for her to say good-by. By the morning of the day she passed through her transition, a sense of anger had lodged itself deep inside of my inner core. I was now, increasingly, angry that the united forces of my Mormon ex-wife, her Mormon bishop, a member of The Church's Seventy in the Salt Lake City hierarchy and one of the L.D.S. Church's legal staff had all combined to keep my children –*Mom's* 'children'– away from *us*. The tragedy was: *My sainted Mom* was dying without seeing them!

I still had the letters in my possession to prove it. All of them had been dated the same day, and those letters from her local Mormon bishop, from the General Authority and the attorney had, actually, each been written on their, respective, official letterhead! It was enragingly obvious that there had been a well-organized, intentional effort meant to disobey the court order of the Superior Court of Los Angeles. The order by the judge had specified that our children "not" be taken "out of the five counties specified." Yet, the proof was there, in my personal files in the form of those four letters. They documented that they –the Mormon hierarchy– had engaged in behavior that left them vulnerable to possible legal action from me. However, I had chosen not to take legal action because I did not want my children to be subjected to the ugliness of litigation. So, I would not see any of my children, innocent of all this, for many years but, *Mom*—sweet, sainted *Mom*—would never again see them on Earth!

Now, as Mom lay on her final bed in the world, the anger over their illegal co-conspiracy, and their tribal-centric behavior increased inside of me with each passing day—as we all waited. The ugly enmity between my Mormon family, and my Catholic family had, now, converged in this, final, tragic outcome. The anger building up inside of me became my darkest rage on the third day, sometime before the noon hour. I knew that, I *had* to do something. I *had* to get away from all the morbid people before I did something we'd all come to regret.

I found myself pacing from one section to another section in the hospital. I went from one floor to another. Eventually, I realized that I had gone by the lobby twice –going nowhere. That's when I realized that I felt like *I had to hide* from my family. My pacing, my wandering though out the hospital eventually stopped. But, I hadn't realized what had happened until after I had noticed: The bloody knuckles on my hands; the tiny specks of blood on the hospital corridor wall; the chips of paint stuck in the drying blood around the open wounds on the broken skin on my hands, and then, I *knew*. I knew that, I had been beating my fists on that concrete wall of the hospital corridor outside of Mom's hospital section! With that awareness, the wetness of my face informed me that I'd also been weeping. Then, feeling the wetness of my shirt, I knew an utter helplessness had totally overwhelmed me.

What finally brought me peace, were Mom's last words. As several of us were standing silent around her bed, holding her hands and touching her gently, Mom softly said—as she looked out into the empty air above her—"I'm going now, I'm going to my mother…"

Those were her last, few words that gave me the peace that, allowed me to eulogize her. Among other things, I said: "Many of you have had your own relationship with her. We're better people because of Aselia Tafolla Acosta, *viuda de Feliz*. I can only speak out of my relationship with her, as a son. I will miss her. She was my best ally. Aselia was one of four surviving daughters of Nicasia Tafolla. Who was a strong-willed, and gifted mid-wife, a *Meshica* healer of her people, who was the daughter of Candelaria Gonzalez, who died minutes after she had received Holy Communion at old St. Boniface Catholic Church in Anaheim, California; who was –in turn– one in a long line of proud *Meshica* women and their French Conquerors. And, now, *Doy gracias por mi madre!*" (I give thanks for my mother!)…

****

Eventually, what became clear to me, is what I needed to know, on the personal level. That was my realization that, *we, as a people*, must finally confront *our* present condition in the same way that I was being forced to face my personal issues about my conflicting cultures. The malodorous condition in which we are ensnared –I'd learned– is the diseased social rotting which results from the violent clashing of closed, bounded and, otherwise, ethnic or, *tribal* worldviews. The common, yet, circumscribed nature of what are still America's separate and distinct cultures was revealing itself to me as a deeply rooted, and personally psychic phenomenon, and I found myself comparing my own family's history with the Mormon community in ways that, I had not considered. I found I no longer valued what I was quickly labeling as purely cultural when it contradicted my evolving Self-Identity.

Over the years this phenomenon manifested itself in unique, and diverse ways. For example, since living with *Meshica* Indians, I no longer value patriarchal attire, especially the phallic, business suite long tie. Now, I always keep my hair cut *below* my shoulders, and my experience in this has made me apprehensive of the motives of our metropolitan peace officers. To my vision, our problem is that we've not yet faced the challenge of the tribal nature of seeing one another only from the perspective permitted from within the parameters of our, respective, bounded or closed social group. But, we all respond from our earliest programming to the affect imagery of how those different from us dress their bodies.

What I've now come to see, is that we have not yet learned to understand one another *as we are,* but instead, we all cling tightly to how we perceive each other is *–as we experience* one another– but, we *only look from within our own closed worldview.* This, I learned, is much like interpreting what the outdoor temperature is, by only the managed temperature, which we each only experience within our air-conditioned buildings. Our Others are not as we perceive them to be *from only within our own limited and closed-off environments.*

But, those perceptions only work from within the various bounded societies, respectively. From within our very diverse but, closed-off worlds, we only experience in previously programmed ways than, from where our collective's more diverse context is able to see. We have all attuned to limited frequencies of understanding that, were programmed into us, many years earlier.

As it was with me on the personal level, we collectively, as a mass personality –as a "civil" body politic– are not yet open souls. Our mass personality has not aligned with our mass spirit. As I had not yet done when Mom went through her transition, our society has not yet risen to America's challenge, and this is the hard work of any culturally diverse national democracy. Unless we do so soon, our beloved America will reap the bitter harvest that awaits any people who practice only an *illusion* of democracy. We each need to face the opportunity afforded all people who experiment on the liberating experience of living in a well-balanced society of diverse cultures, clans, creeds and canon. America is out of balance because America is part of our commonly inherited world civilization. Our problem, in this new century is that, America is the only superpower now and—in terms described earlier—*that* means that, like institutions, America is also about maintaining its place in the modern world. For, a government is also an institution, and exists to preserve *itself*.

The other side of that truth, however, is simply –because we are what we are– the rest of the world will follow our lead, that is: *If we choose an obviously healthier way*. Being the only super power is not bad, in and of itself very much like genealogy *per se* is not evil. Earlier, I referred to Mormon genealogical research, *as Brother Bishop explained it to me*. The point is that, also like being a super power, genealogy is not, *in itself*, a bad thing. Although Mormons may have become genealogists out of an institutionalized historical theology that—I'd discovered—was born of supremacist ideals; if I learned anything as a devout genealogist, it is that if anything does, genealogy teaches that none of us are as distinct, or different from all the rest of us, as "white supremacists" would have us all think.

In my own case, for example, I have had to face the awful truth of my personal genetic and cultural breeding. Exactly as I am a literal convergence of the exploited and the exploiter ancestors, whose DNA make up my own humanness, likewise, we must all collectively find a similar understanding. No matter what heritage we each, individually, are; *we are all* in the same condition as I have discovered about myself. The complication for us today, is the reality of human genetics and modern mass communications. The linking of these two unique factors: Our modern human genetics and today's mass communications no longer allow us the luxury of having the illusion of separateness that fuels fundamentalist ideas of racial, ethnic and cultural purity just because fundamentalist types rank humanity in degrees of acceptance.

Concepts of supremacy –of all *religious* supremacy, for that matter– are, actually, all about *power*. Clearly, America is bullish, and we owe our existence to that way of being in the 20th century

Acknowledging The Rape

world of hostile states. Nevertheless, as we turned into the new millennium, our American superiority, an immense global power that we wield over other people, revealed itself to me as an, actual, *collective weakness.* For, the new twenty-first century world is quickly showing itself to me, far more than it did before, as only one global community—more so than, most of us have ever imagined.

In my high school years, I'd debated over-population in our forums, but none of us participating then ever even touched the idea that familiarity breeds contempt. But, recent years have shown that our mass communications have globalized the effect of our diverse and divergent notions of reality. In other words, irrespective of the reality of war and world hunger, for those who dwell in our planet's modern mega-cities, the complications of human over-population are –in fact– already here. In spite of Earth's vast landmasses, the people are amassing themselves in relatively small geographic areas called, cities. So, 21st century global over-population –I now see– is not about food shortage or, famine.

Over-population is about bad politics. Yet, human over-population is our civilization's greatest moral challenge because harsh notions of superiority are the present civilization's cultural patriarchal context, and as a result, *over-population is actually an issue of our bad management.* But, I see that over-population is only auxiliary to the more basic issue: Having a father-figure's kind of power over others, which, I understand as *"patriolotry.".*

Like my Spanish *conquistador* ancestors, and the later American invaders of their *Alta* California, I learned that—in our modern society—power translates only into power-over others. Yet, ideas of any kind of superiority breed aggressive behavior. So, because of the combination of both over-population and this more primal notion of having *dominion* power over others, our American aggressiveness now looms above this nation—in my inner vision— hovering over us, *as a destructive force,* that is ready to devour beloved America! More importantly, *The Force* that created our species never meant for us to live in such dense circumstances as we now experience. Because of this, blood spilling is expected in our densely populated American urban areas, i.e. in our mega-cities. As previously said, the 1990s bloodletting in non-urban areas indicates a far deeper problem: Our inherited cultural obsession with an aggressive power over others.

But, we can collectively choose to get beyond power over others. On the personal level, I have learned to try another way. It is, therefore, logical to me that we can all choose a better way to go.

We can choose to go beyond our inbred aggressive behavior. Unlike most of us, my experience in the experience taught me that, Paleo-anthropologists—scientists that study the American hemisphere's most ancient societies—tell us, it was aggression that destroyed the ancient civilizations of North America. Hopi oral histories say their ancient ancestral societies were not always aggressive. If that is so, then we can also choose to go a different way than the way which was, evidently, taken by the now extinct *Anasasi*, the *Olmecs* and other ancient cultures, whose also long-gone time of power is obvious to tourists visiting any of their earthly remains. Indeed, it is even now believed that the artifacts and ruins of the *Anasasi* and the ancient *Maya* were constructed to warn us of their fatal social mistakes.[iv]

Yet, secure in the illusion of a 21st century American "civil" or, "democratized" society, we seem unable to be aware enough, to open our vision to a clear wisdom of the Ancients. Ours is still an age where those who can, do violence. Whether we call them "gangs" or "patriots," we live with *our* self-appointed urban insurgents, who have arsenals of automatic and semi-automatic weapons, making war to take back, "their" territory. All our media spin-doctors use other labels besides "gangs," depending on which group is the subject of our mass media news reports. But, if we consider their end result, is there any difference among *any* of them? Sometimes, these groups are called "agents" and at other times they are called "militias." Our metropolitan police—even before September 11, 2001—have been armed with M16 weapons, and are today, increasingly, militarized. Yet, the accepted label for these "peace" officers is SWAT police —now, as this book goes to press—the label is the National Guard.

In short: *In the 1990s, I had discovered that we have been at war with ourselves and we didn't seem to realize it.* Long before September 11, 2001, we were only focused on the past evils done by others to our, respective, racial ethnic and/or, socio-economic group. We today cannot afford to continue to make the same sorry mistakes, which television has allowed us to witness in other less diverse nation states, such as Bosnia, Kosovo, Pakistan, India, East Timor, Liberia and elsewhere. Even after the beautiful unity that all of us experience every time that, America is attacked from beyond our own borders —historically—we, eventually, do revert to our cultural enmities. In truth, both before September 11, 2001 and after, as with those above distant nations, the battlefield is wherever we stand. Now, today, the one difference is that the degree of America's direct combat relative to that of the other global geographical areas has forever changed. Yet, if history is any indicator then—even after today's War On Terrorism is won—we will return to former aggressions because of our inherited cultural bent to assert our massive might over our *others*. The truth is: Our neighborhood circumstance today is no different than others' battle conditions, globally. From the inter-generational passed-on worldview of my *Californio* ancestors, how *they* saw American 19th century Manifest Destiny and how America *behaves globally today*, is the same.

If there is anything being a Feliz son of the dispossessed 18th and 19th century land-owners of Los Angeles and Orange County has taught me, it is that any war is more about cultural domination than, it is about economics. Whether it is happening across the sea, or across the tracks, war is usually waged with economics. But, a war is about ugly, violent, *cultural* invasiveness. Whether we call it other things, war is rarely ever only about the representations of its participants. Historians on the winning side are the only war chroniclers, which we're able to read. My family's unfortunate legacy is an example; for, we were the *Californio* conquerors

In experiencing the experience with the German tourist and the handsome, blond Nevada State police officer, and in some other stories that follow, I learned; our present condition is symptomatic of a hidden disease. The major symptom is a manifest behavior of a deeper problem. For example: I've noticed that anybody, whom we consider as being behaviorally contaminated, we will consistently banish to mainstream's agreed-upon cultural borderlands that lay beyond the imaginary boundaries of what is seen as "real" America. When some tried to deport my father, it was a symptom of a bent toward seeing differences as, "unclean," or as, "untouchable."

We, in effect, quarantine some from others. When we see our others as contaminated, we contain them as if they had an infectious disease, even though our other's behavior actually does no real harm to anyone. What happens is that, by such acts, they challenge our own perceptions of reality. Behavior, *what is*, contradicts our labels. This labeling of peers is the fearful root cause of ugly stuff; like religious excommunication, political incarceration and crimes of hate. Society functions from a place of fear of the unknown. Such is the legacy of our tribal worldviews, and it is manifest in the "pious" verbiage of our political battles in every recent electoral campaign.

Religious prejudices, historically, abound in all of American political rhetoric. But, this is not unique to America. By definition, tribes are families which are held together by their common stories. For example: the great divisions in the Middle East have been heated up over the past century because of this tribal dynamic. Sacred stories define who, "us," is, culturally, and who is, "them." What I call, the Sacred Story Dynamic builds ethnicity in societies and, it is centered in human social classism.

Eventually, the answer came to me out of my own historical research into these issues, and the behavior archetype is none other than, Father Abraham. Historically, I came to see, recently arrived emigrants who wish to assimilate, often do so by covering up their status as best they can. This, I learned, is nothing more than to repeat the old example of father Abraham with regard to his legendary wife, Sarah. According to the story, when Abraham arrived in Pharaoh's court, he lied to Pharaoh, hiding his true spousal relationship with, the legendarily beautiful, Sarah.[vi] This example of the deceit in our mainstream cultural icon of fatherhood is one of many that dominate our world, and all, I believe, are unwittingly, carried into the diverse cultural groups, descendant from that ancient nomadic tribe.

This pattern of obfuscation is as culturally American, in its core, as is the economic classification of nation states as the, "First World" and "Third World," classifications. These are mere inherited ways of seeing, and of being in relationship with one another, and we Americans, are all prone to lie to each other, as a result. We have this bent because we inherited a "civilized" cultural bent to deceive, lie and obfuscate as a personal shield, on the level of the inter-personal.

What I eventually discovered, is that we tend to inter-relate with one another from a context of our inherited tribalism. In that sense, none of us is any different from Afganistan's Taliban: We all believe we are the ones in the right. For example, Mormon doctrine contends that their church is "the only *true* church." In Roman Catholic tradition, theirs is the only line of God's priesthood that is authoritatively held by men on the earth, and so on. The death, demonizing and destruction we have all witnessed all too much of in the ancient lands of both Israel and Palestine –and in our own part of the planet– are a result of this kind of tribalism. This was the root of the horror of the two world wars of the last century, and was also the root of ugly holocausts in America, Europe and Africa.

It is this kind of closed-minded tribalism to which I refer, when I say that all fundamentalist religions feed the deadly plague that I see is currently afflicting our modern American society. Like fundamentalist groups of all kinds, religious fundamentalism will only take America into more, and uglier violence than we have ever experienced, and it is this kind of xenophobic sight that fuels hate crimes of all kinds in our modern society. Xenophobia is merely another term for what I've, here, called tribalism. I'm sure that it is at the root of why Osama Bin Laden said that he objected to Americans being in the Saudi Arabian Peninsula.

Moreover, the mystical culture of my ancestors, especially that which my strong-willed maternal Grandma Nica demonstrated so majestically to my child's eyes as a little boy, was also taken from *me*. I've often wondered, what wonderful truths could I have learned from that great woman, that I was not open to receive from her because I'd been taught by good Mormon people –like the man I'd called the Science Man– that her church was "The Church of The Devil."[vii] All of her keen insight was taken from me because my heart was closed to it by the invasive teachings of old men who see only themselves as being a superior race to all of the other races—men, who, evidently then, secretly believed in the ideas of Arian racial superiority. But that is where I was, however…

Today, my experienced understanding is focused more on our mutual *natureness,* than on my research, or on ideologies. For example, more nature-centered cultures don't esteem aggression, or see it as good, but rather, as a final recourse in self-defense. It is clear to me, from the example of these happier societies than our own, that our bio-ecosystems flourish in mutuality and defy our Euro-centric notions about the survival of the fittest. Because of their excellent example, I now try to focus my vision on being *of* and *in* nature, not on living *off of* nature. Today my work is, largely, demonstrating to others that; the aggressive, competitive behavior within modern society feeds our diseased, classist worldview because of the way the two notions of status and classism often relate.

But, thankfully, the Universe holds no secrets. It never holds anything from us, when we are ready to receive it. Years after my father died, I met an assistant conductor on an Amtrak train, as I traveled from Los Angeles to the Bay Area who taught me this. Her odd greeting was, "You are *surrounded* by death!"

But, her rather strange salutation did not phase me at all because, in my own frame of reference, so many of my loved ones had already passed on to The Other Side. After meeting her, I became a fan of the television show, "Crossing Over With John Edward" because my own deceased loved ones seem to, literally, accompany my writing. Since my becoming a fan of John Edward's television show, I've noticed that my photographs will often have small circles of white light in them around my person, and my photographer friend tells me that film can distinguish different kinds of light energy. So, her greeting was not at all odd to me.

Then, five years later, she greeted me again as I had, again, boarded, yet, another Amtrak in Salt Lake City, then, en route to California saying, "Hey, you're that author!" We both spent some good time on that last trip discussing her giftedness in sensing the energy of the dead that often accompany many of us after they pass, as we go about our lives.

On that last train trip, I told her about my Feliz *Calilfornio* ancestors, and about my recent research in Los Angeles into how they'd both been murdered, acknowledging the cultural rape of my past.

She said, "Truth always finds daylight when *any of us* are ready to see it. Your ancestors must have been helping you all along, from the Other Side, you know. It's probably your new research that, opened up the hidden past to you, and when you're ready for more, it'll come too."

I couldn't help the thought that came into my mind with that last comment she had made: *Truly, The Universe holds no secrets.* Indeed, I had, finally, acknowledged the rape!

NOTES TO CHAPTER SIX

[i] The modern cities of Yorba Linda, East Anaheim, Placentia, and the Anaheim Hills "south to the Mission lands of San Juan Capistrano" once formed part of the Rancho Santiago de Santa Ana that was owned by the Feliz, Peralta and Yorba families. The Feliz family of Los Angeles, who owned the Los Feliz Rancho in modern Los Feliz Village, were forced to vacate the old place by the Mormon Battalion and fled to the land grants that they had to the south in what is today Orange County, California.

[ii] This story is related in my first book, Out of The Bishop's Closet.

[iii] The Mormon Hierarchy, *Extensions of Power* by D. Michael Quinn, Appendix "Genealogies of the First Presidencies and the Councils of The Twelve Apostles (Signature Books, Salt Lake City, UT).

[iv] Fingerprints of The Gods by Graham Hancock (Crown Trade Paperbacks, New York, NY 1995).

[v] Democracy In America by Alexis de Tocqueville (Vintage Books, New York, NY 1945) is probably the earliest treatise which speaks to this phenomenon of our American political system. This is a dynamic that has plagued our democracy from its earliest days.

[vi] Genesis, Chapter 12.

[vii] Mormon Doctrine by Bruce R. McKonkie (First Edition, Deseret Books, Salt Lake City, UT). Interestingly, when Elder McKonkie's reference to the Roman Catholic Church as "the Church of the Devil" became a subject of controversy, The Church of Jesus Christ of Latter-day Saints reprinted a second edition, and endeavored to buy all the copies it could find through various agents. This fact is born out by many personal journals of members of the Mormon community at the time (the keeping of personal journals is a common Mormon practice.)

"I can see in retrospect that, I was manifesting all of the usual traits of having been raped. Eventually, I reasoned that, as it is with any sexual rape, it may also take me years of reflection on my experience to transcend my abuse by fathers of religion. In fact, that is what ultimately happened, in my personal case. The institutional seduction had turned into my cultural rape—in my view—when I saw that *the institution had assumed the role of pseudo-parent over me...*"

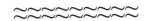

CHAPTER SEVEN

TRANSCENDING MY RELIGIOUS ABUSE

In obedience to an earlier "spirit written" message I had moved to Mexico, and I was living on the *Baja*. I'd wanted for a long time to be nearer to Mom, anyway. Her new place was situated between the two coastal cities of San Diego, and Laguna Beach, California—inland, on the old Ortega Highway. *Mom-Aselia*[i] was now in her mid seventies. So, it felt good for me to visit her more frequently than I had in the past. But, little did I know that, she'd never move to another home from her new dream-house. Yet, at least, she *would* have five years of real happiness there.

My last lover, whom I called Jason[ii] in my first book, had passed on only a few months before I had moved. He had gotten AIDS after we separated, and that reality forced me to confront my own mortality in a 1990 world of casual gay sex. Dad[iii] had also gone through his transition a year before my best friend, Jerry Catan[iv] passed through his transition in 1990. Ten years had passed since Jerry had been an active member of the Mormon ward where I'd served as bishop when I'd left The Church

So, living in San Francisco, by 1990 I'd witnessed sixty-eight of my friends pass on through transition, because of AIDS. Feeling my happy Gay world going in a steep downward spiral, I sought out a psychologist. She had said that, I was suffering "from something like post-traumatic stress syndrome." At that point, a trusted friend in Mexico suggested I move and that, I live on the beach south of Tijuana. So, in light of the recent occurrences in my life, it seemed wise to change my environment. *The Enchanted City by The Bay* was awash in death. Three waves of good friends had each come into the world and gone now. While, I personally tested negative for the HIV virus, any socializing had become too morbid for me there, and I was terrified to go to any of my friends' functions in The City—my beloved San Francisco. It was time for me to heal.

To be completely honest, however, my true immediate goal was more about the ideal adventure of living in another country—as I had done as a Mormon missionary. The location would be perfect to try to continue to make more logical sense of how I now experience the experiences of life. Surrounded by the death of others close to me, I felt the need to make the most of the life that my surviving loved ones and I still had left—and, moreover, I would not have a constant missionary companion around to hinder my "personal exploration." Not *this* time! At any rate, I knew that the old, *Mayan* (commonly called *Aztec*) Calendar, ends at high noon on December 23, 2012 c.e.[v] so, I had come to expect some cataclysmic event would bring about more death in our near future, anyway. It feels right for me to try to understand how to make the most of my Earth time left. These were the actual reasons why I came to live in Mexico...

****

As I walk on, I begin to hear distant drums. The faint, far off sound is a solid, rhythmic beat but, my walking is now synchronized with it. The closer I come to the plaza of that part of town, the louder the drums become. I continue walking, and I begin to hear a strange sound. It sounds almost like a hundred, distant, baby rattlers that are all synchronized with the hard rhythm of the incessant drumming. The deepness of the hard drumming sound becomes intense, and it grows faster paced. It's more aggressive—a nine beat resonation. It causes me to speed up my walk. Then, as I turn a corner, the rhythmic rattling suddenly gets louder. I have to be less than a city block away by now, I think to myself.

I keep on walking, smelling the delicious aroma of food prepared on the outdoor stands. The scene around me is reminiscent of the places I visited and lived in, when I traveled for The Church in Latin-America. The aroma of fresh corn and meat being charred and basted with peppers, herbs and spices on open, hot flames fill the late summer's morning air. The light gray smoke from the food stands lining the street keeps on soaring upward, into the bright and, nearly noonday sky. In perfect pace now with the vibrations of the primal drumming, my legs keep taking me closer to sounds of a primitive time. Whatever it is, it's now just around the next corner.

Everyone around me only seems involved with his or her own activities. To me, it's as if they're all totally oblivious to the rich aromas, to the ubiquitous pounding sounds of large drums, and my awareness that something highly mystical –like the smoke in the air with every breath– is becoming part of each of us. Then suddenly, I realize that, I'm not everyone else here. In spite of similarities with other places where life had taken me, this one feels like complete otherness to me. I'm truly experiencing this place for the first time. Like Dorothy in the Land of Oz found that she was not in Kansas anymore, I'm definitely not in Orange County California anymore, or –much less– in Provo Utah in the United States!

Life here seems more like the days I experienced in Peru, Chile, Ecuador and Bolivia as a new Mormon missionary, in the sixties. It's similar, at least, as far as the cultural flavors that I'm now enjoying. The people, the music, the language, the aromas of the various times of day, and even that certain slowness of time, itself, are all very familiar to me. But, what is no longer the same, however, is that I'm definitely not living as a young, and naïve missionary of the Mormon Church. No, I am now myself. I'm no longer confined to the social definitions of the old faith community in which I was first nurtured, and *that* singular difference is destined to make *this Baja experience* a new one. The reason is me—I'm a new creature! I'm now, finally, prepared for my de-programming!

I'd secured an apartment in the city but, since I'd been invited to stay in a friend's mobile home parked on beachfront property that locals called *Playas,* I did so. In fact, I was on my way to *Playas*, when I came to the wonderful scene on the west plaza on that day. There was a large crowd gathered around a rather imposing, and tall Indian man. His attire, his glistening dark skin and heavy breathing told me he'd been dancing. The tallest person there, he was lean, and he had a perfectly symmetrical and toned, muscular, V-shaped torso. My eyes focused on his hard, heaving, chiseled pectorals, and on his well-defined abdominals. His skin was so dark, I thought to myself that, he must have spent a lot of time in the sun.

How fascinating, I thought to myself, feeling totally hooked.

His body was adorned in the beautiful and ancient vestments of pre-Columbian priestly warriors. The huge headdress, with the serpent head at his forehead was topped with peacock plumes and the longest peacock and pheasant feathers that I had ever seen. I was intrigued by the *connected* way that the slightest movement of his head magnified his presence because of the way that it caused the full length of its plumage to wave majestically. A shoulder piece caused bright reflections of the sun to fill my eyes with all the hues of gold, orange, green, blue and purple from the stones placed in it. It was brief enough to allow for his torso to be exposed, and I saw that he'd been doing the strenuous dancing for years, maybe even all of his life. His dancer's loins were clad only with a thin strip of leather that revealed the massive upper musculature of his long, powerful thighs and the perfectly clean roundness of his buttocks.

The crowd gathered around him, was now eagerly putting money into the drum that he carried upside down, as he went around the circle of people.

He seemed to prance, as he greeted his admirers. His was the grace of an animal in motion—like a gazelle, I thought.

We had all now become a circle. We had enclosed the space, in which this mysterious man seemed to be able to manipulate our senses as if we were all one being, on a leash held by the dancer. All around him, everyone's eyes were focused on his hypnotizing eyes. I looked back over my shoulder and then, I saw that more people had made our body of humanity larger—more dense—than we had been before. We'd been pulled inward with every step he'd taken around the inner part of our circle.

The manly flesh of his full buttocks caught the light of the sun as he stepped forward into the crowd. His wrists and ankles were wrapped with leather bands that had small dried seed pods attached to them. His every step outward, or every wave of his arms, caused all the small seed pods to resound rhythmically. He was barefoot, and I saw that the souls of his feet were black…

I wondered why?

That's when I saw that another male dancer was reverently carrying an earthen pot toward the tall man. He was also similarly dressed and also seemed to prance—gazelle-like—as he came to the center of the vacant circle around which we had all gathered into. The majestic waving of the plumes, the rattling of the dried seed-pods, the drumming of the two primal drums –all of it– was a mix of synchronized sound and colors that were meshed and blended by the physical motion of the two dancers. The second dancer carefully set the earthen pot on the ground and returned to the other side, where he had been when I'd first arrived on the awesome scene. All the time, his prancing captured my complete fascination—as if to draw all of my attention away from the one, who seemed to be the very picture of what, to me, was now a naturally desirable, erotic maleness.

Then, a third male dancer—younger than the other two but, equally as beautiful as the first—came into the space that had become sacred to me. The second man began beating the large drums on the edge of the crowd, across from where I stood, and he looked—no, he *stared*—in my direction.

I felt fixed upon, as if caught in a hunter's cross-hairs.

With that, the first dancer –the tallest one– appeared in my right peripheral vision. While, continuing to take their public's willing donations from *this eager public*, he slowly walked toward my direction.

I tried to get a full picture of his face as he came closer to where I stood. When he was roughly five feet away from me I looked at him.

He nodded back to me.

I don't remember if I returned the gesture because just then, the younger man came over to him and then, handed him an object, exchanging the money filled drum for it.

The tall one looked directly at me again, and *yes*, he smiled slightly before turning away from me.

I felt a sudden surge inside my lower body.

Then, as he took in a deep breath of air, he stood tall, still, and suddenly, he flexed every muscle of his entire body.

He's going to start a dance, I thought to myself.

Standing majestic, he spread his legs apart, fully wide. His was a mighty sight of manly strength—fully balanced. His rippled abdomen was going in and out in heavy breathing as he held up an object, out toward the sun, and I could now see that it was a large sea *concha*. He raised it to his mouth and the resultant sound filled the whole space we all shared there. Facing the bright sun, holding the *concha* upward to its blinding light above us, the sound the dancer made was deep, long and hard.

There was no other sound. There was only the primitive, natural sound of the penetration of air being pushed into prehistoric vibrations. As the air passed through the *concha,* and out into the immensity above our heads, and all around us…

I felt the deep vibration go through my torso, as if my own flesh was now part of his instrument. I had become the sound. As oscillations moved through us, it felt as if we were all made into one soul.

Silence. There was only the silence of a rush of the cool sea breeze.

It was like the sea *concha* had become him. It had become all of us. The penetrating sound continued on as he then turned in the opposite direction then, back—again, toward the sun. Out came the penetrating sound, into the immensity, and through the fleshy core of each of us.

Except for the dancer, we were all silent as we stood there in awe, feeling the vibrations of the powerful sound. The sound had gone in and through each of us there. I again sensed that –in some mysterious way– we had all become one soul. Watching in wonder at what was, to me, a mystical unfolding, I knew we'd been taken into an altered state.

With that realization, in my peripheral vision, I saw other people coming inward where we, the earlier arrivals, had already become a thick circle of humanity. All of us wanted a better view of the alluring grandeur that was now playing out in the sacred space we surrounded, and our density magnified our emotional binding as one soul even more.

The younger, third male dancer had earlier lit a flame in the earthen pot. As the first dancer was sounding the *concha* upward, toward the sun, the younger one who'd lit the flame had begun to play a flute, which he had all along kept facing toward the flame.

Suddenly, the rhythm of the drums began driving hard into us. Instead of a familiar, Indigenous cadence, which I was used to hearing from Native-American drums, here, there was a hard and fast aggressiveness to the beat of the drumming. It was a distinct voice to me but, the change in rhythm also told me a new phase of their *dansa* was beginning.

With that inner awareness, the first dancer flashed from my right periphery, high into the air. His legs seemed to swim through space, as if in an ocean above us. He had flung himself into the center of the circle, coming down right next to the youngest one, who—all along—had played the flute softly, sweetly. Handing the younger dancer his *concha*, his eyes seemed glued on the orange flame. It was as if there was an actual wire stretched tightly from his eyes to the fire coming out of the earthen pot.

Then, the drums suddenly became far more intense—hard. The younger dancer retreated as the first dancer then began circling the flame. His ankle and his wrist movements caused a perfect union of the rattling sounds with the intense drumming. His fixed, and seemingly exact steps took him—cock-like—around the hot flame in clockwise motion.

That's when I saw that the flame had actually moved! The fire, the flame *itself*, seemed to be blown in a clockwise direction too!

I thought to myself, Uh...they must know a lot about wind currents.

Then, suddenly, he quickly reversed direction. The flame followed the dancer, as if there was an intelligent connection going on there!

I thought, no, *that* can't be!

But, then, he changed right back to his original direction, and again, the fire turned too and leaned, as if to follow the dancer, who was still keeping a perfect time with the intense beating of the drums! We were witnessing an unseen force we only knew existed because we saw its results. But, it was a force, which we couldn't see with our eyes as we all watched the evidence of it in complete amazement.

I thought to myself: What magic!

The music was pulsating loudly in our ears. The rhythmic sound and the tall, plumed dancer seemed to be one thrusting and emanating force, pressing itself into our very entrails. Long plumes waving majestically, glistening colors changing hues in the sunlight and the resonance of the drums had all become an experience that I now knew I'd never forget.

Then, the tall dancer stopped moving around the fire, and he began to crouch down on only one knee. As he did this, his other leg raised high in front of him, and his thigh crossed over and just above the flame.

I heard a gasp come out of the mass of people all around.

I wondered, how...how can he do that? My mental question revealed my own sense of awe. Couldn't he feel the hot fire, burning his thigh? Surely, I thought, the heat alone would be unbearable! I surmised that this must be a machismo-motivated demonstration of his masculinity.

With that thought, he showed us all that he was *not* burned. His flesh seemed real sweaty but, just as beautifully unblemished as before.

Again, I thought to myself, but the flame was at the tender underside of his raised thigh! Then, I flashed an old memory: A psychologist friend, years earlier, had explained the meaning of the terms, "cognitive dissonance" to me, and with that old memory, I finally understood what he'd meant, years earlier. What I saw here, didn't compute for me. I could not believe what we were seeing...

The drums were still incessant. With the beat pounding its hard resonation inside of me, I noticed the old, familiar sting of my perspiration in my armpits. I was feeling inner conflict. But, *why?* What caused it?

That's when the one dancing over the flame suddenly began to gyrate his hips around and over the flame as it came up on either side of his crotch. Every sound and gesture meshed into a fever pitch velocity. His voice began to make, groaning and moaning, noises that could barely be heard among all the other passionate sounds.

I felt my breathing intensify.

Pure passion is the only true way to describe what was being created by the sounds of the drum, the seedpods, and now, the sea *concha*, which was being blown by the only woman dressed in native regalia. She also wore a huge headpiece similar to the others' and seedpods and a cream colored dress. When she turned, I saw that on her full back, her dress had what looked like a replica of the Virgin of Guadeloupe embroidered on it.

I thought, a *Catholic* icon? A Roman *virgin*, here, with these *Indian dansas*?

The dancer was gyrating more than ever, and the sensuous sight seemed too uncanny, too inconceivable to me. His thrusting, his gyrating and the look on his face was everything I'd known about sexual orgasm. It wasn't anything I'd expected to see in public—with a Christian *icon* nearby!

I felt the need to remind myself that, this was a union of his bare flesh with the fire! I knew I could have easily been convinced otherwise.

With that idea, the drumming and *concha* sounds stopped suddenly.

All of us, that entire tight circle of humanity then, stood in complete silence. What would happen next?

The tall dancer quickly jumped up in the air and he firmly landed on both feet. He calmly reached down with one hand, and he picked up a flaming coal from the earthen pot as if it were ice and…

I felt myself take-in a deep breath.

…He simply put the bright, obviously hot, coal right into his mouth with his fingers and turned, facing directly at me as he then, took the smoking coal out again. Raising both his hands high above his head, he yelled out loudly. I wondered what he had yelled out in his Native language.

Bursting, we applauded feverishly, as he turned full circle, and *penetratingly* eyed each of us—one by one.

As he took a deep bow, I hoped his eyes would fix back on mine again. His deep bow kept on and on…

Then, raising back up, his eyes did fix on mine, and I knew with that, that I was going to know this man.

As the crowd dispersed, I walked over to him and his two dancer companions. He held out his hand, as if to shake mine.

Close to him now, I also held out my own…

Energetically, he quickly took hold of my lower forearm just above the wrist with his right hand and pulled me to him. Then, as if in a gestured language, his right hand quickly moved up to my right shoulder, and he gently slapped it there. Still resting his hand on my shoulder, his eyes remained totally focused on mine –penetrating into me– as he said what sounded like: *"En-Len'que `NSH-KA."*

A sudden rush ran through me. I marveled within myself, how this gestured greeting from a man whom I'd never met reminded me of the robed vestments of the Mormon temple ritual—I think it was the way he placed his hand on my shoulder. It felt completely natural for me to do the same with my own right hand on his forearm and shoulder.

Then, we hugged, and I said, *"Antonio Feliz, para servirle,"* (Antonio Feliz, at your service). I felt like I'd met an old friend!

He immediately said his own name back to me but then, he added, "*...tu eres escritor y no quiero que tu uses mi nombre,*" (...you're a writer and, I don't want you to use my name).

Shocked at his uncanny insight, I continued in Spanish, saying, "How do you know that I am a writer?"

As our conversation ensued, he told me of several amazing things. He explained that, they were all what I would call "gifted psychics." That, none of them were dancing merely to earn a living, although dancing the Indigenous ceremonial *dansas* of Mexico is how they all lived. He also said that, their main purpose in dancing –wherever they traveled– was not to keep the ancient rituals as an art form. Although preserving what I understood to be folk dances, their *folkloricos*, are a by-product of their work. He explained that having a cultural impact was not their major purpose.

As he talked, I found myself looking deeply into his clear, light brown eyes. He seemed to have facial features that, I had not associated with Indians. His eyelashes were of a double thickness. The long, full eyebrows perfectly framed his eyes on either side of the most masculine nose that I had ever seen. Though dripping with heavy beads of perspiration, at this close distance, I saw that his skin was clear of any blemish. His face had a shine that actually reflected the sun in my eyes, and his dark-chocolate skin had a reddish hew.

Suddenly, I felt the warmth of his right hand in the center of my chest. It seemed warm, like it had a palpable magnetic quality. It was as if his hand, actually, radiated energy into my chest's core.

He went on, "know that the dance is a spiritual vehicle. It is as much the practice of religion, as is the Christian celebration of the Last Supper. We are all warrior/priests of the *Meshica*, otherwise known in the world as the Aztec people..." He continued explaining that their dancing that day was—in part—a love dance with the sun, the air, the water, the earth, and of course, with the fire. He spoke most respectfully of the fire.

I asked, "So then, you were not just being macho in allowing the flame to touch the flesh of your body?" That's when I realized he was taking his hand away from my chest.

"We are warrior/priests of the *Meshica*. Our's is a purpose that is designed to help The Great Mother," he answered, stomping his foot on the earth, "we help Her remember that The Venerable Mother of us all yet has believer children living on Her skin."

"Why do you need to do this?"

"Have you not seen the pollutions? Have you not smelled the stink? Do your ears not hurt with the noise of the European man's ways? Are you not sickened by Europeans taking more than they need from out of Her? Are you so much the European, yourself?"

I only nodded, feeling a tinge of shame.

"Since the great earthquake…"

I assumed that he had referred to the massive Mexico City earthquake that had happened back in 1986, but I wasn't sure. Not wanting to interrupt his explanation, I didn't inquire further. I simply listened.

He went on, "…in what was once the ancient city, you call it Mexico City, it is named after our people, the *Meshica*…" His long, thick, shining black hair easily fell on either side over his big, broad shoulders, glistening in the sunlight.

"But," I interrupted, "why didn't Mexico City get named Aztec City? I mean, if that city was named after the people living there when the Spaniards came…"

With that, all the other dancers sat down with him and me at a table on the plaza. The other Indians all listened as my tall friend explained…

"Aztec," he said with a hint of sternness in his chiseled face, "is the name that the Europeans gave to us. It is their word. It was never a *Meshica* word and, it was never our name." His arms and hands were hovering over the tabletop as if it were a map of the land of which he spoke. "Because we called the land of our origin *Aztlan*, the Spanish called us *Azt-ecas* because we had come from the place called *Azt-lan*. What the Europeans most wanted was to destroy all of our memory of our culture, to destroy all memory of our religion –our union in the natural world– and finally, to destroy all memory of our social reality as the *Meshica*."

Suddenly, I thought of how "*Aztlan*…" resembled *Atlan-tis*! I knew that the suffix, "*tis*," is Greek. So might, "*Aztlan*," be the legendary *A[z]tlan-tis*? "So," I asked, "how did the name *Mexico*, come about?" I again noticed the splendid form of his face. His total honesty was open. I realized he'd focused on listening intently. His facial expressions were all very consistent with his words. I detected absolutely no deception at all. His presence was the epitome of a man with a total clarity of conscience.

"It was during the struggle for independence. Our people, the Indigenous of all of this land, are the people of the revolution in Mexico. In your *Aztlan*—on the *Norteamericano* side, in *el norte* (the north)—the Indigenous of this land did not succeed in their resistance of the European invaders. On your side of *la linea* (the line), the Indigenous of this land were all put on what you still call reservations—the *prison lands*—which are the least desirable parts. While, contrarily, *en este lado* (on this side), *Aztlan* has been kept for the most part; for, our struggle for independence was to be *Meshica*, in spite of the ugly power of the European. On this side of *la linea* (the line), our revolution succeeded to a greater degree because our founders officially adopted the *Meshica* political identity. Sadly, however, we have now joined with the European and made a mixed people, and thus, many have lost our first identity."

"*Mestizos?*" I asked.

Nodding, he added, "…Yes. Our revolution was a struggle to first, retain our original identity as the *Meshica* so that the future generations will remember who and what we are –to once again, call ourselves by the correct name of most of our ancient people. The ancient way of saying Mexico is *MAE'sheeko*; for today, we are the *Meshica*."

I asked, "then, why use the European pronunciation? Why is Mexico, pronounced MAE'heeko? Why is it not MAE'sheeko?"

"Unfortunately, with the second part of retaining our first identity, we did not succeed. We married the European –unlike most of you *Norte-Americanos*– and, as a result, the old way has been lost because of the Christian prejudice against the older traditions of the *Meshica*. As you said, we are mestizo—but, we are still *Meshica*. Sadly, by the time of the last big revolution, most of our people had forgotten our mothers' tongue. We had all adopted the ways of the European men in much of our daily living. Sadly, how we now talk is only one way in which the *Meshica* have, today, meshed with the presumptuous Europeans who invaded us from across the sea."

The others listening at the table nodded in their agreement. One of them added, "*Pero somos Meshica y Meshica seremos*" (But, we are *Meshica* and *Meshica* we will continue to be).

Then, his look became even more intense, and leaning over the edge of the table toward me he added, "Here, south of *la linea* (the line), we did not get put on 'reservation land.' Here, we made the entire nation into *Meshico!*" The beaded sweat fell from his forehead onto the table.

Again, all of the other men around the table added their own obvious approval of his words, nodding and looking at each other in agreement. One of them added, "There is a traditional Mexican song which goes, `Viva Mexico! Viva *Mexica!*' It is our way to remember who we are."

"Still," I asked, "Why is it that I've never heard about the *Meshica* before your words to us all here, today? Why did I only learn about the *Aztec* nation in my youth? Why does every person who ever spoke to me of your beautiful dances –in schools in Alta California, my family, who all eventually come from either the state of Sonora or Guanajuato– all of them have only called your dances, `*Aztec* dances?' Why?"

"It is the European who has recorded the story of the history you have read. It is the European who wants to forget what we were, and what we still remain. The European continues to refuse to acknowledge the consistent existence of the Indigenous peoples on the land, generation after generation. For, my friend…" suddenly, he broke into a big smile, "…such an acknowledgment would recognize the, actual, failure of the European invasion. Such a way of seeing us, is to understand that the colonization did not prevail, after all. The European seeks to save face."

All of us, very quickly, became extremely good friends. Over a series of many conversations, I was told that they traveled throughout the North American continent as a group. They took their *dansas* wherever they sensed the need to inform the spirits of their ancient ancestors that, their kind still live on this land. Unless they already knew someone in the area, they'd camp out on the edge of the cities they visited, and perform in the town centers during the mid-day, when the sun was fully risen.

Their dancing is ceremonial. It's priestly; sacred, in the true sense, in that they dance on behalf of the human masses that do not. According to their ancient tradition, all peoples who live on this entire continent need the benefit of their *dansa* to the four elements and to Father Sun. If they did not still do the sacred dance then, eventually, the spirits that keep watch over us all would inform Great Earth Mother that her children no longer inhabit Her valleys and mountains. This would be catastrophic because She is pained by the vast pollution put upon Her in more recent times. In their view, if Her devotees no longer lived upon Her then, "Great Earth Mother would clean away all the pollutions with the burning earthquake, the falling stars, the whirling pillars, and with the icy storms, and overwhelming waters. She would easily sluff us all off, as any would do to parasites, who persist in consuming living flesh. For, indeed, that is how we humans have misbehaved upon Her skin."

The major purpose of their visit to this densely populated metropolitan area near the Mexican-American border today was no different. Their camp was relatively close to the beach place I stayed at over the weekends so, it felt natural for me to stay there with them most weekend nights on the beach, instead of at the mobile home near my friend's house at *Playas*. Besides, there was no denying my intense attraction to the tall dancer…

So, for three months, I lived with those dancers and their extended families. Through that warm association, they'd come to mean much to me—especially the tall dancer who had asked me not to use his name in my writing. His masculinity was as unrehearsed as was his freedom to manifest a primitive eroticism. But, most of all, I was attracted to his genuine complete lack of guile, and his profound sense of community. I later learned, to my deepest joy, that his sense of community is what motivated his request that I not use his actual name when he asked me, "why add glory to myself when my work is to better the life of us all?" I, therefore, do not reveal his name here. I promised to honor them all, as a collective, even though he and I had developed a "special" relationship.

He said once, "…you will write only the good things about me. Yet, I know that we are all not *that* good all of the time. I am a man of passion. But, my passion is meant in a healing way, and I have no need to be misunderstood; to be seen as being different than most others, by those who read your words. Those of the European mind are incapable of knowing me without also having my tools. And, since my tools are not their tools, it is best that they know all of our people through you—not merely me."

I quickly became aware that his term "*tools*," wasn't meant as a mere metaphor. They all lived in the understanding that their honesty was a veritable tool used, like a metal grip, to hold their person-hood intact. I soon learned that being clear, open and honest in his relationships was a result of him seeing personal integrity as his tool for spiritual evolutions.

They each demonstrated by their individual behavior that personal integrity was indeed, a tool used by each one to strengthen and invigorate their essence. As one of the older men in the group said to me once, "it enforces our individual existence in the modern world. For, the world in which we journey is a place that tears one asunder." While playing, this one man in particular, was definitely a trickster rascal, but yet, that kind of illusory behavior in all of them only happened in games and jokes around the happy night campfire. His playing with me was always exactly that, *playful*. Unlike any past experiences—that I'd had while growing up—his playfulness didn't come from any warped competitive need to win. His humor —likewise—had no hint of either sarcasm or, satire. I don't believe they can imagine what it's like to tell a lie, an untruth or, far less, to intentionally deceive another for personal benefit, greed or gain.

All these people are of a natural brand of honor, sobriety and soulfulness. The trickster was, I later discovered, the one accepted by the rest as a wise man of the *Toltec* tradition. Yet, unlike this man, my tall dancer friend didn't seem to respect the usual social roles and boundaries that my own traditional European cultures had created to reinforce the male/female dichotomy in things, erotic. Though he obviously had a mate, who had given birth to their two children, his ability to also express his raw eroticism verbally with me, *in her presence*, was beyond any of my own personal inhibitions. After having lived with them all, I can't apply the usual stereotypical labels that, American society uses to maintain the illusion of a male/female dichotomy in our common, *natural*, human sexuality…

One night, my dancer friend lay beside me on the, still, warm sand. He was verbally flirting with me, with the mother of their two children standing close enough to have heard him. Among other things, he had asked me to join him in swimming naked under the full moon in the ocean. "Let's get naked! Sister Moon is full tonight, Antonio!"

"It's too cold for me," I said shaking my head. I tried to hide my increasing excitement with my forearm, as I watched him take off his pants, and his shirt. My reflex reaction was to look away. As I did so, my vision focused on his sweet mate; who was covering her mouth, as if she were embarrassed, and really trying to cover up her spontaneous laughter.

He kept on stripping in front of me, without any change of facial expression. Without any hint of shame, he quickly disrobed right there.

I was terribly confused. I wondered if she thought that my reaction was humorous or, whether she thought his nakedness was comical. It occurred to me that she had only seen *my reaction* as comedy. That was when I realized my sense of otherness around the dancers and their little band. For nearly nine years, since leaving The Church, I had seen myself as being liberal and open-minded. But here, finally, I was forced to see how much of a prude I still was—in truth. Moreover, I had also believed myself to be adept at reading facial and other non-verbal body language in others. However here, now, I found myself completely baffled at my inability to read either his or, her non-verbal messages, for that matter!

From my place on the sandy beach, I watched his glistening form dive into an oncoming dark wave, as it broke into a deafening roar of white foam under the brightness of that white, full moon. Beyond him, the entire surface of the water seemed to be a mass of living black glass.

Turning aside, I saw that she was also watching him play in the glittering and thundering sea before us. Her whole person reflected the light of the moon. It was as if her whole body, itself, was a light. She was all a-glow! Standing there, she was personified luminance. At that moment, I understood the depth of her passion and love for him.

Who are these people? I wondered quietly to myself, what was she thinking about?—About him?—About us? I *had* to ask her how she felt about the erotic overtones he had initiated in our earlier conversation before he had stripped, and run into the dark water. So, walking over to her, I began, "You know, I was an ordained priest and a bishop for many years, and I was married for fourteen years in a marriage with a woman. Does the way he and I talked, offend you? I do not want to offend you."

She stoked the campfire without saying a word.

The incessant sound of the waves seemed to get louder.

Then suddenly, she looked right at me in total silence for a moment. Then, wind blew her long, singly braided hair to one side, and she turned and looked out on the vastness of the water—a picture of purest dignity!

Out in the black water, directly under the path of a reflected full moon, he waved back to where we were. His naked body was bobbing up and down in the shallow part where the last wave had just left him. Between the thunder of the breaking, black waves his *gritos* (yelling) were as wild sounding as I had ever heard from him. His beautiful manliness was authentic, full of energy and totally honest.

His wild abandon electrified every inch of me.

Then, as if reading my mind, she finally turned back to me and then, she said, "Yes, Antonio, he is beautiful. No?"

All I could do was nod my head in agreement. But, I needed to hear an answer to my question from her. I needed to know if my, now obvious, inner responses to his erotic invitations had offended her. I felt myself quiver with excitement and apprehension…

After another long silence, she looked right at me and said, "You are a funny man. Why do you not share your man energy with him? He knows you want to do it. He has told me that is your desire. I know that he wants to mesh his energy with yours. But, I see that you refuse his invitations to you to lay with him." Laughing, she added, "It is as if you are a baby who is hungry, but who refuses to accept the nipple of his mother! You silly man! Her laughter went on, only getting drowned out by the loudness of the crashing waves of the black ocean behind her.

Stunned at her openness, I asked, "It would not trouble you if he and I were to lay with each other in the way he and you do?"

She just laughed all the more, and began again to stoke the fire for washing pots, pans and eating utensils. After a while, she began to laugh again, and said, "To speak of such things is to calmly discuss the shades of color of a man's shit or, to talk about the bitter aromas where the men urinate…" Her continued spasm of laughter didn't let me understand the rest, as she just laughed, and worked.

I was in awe of her openness, in awe of her absolute honesty.

Then, a roar of the breaking waves—as if to punctuate her words to me—totally drowned out the sound of her laughter...

It had never occurred to me that sexual divergence, in a coupled relationship, could be seen without a hint of shame or guilt, whatsoever. That, a relationship wherein the partner actually desires that which gives sexual joy to the other, whether it includes them or not, could even exist with no hint of jealousy. Her words had only chided me for my desire to understand their private relationship more than for my erotic response to him. They implied that, she viewed his erotic teasing of me as being as natural to him as is defecating and urinating to anyone!

My mind was still filled with only that one question: Is she actually not offended by his obviously homo-erotic overtures toward me?

Then he came back near to where she and I were talking.

I couldn't wait to ask, so I moved closer to him in order to be heard above the sound of the breaking waves.

As he dried himself off with a towel, in spite of my arousal by his nakedness, I began to review for him, as best as I could, about my brief conversation with her. Probably sounding incoherent to him, I ended it with, "Am I just totally unaware or, did she actually communicate to me that she doesn't care whether you and I…"

His laughter burst out interrupting me, as he fell hard on the blanket where I sat. "What is it about you of the European mind? You seem to analyze and try to find reasons for shame over things that are natural to us all. Do you not experience your body in sharing energy, in the same way that you experience your body when you squat and shit or, when you stand and let the urine pass out of you?

My body began to shake hard with sexual tension.

With that, he reached out his left hand, and he thrust the palm of his cupped hand over my awakened genitals.

Sheer contradiction flooded my being. I looked back at her.

She just kept on with her work, as if unaware of his hand.

But, I still needed to know if she had seen us…if she had… no, *whether* she'd been watching us.

She hadn't, and more importantly to me, she still wasn't.

"The conflict of your body, and of your European mind, is centered in here." His hand felt warmer than any other sensation I could feel, "here, in your man-fountain-of-life." His hand began to massage my entire pelvis and groin area, "this is the vessel, the bowl of life, the place of creation." As he cupped my cheeks and hips on either side with his large hands, his voice was suddenly very deep, "and, this," he said massaging my whole butt with a strong kneading motion, "this is the source of what you and I can create together. It is the same in both us men, and in the women also. It's your matrix." His hands hovered—grazing my hot skin—hunting.

My erection completed. Again, instinctively, I stole another look to see if she'd looked over at us.

With that, he moved his massive torso over, and in doing so, he blocked my range of view between her and us. "Your body knows what it desires," he breathed into my ear, "what your body desires is of no consequence to your mind. It is, therefore, of no consequence to her." Then, with his right hand, he took my hand and he gently placed it on his fully erect organ, and then said, in the softest voice to me, "it is only of consequence to this body that is next to your body. It is not even of any consequence to my mind."

I felt my exhaled breath become a moaning, as I sensed an inner rush of my hot body fluids. The tingling feelings inside of me increased rapidly until they pulsated out in waves from my core. Can she see my hands? With that thought, I moved them upward to his tight, muscular waist. Ever so lightly, I rested my hands there, on his writhing mass.

"Allow your naturalness to meet my own naturalness. Let us become like our Mother Earth. Let Her be one through us, here, together; me in you, you in me. Recall that I am you and that, you are me: Remember Antonio; you are Another Myself. Your body is this body, and this body is your body. I am Another Yourself. We are both Earth. Do you see?"

That did it. Something inside me exploded.

"Now," he went on without stopping for my answer, "allow your male naturalness to meet my own." His huge, long, hairless legs began to wrap around my own. His strong arms took both of my hands and then, he placed them firmly on his powerful, unclad loins, "This is my matrix. Know it. I want you to know it." His breath, and writhing hardened.

I was now under him. Silken, smooth skin was all I could feel. Looking up at his big, beautiful smile, the same smile that had seduced me from the beginning, both of us were grinding deeply into each other's flesh. I tasted the saltine aroma of his skin. His taste intoxicated me.

He moaned and moaned.

Deep moaning from deep within both of us went on and on.

I was now, also fully engaged with my hands.

Then, going lower, his long, black hair sensually brushed across my hardened nipples. Rushes of energy swept over all of me.

Had I been conflicted? Was I split apart? Yes. But, right now, those puritanical complications didn't matter at all to me. All that mattered to me now was the present. There is no past; for, it is all gone. There is no future; for, none of it has yet come. All that is, is the now, the present!

I awoke in the early pre-dawn shadows, before the first light of day announced the coming of a new morning. The constant sound of the ocean helped to keep me between both, the sleeping and the awakened states of being. The man who had forced me to face the contradiction of my cultural socialization and my honest hormonal realities lay asleep next to me. A child-like absence of guile radiated from his face as he breathed slowly in my ear. How wonderful it must be, I pondered to myself, to be raised without the encumbrances of shame, guilt and other tools of "civilized" propriety with regard to things erotic. His words hung in my mind. He had spoken much after our sharing of energy about how our bodies each have their own will –how, human flesh is intelligent; how, it makes its own choices without the *thinking* mind.

He had said, "Mind has nothing to do with the bodies we are. Our flesh bodies only inform the mind of what they desire by their physiological responses and our mind considers it involuntary. Yet," he'd said, "it's all voluntary, as far as the body is concerned. The living flesh is aware on its own," without our conscious awareness. "The European mind cannot understand that our bodies do not seek approval from the mind. The European mind sees itself as superior to the world of nature. The world of mind," he'd explained, "is only different, it is not superior. Mind is not even the world of spirits, and mind knows nothing about the powers of the making, exchanging and sharing of our human energy without the physical body. The problems we have in our world today often show themselves when the mind builds rules for the honest responses of the physical body. But, all that happens is that—you dream—you mentally impose an illusion of what is the common world of nature. *Rules from the world of mind; they tear the cloth of existence in the world we live in.* Rules for the stuff of Mother Earth are like a craziness that insists the sky above must be green as the emerald today, because that is the rule."

As I lay there, still feeling the warm, after-throb of pleasure, I caught a glimpse of the mother of their two children. She was getting up from where she lay with the children. The shame of my old post-Victorian, middle-American imprinting, suddenly came to the surface. My mind went backwards. How would I relate to her now? Does she actually take no offense at what has happened here? I looked at his serene, sleeping face. With his eyes closed, it was easy to believe that –with him– what you see is what you get.

A faint but definite smile came across his face, yet, he kept on sleeping. In an instant, his covered eyes seemed to move rapidly as if he were dreaming.

Suddenly, I was aware that my heart's core had been pulled by the magnetism of this man to whom I felt bonded now. The force, which I felt pulling me into him, was my clear realization that what *should* be the case wasn't even an issue with this amazing group of people. This beautiful, sexual man, and the others—including the mother of their two wonderful children—*had never used the word "should."* I finally knew that I, indeed, needed him now because I understood that, for them, there is only what "*is!*" For them, the only truth is what is! I wanted that. For them, there was no "*should*"—it didn't exist in their language. In their vision, "should" is too abstract. As with any abstract, "*should*" is a concept that is not complete.

He had agreed that there was a past that had been but, that "the past is no more." He had said that in their language, the term "should does not exist" yet, the significance of that fact had not at all registered with me—until now.

At that moment –as I lay beside him, watching him sleep– I knew I was in awe of such a genuine way of being. I was in awe of how honest –truly open– living is for me, here, with *them*. Above his wind blown, black hair –in the still dark distance– the ocean waves relentlessly burst open against the sandy shore. What contrast there was between the serenity of his sleeping face and the violent forces of nature in the Deep. As an especially loud breaking of the waves thundered, I knew I wanted to know more of this way of envisioning.

With that thought, I turned to see what she was doing over by the rocks. She'd already begun to add more wood to the fire for our morning breakfast. What can I do now? I asked myself, what can I possibly do to ease the awkwardness I still felt about us all.

As if sensing my thoughts, she suddenly looked up at me. Her warm smile and the big wave of her hand told me that she was feeling no different than before it all happened.

Such freedom! I *had* to understand more about his way of being. I tried to get my clothes on, and I got up as gently as I could. I didn't want to wake the man who had now, so quickly, become such tender, sweetness to my soul.

Over in the distance, she calmly motioned to me, calling for me to come over to where she was. She poured a cup of coffee that she'd, obviously, freshly brewed for everyone.

So, I began walking over, while she put the tasty chocolate and cinnamon flavored coffee on the flame-heated rocks to keep it warm. As I walked closer, I couldn't find the words to break the ice that I still felt in my newfound awareness of our circumstances. The anxiety within me was building with my every clumsy step in the sand. My heart felt a sense of love, of *sisterhood* –yes, sisterhood!

"*Buenos dias,*" (Good morning,) she initiated, "the new coffee's ready for you."

"*Buenos dias,*" I responded hesitatingly.

As if fully aware of my anxiety, she just waited.

"I can't thank you enough; truly," I began, "for your warm hospitality," I said, "…it's still a little odd for me, though."

"*No hay de que*" (It is nothing) she said, handing me a full cup, "you are now one of us," smiling broadly, "Antonio, you are family."

My mind rested on her last word: *family*. It felt comfortable with the aroma of the coffee, packed with chocolate and cinnamon. As I took a little sip, I pondered over the complete innocence with which she related to me. There was no hint of jealousy, no conflict, whatsoever. Her complete acceptance of me had none of the typical dysfunctional character traits, which were all part of the puritanical upbringing of my early formative years. The comfort I sensed with her was, indeed, like that of a sister, and it clashed with my sense of what I could now only describe as the truly bizarre.

"Speak," she commanded suddenly, "your face speaks more than your mouth."

Her directness reminded me of the ways of some of the women in my extended family. With that mental comparison, I asked, "Do you always prepare the meals?" I had to know if the roles within their family were like those of my parents', and like the ways of the rest of my Dad's relatives in Mexico. My extended family had always seemed to be more oriented to what I had learned to call "traditional family values."

"No," she responded. Then, after some rather obvious inner reflection, she went on; "sometimes, the others do those things. So, tell me in your family, does only one prepare the food for the entire household?" That, somehow made her burst into laughter as she went on, "that would be too much work for one person!"

I shook my head, "*no,* " in a mortified awareness of the, now, seemingly ridiculous nature of my question. "No," I went on after another sip of the delicious hot coffee, "I mean to ask of it is always the women among you who prepare the meals for the men, or do the men also join in the more domestic chores?"

Her answer seemed so matter-of-fact, "When one has shared energy with another, it is best for others to prepare the first meal. Is it not more practical than, if the one who has shared energy all the night before, to also prepare the breakfast?"

Did my having shared sexually with him mean nothing to them, except that someone else *besides him*, would know to take care of getting breakfast ready the following morning? My mind was whirling. It was suddenly clear that I wasn't even thinking along the same line as she was. She seemed oblivious to my confused inner thoughts. Our worlds are too far apart for efficient communication, I thought to myself. Both our frames of reference were incongruent with the other's envisioning. I had to think about her response alone.

So, after politely excusing myself, I started a long walk along the beach. I had so many questions…

Where was all the anger? Where was the ugly jealousy? Where was the pain that would reign in similar circumstances in the families of my childhood? Can it be that, here, in this small band of loving people, what is celebrated is a joyous participation in the pleasures of nature over any *possessive* claim that a spouse might have on a partner? Had they even vowed to be monogamous, like other couples I'd known? Or are there really no scruples here about with whom, and when one makes love? Does everyone else simply chip in on all of the domestic chores when their partner is sexually indisposed with another person? There had to be more to it. There is some basic way of comprehending here; on whether an assignment of morality applies, and it *greatly* differs from my old church way.

As I took my first steps out of the campsite, I soon realized how confused I was. The sand felt cold between my toes as I walked in the morning's overcast light. Theirs was definitely not the typical Mexican culture that I'd been exposed to when our family had visited our relatives residing in Mexico when I was a little boy. These fantastic people were nothing like any of my family's relatives! They were not filled with the old rigidities of the 20th century. That's what felt so terrific to me!

My relatives seemed more conservative in their way than even some Utah Mormon people I knew. Although I knew that they weren't married to one another legally, my hosts were married where it actually mattered –in their unique mass soul. Their affections were not tangled up in the rules of conduct that had been so much a part of my childhood socialization experience. With that idea, it hit me…

Of course, I thought, as I walked onward; these are all *Indian* people, and as a result, my proprietary notions didn't apply even in their coupled relationships any more than they would in other areas like real estate, for example. I decided that, petty jealousies had no visible existence within these honest and nature-centered people.

Finally, the one question I rested on, as I kept walking further away from their camp was: Did these men and women actually not see recreational bisexuality any different than any other normal human bodily processes? Was sex that *simple* to them?

The salty, wetness of the morning air felt like a shower that was cleaning my innermost being. His words returned to my mind. He'd said, "If it is not what the European thinks is 'messy' then, it is not good. Eat with the fingers and it is good. Wrestle until the hair gets all tangled and it is good." The memory of his seductive words led me to reflect on the previous evening's passion. All our sharing of our male energy *had* been good and messy –with sand, sweat and all the other stuff! Opening my shirt, I smelled the dried semen on my bare chest. With that, I heard the cackle of my laughter above the incessant roar of the crashing waves.

After a spasm of more laughter, my thoughts returned with increasing clarity. I had never considered shitting and pissing as pleasures to be enjoyed. These had always been mere need functions to me. Bathroom activity had always been undesirable and of no value. I noted how I use the word *bathroom* for rooms that have no bath in them! I remembered being taught that pissing was a mere biological device that served our physical need to rid our bodies of unhealthy waste. I remembered the exact moment, when I had been taught that idea by my first primary teacher: It was in the Mormon Primary class years ago and –with that thought…

A thunderous wave crashed against the rocks to my left.

I stopped walking; stunned by the way *the very ocean* now seemed to speak to my heart's core. So, I thought, if pissing was meant to also be pleasurable then, what about shitting? In the midst of these questions I realized I'd stopped walking. I felt the sensation of tears falling down my cheeks. Father Sun was now changing the colors of the ocean, the sky and sand. Walking On Water had begun His sky-bound journey…

Many other thoughts rushed through my mind on that walk. One, the tall dancer and one of his companions had talked a lot about, was how "reality is created by our agreements." I recalled similar wording, written by me years earlier, when I'd received a message that my psychologist friend had called "spirit writing." Both the tall dancer and the other man had advised me to ponder their words on certain agreements that, they had reviewed with me several times since I'd first met them. What I didn't understand was why they said to "ponder the[ir] words," while I pissed! What was *that* all about?

Hell, my bladder needed to be voided now, anyway. With that thought, I turned, and walked over to the vegetation beyond the coarse sand, and away from the ocean. I tried to become aware of sensations inside of my body as I unbuttoned my fly and spread my legs. The now increasing warmth of the breeze, as it blew against my genitals, reminded me of how the dancer had talked about making love with the wind spirits. The idea eroticized what I was doing, as daylight quickly became much brighter. The brilliance of the sun was peaking through the clouds now.

The sensation of fullness was, somehow, far more powerful inside me than I'd ever felt before. I noticed how it all came with a heat and a surge that gushed itself out of me, like the stream from a hot hose fully open—out into the cooler morning air. My forefinger connected with the pressure against it, as I held my natural orifice out, away from my shirt blowing in the breeze. I had never been aware of the similarity between these sensations I felt now, and the powerful thrusts of ejaculate during orgasm. Shooting pulses of pleasure hit my groin because of the surging of fluids through my inner thighs. When the wave of pleasure ebbed, the yellow puddle was a steaming, golden stream between my two feet.

I heard myself let out a huge sigh, and I laughed out loud again. Hell, it felt great! I wanted to feel it all over again! So, I dropped my pants and thrust my pelvis out –away from my ankles. I began again by relaxing the taut muscles inside my groin somewhere between my anus and my testicles. Then, just as the yellow stream began again...

Waves of hot air swoosh over me like hot flowing blankets on my bare skin.

Interrupting the hot yellow flow, the excitement building within me demanded more. I wanted to feel more of the warm wind blowing against my bare thighs. With that thought, I quickly took off all my clothes. Standing there, with my legs spread, I began to make love with the wind spirits, as the dancer had taught me. Balancing myself with my hands at my sides, with my knees slightly flexed, I thrust my pelvis back and forth in the erotic motions of lovemaking. After grinding my hips in the warm wind for a while, I realized that I'd thrown my arms and hands high, above my head. The caressing pleasure of the warm summer morning wind moved in and around my upper thighs and shot up, wrapping itself around my butt. Letting go of my penis had caused me to be aware of feeling it lengthen and thicken. With the wind bellowing around me now, making a major mess of my now longer hair, I suddenly became aware that I had never before experienced taking a leak naked—or, "*natural*"—as the dancer had said pissing, "is meant to be experienced!"

The wind had felt unusually warm. This is the moment I knew, for the first time, that my erections have their root deep in the underside of my torso, down where some traditions place our energy connection with the earth. I could feel where all the muscles meet between my anus and my scrotum. Suddenly, the rush of fluid seemed higher up in my abdomen than ever before. Then, with my semi-erect shaft still swaying in the wind, I felt the gently thrusting stream inside of me. As I felt the last of my urine hurl against my inner walls, the sensation came –wildly– and, finally, my bladder was totally emptied.

There was a quick, and an almost imperceptible, throbbing. It sent awesome pleasurable sensations shooting from my anus to my scrotum that I'd never known before. It was met at the base of my organ by an even sweeter pulsation rushing down from well below my belly button. When all of it had become a small golden trickle, I just stood there in absolute amazement. The wind, still moved over my nakedness, but now, it felt chilled. However, pissing had never been an explosion of pleasure, and from then to this day, this frequent function has been far more than "merely eliminating waste."

Had awesome sensations always been there? My thoughts began to rush again. What was it that now made these familiar, old physical feelings more real to me than before? Was it what he'd said? Did our, "Mind," in reality, have "nothing to do with the bodies that we are?" Was it true that our, "Bodies only inform the mind?" His words came loudly into my mind with a strength-of-force that was uncanny to me. "To make rules for the body's functions is to impose illusions on what is the real world. Rules for Earth's stuff are like a craziness that insists the sky must be green as the emerald today, because it is the rule."

That's when it hit me. My dancer friend had instructed me to "ponder" what he had taught me about agreement…then, with that idea, I knew the reason he had said that, *agreement is the core of creation.* Like a post-hypnotic suggestion, his words were making a lot of sense to me now. My struggle had been clear to him. It was now becoming clear to me: I was struggling "to become free of being *domesticated* by all of the ways of the invader European mind" –European *agreements!* *Becoming free of domestication* was the essence of the dancers' "agreements."

Father Sun was now beginning to push His light through the marine layer that had been our night's cover. I took the sweet grass he'd given me out of my pocket. Stopping in my path, so as to block the wind, I lit the braided herb with my lighter. Even in the wind of the morning, the sweet aroma of the sacred, braided herb filled me as I brushed the smoke onto my head and heart with my hand, as he had shown me. I began by honoring and greeting the Four Directions: Where the sun rises; Where the sun goes, at the end of its daily journey; Above me, and also Below me. I remembered his words: "Follow the sun," and his tale of how the sun was made –how two men had become "deities" and gone into the light.

There, as the now green waves pounded their mantra against the sandy shore, I knew that I was grounded in my own place in the world. *I am the center.* He'd taught me to see myself as being one with the sun; to say, "I am One. Earth is my mother and the Sun is my father. All creatures are my sisters and my brothers."

Then, once more, truly as if the Universe was punctuating Its encoded message to me, a huge roar announced that a powerful wave had pounded itself against the rocks that went out into the water from the shore.

I thought, were they *right*? Can the elements, *Themselves*, actually *communicate*? Is that vast ocean truly *alive and intelligent*?

His words resounded in me, and I realized that he *was* right. *My world is my own creation*! If I am a child of the sun then, why could I not be a center also? Why am I not also as much a creator as any deity because –according to his legend– the sun was once a god, Himself, who had become Father Sun. The ancient *Toltecs*, indeed, *had* called their Pyramid in *Tenochtitlan*, "the place where mortals are made into gods"—after all! To me, this was pure Mormonism!

Finally, because of that one awareness, I felt able to respond to the world around me because I am the Center. Not that I felt any sense of control, but I'd come to know I was not out on the edge of reality. *My world had suddenly become a simple manifestation of me*! I'd begun to self-identify with all that surrounds me. For the first time, I knew that I was able to respond to what he'd called, "the world" because I AM its center. The *Meshica* had taught me that "each mind is its own world," and my acknowledgment of my own mind's role in the creation of it, is to know that I am the *responsible* part, the *creative* Center of it all.

Father Sun was at His full brightness now.

I put my clothes back on, and before finishing, I realized that I'd been dressing reverently –as, had once been my custom– when dressing for a religious service. In that moment, I knew that I was putting on my shirt with the same sacred attitude with which, I had done years earlier when dressing in a Mormon temple after a sacred ceremony. With that awareness, I understood that my entire world had, again, become my Temple! Finally, I'd been endowed to be wild again—to be undomesticated again!

Walking on, now, the dark, wet and coarse sand of the beach on the water's edge was squeezing itself between my toes. The wind was blowing my light clothes tightly against my body. Walking on through the saltine aromas of this place, I knew that I was trying to make better sense of the differences in the way that these new friends responded to all things natural compared to how I was, emotionally, programmed to respond to nature. The pleasurable sense of my, now, voided bladder, brought me back to the sweet memory of the previous night's lovemaking. The sense of throbbing, still in my groin, was a persistent after-pleasure of the awesome wonder of a man who had become infinite sweetness to me.

These loving, kind and totally honest people –with whom I ate, danced, slept, played and loved– had challenged the heart of my training in social propriety. These *Meshica* Indians, by simply being themselves, challenged the purpose and meaning of all of the social roles, which had been invasively imposed by my old organized—by an institutionalized—religious heritage. Mainstream's conventional behavioral rules on sexual "purity" no longer felt right to me. The customs of propriety by which I had been raised had, finally, become clear to me. By the time I approached the campsite, my friends had finished their coffee, and the overcast marine layer had completely dissipated. Approaching them—it's, now, light enough for me to see their joyous eyes and happy smiles!

Suddenly, I realize that, I'm actually, *running* toward them!

****

After September 11, 2001, our dangerous social constructs manifest an arcane religious fundamentalist quest for behavioral, or social, and territorial purity. Arcane, because the proponents that, I refer to, have not changed at all in their basic view of human inter-relationships since the days of their origin in Middle East patriarchies, which produced all of today's fundamentalist Judaism, fundamentalist Christianity, and fundamentalist Islam. Irrespective of the religion, the fundamentalist way to envision sacred stories is *literal*, and in light of the globalization of the planet, fundamentalism is irrational in our, increasingly inclusive, social context.

After September of 1990, the *natural* way of my *Meshica* friends in Mexico had, likewise, made more sense to me than my past mentors. I could now see that their Indian ways were, at least, all congruent with my growing awareness of who and what I am. It was apparent to me that, these *Meshica-Toltec* ways had what I considered, *the important things,* right. This is why all of the men in their band consider themselves, each the true father of each child! Now, my experience had given me a taste of *how separated from nature the cultures of my second womb had molded me to be.* To all of these genuinely happy souls, *my sexual proclivities were seen as a spiritual asset to the group soul of this little band*! Because of their celebratory example I was, thus, finally off—becoming less domesticated myself! They had set me on my way toward becoming a more open soul.

I had also now seen that I had definitely been the victim of a religious institution's, actual, religious abuse of me. But, by seeing their example, I could now see how I might actually *transcend* that abuse. I knew it could take many years of personal reflection on how I had experienced prepubescent experiences. For, as I have learned since then, those years in The Church were the years when my ability to understand had been severely limited by what the late Joseph Campbell had called a "second womb."

I will always be grateful for his keen insight because it was my exposure to his writings that let me know that, there was a greater truth beyond our closed community. Joseph Campbell's books were the first that gave me hope that, the abuse of those years could be transcended. Indeed, it was Joseph Campbell who had taught that, the abuse of those earlier years had existed precisely, *to be transcended by me*! What Campbell called the "Hero's Journey" had been my own experience and, more importantly, I now knew it! Now, I had finally learned that, experience in the experience is the bearer of the most important wisdom, after all!

As mentioned earlier, "hindsight is 20/20 vision." I can see in retrospect that, I was manifesting all the usual traits of having been raped. Eventually, I reasoned that, as it is with any sexual rape, it may also take me years of reflection on my experience to transcend my abuse by fathers of religion. In fact, that is what ultimately happened, in my case. The institutional seduction had turned into cultural rape —in my view—when I saw that *the institution had assumed the role of pseudo-parent over me.* The clincher, for me, came when I saw that, in this way, the hierarchies of my former religious institutions were able to program my emotional responses to my experiences, and set my future use of mental default systems, accordingly.

The violation of this particular institutional invasion is that, its heterosexism is designed to devalue, and even to depreciate, my naturally rooted sexual orientation. The shock of learning what, my truth was—what Professor Walter L. Williams refers to in his ground-breaking book, The Spirit and The Flesh *Sexual Diversity in American Indian Culture*, as a "*berdache*" tradition—could have been far more traumatic because I realized: *I am a, "berdache*!" I realized that, 18th century French trappers would have called me a, "*berdache*" too! Fortunately, I learned long before this realization that, there is nothing "small," or "diminishing" about a real deity. I knew that, when any doctrine leads to envisaging my fellow humans as "less than" I believe I am then, its Source is, clearly, *not* The One Divine God, of Love.

Along the way, choices put me in the company of an Indian holy man called *Red Feather* who named me, in his old language, telling me—in English—that I'm called, "*Keeping The Gate*" by him. Years later, another Indian wise man would further inform me that I am; "'*Keeping The Gate' because* [he'd say] "*you are a 'two spirit* man' on the Gate between two worlds. Antonio, the fact that you are a two-spirit man, is a good thing. It is our blessing." At least, my sexual proclivities were not seen in any of the faith communities of my past, as being an "honorable" characteristic—much less as an "*holy*" characteristic that, is a spiritual group's traditional reason to celebrate! This was acceptance—no, it was a *celebration* of my nature—one that, I had not found before! Now, I was enabled to envision from their far healthier *Meshica/Toltec* Indian way to see what and how I am. Now, I knew why I'd always felt drawn to those things, which most institutional forms of religion had, historically and consistently, appropriated only for themselves! The *Meshica/Toltec* Indian way had revealed the truth to me of who and what I am. That, the Christianity I had known, hadn't been able to reveal it to me!

My true sexual orientation was [*their*] "...*blessing*" because *it signals* to them that I am "*a two spirit man;*" that, *I live in two worlds—in this common world of nature and, in the world of spirits*! I finally saw the reason for the uncanny way that I experience the experience of living, in paranormal ways, which is by far, my earliest memory. To them, my *natural* sexuality is experiential evidence of what I had been raised to call "spiritual giftedness." To them, my attraction to other men is what *evidenced* the *propensity in me* to the paranormal! Finally, I could wrap my mind around my life—make sense of—what had always been my reality! Finally, my *existential truth* made *spiritual sense*!

NOTES TO CHAPTER SEVEN

[i] I am the son of Aselia Acosta; who was the daughter of Maria Nicasia Tafolla; who was the daughter of Candelaria Gonzalez, who was killed by a truck minutes after she had received her last holy communion at St. Boniface Catholic Church, the oldest Catholic church in Anaheim, California; who was the daughter of *Meshica* women, whose birth, marriage and death records to the occupying French army officers had been burned by the Mexican Revolutionary War embattlements of 1912.

[ii] Harry James (Jimm) Kinney; the man to whom I refer in Chapter Six.

[iii] I am the son of Antonio A Feliz; who was the son of Antonio Feliz; who was the son of Jose Antonio Feliz, the same who was shot by a Vigilante possee, some of whom had been members of the Mormon Battalion, which had invaded his ranchos and the ranchos owned by his Peralta, Cota and Yorba families; who was the son of Manuel Celestino Feliz, a judge in Californio days during the conquest of California by the invading American Army of the West; the same who mediated between the Angelino pueblo civic authorities and the occupying army's leadership by hosting the signing of the Treaty of El Campo de Cahuenga in his adobe [see Neal Harlow's California Conquered 1846-1850 (University of California Press, 1982) page 231]; who was the son of Don Josef Tomas Feliz, who originally built the adobe at El Campo de Cahuenga; who was the son of Don Jose Francisco Feliz, the same who built the old adobe that is currently near Los Angeles' Griffith Park and, who was murdered by members of the Mormon Battalion in late March, 1847 for control of the estates owned by this last of the Los Feliz dons of Alta California; who was the son of Don Jose Vicente Feliz, the founding military head (*comisionado*) of El Pueblo de La Reina de Los Angeles the same who led the colonists to what is now the San Gabriel Mission from Los Alamos, Sonora who was a direct descendant of either Jose Blas Felis or his brother Geronimo Felis; the sons of a Spaniard who had escaped to New Spain to "escape the Spanish Inquisitor." It is said that, Los Feliz of Los Angeles used "Felis" as a spelling in the 17th and 18th centuries because medieval ancestors claimed only a French allegiance while others used "Felix" as a spelling because "we descend from Felix of the 1st century "c.e.—a governor of ancient Rome, "who represented Tiberius Cesar in the Germania of ancient Rome."

[iv] I called this man "Jeff" in my first book, Out of The Bishop's Closet, *A Call To Heal Ourselves, Each Other and Our World* (2nd. Ed. Paperback, Alamo Square Press, San Francisco, CA. 1992).

[v] Since, this pre-Columbian calendar ends at "high noon, December 23, 2012, it has always been significant to me that this happens to be the birth date of Joseph Smith Junior. He was born on December 23, 1805 and, whenever he was asked by his followers to expound on the coming of the long promised Millenium of peace, his responses would be about his birth date—December 23rd.

"We can collectively make hell into paradise because as is the macrocosm, so is the microcosm. Each of us is an energy vortex in which transmutation takes place. So, like the tiny creatures in our physical, human intestines metabolize our food into our individual human body cells, in like manner, humans metabolize fear into love. This is because, whether we believe it or not, emotions are elements of human consumption. Some of us have done this already, and *are already in a paradise,* and the rest of us *are unaware*!"

CHAPTER EIGHT

I AM
ANOTHER YOURSELF

We had met each other at a 1992 national conference on World Peace and Global Community, where he had been the keynote speaker at a gathering of workers in the global peace movement. Although, the vast majority of the presenting speakers were there from the World Church Temple School of the Reorganized Church of Jesus Christ of Latter Day Saints[i] headquartered in Independence, in Jackson County, Missouri, I'd assumed from his surname—noted on the official program—that he had been raised spiritually, as a Jew. Yet, over the years I have come to see that he does not take the Torah of his ancestors, literally.

Joel, I have come to know, is another person on the way of becoming open souls. As he stood, speaking before the crowd of more than three hundred of us who had just finished dinning, I found myself examining. Like a laser is made to do, I felt myself scan his every gesture, his facial expressions and body movements during his keynote presentation. My precision in this personal obsession with public speakers is from the fact that much of my undergraduate work at B.Y.U. was in theatre and in public address. Hence, when I am in an audience, listening to a public speaker, my propensity is to experience a public speaker from a professional, or a dispassionate analytic perspective. Over the years, I'd learned to do this in a quiet fashion, and to not discuss my observations afterward because I've learned that none of us enjoy being criticized by others. But, little did I know how unique this experience would be for me—especially, in light of my university training in communications.

My undergraduate B.Y.U. formal training in inter-personal communications usually has me observing the far subtler manner of a public speaker, and the result is that I often receive a much more complete view of what the public speaker is about. The rest of us can normally decode only the message being encoded by the very highly practiced facial/body movements, gestures and even other types of physical expressions. However, I had learned years earlier in theatre classes that *this* is only what the public speaker desires. The speaker, after all, is the one who is consciously *encoding*. If the encoding person, who sends the message, is not an open soul then, a hidden, or an unspoken message of their actual intent is disguised by the ability of the public speaker to camouflage her or his actual intent.

The rest of us will usually be receptors of only their encoded message, which the encoder desires to send out to us. But, there are those among us who, with training, have learned to decode what some public speakers either desire to hide while, others aren't aware of the other ways, in which we all encode out to others. I refer to the human energy field—a radiance of energy often seen as light.

The human energy field –or, what New Age thinkers might term the human aura– is constantly sending out honest messages, encoded in its language of light. It is a language system, which utilizes an alphabet of colors, to those who have sufficient ability to read it. *This energy field is speaking out what each of us is feeling inwardly; it may be considered the mouthpiece of the soul because whatever other encoding systems we use to try to send out messages to others, this encoding system is never turned down or off.* If there is someone in the audience of an event, in whom the ability to decode the human vibrational light energies has been developed then, she or he will usually be able to do so. As a result, the more complete inner message will be communicated; whether the person who is doing the encoding consciously wishes it, or not.

My *Meshica* friends had taught me in Mexico in 1990 to be open to this unconscious language of light energy with which we all speak out. Most interestingly, to me, Utah based Mormon scripture contains a verse that –at least in the language of metaphor– seems to allude to the existence of this ability to be sufficiently open to this honest language system of each other's soul. The scripture, which Utah based Mormons believe is a vision of a highest heaven, reveals interesting facts about this process. It declares: "They who dwell in his presence are the church of the Firstborn; *and they see as they are seen, and know as they are known;* having received of his fullness and of his grace."[ii] Here, the vision of the L.D.S. Three Degrees of Glory –the Afterlife in the Mormon cosmology– promises that they who are in the highest degree will be able to, "see as they are seen," and also, "know as they are known" —but, *by whom?* From whose perspective do they perceive us? *Who* is it that, "know" us as we, "are known" by *Them?* By *Who?* Simply: It is *They* who have the ability to see and know us in a way that is unique to their dimension of existence, one from where that kind of knowledge is engaged.

They are the ones who can "see [us] as [we] are seen [by Them] and know [us] as [we] are known [by Them]." Our bodies of light—for lack of a better term—are no different than the bodies of those having this ability, who's place is now in those dimensions of light. But, an Earth-bound soul—who is often prone to dishonestly deceive—is truly at a disadvantage because of her or his propensity to lie. Our physicality usually does not let us. This is because, like the light of fire, the human energy field is also an eternal element.

The human energy field is the force field of the soul. As long as the physical body lives –or, is *enlivened* by this energy– dishonest persons who desire to deceive or lie, will be seen by mortals, who are trained to perceive the human aura, as he or she is seen by *immortals*. This force field of the soul allows her or him to be known, as they are known by all who read their aura, irrespective of private desires to hide anything from any others. She or he will be "known as they are known" by the immortals, and will be "seen as they are seen" *by all others with the same ability to see.* Although still mortal, some can see through deceit even though the celestial dimension of existence is not where we –as a civilized society– are today.

But, I have affirmed in this book and elsewhere that, our present condition can be changed—that, our social condition can be transmuted. The key is for us to each self-identify as the planet, as the One being we call Earth. We can collectively make hell into paradise because as is the macrocosm, so is the microcosm. Each of us is an energy votex in which transmutation takes place. Like the tiny creatures in our physical, human intestines metabolize our food into our individual human body cells, in like manner, we metabolize fear into love. This is because, whether we believe it or not, emotions are also elements of human consumption. Some have metabolized fear into love already, and *are already in a paradise* while, the rest of us *are unaware.* But, we do not need to wait for a deity to transform this world. *We* mortals can just agree to it; because *agreement is the active principle in group prayer.* Though it is mostly practiced by Christians, group prayer is a vehicle that truly activates generative principles. We engage them, through inter-personal agreements, and this dynamic—a simple agreement of more than one, united in the chordant harmony of Love—is how we evolve a critical mass able to invoke the chordant vision that the Christian tradition claims:

"AND I saw a new heaven and a new earth: for the first heaven and the first earth were passed away; and there was no more sea.

"And I John saw the holy city, new Jerusalem, coming down from God out of heaven, prepared as a bride adorned for her husband."

The above vision, which most Christians understand as a prophecy about the final earthly triumph of good over evil, is –to me– a beautiful metaphor about the final result of a critical mass of open souls. In fact, I affirm that the process *has already been going on,* and that, it is now processing at a far faster rate than before the current huge paradigm shift began, and that: The dynamic of Earth's transmutation is already engaged!

Then, –since we can make a hell into a paradise, and also since some of us, involuntarily see our Other's human energy field and even, other beings of light– it follows then, that, *the metabolic transmutation of fear into love is already engaged.* Who ever said that the process of our transmutation would come all at once? The logic that our home planet's transmutation is already engaged has been a comfort to me, since my days as a recently ordained priest in the old Porterville ward of the Mormon Church. From that time, I've actually experienced an involuntary ability to see the human energy field. But, it isn't a constant gift for me, though. It comes when the person whom I am, "reading," is energized on a favorite theme or topic. This first meeting with Joel, was one such experience...

****

Our keynote speaker was a light-skinned man with full, shortly cut black hair. His face had hints of healthy pink tones with lips made red by the brightness of his white teeth. Clean-shaven, he stood about five feet/eleven inches in a dark suite, with eyes that glistened as the light on the hotel rostrum reflected in their moisture. Noting his clear, unblemished face, I surmised he couldn't be any older than thirty-two. As I continued listening, I focused my intent on his person, finding myself in complete agreement with the sense of empathy in one of his parables. Then...

With that intent, his whole person seemed to begin to glow. His countenance became luminous. As he spoke, I was lost to the logic of his words because the radiance from his face and chest was pulsating out a bright, yellow-white glow in his energy field. It actually reached out, over the audience sitting below where he stood and extended out over all of us in that audience. I don't remember exactly what he was saying at that precise moment but, I've never forgotten the inner sensation, which I experienced in the experience, because I decoded his encoded radiance as the emotion I'd come to know as the kind of Love about which, I write. This, I was enabled to do because of the teaching of that *Meshica/Toltec* wise man in Mexico in 1990: "*All humanity is One being. Collectively, we do what all living beings do—we metabolize the emotions we feed on.*"

With that recalled idea, I knew that I wanted to meet that man. So after the end of the session, I tried to go up to the rostrum to see if I could introduce myself but, I was overtaken by another man, whom I'd also wanted to know, who'd interrupted my walk up to the front of the ballroom. When he and I had finished, I couldn't see the Keynote Speaker anywhere. So, having to return to the vendor's area to sign my books and greet others, I left the hotel banquet room.

But later, while I stood and spoke with the same man who had chatted with me earlier by a dinning table, our Keynote Speaker came to my vendor's display, so I excused myself to the man that I'd been conversing with, and I held out my hand, "My name's Tony. Thank you for your message tonight."

Up close, his smile was the brightest jewel of his presence, and as he also held out his hand he simply said, "Joel," looking directly into my eyes. His grasp was firm and definite but, the most exquisite surprise was the healthy and pristine glow of his skin.

Instinctively, I picked up a copy of my first book and having signed it, I handed it to him, "here, take this with my compliments. I'd be interested in hearing from you about what I've written here. My number is in it."

"Thank you," he answered through his smile, "I will call you, promise." Then, after a few pleasantries, he left.

That was the beginning of one of those rare friendships that have –in most respects– made my life like a paradise on earth. Some live in bliss because, as it is said, *Ignorance is bliss*. For these, life can only be an illusion because, to truly *see*, requires a knowing; it demands an inner awareness. For such, life becomes paradisiacal by transcending the reality of which we are all too aware. Hopefully, in the preceding chapters, I've been somewhat successful in my effort to reveal how this has happened in the experience of one person —*myself*—through these experiences from my personal journey.

Joel is one of the many people in my world who is genuinely also endeavoring to travel the same way that I try to journey. There are numerous others in my world, who also seek the vibrational frequencies of Eternity in the same intensity as I. Some have been exposed to the reader in the stories that encompass the pages of this book. Others are not told of in this book for reasons, which I respect; but, that does not mean in any way that they are any less driven to go on the way of becoming open souls. For now, here, I only offer the above experience and the following two other experiences with this friend, and one with another man, which have taught me that each of them is also Another Myself…

A few years after we had first met, Joel and I were hiking on a mountain trail near his home on the part of Los Angeles that was once part of the old Los Feliz Rancho of my 18th and 19th century *Californio* ancestors. There was a perfect half moon –a *Meshica* symbol of equality– because Sister Moon then, lets Herself be seen as here, and not here, equally. The night seemed to be especially bright because the light of the moon made its glistening way along the surface of Silverlake Reservoir, below from where we stood. The black silhouette of the trees, shrubs and housetops—below the half moon, on the hillside across the lake from us—was contrasted with the bright colors of the night. The infrequent streaking clouds showed off the high energy colors of dark blue, purple and violet as they slowly made their way across the face of the moon in the black sky. The entire scene created a moment filled with portent.

It was one of those moments in time when Eternity seemed to be aware of us, and we could both feel it. Like many close friends, we embraced and looked over the awesome evening scene, in silent contemplation. Before standing there silently, we'd been engaged in conversation about how we both often envisioned what the future day might be like when we become a society of open souls. Joel holds a doctorate in political science, and yet, I knew that his life was more about becoming an open soul than about politics, *per se*. He'd pointed out that we were standing behind a mansion that was –at the time– owned by Madonna.

"How fitting," I said, "that here under the light of Sister Moon, who is down there, 'Walking On Water,' we stand looking out over a large body of water in the shadows of a celebrity's home who is a modern icon of woman." I found myself openly explaining to him that, in my former community of faith, I'd been taught that the future Millennial society of Love and peace had been named, "ZION —THE PURE IN HEART" in L.D.S. scripture. I began to comment to Joel how I, now, see that, while all institutional religions claim to foster society's becoming pure in heart *regarding Love*, they usually fail to stay true to this purpose. That, the behavior of purist-centered mentalities among fundamentalist religions has only made people pure in the *externals,* and I said out loud, "the term used by my former Utah faith community interprets what constitutes 'the pure' by their externally-based vision. Did I ever tell you that they now officially replace the original term 'white' with the word 'pure' in their current version of the Book of Mormon?"

"What do you mean?"

"Well, they recently changed that wording in reference to a key verse that says that, people like me –the Lamanites, or Native Americans, Indians– will 'become a white and delightsome people', to 'become a *pure* and delightsome people.' It's racist!"

"Now Tony, that could be the result of other factors too."

"Yeah, Mormons don't see it that way either, but what ever their reason, I don't worship a god who sees who is 'pure' by whether they're 'white.' Don't you see? *Using* the term 'pure' in the same context—*for what before was* 'white'—not only changes the canon, but it *equates* the one term with the other. Because the subject of the verse is racial, it now implies that being 'pure' is *actually*, equated with 'white' skin! What I work for –just as you do– is a society that is pure where it counts: In the heart. Ironically, that is what that other scripture declares—the one calling Zion, 'THE PURE IN HEART.'"

"But, those verses changing 'pure' from 'white" skin really are the only verses that they changed?"

"Well, historically, many other verses in that book are also altered."

Still hugging me, he quietly asked, "Do you mean to say that they're wrong? That they don't get it? Or, are you say…"

"I don't judge them anymore for this faulty envisioning," I interrupted. Then, I went on, "the ancient Qabalah teaches that the first thing we must lay down at the entrance to the temple is our bent toward judgment or criticism because both of 'these are loveless proclivities.' I just wish that they'd be more open, more honest, that's all. I learned long ago that, while I usually speak my truth boldly, truth is spoken out of my life's purpose, because being open and honest is part of the way of becoming an open soul."

"It sometimes gets others a bit angry with you though, don't you think, Tony? I mean, truth telling can come across to some as being a bit judgmental."

With that, I pulled away slightly to see into his eyes. "That's only because the shoe fits! I can't be quiet, and I'm sorry for any pain experienced in the experience by another. But, Joel, I have to put my own vision out into the chaos of the Universe in this dimension –especially in my inter-relating– because that's the way I cast my energy into the chaos, so that the awareness, which is within me, is acknowledged to the spirits. How can I expect the dynamics of Love to sustain the spiritual evolution of the mass consciousness that my personal relationships manifest? If a human relationship is a mass consciousness then –if I don't take the initial step of letting my inner awareness have its voice– I'm not being in the world as I am, in truth. Yes, sometimes my relationships are very strained by my efforts to be open and honest, but ultimately, I want my loved ones to know *me*. If I hide my truth from them then, they can only know a person whom they *imagine me to be*."

"And," because we do know you, Tony, our Love as friends can sustain the relationship," he added.

"Yes! Joel, you know I need to be 'known' outwardly as I'm 'known' inwardly because that opens me, as I journey with my fellow travelers in life. Besides, how can I effectively share my vision with others, if I'm obfuscating, hiding something from them? You know the importance of being open souls." I had just finished explaining what Zion is to Mormons and that, *that* is my goal on Earth. I asked, "So Joel, what—as a Jew—do *you* believe on the idea of a coming millennium of global peace and harmony?"

"Well," he said, raising his full eyebrows with an ironic smile, "this isn't exactly the official Jewish position…"

We laughed.

He continued: "But what I believe is that, the coming of the Messiah, if you want to call it that, is a collective process. To me, that actually means that, everyone has to take the same level of responsibility that, say, Jesus took."

I said, "Didn't you once tell me that 'the point of it all is to become saints'?"

He nodded back his affirmation.

"Joel, that's why the Mormons call themselves Latter-day Saints. In the Roman Catholic tradition, that's what they call the 'mystical body of Christ.' For Roman Catholics, the reference to the mystical body of Christ has to do with their mission to evangelize the entire world. Catholic *means* universal, or inclusive."

Joel answered, "One of my favorite Jewish prayers speaks about a future day in which '*God will be one and his name one.*' To me, that means we'll eventually reach a point where religions won't clash."

"Do you really believe that?"

"It's what I'm working for."

"Well," I responded, "I don't think religions are going to do it. I think that they're the old way. For me, the term religion means 'to be bounded to the past, again.' So I don't think that religion, in that sense, can be the solution. They're blind. None of them teach the inner truth. They teach ritual and ceremony and tradition."

Joel looked thoughtful and then, he spoke, "It depends on how you define religion. Gandhi said—and I agree, that—there are as many religions, as there are people. There is a lot less uniformity in people's beliefs than meets the eye, Tony. I try to use the word *spiritual* to talk about this kind of coming together. Fundamentalists —and other authoritarians—have given religion a bad name for a lot of people. In any case I believe that, through communication, and dialogue and openness, we can achieve universal understanding across religions."

"That's not the answer," I replied. "That's the *process*. The answer is to discard the literal interpretation of any canon or sacred story, which implies that there can be only one truth. I'm talking about tearing away what amounts to the itchy scab of the open social woundedness on the human emotional body."

"Well," he smiled, "I'm not sure I'd use that metaphor." We laughed.

He continued, "Religion may bind us to the past, but I just think we need to be gentle with the past as we create the future."

"Yes, it's got to be done gently, but it's got to be done. Society is really sick, Joel. Society needs a healing—big time! You have to acknowledge the problem, before you can even know that you need to choose to go a different way."

Joel nodded in agreement, and then said; "But, you and I both know, that encoded in all of the world's major religions, along with the patriarchy, and all the other negativity you write about, are the same universal principles that we both want to see realized. Tony, that's why I think the work of the Dalai Lama, in participating in so many dialogues between many religions, is so important—for example, in pointing out the host of all the experiential similarities between Eastern meditation and Western prayer. It's a work that truly gets below the surface of the differences to the universal truths beneath."

"For me," I said, "the issue is not whether we need to be nice to each other in our different communities of faith, but whether we allow each other the same protection of rights that we each want. *That*, to me, is what being an open soul is all about. When we can all mutually come to an honest agreement to respect each other's rights of belief, *and put our civic work where our mouth's rhetoric is* then, we are truly saying; "I am Another Yourself."

"Well, then," he said quietly, "I am Another Yourself."

My dialogue with Joel strengthened my personal conviction that, until we have a critical mass of parallel thinkers who envision from the same perspective, we're just going to be hiding away in our own private islands of paradise in a world that's like a hell.

I had months earlier related the story to him of my 1990 first encounter with the *Meshica* in Mexico. We had often talked about how their more ancient *Toltec* wisdom teaches about the Mastery of Intent, and Joel responded to my comments that night by simply saying to me, "It really is all about how we envision, isn't it, Tony. As long as you can retain your view of all of your relationships as being mere reflections of yourself, you will probably use respect and compassion in how you inter-relate."

Walking on a little on that little trail we'd taken before, we'd stopped to enjoy the moonlit view. I said, "Joel, I'd like to relate an experience I had not too long ago in Salt Lake City."

Stopping by a promontory that allowed a glittering view of the city below us, he got down and sat on the earth. "Okay, tell me the story."

Sitting down next to him, I began, "I've told you about the six distinguished Latter-day Saint scholars back in Utah who all recently got excommunicated from the Mormon Church, didn't I?"

He simply nodded.

"Well, that entire experience that I've told you about in that Unitarian Church honestly happened. As I sat in that side chapel at the Unitarian Church on 1300 East in Salt Lake City, listening to Paul and Margaret Toscano respond in a public forum to his own excommunication from the Mormon Church, I saw them." I felt the tears well up in my eyes.

Joel put his hand on my shoulder; his face radiating his caring. He knew how much this experience has impacted me.

"Joel, I saw two beings of light sitting exactly opposite to Margaret and Paul, as if they were listening to their testimony. It was like seeing two humanoid forms made out of *fire*, Joel. You know how a candle's flame is usually a yellowish golden color?

"The color of the light of a candle's flame, you mean"

"Yeah."

"Now, I know why you love candles so much."

I felt the smile on my face. His empathic perception of my

way of remembering this experience was just like him. "Joel, in the places where a photograph would manifest shadows on the body of a person, the light of these two humanoid forms was that same color of golden yellow. But, in the areas on the form of their bodies where our natural vision in this dimension is prone to see as being lighter in color, the light was brighter than the bright sun in our sky. I'll never forget what I saw there, Joel. If seeing is believing then, I really believe. Do you think I'm crazy or…?"

"Tony," he interrupted, "if we can accept that airwaves can contain television signals that reach our television sets then, I think it's acceptable to also believe that we can also be composed of light energy that can't usually be seen by us any more than a television network's video signal. I don't think it's crazy at all."

I felt the tears begin to role down my face.

"I think I've told you, yes, I have. Joel, do you recall that, all along my way after I had left my organized religious communities, I've consulted either a psychologist, or psychiatrist to be sure that my other-worldly experiences are not a product of some weird chemical process in my brain, or some really bad *mota*!"

Joel's uniquely bright smile became complete. I could trust him to always respond to humor.

"Anyway," I said, wiping my tears, "I've been careful to know that the Source of these phenomena in my life are from a place other than my brain." I'd stopped tearing, and I felt the now familiar sense of peace in my solar plexus. I looked into his eyes. I thought: So what if it *is* a product of my mind? After all, the laws of modern physics *do* allow for mind to be an actual place occupying space. The *Meshica* had even taught me that some forms of schizophrenia are a giftedness that opens an inter-dimensional channel. "But, Joel," I added, "I do think that our brains are a part of the dynamic because –at the very least– *our brains are the physical decoder of other-worldly phenomena.*"

At that instant, the bright moon was reflected in his eyes, as his semi-shadowed face seemed to glow.

"So," I went on, "when I saw those beings of light –without knowing whether they were some out-of-body manifestation of the light bodies of the two speakers on the stand– all I could fully see was that, they were two *additional* beings from a world of light. Joel, they were made of light!" After taking in a deep breath, I went on, "I turned to a friend sitting next to me to see if he'd seen it too. Uh, I've mentioned Jon to you before, haven't I?"

Joel nodded.

"Jon was sitting there to my immediate left and I whispered, nudging his side, 'Jon, do you see...?'"

"Jon shook his head, as if to say, 'no', and he whispered back, 'Tony, what is it?'" With that vivid memory in my mind's eye, my tears began to flow again. "Well, at that point, I turned back to see more, and they had both vanished from my vision."

"Who do you think they were? Why were they there?"

"Oh, I have no idea. To me, the important thing is that I really *did* experience the experience. I experienced it in a way that enabled me to read a more complete picture of their message than did others in that audience. Because of how I there, experienced the experience of those beings of light, I'll never forget the comfortable, happy, peace, and the sense of fullness—as long as I have human awareness."

"So, that real paranormal experience has great meaning for you," he said with an earnest look. But, this, was not a patronizing comment; that isn't Joel's way. No, this good friend has a large capacity for empathy. He understood, and he simply wanted to validate my experience.

"Well, I don't think I have any chemical imbalances and all the psychologists I've consulted say that I am part of sixty percent of our population."

"You mean that sixty percent of us experience the world like you do? Tony, do you know what you're saying? His eyes were such aglow. "You're speaking..."

Interrupting, I said firmly, "Yes, sixty percent of us. But, what it speaks out loudly, Joel, is that there really is a dimension of reality other than our world. It is a world of light. It's a world where one's own personal integrity is the *norm*. My experience, of the experience of those two beings of light, is a confirmation of what physicists now say about the nature of the Universe. To me, the experience itself, is a phenomenology because it *speaks*. It is saying that –because it is, as it is– my purpose in living is to be attuned to the peace of that revelatory moment, which has since then gone into my world of memory, as a guide for my journey. Because I experienced the experience in the peaceful, joyous and harmonic way that I did, if nothing else, it is evidence to me of an actual world of chordant light, which I not only sensed with my vision but, with my entire body. It's saying to me that this other dimension is, actually, made visible to me for some, yet, hidden reason but, because each experience like this one brings me physical health, I'm generously blessed."

The light of the moon was, now, coming from behind his face, and...

I went on saying, "In a way, I guess that, if the old saying applies, 'It takes one to know one' then, this phenomenology of mine is saying something about my own nature. But, more than that, I was recently reminded by my friend, Sergio, that *the difference between a signal and simple noise, is that a signal will repeat itself.*' As you know, Joel, the many ironies in my life so far, actually amount to the same old message repeating itself to me; communicating that I and you and all living forms are also beings of light! And, what does that message take us toward?"

"Awareness," he said firmly. "If it says anything about you, Tony, it says that you've been taken to a unique place of awareness. Where do you think it takes us toward?"

"Yes. I mean…I don't know where it really takes us." To myself I thought, I hope-I believe-I trust that *is* where it takes us. "Yet," I said and paused…

The moon was falling quickly now.

"Joel," I said looking right into his eyes, "because the first response in me was a sensation of rapturous peace, I can only see it as being from a generative Force. My health is good, my body has truly been renewed. But, you know, evil doesn't have that effect. Evil, I've come to know, is not creative but, on the other hand, evil is a destroyer. You know that the things that I am trying to be about are all creative in nature. At least, if how I am now, health-wise, after experiencing the experience, is a measure of what the meaning of those two beings of light is then, these experiences are obviously generative in nature. However, far more than anything else, that one phenomenology is saying to me that –because the phenomenon was two beings who both appeared to be made of a kind of firelight, and also since they manifested separate from the two speakers– they were from a world of light. That is what I feel about it. With only that data, Joel, and with nothing more to go on then, it seems safe to assume that that message will, at least, lead us to a world of light because those light beings came from such a placc."

"Heaven?" he asked with that smile that always told me he had some off-the-wall perspective.

With that, both of us immediately exploded in loud, raucous laughter.

Loud laughter was always my response to that look from Joel. After regaining my composure, I finally said back, "I don't care if those light beings are actually alien creatures from some other planet, or something. That scenario, at least, would fit a 19th century cosmology Joseph Smith, Junior provided for today's Utah based

Mormon community. By the way Joel, did I tell you that Mormons have believed since the early 19th century that aliens *do* live on other planets? That was long before the rest of us believed that idea. I recall that, just forty years ago, the idea was pure fiction."

Joel nodded, "Aha."

"Wherever the journey takes us, Joel, you have to agree: Life is an adventure!"

Joel got very quiet then, he said, "There have been times when I have been in great physical pain, and I have meditated, and I have felt the essence of myself that is not my material body; something that I know is in me, and also throughout me, and around me, and connected with everything else in reality. That, *comforting presence* is what I know of God and heaven. It's the love, which I've seen, felt, given and received throughout my life. It's the flow of the energy, or spirit among everyone and everything, and it's by far the highest possible good and purpose that I can imagine. This now happens whenever I meditate, whether I'm in pain or not. It's been called Heaven, God, Love, or Nature. In other words, Tony, I may not see the light that you see. But, I feel it."

"So, do you mean; you experience it, Joel?"

"Yes. When I turn my focus outward I send that energy out into the world. That way of being 'on Earth as it is in Heaven' is what I call Topia. It's my word for Zion."

Although we two had come from very different paths, my experience with Joel showed me that; he and I had now arrived at the same place of reckoning. But, most of all, it wasn't his ideas, but his "fruit"—his own gentleness—that communicated to me where he was coming from.

****

About a week before that experience with Joel, I had met Another Myself in, yet, another synchronicity in my life. This was the time of my life was when I'd initially moved back to southern California. I had made a decision to get a private mail box in West Hollywood because I still didn't know where I would finally settle. So, it was only the third day after driving my rented U-Haul truck into my current neighborhood that I was reminded that some in this world are angels who live among us—serving our spiritual need for otherworldly phenomena—yet, being sensual, physical humans...

****

I first saw him there as I walked westward on Santa Monica Boulevard in West Hollywood. I could see him across the street I was crossing, in a lotus position on the curb with forms laid out next to him. I wondered what he was doing, so I walked closer to him after stepping onto the sidewalk where he was sitting. I could see that he was absolutely one of the most perfect specimens of male beauty that I'd ever seen. Suddenly, he turned toward me, and the expression on his face reflected a person who'd just seen a long-lost and cherished friend.

I kept walking closer, feeling a big smile come onto my face. I wondered to myself, who is this person? Do I know him?

With that thought, the young man, who seemed now to me to be in his mid twenties, began to get up from his place, yet, he kept his gaze focused right on me.

As I approached within about three yards away, I felt my heart pounding. He's so beautiful, I thought to myself.

As he kept looking at me with what I would later come to call his mesmerizing or, his intoxicating look of sheer joy, he began to open his arms, as if to give me a hug, and took a step toward me. I could see his face better now. His face looked like a cross between Brad Pitt and Val Kilmer. Standing up now, I saw that he was easily, over six feet tall, with no facial hair and a carpenter's musculature that was obvious to me, even though he was fully clothed in jeans and a simple T-shirt.

His smile was completely contagious.

I couldn't keep from smiling. It was like I *knew him*!

Now, walking right up to me, he was the picture of—the epitome of—brotherly friendship and sincere affection.

Suddenly, at just a few feet away now, I felt a very familiar sensation. Was he truly someone whom I've known before? He did look familiar but, who is it? I stepped closer without hesitation. If anything, I responded to his friendly overture as if I knew that we'd been long-lost friends. Maybe, I thought, he looks familiar because he resembles a movie star. My arms were now, opened up to hug this complete stranger on a busy boulevard in the city!

We hugged ecstatically—like two old lovers who had just re-discovered each other in an old sentimental black and white film!

"Ohhhhhh!" he moaned out loud as we two –two complete strangers– embraced there, in the way that only old friends do. After several seconds of bliss there, on that busy sidewalk, he added, "and he gives good hug too!" His hands were massaging my back, in a way that told me he was well aware of the art.

"Hey, buddy," I responded, "do we know each other? You look so familiar to me!"

Stopping for a second to look at my face, he answered, "I know that's not just a line." Still in a full body embrace, he added, "maybe we should get to know each other– again."

With that, I noticed the papers and forms that he had on the sidewalk next to him. "What are you doing out here on the street?"

"Oh, I'm just registering people to vote. Hey, are you a registered voter?"

"Actually," I said breaking our embrace then, and stepping toward his forms on the sidewalk, "I'm on my way to open a new mail box. I just moved here from Utah…"

"Utah?"

"Yeah. Let me go get my new mailing address set up and then, I'll come back and register with you. Okay?"

After finishing my business in the area, I returned to where he still sat in his lotus position. After registering with him, we talked for a bit to discover if –maybe– we actually had met somewhere in our past. We decided that we hadn't but, that we wanted to know each other better. So, after about a half-hour of talking there on the street, we went to his car, and eventually, went to his place in Venice Beach, California.

It turned out that Atundra had also recently moved back to southern California from the Pacific Northwest. He'd spent several years with the Rashnish, the now late guru of a commune in the State of Washington. Atundra was the name the Rashnish had given to him after he'd moved there from a different commune in Australia. I learned that Atundra had been like a right-hand-man to the famous and controversial Indian guru of many thousands of disciples, and I soon became aware of his highly evolved and keen psychic abilities. He told me that, his original name had been Sergio, so I ended up calling him Sergio instead. It seemed to me that, he was a little more comfortable with Sergio than, with Atundra. But, the interesting characteristic Sergio had, more than his masculine and physically sensual beauty, was his well-honed psychic/spiritual ability, which he'd perfected by the Rashnish's personal tutoring.

Sergio had developed the ability to read another person in a way that allowed him to verbally articulate their innermost, intimate and their most significant emotional conflicts in the context of that moment in time. On the Santa Monica Freeway in Los Angeles, on the way to his place, he suddenly began to relate to me *–as if he had personally been a part of the experiences–* as if he had personally participated in all of the wrenching and emotionally challenging contradictions of my life. He spoke as if he'd been there –at my side– during all of those years of my depression, terror, anger and disillusionment. Eventually, Sergio moved in with me, and there were countless times when we'd enjoy a sunrise or a sunset on our third story balcony, only to have him break into a stream of words that came out of his readings of me. Those times were wonderful days of many paranormal experiences, excitement and revelation.

It was natural for me to try to get Joel and Sergio to meet each other because of my affinity with both of their, respective, profoundly spiritual ways but, the timing had never worked out. Then, a year after I had returned to California, I had done a book signing at A Different Light Bookstore in West Hollywood and Joel had been good enough to come and support me. After the event, Joel and I had gotten a little bite to eat at a restaurant on Santa Monica Boulevard, and as Joel and I were leaving the place, I saw Sergio walking toward us from across the street.

Right there, on the island between the east and west traffic, we all met, and I was able to finally introduce these two important people in my life to each other. We decided to all go with Sergio to his new place, just north of where we were at the time, for a brief visit. On the way there in Joel's car, traveling behind Sergio's car, I said to Joel, "this is the man I've told you about. He's the one that I hugged the moment we met."

"The psychic guy?"

"Yeah, Joel. Brace yourself for a unique experience in what you like to call the paranormal." With that comment, I noticed that the wind had picked up because all the palm trees started swaying a lot in the wind. "Look at those trees, Joel."

"It just got pretty windy," he said calmly, as he turned off the motor in front of Sergio's apartment building.

"It's the wind spirits," I said, as I started to open the car door on the passenger side. The sense of some ominous portent filled my soul.

Walking up to the main front door, Joel asked, "is that what the *Meshica* Indians would say about our southern California hot Santa Ana Winds?"

"Well, Joel, all of the Santa Ana Winds *do* originate in the ancient sacred place, which we now call the 'Four Corners Area' –the ancient holy places of several Indian societies, including the ancient *Meshica*."

Opening the front door, Sergio welcomed us, and looking out into the windy night around us, he added, "the spirits are out tonight!"

In the course of our brief visit that night, exactly what I'd suspected would take place happened, as if perfectly on schedule. However, it didn't happen until I left the room for a few minutes to go to the bathroom; so, as a result, I don't know exactly what Sergio had read in Joel. I was only able to catch the last part of his reading as I walked back into the living room...

Joel was sitting on the floor. His face was totally transfixed on Sergio as he listened intently.

"...and, unless you deal with this now, it will continue to be an obstacle to your purpose for being." Sergio had finished.

"Oh, I missed it!" I said, sitting down on the floor with them, "why didn't you wait for me to come back into the room?"

"This was for him; not you, Tony."

"Tony," Joel exclaimed, "he just...he just..." Joel couldn't calm himself. He was completely taken by the accuracy of Sergio's words. "He hit the nail right on the head, Tony!"

"Told you," I said simply.

****

Indeed, there truly are angels who live among us as mortals, who are messengers of inner wisdom from a place beyond any of our cultural moorings. They're at work here, helping many to evolve into that long-promised world of harmony, peace, Love and light.

Today, as I sit at the keyboard and press the keys that make the black symbols we call words on this page, I remember another man who has shown me that he is also Another Myself. Although he and I never used those words because I had not yet met my *Meshica* friends, like Joel and Sergio, the man whom I call Don in this book is also on the way of becoming open souls. As mentioned in the story below about how he and an old friend from Utah –Jon, another opening soul– had made an agreement with me that created my first book, Don had worked with me in the design of and final editing of the project. It was almost a book...

****

One night, before the night when we loaded his U-haul, Don had asked about my plans for my next book. This conversation took place, only days, after a rather bizarre two week road trip that was filled with intense, multi-sensory connections, and with a series of otherworldly paranormal forces. But, that story isn't told here.

I answered by mentioning the parts that had been edited out of the manuscript of my first book before he'd begun to assist me in the final production work. Then, with that certain inner awareness –that sense of knowing– that what I was about to say would actually, come to happen, I hesitatingly spoke what I felt: "Don," I said, again, feeling that unique and strong sense of confirmation within –in the region of my solar plexus– "I can envision myself, sitting at my computer, working on the project."

"Okay," he said. "Now, describe it. Tell me what you see."

Deciding that I would have some fun with him, I said, "I see that I'm naked..."

"Seriously, Tony."

"Seriously," I quipped. Then, I went on, "I can see out from a large sliding glass balcony door and window in front of me. I can see that I'm upstairs –maybe a second floor place. I'm looking out over the balcony railing, at the verdant trees and thick shrubbery, with a large palm tree standing tall from out of all the green below –like an erect phallus penetrating the clear, blue horizon."

"Okay," he responded, "anything else?"

"No," I said simply. Then, after feeling that sensation again in my solar plexus, I added, "...except for maybe a few birds, who will be happy to visit from time to time. I don't believe in having pets, unless it's the animal who chooses to come to me, to live in my home; not the other way around. So, I welcome wild birds, if they choose to come. In that sense, the wild birds are my pets."

That conversation took place in 1988. As this book goes into its final editing, it is the Spring of 2004. So, even writing these lines, is a response from the vast enfoldings of Bohm's implicate order that existed when Don and I spoke out loud about where my choices would take me. Today, as I sit and look out at my fragrant tuber roses on the balcony, framing the exact scene that was then, yet an enfolded reality which I had envisioned roughly fourteen years ago, I wish I had kept in touch with Don.

I wish I could show him here, in person, how my present is an exact reflection of the envisioning we did nearly fourteen years ago! With that nostalgic idea in my mind, a familiar group of wild robins that seem to enjoy my balcony as much as I do, fly down from the giant tree across the street –where I saw the lovely *lady of light*– and perch themselves on my balcony railing.

My mind wanders to the wonderful and awesome way we'd experienced the experience of those days, when my evolving way of being in the world had first become engaged. One day, when Don and I were on that two week road trip, he'd recognized a large granite rock from my dream-world. I'd told him the previous day that I'd dreamed of it "protruding out of a mountain." When he'd found it in a mountain area in the Sierras on our camping trip, he'd said simply, "I found the large rock protruding out of the side of the mountain in your dream." And, sure enough, after taking me to it, it was easy for me to recognize the entire scene.

Well, I think Don, now, would also recognize today's emerald colors against the blue sky –including the phallic-like palm tree– which make up the scene just out of my second-floor apartment. I wish we had kept in touch because I know we'd probably both laugh raucously about this absolute synchronicity! He'd especially enjoy the beautiful and friendly wild robins, I think.

****

So, Don –if you read this, you know who you are– I affirm that agreement really is the core principle of all Eternity! And, Don, all those spiritual phenomena that, we experienced together were the first part of a long, and a recurring phenomenological pattern that continued since we put that first book together. Little has changed since my excommunication. Do you remember that ethereal mural that makes up the three walls of the Celestial Room—as one enters it from the other chambers—in the Los Angeles Mormon Temple?

Now, recall the remarkable mural on all the walls except the one from where one enters that beautiful room. As you know, a Celestial Room of a Mormon Temple is designed to re-present an environment that speaks out the peaceful harmony of the Celestial Life. That mural was of an ethereal, misty garden, complete with juniper, palm, magnolia and other temperate/semi-tropical trees, shrubs and plants painted in muted violet, blue and pink hues. The mural's artist had also multiplied the misty horizons of vegetation silhouetted in foggy high-energy colored layers.

Close your eyes now, Don, so you can remember how its layered quality allowed for tremendous depth to be perceived in that mural, which greets anyone entering there, from the west. Well, this morning, as I turned around on my east balcony, after facing east, I went to open the screen door by sliding it over the two layered glass door –which was still positioned opened– so that the sliding door's additional two layers of glass entirely covered it. In other words, four layers of glass were facing a misty morning sun, creating a multi-layered reflection of the treetops.

So, instead of actually opening the screen door, I stood there and felt a surge of energy within me respond to the multi-layered scene reflected in the glass window, and on the opened glass door behind it. The effect was a beautiful reflection of my second-floor view of all the tops of avocado, juniper, magnolia, rubber, weeping willow and palm trees! I stood there for a long moment because today, being one of those heavy, wet, foggy L.A. mornings, the view reflected on those four layers of glass had the same awesome effect as in that huge Temple mural. The scene before me re-created what is seen, as one walks into that Celestial Room in the Los Angeles Temple from that Temple's western chambers. So, even as I write these final lines, the Universe is speaking out its harmony to me, and the whole world has become my Temple! Don, don't dwell on what others have said of me.

Contrary to what some others have disparagingly said about how I now experience the experience, I hope you can tell from the stories in this book, that there definitely is a major phenomenological pattern in my life –a true signal– because it is a pattern. Mere noise, remember, doesn't repeat itself. Mere noise is constant. But, Don, an intelligent *signal*—a signal will always be a repetitive and consistent pattern! Think of it, Don...

No matter in which cultural context –or what worldview– in which I experienced the experience, the signal was consistent, it was a true pattern that repeated itself. For example, as a young Roman Catholic boy, and even much later when it directed me to one of the Bishops of the Holy See for their rite of confirmation,[vii] the message of the phenomenology came in an intelligent pattern. As a Mormon, over and over again, the same message was also manifest for me in the same pattern. *It was a phenomenology about a parallel world of light and, on our natural Oneness.* Then, in the Reorganized L.D.S. community based in Independence, Missouri;[viii] the same intelligent pattern was manifest in their unique context of spiritual giftedness –with a different view on spirit writing than is the worldview of Utah based Latter-day Saints– but, the signal, the message, was again the same as always. Finally, when I lived among the *Meshica* in Mexico in 1990; the same signal was repeated but, it came in a, yet, very different cultural context. But, the inner message always came to me in the same, consistent pattern! This phenomenology tells me that it is *not* mere noise! It is a definite signal from the enfolded

Universe—irrespective of what some may have said about me to dissuade you from any further involvement with me!

That signal is the same signal that I've been receiving from the compassionate Universe from the earliest day of my childhood's experience in the experience. It is a signal that screams out the singular message that, after all is said, written and done, the only important matter left, is Love. It is a signal from the world of light that is saying that the Unifying Field is Love, that The Force –which exists in and through all things, which have been, which are, or ever will be– is manifest in this mortal dimension by our human mass consciousness. I've learned to read the encoded signal.

The signal is constantly saying to me –over, and over again– that The Force is comprehended by us as Love, as *Itself*! Just now Don, as I came in from my balcony to finish writing this paragraph, the Universe used the language of *beingness*—of what actually *is*. Our compassionate Universe here presented me with my past, in my present, as if to foretell my future by reflecting old affect imagery, saying: I came from an environment of Love, I am still surrounded by a context of Love, and the layered misty horizons speak out a Divine promise that Love will eternally increase.

However, Don, my world of memory speaks out honestly –and loudly– recalling that the kind of Love of which I write will not increase because of religious institutions. How I've experienced the experience has taught me that all institutions are about *their* self-preservation, first and foremost. That, they all teach about Love, but that, they're not capable of *being* Love. It is we who are naturally, *living* creatures, who are able to generate the Love of which I write here. The reason why I have written in this book that our civic life is where we can learn to grow into Love—rather than in our religious life—is simple: It's in our *secular* world where we *do* all inter-relate with others who are *not* also products of our, individual, respective, second womb environment. This is why I've written elsewhere[ix] that our democratic republic is where, I believe, we truly have the best opportunity to evolve into a society of open souls. You can read one of the same signals too, Don:

Examine the top, external architecture of our nation's capitol building in Washington, D.C. Don, you've probably also noticed that its dome is capped with a huge statue of an Iroquois *woman* in full Native regalia. This is no accident, Don. It is a testament to us all that, our beloved form of civic life –in contrast to most of our own religious lives– was, in fact, borrowed from the older, pre-American Iroquois Confederation by the 18th century, Euro-centric founders of our constitutional government. Recall that all our legislated "civil rights" are merely an attempt to institutionalize what are *already our inalienable* human rights. Even our civic monuments speak it out! That, empathy must be seen as if being on top of domination—for the Capital dome is a phallus—saying that, openness to diversity invokes unity in the Mass Mind that, we are.

Everything that has happened, as I have journeyed since I last saw you, Don –yes, everything– speaks out that same message which, matters more than any institution, politic, ideology, theology, dogma, tradition or canonized document; for, all of these are only contextual manifestations. That all-important message is: The Universal Integrating Force in all forms of life who have lived, who now live, or who will yet live in all dimensions of time and all eternal space –that All Inclusive *Force,* that I AM– is the Source. It is the Source of the call for us all to travel on the way of becoming open souls. Nothing else is more important for any of us to understand. Nothing.

NOTES TO CHAPTER EIGHT

[i] The official name of this global faith is now, Community of Christ.

[ii] LDS Doctrine and Covenants, Section 76: verse 94. (italics added)

[iii] Revelation, Chapter 21: verses 1-2; King James Version of the Bible.

[iv] Ibid., Section 97: verse 21.

[v] The Pearl of Great Price, Book of Abraham, Chapter 3; verses 3-19 discusses the Mormon cosmology and reveals the "planet" on which the earliest apostles of the Mormon community taught that Father In Heaven dwells. They took their text for this doctrine from the discussion of the suns in this reference, wherein it states, "…these are the governing ones; and the name of the great one is Kolob…therefore Kolob is the greatest of all the [suns]." In fact, in currently accepted L.D.S. Mormon ways of envisioning, the earthly inhabitants of the city of ZION will inter-mingle with the angels who reside in the presence of the Son of God when he brings them with him at His Second Coming.

[vi] I highly recommend Dr. Joel Federman's website: www.topia.org

[vii] The story of that miraculous experience in the Roman Catholic Kansas City Cathedral is told in my first book, Out of The Bishops Closet.

[viii] Community of Christ

[ix] The Issue Is Pluralism, *A Call To Greater Pluralism In Civil Marriage Law*, by Antonio A. Feliz (Editorial Los Feliz, Los Angeles, California, 2000).

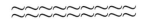

"She was born with complete male sex organs, externally and internally, and she was also fully equipped at birth with all the usual female sex organs, with the one exception of a uterus. Her vagina, labia, fallopian tubes, ovaries, etc. were as much developed as were her penis, testes, prostate gland, etc. Her vagina was where the rest of us have only a rectum. All of these are physiological facts of Mary Jane's physical body at birth.

"This was the actual truth of her life, which the highest ranks of the Mormon hierarchy that she humbly trusted, were so adamant about...and, like Galileo's Roman hierarchy, Mary Jane's also chose to excommunicate her, rather than, to value her testimony born of her experience..."

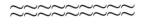

CHAPTER NINE

SCIENCE ALIGNS
WITH ANCIENT WISDOM

From my earliest memories, I knew that I was *queer*, in the broadest sense of the meaning of that word. The way, in which I had experienced the experience of all my past circumstances—and, my responses to all of them—had revealed a pattern in all my previous personal choices. That moment in 1979 was when the Universe first endowed me with a vision to see all the hidden motivations of my earlier life choices. It was when I first knew where I'd come from, why I am here and where my journey was now headed. It was when I found that *both* science *and* mysticism had the answers...

I often reminisce on that remarkable epiphany I experienced in 1979, when I worked for the L.D.S. Church Offices. I had been standing there, very early on that day, in front of the massive South window—the huge mezzanine one that oversees the main outdoor waterfountain—looking out from inside of the South Entrance to the L.D.S. Church Offices tower in Salt Lake City, Utah. It happened the first Monday after my last trip to South America—that final, fated, three-week voyage with my then, new supervisor at L.D.S. Church Offices and I sought solace and strength.

It had been on that trip wherein Brother Bishop had revealed the disgusting secret doctrine about how it is that, all the men who become members of the L.D.S. Quorum of The Twelve[i] are all, each biologically related cousins, or related by marriage. My soul was still in a swirl about the "*implications*" of our hidden doctrine about a "royal" *family* –about a religious oligarchy– that claims Jesus as a common ancestor. D. Michael Quinn, the most widely read historian of L.D.S. Mormon history, would do the unthinkable (years later) by publishing the genealogies of all the L.D.S. First Presidencies, and all of their Councils of The Twelve.[ii] Yet, L.D.S. still don't believe that their church is presided over by men who are all each other's cousins, but in 1979 *I did.* So, I sought solace, and strength...

That huge south plaza waterfountain, with all the glittering sunlight in an early morning dance throughout its water, had always been a pleasant sight to gaze on before going up to my office. The sun's brilliance was shimmering like a trillion little dancing gold and white lights. This was a place where the dynamics of nature, physics, and the Topian[iii] ideals to which I had dedicated myself many years before, had always seemed to come together for me. Like in the old Quaker hymn that teaches about life, that moment was precisely when, overlooking that waterfountain, I saw that, my life had begun to "turn, turn, until…" I'd, eventually, "…come out right!"

****

The words came softly into my mind as a definition that I knew was about the *water* of that waterfountain. Because the words defined the word, "concord;" in that one instant, Divine Intelligence had opened a sense of purpose for me as I journey on in the dominant civilization of our modern world which, in my college years, I had come to understand as a constant personal struggle. Because of my constant struggle to be a good patriarch, which was not *my natural bent*—to me—life, itself, had now become like going up on a *down-*escalator. However, *this* was the re-defining moment from which, I would never again perceive life in the same conflicted, contrary, confused and constraining ways…

After I felt those words, like a vision, the revelation became majestically manifest in the wondrous waterfountain's water below me on the South Plaza. In the center of all the hustle and bustle of people there, majestically, the water was thrusting, it was pushing upward. It was *all* so alive! It is so dynamic, it impacts all who see it—and, in this way—its very phenomenology imprints itself on all of our common sub-conscious senses of our human psychological, emotional and social cohesion. It is subtle, so subtle that, it registers only on a sub-conscious level. All confronted by it –when seeing that waterfountain's surging form– must know on some level that, *it is a constant—it is a continuous combination of innumerable single chemical units in a dynamic that shapes them all into a collective phallus of water that penetrates the air above it.*

This affect imagery is so subtle that most passers-by, that see it, don't get the message that *is* the waterfountain, *itself,* speaking out—myself included. I'd passed by that magnificent feat of modern water engineering many times before without having its language of *beingness* register with me. But, this time, its phenomenology spoke out loudly to my conscious mind. Whether its designer had intended it or not, on *that* one particular day, I listened—literally, assigning a personal meaning to the experience—by listening to the language *of the process that is that waterfountain*. That, inter-relating dynamic –between me, and the *dynamic* that *is* the waterfountain– changed my life forever. But I had no idea how much I'd change, as a result, of that clear Divine intervention.

In retrospect, the defining words that had endowed me with a new way to envision had opened up the message of the waterfountain to me. The thrusting water, *itself*, became the theological metaphor of "Priesthood Keys" that forms part of both Roman Catholic and Mormon dogma and doctrine. Suddenly, each individual molecule of that water became *"like unto"* a single key! Life for me, before that moment, had been about seeking, honoring and holding sacred that which 'opened closed doors' for myself, and also for my family. Specifically, what I had sought for, was the possession of Keys to cosmic doors that, open to a direction—that I'd been taught was 'the one and only way' for a man who tried to be a saint—to experience the universal experience of life. I had sought Keys to mythical doors —*cosmic keys—that I had been taught are now accessible only in my employer*, The Church of Jesus Christ of Latter-day Saints—a *man-made legal entity*, a "non-profit institution!"

Like in the Roman Catholic tradition, Mormons also tell of 'Keys of Priesthood' [Keys of the 'Kingdom'] and both faith traditions historically assign a meaning by understanding the term 'Keys' as representing keys one would use to open doors. However, when those clear, and defining words came into my soul defining the word "concord," I had already decided that life could not actually be about *exclusive access* to what is the general or, *The* Ultimate Universal Human Good. By then, I had already come to comprehend that, all common views within human societies that are based on a line of priestly ordination, or on a genealogy, were now all incongruent with my opened awareness. Those ways to envision were all now far too *hierarchical* in nature for me.

I had discovered that, my Beloved—The Church *I'd loved*— had betrayed me. My heart had been broken by my discoveries in the Church Archives, and Brother Bishop's shocking revelations had confirmed my horrified fear. And, as it always is when anything is broken, my heart had become totally *opened*. The experiences of my past, up to that moment, had spoken out logically to me. I, finally, understood! *They had been a veritable language* that, I'd not heard before that moment because all my previous training had otherwise programmed my attunement to the Universe! *Inner attunement,* now replaced the old ideal of "worthiness":

The Universe—from which my inner self was by then, open enough to learn—had communicated the understanding of Eternity to my soulful self, and with that experience, I turned toward another way of being in the world. As a result, of that new awareness, the meaning of 'Keys,' suddenly to me, became "*keys—as in diverse keys of harmonious music!*" Like all of the molecules that made up that water—pushing itself into the form that that waterfountain had been designed to shape—keys of music, that harmonize, all do the same thing! Priesthood Keys also form themselves into an entirely new thing, as do multitudinous tiny water molecules that harmoniously formed a thrusting phallus when the fountain was first made.

A chord of music is made up of a full range of musical keys that harmonize by using their diversity of sound. Suddenly, I saw that, *inner* ways of being—self-relating—fit theological Priesthood Keys metaphors better than, do the *external* keys interpretations that open doors from the outside. Like the molecules of the water that had each formed themselves into that water's form, diverse Keys of *musical chords* would also more accurately symbolize the ultimate purpose of my life now, as I had been raised to seek it from my youth —personal, or *inner* and global, or *external* peace!

I had been raised to understand the ideal of a City of Zion as the realization of God's version of Plato's Utopia. Even though I'd learned years before that, our social sciences –born of our Western civilization– had declared that ideal non-existent, and anachronistic to our nature.[iv] I had personally known inner power by the mere hope of Zionic ways of living. Because of that one reality, I'd always sought to better see what could be meant by the words, "Keys of The Holy Priesthood." So, what I knew in that moment was the actual Zion, as it was reflected in all of the dynamics of that waterfountain. Finally, I was enabled to envision myself, and the rest of the Universe as being what our social scientists might call, "Topian." "Topian" —instead of Plato's word, "Utopian"—because, to all of humanity's common ways of envisaging, "topian" (the freedom of harmonious residents in a City of Zion) ways are not an "impossible" ideal toward which humans can evolve. As I've said earlier, I've always been "a queer sort." Long before that pivotal day in 1979, I had rejected the assumption of Zionic, or *harmonious* living, as an "impossible" goal.

However, until that awesome revelatory moment, gazing out on that waterfountain, I had known only the external language of the Priesthood Keys theological metaphor. Because of that institutional programming, I only comprehended 'Keys of The Priesthood' as keys that open doors. What had always struck me was; most people are excluded from access in the older interpretation because—by using an *external* keys affect imagery—we envisioned with programming that was more about exclusion than inclusion. External keys only open and close access to the sacramental blessings so, significantly, those keys shut most people out. *Doors are exclusionary, making the metaphor exclusionary.* This had always been a dilemma because, essentially, this is sin: In other words, it is a *judging of others.*

Yet, what I had waited decades for, was *attunement*! What had always puzzled me during my questioning adolescent years was that I'd been raised to believe that the ideal of a Millennial reign of Jesus Christ would, necessarily, include non-Mormons too, and thus, The Millennium *must* be about harmony, or about *unity in diversity.* Mormon Millennium theology has never been exclusionary. Yet, the *policy* of The Church, *as an institution*, is totally exclusionary. The response came in the trillion little gold and white dancing lights of that water! With that experience, theological Keys suddenly became "*like the molecules of that water.*" I suddenly saw the molecules of water as diverse keys of music that are harmonious enough to form one sound—the *attunement of a musical chord.*

In an instant, the Universal vision finally allowed me to see that the innumerable molecules of water of that waterfountain were each "*like...*" keys of organized sound that combine harmoniously into a single *musical* chord! I easily saw that none of them were excluded. Each separate molecule was *included* by the concordant *beingness* of that one fountain of water "*...and, thus,*" I was taught, "*...are any true Keys of the Holy Priesthood...*!" Knowing my life purpose had, finally, evolved by a new way of envisioning the far older Keys theological metaphor—one that, all Mormons had clearly inherited from other older traditions than Joseph Smith Junior's 19th century theological vision. So, envisioning now, in a different way, revealed what I'd come to understand as a "higher truth."

The Universe had now chosen to use a visual aid to give me further light! The knowledge I had gained years earlier that, Keys of The Holy Priesthood "*are about attaining a rich harmony among differing parts*" finally found a visual manifestation in the different notes—or, *attitudes*—of a harmonious chord of music. My vision was suddenly able to see that *the old way of interpreting scriptural terminology excluded because of sinful judgment, while this way of envisioning opened up an inclusive way of reading all our L.D.S. Standard Works*! The Millennial world would be one of *attunement*! What I knew decades earlier had finally found expression but, it had not expressed itself in The Church's policy, or by its teaching. It had revealed itself as I became attuned to *Nature*, to the *natural* force of water in the world. In hindsight, this fact is highly significant to me.

****

The threaded message of this book is only one: It is that our natural world is speaking out its wondrous message to us! In this experience for example, there was a field—or, a body of water—that made up all of the stuff that composed what human engineering had formed into that powerful waterfountain. Likewise, I am saying that there is a field that vibrates –like the energy of that waterfountain– in, and through all that is. Its specific vibrational frequency is the place on the spectrum of all Eternity from where all that is manifested in our common natural world originates. If any chordant sound can lift and, otherwise, cause human beings to transcend this dimension by taking us mortals beyond our limiting cultural biases and boundaries like harmonious music can then, why can't we all learn from that phenomenology? So, I ask: Wouldn't the Keys of a truly universal priesthood *that is diverse, yet, chordantly harmonic*, both elevate and exalt the human soul? Isn't it *natural* for us to consider Priesthood Keys like a harmonic musical cord because isn't all good music, actually, the organized sounds of Nature, *Herself*?

It is our human spirits, who transcend this world, not our organizations! Attunement with higher worlds of light is not about institutions, it is a phenomenon of *natural* beings. I see all plant life and then, I see that it is natural for human Earth matter to also reach for the stars. Our human body chemistry is the stuff of which the stars are made. But, we humans create all the institutions, and yet, we do not yet know how to duplicate the same processes, which the Universe uses to make raw "star stuff" into us! So, to me, it is also logical that, attunement is not a phenomenon which any institutional forms are capable of accessing because institutions are only abstract things. All organizations are impotent to penetrate the profound and lofty dimensions of light. Conversely, it is us, individual humans— who, can and who, truly *do evolve ourselves* into more harmonious vibrations, by each individual life's experience—who, can access all time and Eternity, as the keys in a full chord of harmonic sound can evolve any one musical key by enhancing it with diversity.

There is a vast field of which I write here; it facilitates our own human mass interconnectedness. This is as much a reality, as it is true that, *that* waterfountain's water allows for a phallus to form; that, the Electro-magnetic field allows for all electrical currents to be, and that the magnetic field allows magnets to be magnets and; that, the field of light exists so that photons of light can exist. With our modern physicists, I ask: Why wouldn't the same principle apply to *all* fields?—especially where a true, healing priesthood originates? Deepak Chopra, the medical doctor who first awakened our Western medicine by popularizing the wisdom of older ways of healing, is one who writes on this idea. He writes:

"Before there can be a photon of light, there must be the field of light; before an individual electron, the field of electricity; before an isolated bar magnet, the earth's magnetic field...When we see light, our brains are actually selecting totally abstract qualities from out of the field and interpreting them as light. In fact, everything we see, touch, hear, taste, or smell, has been selected from the infinite reservoir of vibrating energy in the field. [It]...*is an abstraction that we shape into things.*"[v]

This view is no different than, the Kahuna envisioning of *Huna* traditions of ancient Hawaii.[vi] Ancient Hawaiian Kahunas were well known for their powerful ability to call forth changes in the weather, precisely because of this *shamanic* knowledge—because of this single, creative attribute!

When I had first read Chopra's words, I marveled at how parallel they were with the way my *Meshica* Indian friends in Mexico had also explained their perception of reality. The elder of them had said to me that, "we all swim in the same ocean...!"

After I had realized (days later) that the old man had never actually swam –except to swim underwater– I asked him if he meant that, "'we all swim' on top of 'the same ocean?'"

Laughing at my question, he immediately answered back, "No Antonio, *we are the ocean*!" Then, his laughter went on and, on.

Rabbi Elias Gewurz also wrote about these scientific, yet mystical, ideas. This 20th century Qabalahist, unlike scientists of the Western tradition, easily accepted the paranormal along with what is empirical *evidencia.* He wrote that, "Space...is equally illusory. Spirit is not separated from spirit by distance; but by discord...spirit is...united to spirit...by the affinity subsisting between them."[vii]. All these, and other wise ones—worldwide—teach of another wisdom than, do my older mentors. These do not see as most of us do, and when I realized this I, finally, understood that, my old Utah based Mormon mentors did not see as *true* mystics see.

Even Dad used to say that, "...those who use theatrics and repetitive affect imagery only masquerade a type of mysticism, while at the same time, they will fear genuine mystics." Dad was into the old Rosecrucian mysteries for several years. Mysticism, I guess, has always been a part of my Feliz family's legacy.[viii] There is a certain awareness of giftedness that is passed down in our family, I believe, through our genetics. Mom and Dad both, in their own respective ways, both demonstrated otherworldly gifts. My children have often demonstrated that they, too, have inherited these same paranormal phenomena, and I know from my own personal experiences that, the mystical is part and parcel of my own *beingness*. But this giftedness has been a blessing and a curse also.

When all of my loyalties were still bound to limited Mormon ways of envisioning, it never hit me as a positive factor in our family. I distinctly recall hearing Mom ask Dad when I was eight years old,

"All Mexican mothers give their children their blessing by laying their hand on the little one's head. Why, because we are in The Church now, is it not a good thing for a mother to bless her children as in the Mexican tradition?"

Her question, which I had only casually overheard, wasn't significant to me until well into my adult years. I had been taught to be grateful that the Mormons had sought out my father "to free us from the church of the Devil." Yet, my experience in the universal experience gives me comfort to now realize that, my propensity for otherworldly phenomena has a genetic origin.

More recently, I have been exposed to an ancient Italian wisdom that teaches the notion of one's propensity to the paranormal as being carried through what amounts to our inherited biological chemistry, our unique DNA.[ix] But, in the context of The Church, I seemingly only had this giftedness manifest "out of *obedience*." In The Church I'd been taught that "gifts of the Spirit" only result from our *obedience*—or from our behavioral commitment to priesthood leaders' counsel. So, because I had experienced the other-worldly phenomena as a common thing—when I had meditated in the upper rooms of Mormon temples—I had fallen into agreement with the worldview of the claimed "Mormon monopoly on authentic things" from the Celestial Worlds. I had believed that, all the otherworldly phenomena happened to me because of the sacred place, *itself.* I was taught it wasn't about me but that, spiritual things *happened* because of where I was—*in the L.D.S. Temples.*

Temples, in the global Mormon community, are not your typical Mormon meetinghouse, or chapel. We barely approach an understanding of the inner significance of a Temple to Utah based Mormons, if we consider how Ultra-Orthodox Jews might view the ancient Holy of Holies. That Holy of Holies was closed off, even from common priests, within the walls of the Holy Place, and the Holy Place, was closed off from the rest of Israel, being within the Court of Israel of the old Temple of Solomon. Such a chambered place is not a synagogue or a church wherein *public* worship took place. Tradition says that it was the one place, where the God of Israel made His presence known to only His *high* priest. It was the dwelling of *Yaweh*. This idea defines Utah based Mormon Temples.

However, since leaving The Church –since the doors of L.D.S. Temples have been closed, to me– the visions of the day and the dreams of the night have not stopped! The spirit writing has become clearer, easier and far more instructive than ever. The intuitive ability to discern what another feels in contrast to what they say to me is still there and the gift of prognosticating the future of a given process is undeniable. My close friends know how I live my life; they know, because they have been with me when these gifts manifest, that Spirit is yet my guide—even now, shut out of a Utah based Mormon "House of The Lord."

Today I know that my faulty logic was, actually, a classic result of my old religious fundamentalist discipleship training that is commonly used in some religious hierarchies as a mere means to manipulate behavior for group discipline and order. In my case, Mormon ecclesiasts called my disobedience of their rules, and my eschewing of their priestly authority over me, "grieving the spirit." But over time, deep in my soul's core, I came to know that all that was grieved by my actions was my own spirit. I'd ignorantly believed the much touted wise "counsel" of my "priesthood leaders" as actual wisdom—without testing its wisdom for myself *by my experience*. Indeed, what would happen if the same spiritual gifts, that I had experienced, happened anyway—if I were not still an obedient member of my community? What, indeed, would *that* mean?

Among other things I, eventually, discovered by all of the questions often heard in Mormon circles that, it would mean more questions would come. For example: A common Mormon question would be; "Why do Native-American Saints experience spiritual gifts more than Anglos do?" After leaving those circles, I learned that, in older societies than those shaped by one of the three great religions, descendant from Abraham, these psychic abilities are, *expected,* when designated by the Universe through some omen, like, my sister Maria's: Maria had been born "with a veil" –a membrane– designating to the mind of Mom's midwife, our Grandma Nica that, "a child of giftedness [had] come" from the place of light into our family. And, it was Grandma Nica who had taught me, when our home was honored by her daily presence that, "our family is a family of healers." However, another truth I quickly came to was that, we *all* have the Gifts naturally. Only, some are socialized early on in life to unlock them while, others, are programmed in those first defining years of life to stifle and repress their giftedness. The difference, I saw, is *cultural*!

So, I've come to know that there is a certain holiness gained by a person working on personal integrity and that, the inevitable disagreements with anyone's religious institutions are, actually, often opportunities for true spiritual development. I'm describing the way of ever-expanding souls. As has been related in other chapters, my experience with the experience of unseen inter-dimensionalities has been a *transmutational* process. In the language of physics then, it is to observe the unfolding here, in the "explicate order," what was previously enfolded elsewhere, in the unseen, "implicate order." I affirm that this way of living, this experiencing of inter-dimensional transmutation, is the reason why I am still alive today. I am living proof that there is a, literal, physical renewal, or a rejuvenation –a *regenerative sanctification,* if you will– that is derived by following a path that lends itself to living life in this way.

The path I've taken has been my mentor. Life is not a school. Life is a journey. It is a path, a *way* that teaches. This is the truth that is, ironically, taught in all Utah based Mormon Temples because the classic metaphor of a sojourner is played out in the Mormon Temple Endowment ceremony. Latter-day Saints are taught in their holy Temple to learn "from…" his or her "…experience to discern" what is "good" and what is "evil" as they symbolically, "journey," from room to room. Much more is said of this very important distinction elsewhere. Here, however, I offer this:

This distinction, in how to experience life, reminds me of how I, now, usually enjoy facing backwards, whenever I ride a train. Experiencing the train ride this way is like the phenomenology of living. Like life, what we see as we sit next to the window –as the train pulls us onward– is the territory in which we've already entered. Like this way of sitting on the train reveals, the reality in which we find ourselves, at any time, is created by us all before we, actually, experience it as truly happening. This is not only now accepted in theoretical physics, but it is also a foundational principle of mystic traditions, worldwide. I bring this up because there is a fundamental lesson for society in the metaphor of sitting backwards on a train: We are now in a paradigm shift that has its beginning in our *past* choices but, the future is determined by our *present* choices, as a collective society in life's journey. We learn as we examine our journey.

The ugly horror that, we see all around us as the violence, the bloodletting, the "nice boy" massacres and all the hate-filled terrorist rhetoric of our time –as previously stated– is only the shaking death rattle of a dying worldview. We are in one of those moments in time when humanity is going through a massive shift in our paradigm. The time has even come for us to envision differently regarding our entire way of knowing. This includes notions of reality, even what it is that constitutes a male and a female human being, for example.

In our world today, scientists are becoming more aware of the ways in which chromosomes determine what sex we are. We think we know what sex is, but what sex we are isn't only about our genitalia. Today is a New Age! My *Toltec* friends call it the "SIXTH SUN," and science now says that our sex and sexuality are also about chromosomes, and even other less talked-about factors…

****

Mary Jane's story is one that is emblazoned on my mind, as the example of what I've elsewhere called the Galileo Phenomenon.[x] All she wanted was a dialogue with her church fathers. Yet like Galileo, Mary Jane was also brutally rebuffed and excommunicated for speaking publicly about the truth of her life. The objectionable fact about her life was that, Mary Jane had been born an almost true hermaphrodite. Mary Jane was born with complete male sex organs, externally and internally, and she was also fully equipped at birth with all the usual female sex organs, with the one exception of a uterus. Her vagina, labia, fallopian tubes, ovaries, etc. were as much developed as were her penis, testes, prostate gland, etc. Her vagina was where, the rest of us, humans have only a rectum. All these are physiological facts of Mary Jane's physical body at birth.

This was the actual truth of her life; which, the highest ranks of the Mormon hierarchy she humbly trusted were so adamant about. She was not to publicly discuss them. Like discoveries, which drove Galileo to seek an open dialogue with his own religious patriarchs, Mary Jane's physical body's reality also drove her to make sense of it all, by seeking wisdom from her spiritual leaders. And, like Galileo's Roman hierarchy, Mary Jane's also chose to excommunicate her, rather than to value her testimony, born of her experience. They also chose to publicly deny her existence as well as anyone also born inter-sexed as manifest evidence of a reality—a reality that, is not yet understood.[xi] In both cases, the institutional response was refusing to dialogue on the implications of the new data brought to them by a lay person, who was not a part of their powerful hierarchy. And as will be told below, the newly discovered data was seen as most heretical because it contradicted Mormon tradition, which claimed that only two human sexes exist here "*and in eternity*."[xii]

The Roman Catholic Church, historically, has fought against the world's major scientific breakthroughs of new knowledge, when those discoveries went against its then, prevailing institutionalized theological "truth." In both cases: Persecuted truth seekers are harshly condemned by the established religious authority. But, those caught in this chasm between reality and religion usually only sought a dialogue on a new way to see reality. So sadly, Galileo is only one example of this practice of religious hierarchies, and as stated above, our history books are filled with many, many, more similar examples.

Mary Jane also felt a need to express her frustration, and she began to speak about her questions in public. We, in fact, met on one such occasion, and striking a good friendship based on our mutual individual experiences, she gave me permission to tell her story here. To me, Mary Jane's search for additional knowledge is not unlike the fabled Eve in the sacred story of Eden—Eve was also a seeker of knowledge.

Mary Jane's need was about her gender and sexual identity. But, she discovered along the way, that –although Mormons are often the most highly educated among their peers– the Mormon men who lead their faith community quickly repress any public scientific penetration of reality that seems to differ with their own established doctrine. To Utah based Mormons, one's assigned sex is not a mere mortal phenomenon because they teach that, one's own personal sex already existed in a "pre-existent" spirit world *prior to earth life*.

When she and I first privately discussed this part of her life, she said, "Tony, this is not as unusual as you may think."

"What do you mean?"

"My therapists tell me that there is a study going on in Utah because they noticed a high incidence of this type of hermaphrodism in the three major metropolitan areas that are geographically situated around Salt Lake City, Utah."

"Wow, along the Wasatch Front! But, why don't we hear about this in the media? Why is it that, although I've lived over thirty years here, I've never heard anything about what you say to me is 'common?'"

"Don't you see, Tony? The fact of my existence flies in the face of our commonly accepted view of how things are. We're all raised to believe that humans are either male or female, with no other option in between. Have you ever known anything in the natural world that is that separated by distinctions?" She waited for me, as I pondered her question.

I kept thinking, to myself, about the question for a bit, and I had to agree with her point, so, I said, "no, not really. But," I added, "why were you raised as a boy by your mom and dad, when you say you've always known you were far more than just one of either?"

"Oh, come on, be serious. In Utah, a male-dominated and male-centered society, it's clear that when a parent has to actually decide –to choose– between whether the new baby is going to live as a boy or as a girl, the choice is already made by the biases here against all females."

"Then," I began to ask her, "why did you choose to became a woman, after you'd been a man? I mean, you are part of this society; like me, you were also influenced by the biases toward males. You'd served as a Mormon elder, as a missionary, and then, you even married a woman in the Temple. Mary Jane, you just told me that you've even fathered two boys! In other words, you'd already known what it's like to have a full *male* experience as a part of the ordained priesthood in the church, and as one of the ordained, you must have understood that the change would take you out of the privileged class here. You must have known that the choice to become a woman would forever hold you down in an underclass here. You knew that we, Mormons, don't ordain women."

The look on her face was one of incredulity. "Tony, you didn't let your ordination as a bishop stop *you* from choosing to be yourself on the outside *because* of your need to be who you had discovered you *really* are, on the inside. You also changed your own identity from a heterosexual man because you *too* had found your sexuality was more than just that of only a heterosexual man. Tony, your truth encompassed your natural personal world, which living as a heterosexual man denies, devalues and tries to destroy." Her perfect smile told me she had confidence in her logic.

And, I felt my lack of reasoning duly rebuffed.

"My gender identification is no different," she went on, "because it demands the same congruity, integrity and cohesion as does your own; only my search for true alignment with my soul also involved my sex, not just my sexual identification." Mary Jane's smile returned slowly. Then, after she saw that I'd understood, she beamed out the largest smile I'd ever seen on her! Her face, literally, glowed with confidence.

With that, I finally knew that both of our choices were the same. We'd both opted for a choice toward a personal, and a social authenticity. We'd both chosen to walk on the way of becoming open souls, open to whatever way of being that life brings, in spite of the tradition in which we'd been raised. Both of us were open to learn from life's journey!

****

The wisdom, which our modern civilization has inherited from the arcane theologies that stem from the mythologies of former old world times, is no longer a healthy one for us. It is time for us to think more rationally, to reason what has taken place, rather than to only accept what has been said or, even *written*. This is a new age now; one in which the dawning of a great new way of envisioning ourselves –including all the inter-sexed– and our common world can transform humanity forever. If we envision in a more nature-centric way, we will find meaning and blessing if a home in our community receives an inter-sexed baby.

I say that, because I have lived with nature-centered people. I have come to understand something of the differences in how they see the world, and how I was first socialized to see the world. For example, I can say that all the nature-centered people with whom I have inter-related do not think of themselves as being separate from their environment. It had never occurred to any of my *Meshica* friends in Mexico, for example, to envision themselves as mere "observers" or "knowers" of their world.

I am suggesting that our ways of envisioning must evolve. That, the reality into which we were each, respectively, born is but an acquired illusion to which we must each die before we can be re-born again. Our inherited imagery must make way for an expanded, affect imagery. I am saying that we must each die to this civilization. In the socio-political movement that he led, Ghandi termed this truly active dynamic "non-cooperation" but then, what does *this* have to do with the inter-sexed?

To me, the call from the blessed Jesus figure in the Christian New Testament is for us to eschew conformity to all cultural forms when they reinforce a bounded way of envisioning others. That's what the Jesus character was about in all the sacred stories about His journeys. In the sacred Christian canon, Jesus is reported to have openly rejected the cultural definition of what constitutes a family that was predominant in his own time and society. To me, the inter-sexed, more than, Gay men, Bi-sexuals, or the Trans-gendered and Lesbians, open His meaning to us:

"*Then one said unto him, Behold, thy mother and thy brethren stand without, desiring to speak with thee,*

"*But he answered and said unto him that told him, Who is my mother? And who are my brethren?*

"*For whosoever shall do the will of my Father which is in heaven, the same is my brother, and sister, and mother.*"[xiii]

Jesus had here, reportedly, *organized a new non-biological family for himself,* and did so in direct affront to a biological, nuclear family. This is significant to me, as a Queer man because I've learned that, the Jesus figure of the Christian tradition, like the Buddha in Buddhism, or like Krishna in Hinduism is the template for us all to pattern ourselves after. So, to me, His, above call is to what Gandhi called non-cooperation with an abusive social system. Seen in this light, such non-cooperation is the epitome of courage. Thus, a call to sainthood is a call to non-cooperation with the present definitions of what constitutes "the traditional nuclear family."

So, I affirm that the cosmic call to be "born again" is a call to be delivered from the dominant worldview of society. Recall that the late Joseph Campbell wrote that the ways in which we picture—or, envision the world to be—are our worldviews. All of the holy ones of the planet knew that our diverse choices and worldviews are, at best, extremely dangerous scripts for the cosmic play of life. Our worldviews program us with default dynamics that we play out in individual times of stress.

Remember those two sick, trench-coated, young men in Littleton, Colorado, and how their behavior was in retaliation for how they had all been mistreated. Even the horror inflicted by those September 11, 2001 terrorists had its cause in their warped sense of being culturally bullied by our American Pop. Culture. All of these were simply playing out the scripts that had been written for them, in spite of all the extras on the stage of life with them. Let us remember that all our sacred stories, like our holy rituals, are potent symbols of cosmic concepts and are always best taken as metaphor. This is why the true mystics of all cultures and societies begin their great spiritual journey by going within *first*.

As stated earlier, the Jesus figure—whom I believe, also took the form of Krishna and Buddha—is the template for us all to emulate. If those who abused parishioners truly believed this then, would they have abused?[xiv] I think not. His message was more about our personal, and thus, our group soul's *attunement* –as in the diverse Keys in a musical chord– than, about keys that close doors to exclude those judged, by their—today notoriously sinner priesthoods, as being morally unworthy of their sacraments.

Using Keys that can close others off from where we are, is a clear metaphor of the control of our Others. However, the metaphor of a Christ figure is the greater wisdom! The behavior and biblical words of the Christ in the Christian gospels sang out the chordant, and harmonic virtues of an open, receptive, feminine and forgiving nature; while, the institutional forms celebrating these ancient stories are all patterned more after external, cultural perceptions of only the male principle, i.e.: Aggression, control of any social situations, domination of others, *justified* retribution and power—not, as an energy but—power, as an Inquisitor's brute force.

Conversely, the Christian mythology that I have loved since my earliest childhood days manifests a great truth: The Jesus figure only wore the body of a man but, his inner *beingness* is womanly. In other words, all the cultural systems that have produced the beautiful, and centuries old Christian iconography assign femaleness to the traits most often attributed to their version of The Christ. I am sure that this is the reason why European Christian iconography has often depicted the Jesus figure as a person of androgynous traits. So, if we want to benefit by the elements, which our common culture deems feminine within each of us then, let all try to emulate the Lord of Compassion! For, there is a good reason why He is often depicted femininely:

We see things feminine as *internal,* and things masculine as *external.* This femininity is also found throughout all of the ancient traditions that seek truth. For example, in numerology seven is a sacred number, and significantly, in scientific disciplines it is also a *prime number.* Mystics record that Jesus was penetrated seven times on the cross: One for each hand, one for each foot, one for his side, and one in each wrist to secure his body on the hanging cross. The final penetration in the side of the Man of the Cross is said to have "let out water," and most significantly, the side is the same place on the human anatomy where the fabled Adam is said to have *lost* a rib for the creation of the Woman. This, at least, is true according to the second version of the Genesis stories.

So, as Adam gave birth to Eve from his side in the later myth, Jesus is written of as, likewise, giving birth to a new faith covenant through the opened, fleshy heart-wound in his side. Here was an ancient, archetypal symbol of a delivery, of a birthing –or, in light of the "water" that burst out– of a cosmic, orgasmic union with The Infinite. It is no coincidence that, in this story, the final wound in His side became the ancient, or the archetypal, symbol of the Greatly Revered Mother: Herself, fleshy; as if the various layers of his torn abdominal wall had then become the open labia of Her Motherly Womanness, giving out her waters, ready to deliver the new and better creation than had been, ancient Rome. Yet, what have we inherited from those who wrote the story of the cross? We have inherited nothing less than the old Roman Empire, over and over again –generation after generation– and, we called it by a long series of new names. In today's media, it is the "New World Order."

Celebrating the feminine principle, in contrast to only the brute masculine principle is a strong, and it is a recurring theme in the religious iconography of many of the planet's most ancient traditions. These, were supplanted by the old father god of thunder and war. We only need to study the Roman iconography of the Mexican patron saint, or *La Virgin de Guadeloupe* to see; what the Roman Catholic mind perceives as "rays of glory and the traditional purple-blue robes around her person". This is, in truth, understood by the more ancient *Meshica* worldview to be the fleshy, eroticized vulva of their dark-skinned Earth Mother; the ancient, *Toltec, Tonantzin*—"the revered mother." In their guilt-ridden, male-centric perception, the Fathers of Christian Catholicism cannot imagine that, a Divine Intelligence would dare to manifest *holy woman* in such a way! They would all rather repress an image that celebrates things natural. They give their devout a mere abstract of the fullness of meaning offered to their soul mass by their most sacred Mexican icon.

Where does all this put the former believer in the well-kept lines of a continuous priestly authority? What does it do with the genealogies of Jewish Levites, or with the ordination chronologies of all Catholic Bishops and all Mormon Elders? These are the hard questions that helped to form my personal sense of purpose after my excommunication. Those basic questions have led me to note that, the formulation of all these lines and genealogies are, in effect, for group authority and that, these things truly are great evidence of *institutionalization* but, of little else. What, after all, is the real worth of any documented record of who laid hands on whom, and in what order if it isn't to merely *legitimize*—to *institutionalize*?

For example, in Utah Mormon circles, there is a phrase used by the high priest as he seals a couple kneeling at the altar in their marriage sealing ritual: "…legally *and* lawfully wedded…" To the Mormon institutionalized worldview, "legal" has to do with time –with the law of the land– while, "lawful" refers only to the law of Eternity. To true believers, to those looking to their Temple ritual to unite them as a couple for all Eternity, I say, we *are* in Eternity now. If you could see this world as it already is then, it would appear as an ocean of light. Joseph Smith Junior taught that, in its "celestialized state," Earth is "a sea of glass."[xv] I'm saying that we are inundated, or immersed in an ocean of light –we move and live inside of a vast sea of glass– inside *crystal* in which we all "…live, move, and have our being" –*in* a sea of glass, *in* a crystalline ocean of light. Truly, we *are* the ocean of light!

The *Meshica* taught me that our planet is not made up only of fire, water, air and earth with the plant life growing out of it. We, the diversity of its mobile life forms, which all move and exist within our planet, also are the planet –every bit as much as its land mass and its vast oceans are the planet. This is especially true if we take the perspective of astronauts in space that can see the pulsating rhythm of this blue orb through its outer layer, our atmosphere. And, Rabbi Gewurz reminds us that,

"Speaking of matter, we [think] of tangible material such as we can see or touch or recognize by the physical senses, but air is matter and, we live completely immersed in it and in…finer elements than the one we call air."[xvi]

These "finer elements," I suggest, are *us*. Reiterating the words of Deepak Chopra: They're, "an abstraction that we shape into things." I, here, refer to our bodies of light, and there is evidence of this in our personal lives. Think about it:

Before you, the reader, knew yourself in infancy as being either a boy, or a girl, you already knew that you existed. Your *unconditioned awareness of being* had no label, and it never has had labels. Your own *inner, uncorrupted self* has no conditions. It is you, simply knowing: "I AM." Your inner unconditioned awareness of being, that you are –that sense of I AM– is this liquid light of the world which manifests all the inner conceptions that you have of yourself. Your own inner conception of yourself then, automatically determines the exact expression you have conceived yourself to be. This is the most sacred place where Einstein's General Relativity meets all the true mystics and sages of our diverse species. This knowledge, or this awareness of being, is about being the, actual, Creator of the World—*us, Ourselves*! That is why the *Meshica* are correct when they teach us that, "*Cada cabeza es un mundo.*" (Each mind is its own world). This is the reason why I write about how I have "experienced the universal experience."

This may sound like new age "fluff" speak to some but, how else would anyone account for the amazing way that I've experienced the same experiences that others also experienced? The theory that works for me is that, I created my own world; my experiences in life are an art form, from my own mind –from my unique and my, literal, *world*. My life is so fantastic that, if I had not experienced the same experiences that others experienced *as I have* then, I probably would not believe it because my experience isn't often confirmed by the experience of most other people around me. But, I know I'm not insane. I merely see what others do not. As evidence to this, I offer the usual fact of multiple witnesses to car accidents: These witnesses always experience the experience *differently*.

Moreover, what is affirmed in my personal phenomenology seems to agree with the discoveries in modern physics of the 20th century. For example, physicist, David Bohm, extensively discusses the "explicate" or *unfolded* reality in contrast to the "implicate" or, the *enfolded* reality. In the quantum field theoretical version of causal interpretations—which I learned through a friend whom I met synchronisticly in San Francisco—an elementary particle is a visual manifestation of an underlying quantum field. This tiny particle –the quantum– in David Bohm's view, "is a representation" of "the underlying quantum field into a localized region." Likewise, "the annihilation of the particle is the *unfolding* back into the field." This is how Bohm explained the highly complex reactions of elementary particles as the "*enfoldings*" and also as the, "*unfoldings*" that, he observed to take place within a dynamic background.[xvii] To me, this describes birth and death, itself! David Peat explained that:

"The explicate order corresponds to the Newtonian vision of nature…the explicate order could be thought of as an extension of the order of Cartesian coordinates introduced in the first half of the seventeenth century. In the explicate order, bodies are exterior to each other and react to local forces. By contrast in the implicate order, structures enfold each other so that one structure can be simultaneously internal and external to the other. Since all (physical) forms unfold out of the same ground…their whole dynamics is a function of the implicate order of the unfolding of explicate (physical) forms."[xviii]

In these scientific terms, I can definitely agree that Einstein was correct. The unified field does exist! My view, however, is also informed by the mystical, and so, I would add that Einstein's unified field is actually what we all call, "Love." I don't speak of what is understood to be romantic love but rather, my reference here is to that Love, which is the basis of all that is, including every single one of us. Remarkably, we humans are all created in a way that enables us to actually *feel* Love. I believe *we can feel love because love is a part of the spectrum of particulate light matter*. If I am correct, then we feel what is understood as the fundamental basis of all that is: The Unified Field. To me, *That* is what we each are!

What I'm saying is that whether we call it: A field, spirit matter, The Force, or Love, the fact is that experiencing *It* is the true business of our mortal life. If "God is love", then, to me, it follows that the Unified Field is Love. Clearly, anyone that, truly Loves can understand that; the kind of cosmic intimacy that is generated when Love is felt is a natural drive. The *Meshica* say it is all around, and even through us, all of the time. We, in our purist nature then, are Love, and Joseph Smith, Junior taught: "the first principle of heaven is to know the nature of God."[xix]

So, to "*know…God*," it seems to me in the 21st century, is to experience the experiences in the phenomenology of Love –by our act of choosing to be on the way of becoming open souls– and, therefore, Love—itself—is our common, ultimate life purpose. I've often said to my friends, when they ask why I am a friend, by saying, "There is purpose in it." This has always been my meaning; for, I had learned early on in life that friendship really is the most sacred of relationships. When any of us inter-relate out of honest Love, we experience all the energy and all of the intelligence of nature because all things are also made of Love. Wherever there is Love, in that unique place there is a potential for anything! Conversing with a mixture of the languages of mystics and of modern physics then, where there is *anything*—even the smallest subatomic particle, there is Love and with that Love, there is also the potential for all of the qualities that we assign to The Divine. For, this is What we are!

In a previous chapter, the problems of the world of ugly hate are explained as what we, together, have all created. This is because, as Jung explained, the "mass mind" impacts the reality in which we live.[xx] So we, together, are The Creator, and this idea is evidenced in the current theories of modern physics. In fact, these theories are all actually about possibilities, and it is possibilities that true faith is all about. Faith then, is a vibrational frequency.

Science tells us that everything is in vibration. So, *because everything is in vibration, we are all inter-connected as One, through our diverse and chordant harmonics, as a mass consciousness.* Our human inter-connectedness is, essentially, our agreements. What we truly agree to, therefore, is what ultimately, is unfolded out of the great, and yet, enfolded Universe. As our template, the Jesus figure of the Christian gospels is reported to have said, "Again I say unto you, That, if two of you shall agree on earth as touching anything…it shall be done…"[xxi] All things are possible to those who Love and, truly *agree* to it. This is *attunement among human beings who Love.*

This is the understanding that has influenced my life since the days of my mother's earliest teachings, while I sat on the kitchen counter listening to her answers to my difficult questions as she went about her wifely duties. Then, later in the mid 1980s, I received a spirit written message, which confirmed this idea that, Agreement is the core principle of all Eternity.[xxii]

I've known since that day, that agreement will be the way, when, and how the common world will transform. In the *Meshica* worldview that I learned in 1990, we humans are each unique worlds of dream and memory. They teach that, because each of us is our own world of dream and memory, our common world is both, happy and violent. As a result, the *Meshica* choose to perceive all creatures in their entire environment as equally valid as the other, and it is why the ancient *Meshica* would customarily accept the symbols of the older societies that they conquered into their *Meshica* pantheon. Ancient *Meshica* spirituality was open.

This worldview is at the heart of why all my Indian friends speak reverently to any animal or plant that they might eat. This is an ancient tradition, one from which our more recent "blessing" of our food at mealtime is only a remnant. They, however, would see their siblings on the table, that I might set, and they would understand that all of us, including the very food we ingest, is One. When we eat food, in their eyes, we eat ourselves, not forgetting that we are all Love. So, when we eat, in their view therefore, *we eat Love*. Again, I can't help but believe that this ancient notion is the distant thought behind the faith tradition of transubstantiation in Roman Catholic dogma—for, God *is* Love. Indeed, as if our mass behavior in the aftermath of September 11, 2001 were a prayer to the cosmos from the global human collective that we are, we immediately collectively recoiled. Again, we finally began to treat each other as One—acting as a mass collective of Love!

This is because truly being One is our ultimate reality, it is our bottom line truth. Our business in life is to –step by step– find ways of returning to that Self-Identity. By ever-increasingly trying to envision our Self-Identy as being inclusive of our Other, we are then, "…added upon forever." In the language of all of my former Mormon Christianity, being "added upon" is the ultimate purpose of being alive. If the process is an eternal one then, it is what Joseph Smith Junior called "eternal increase."[xxiii] Each party to any given relationship –in all the worlds, in the language of the *Meshica*– is as valid in that relationship as is each of the others. Each one is worthy of acceptance, as part of what defines Them all.

This realization has also transformed how I now interpret other metaphors I'd learned in my youth. For example, instead of seeing in the old Mormon way of "eternal increase" as meaning to have off-spring *sexually* forever, my sense now is that Utah based Mormons miss a far more reaching opportunity in their founding prophet's cosmology. I am here suggesting that the process of what he, in the 19th century, called "eternal increase," may better be likened to two stones being tossed into a placid pond. Each stone creates a unique surface ripple that causes waves in an increasingly larger circumference that, eventually all interpenetrate and mix with the other's ripples. The two separate vibration systems manifested there, on the pond's surface then, become *only one, massive, vibrational pattern*. The two opening systems, in fact, become a new pattern that allows the first two to then, become One. As I see it, in this way, no matter what sexes each couple is composed of, all of us can attain an "eternal increase."[xxiv] This is because, like all sacraments, the Utah based Temple sealing ritual is a metaphor that points to a reference. To see Mormon cosmology in the traditional L.D.S. Mormon way, now, feels like a vain attempt to take a lowly cultural perspective, and to change it from being a metaphor from which to learn a reference, into an imagined "fact." To me, the now arcane, heterosexual church is repressing an expansion of how to understand, "eternal increase."

Consider the sealing of couples as a holy metaphor: In the above example, the two patterns are able to become one larger and distinctly unique pattern because of the true core creative principle of all Eternity: *Agreement*. The inter-pattern of the two circles is their agreement. What is agreed upon is always what is created. This can be seen throughout our common, natural world. For example: A single sperm penetrates an egg because there is intelligent agreement for it in the chromosomes. We are also coming to understand that, there is a link between emotion and health. The mind and the body agree, and thus, they—together—either create disease or wellness. What we come together on, or about, is what gets unfolded out of the Mass Mind's enfolded Universe. If I am correct then, the question is: What is the kind of future you and I now agree to create? Do you want to keep your loving relationship after one of you passes into transition? If so, I agree to it also; so, expect it! To me, this is our agreement! *Attunement* is a more" far-reaching understanding…"

But others say to you, "No, you need permission from the fathers of religion." Yet, your inner awareness has never asked permission to express that which you are aware of being. Why ask permission now? Your need to seek permission is only because that is how you were first domesticated to react to such a question. So, consider this: If the entire world should agree that a certain thing could not be expressed, and yet, you became aware of being that which they had agreed could not be expressed, you'd still express it one way or another, at least, in your own mind, and memory. That is because each human soul is a personal sovereign, a being of free will; as the *Meshica* taught me: Each human being truly is a unique world. The Kingdom of God isn't some church hierarchy, or organization. The Kingdom of God is within you and me because *our light bodies are us*, and it is within every other being also. We are each sparks of The Kingdom of God. *What is wrong in one circumstance, is right in another*! That is why the only evil, which I now see as truly evil, is that which does not honor the dignity and sovereignty of each of us.

Only one who does not realize that the personal dignity of his, or her Other is truly his own, would willingly and deliberately do violence to their fellow human being. That is because, in their core, they do not self-identify with their Other. They do not envision as the true mystics of ancient and modern times. They have fallen into agreement with the illusion that they are a separate entity from their Other. Such a one is not aware that their Other is Another Themself. Theirs is the same state of mind, which is obviously experienced by any modern terrorist.

When the *Meshica* warrior/priests and the *Toltec* wise man first introduced themselves to me in 1990, the greeting each one of them used translates into our English as: "I Am Another Yourself." What hit me most about the greeting, when I learned the translation, was how *the act of saying it* to another is, *itself,* meant to create *in our inter-relating* what is the reality in the unseen world. The greeting is a Key of the best part of The Holy Priesthood of all "dispensations of time" because it invokes the enfolded implicate order by calling forth priesthood's true nature into an unfolded explicate order, where any relationship is experienced—*here.* Their salutation engages one's personal Self-Identity with *the entire* Universe, if it is understood.

And, if it is understood then, it informs us that the reality of the world of light is Love. It's the kind of love born of empathy; and, that is extremely significant to us because empathy is an accepted way of describing the attitude of soul, which is reflected in the above greeting. Recall that, to the *Meshica,* each mind is its own world. Thus, the way that the *Meshica* follow to avoid the collision of two or more worlds is by an empathic attitude of soul. This way of inter-relating will call down the nature of the enfolded implicate order, which we have learned about through the metaphor of heaven in all the canon of the world's great religions. Eventually, this far more natural way of inter-relating will then manifest in our common world –here, in the present hell-like unfolded explicate order– as Paradise and as the highest good.

As has already been stated herein, this is what it is to be truly human; because to be humane is to manifest Love in our world. And remember, God is Love. In other words, the unconditioned inner nature of humanity is, literally, to *be Love personified.* That is why *we can* change the world! We have the ability to re-make our reality. We have the ability to rise out of our inherited hell. The implicate order, is constantly being redesigned by our behavior here; by our individual and collective emotional and psychic response to what the explicate order, or *reality,* currently manifests. The phrase, however, that "there is power in numbers" is a key. Mass holds increasing force, depending on the size of the mass. This is true in outer space, and I am saying that it is true of inner space as well, and this holds tremendous implications for us in our present time.

That is why I say that the power of our Mass Mind is stronger than any other force in the Universe. The ability of the collective mind to impact natural reality is a recognized factor in the study of paradigm shifts. This is why it is carefully observed by any that seek to influence the masses. Our savvy media moguls know how the persuasion process works, and marketers call one of the marketing tools for its engineering "opinion polls." What is key to understand is that, *a critical mass,* or a sufficient number of parallel thinkers –who are each of the same mind– is what changes the design of the implicate order [the future]. My hope is to manifest, or demonstrate it by the various stories in this book. For, I perceive that this is how our involvement functions in the creation of reality. In fact, there is an entire science based on this knowledge, which seeks to understand how to better respond to public opinion.

In our modern era of the theories of Einstein, of relativity and of quantum physics, it doesn't take a prophet to see our species' future. It takes the ability to comprehend sudden paradigm shifts as being a social manifestation of the dynamic which, in Lucas' Star Wars film efforts to produce a new mythology, translates into "a movement in *The Force.*" Being a successful seer in the present 21st century only takes the ability to recognize where we are headed. But, the seeing is not from a prophet who is outside of ourselves; sources of prophetic wisdom are *within us all.* It takes a connection with the Eternity *within ourselves* to clearly see that, the end of things as they now are, is fast approaching. The truth is that each of us is what any Mormon would call a, "prophet, seer and revelator." Each of us is like a radio, or a television receiver, of sorts. All are on the same journey of the mystic seer. All of us seek truth whether we're aware of it or not. But, thankfully, truth seeking is also the work of science.

Indeed, the scientific method is a far healthier wisdom than the more sluggish ways of *institutionalized* tradition. Science is the process that has allowed us to sufficiently examine ourselves, and our world. Science has led us to know that some aspects of our inherited civilization are toxic to the planet, as a whole. Yes, the use of science by ancient and modern patriarchs is largely to blame for our playing the dis-harmonic instrument of humanity's inhumanity. Yet, it is also science that today informs our mass consciousness with modern quantum physics, general relativity, and about the impact of our Mass Mind on the evolution of reality.

This last knowledge –that our Mass Mind *does,* actually, impact the evolution of our reality– is what drives us to *perceive ourselves as the creators of reality.* This way of envisioning is the epitome of being authentically human! I have had this truth revealed to me in many ways and through many other people, and some of those learning experiences are told in the stories in this book. But, in order for us to truly create "a new heaven" and "a new earth," a critical mass of us humans must learn to experience life differently. For, the malodorous reality is that all of us –to one degree or another– experience mortal life as if we're under siege. Indeed, it is how we *perceive ourselves* to be, which will bring about this prophesied massive transmutation. This brings us back to Columbine:

One of those unfortunate victims at the ill-fated Columbine High School was Rachel Scott, and it is significant that before she was killed, she had outlined her view of compassion in a thoughtful essay. She'd written how a "chain reaction" could usher in a new world. In her clear adolescent wisdom, Rachel Scott probably saw that a critical mass of us must learn to envision –to perceive– differently in order for us to change hostile environments. Young Rachel Scott understood our options well.

In 1985, I also saw, that we each need to find ways to act differently if we want to be part of the transformation of humanity. So, I gave Mom my new 1985 Camero; I signed it over to her, vowing that I'd from then on, be part of solutions to our polluting instead of part of the problem. I had seen how much our fossil fuel emissions contribute to planetary changes. Since then, whenever I'm on a train –traveling parallel to the freeway– it is obvious how society has not listened to the wisdom of scientists who warn of our depleted ozone. We believe that, we "need" bigger cars in order to navigate like giants through the danger zones we call freeways.

Even from *before* September 11, 2001, we have habitually acted as if we are under siege. We are yet unaware. For example; long before our current terrorism was underfoot, instead of medium cars—like my last one—we have been accustomed to climb into our tank-like sports utility vehicles before we go out onto the world of giants. We call this world of giants our "freeways" because they are now infested with these gas-guzzling giants. We all say to ourselves that; "an SUV is safer because it can withstand hard collisions." This isn't because of any terrorist. It is because of our collective mental sicknesses in our *mass consciousness*.

Because of a diseased condition, we—collectively—do not even see our others as they truly are. We don't say to ourselves, "there goes a mother and a child." No, we say, "there goes an SUV." Like snails, feeling as if under siege in the "freeway" world of giants, we all identify with our human shells—our tank-like SUVs—more than we do with the other human beings. As this book went into its first editing stage, a new television commercial denounces SUVs as contributing to the terrorists because of their tendency to use huge amounts of gas. So, it seems to me that, the late Rachel Scott—the Columbine victim mentioned above—had a better vision of who and what we each are than, evidently, our human *mass consciousness* does. But, I still have faith in the Mass Mind...

In the winter of 2003—as this book went into its first edit, the world grew closer to war over Iraq—it seemed that a critical mass *was* becoming aware. Millions of "Rachel Scott" types, in massive, global peace demonstrations manifested our human collective's huge paradigm shift. Then, in the Fall as a courageous American military, increasingly, returned back home in more and more body bags than standing on their own, others began to wonder if we had not been "tricked" into going to war, in the first place. The media had begun to look more critically at the original Whitehouse spin on the George W. Bush Administration's reasoning for our deposing of the Iraqui dictator, Saddam Houssein—rather than, only continue to seek out Osama bin Laden, in and around Afganistan and Pakistan.

Most European nations were not with America. Humanity, it seemed, was finally beginning to see military responses for what they are. Like only a few other moments in time, in 2003 and later in 2004, a critical mass quickly realized that *military responses are not the most desirable options*. These anti-war events may have been evidence of the start of a final transmutation! Only time will tell if it was another small change, or whether it was the beginning of major changes. Either way though, ancient *Toltec* wisdom says that, the "SIXTH SUN" has dawned, bringing huge transformations with it!

NOTES TO CHAPTER NINE

[i] The Quorum of The Twelve in The Church of Jesus Christ of Latter-day Saints (commonly known, worldwide, as the Mormon Church) is the primary entity of ecclesiastical leadership of this Utah based religious organization. In fact, in the succession process of the highest leader of this church, the man who becomes the next President of The Church of Jesus Christ of Latter-day Saints (upon the death of its President) is the President of the Quorum of The Twelve by virtue of his being the presiding officer of that body. Thus, in a very real way, it is the Quorum of The Twelve in this religious organization that, actually, heads the entire hierarchy. This is not the case in other religious institutions that claim to descend from the Founder of Mormonism, Joseph Smith, Junior. For example: in Community of Christ [the second largest religious organization that claims Joseph Smith, Junior as its origin] the succession process is rather different. The President of Community of Christ is not required to have been a member of their Council of Twelve Apostles but, rather, is designated by the President who is to be succeeded during his tenure and then, is ratified by delegates to their bi-annual World Conference by conference resolution. Thus, in the case of this denomination, their President does not take leadership of the institution by virtue of having been one of The Twelve Apostles nor, because of biological relations.

[ii] The Mormon Hierarchy, *Extensions of Power* by D. Michael Quinn, Appendix: "Genealogies of the First Presidencies and the Councils of the Twelve Apostles" (Signature Books, Salt Lake City, UT 1998).

[iii] This term is discussed in length in another chapter. Although, I grew up understanding the ideal with the term "Zion," "Topian" is used here, in place of the Mormon terminology "Zion" because the Mormon use of this biblical word holds a modern interpretation about land and "Zionism," as it is currently understood in the Middle East. Here, "Topian" has reference to the ideal of a diverse humanity living in peace, love and harmony, and it has no reference to land, territory or the modern concept of Middle Eastern "Zionism."

[iv] "The Prophecies of Nostradamus" Produced by American Video. Nostradamus is quoted as saying in 1560 that the term was original to Sir Thomas Moor of England.

[v] Unconditional Life, *Discovering the Power to Fulfill Your Dreams* by Deepak Chopra, (Bantam Books, New York, NY. 1991), page 207.

[vi] The Secret Science Behind Miracles, *Unveiling the Huna Tradition of the Ancient Polynesians*, By Max Freedom Long (Devorss & Company, Marina Del Rey, CA. 1976).

[vii] The Hidden Treasures of The Ancient Qabalah Volume I, by Elias Gewurz (Yogi Publication Society, Chicago, IL., 1918).

[viii] See Los Angeles Times, Sunday Magazine article titled, "*The Curse of Los Feliz*," January 3, 1995, Metro Section, page 3. This is a Feliz family legend about "*Dona* Petranilla Feliz" (Petra Feliz) and how she responded

to the swindle that disinherited us from our ancestral lands in the late 19th century. It explains why the Griffith family who's ancestor, had purchased much of the land, to this day, fights to prevent the City of Los Angeles from charging entry into this large city park that was once a part of the old Feliz Rancho. It is also why the Baldwin family divested itself of the old Los Feliz Rancho after having suffered the "consequences of the curse."

[ix] Italian Witchcraft, *The Old Religion of Southern Europe*, by Raven Grimassi (Llewellyn Publications, St. Paul, Minnesota, 1998)

[x] *The Issue Is Gender Equity*, A Paper Presented to the Salt Lake City Unitarian Church Support Group for Former Mormons, by Antonio A. Feliz. This paper has since been published in paperback form and titled, The Issue Is Pluralism, *An Urgent Call To Greater Pluralism In Civil Marriage Law* (Editorial Los Feliz, Los Angeles, CA. 2000).

[xi] Ibid. See also: *The Development And Diversity of Human Sexuality: A Biologist's View*, 1993 Sunstone Theological Symposium, Salt Lake City, Utah by Dr. Duane Jeffery, page 333. Inter-sexed persons are not to be confused with Trans-gendered persons. However, the phenomenon is related to trans-gendered persons, in that, it is where some humans are born with ambiguous sex organs.

[xii] See Journal of Discourses; Brigham Young often taught this in the 1860's.

[xiii] Matthew, Chapter 12, verses 47-50.

[xiv] This is in reference to the 2000 Roman Catholic child abuse revelations.

[xv] Doctrine and Covenants, L.D.S. Section 77: verse 1.

[xvi] Op.Cit.

[xvii] The Holographic Universe by Michael Talbot (HarperCollins Publishers, San Francisco, CA. 1991) page 46.

[xviii] Synchronicity, *The Bridge Between Matter and Mind* by F. David Peat (Batam Books, New York, NY., 1987) page 171.

[xix] The Words of Joseph Smith, *The Contemporary Accounts of the Nauvoo Discourses of the Prophet Joseph*, Volume Six, edited by Andrew F. Ehat and Lyndon W. Cook (Brigham Young University Religious Studies Center, Provo, Utah, 1980) 13 August 1843, page 241.

[xx] Ibid.

[xxi] Matthew, Chapter 18: 19.

[xxii] Hidden Treasures and Promises, The Restoration Church of Jesus Christ, Salt Lake City, Utah.

[xxiii] Op.Cit. Section 131: verse 4.

[xxiv] Ibid. What most Mormons do not know is that these particular three verses in their scripture (D&C 131:2-4) comprise the only part of their entire canon [the Standard Works] that, as it is written, "eternal increase" means marriage. They are in parentheses in their scripture for a reason. The quote in question reads: *"And in order to obtain the highest, a man must enter into the order of the priesthood* [meaning the new and everlasting covenant of marriage]; *And if he does not, he cannot obtain it. He may enter into the other, but that is the end of his kingdom; he cannot*

have an increase." The parenthetical statement is in the L.D.S. <u>Doctrine and Covenants</u> as it is published today, but, is not in the original archived document, which I personally read, in the late 1970s.

This verse is the only one of their canon that is the basis of their official doctrine and policy that only heterosexual marriage is of Divine origin. My sense is that, since the archived records also state that Joseph Smith "sealed men to men" as "equals" in the early 19th century. Then, this single written comment—compiled in Utah over twenty years after the fact—was probably not originally meant to be limited only to what this man's 19th century anti-mainstream Christian rhetoric, considered this "order of the priesthood" to be. Why so?

It is a documented fact, that Joseph Smith, Jr. [whom the current L.D.S. canon claims was the author of that single defining parenthetical statement] is the same Joseph Smith, Jr. who performed his first marriage ceremony out of a defiance of the Christian clergy of his neighborhood. Who had claimed that he –"the Mormon prophet"– had "no authority to marry" couples in their Christian community. This was when the little church was headquartered in Kirtland, Ohio in the 1830's. The specific parenthetical statement –reported only by one of Brigham Young's closest friends, William Clayton– is claimed to be part of a personal discussion between the two. It ended up as a verse in the L.D.S. canon decades after Joseph Smith Jr. had been assassinated. If it is what it is claimed to have been—personal—then, it was probably not meant to be otherwise taken.

I suggest that, Joseph Smith, Jr. was not speaking of marriage in the 1830s, as marriage was understood by his contemporary mainstream Christian denominations. He had no need to do so. His behavior in performing his first marriage was, I believe, a gesture meant to communicate that his own particular priestly authority went far beyond what the Christian community, of his time and society envisioned, as to; a) What marriage was; b) Why the then, evolving sealing ceremonies of the, yet, future Mormon Temples were to become part of the Mormon equivalent of most Christian marriage rituals and; c) Why later Temple initiated Nauvoo Mormons did not believe that Christian Marriage was enough. To any student of the cosmology of this "Founder of the Mormon Church," the limiting of what he introduced as the Sealing Power of Elijah to heterosexual marriage, is akin to a Roman Catholic Bishop of Rome [the Pope] saying that he is not "the first among equals" of those who also claim a Catholic or, an episcopal sacerdotal authority. It is anachronistic to all that his theology claimed in this period. To Joseph Smith, Junior the Sealing Power of Elijiah was (in the words of President Harold B. Lee to me) so "far reaching" that it can't be limited to the mere marriage customs of his time—much less, of our own day.

Theologically, Sealing Power is a *power*. It is not a priesthood office nor, a "priesthood key." This is why it is never spoken of by L.D.S. authorities as an "authorization" or, as an "office" to which one is "ordained" or "set-apart." The Sealing Power of Elijiah appropriates to itself—as a theological institution—something that I affirm in this book is the core principal of creation; i.e.: The Principal of Agreement—which is, literally, a generative *power*. Sealing Power then, has nothing to do with the external [public] institutional church. It, by definition, is claimed to be more "far reaching." It is a *power* that, theologically, is independent of all institutional forms. This theology dates back to the earliest days of the Mormon community, and in fact is why, the modern day Mormon polygamist groups claim they can "seal" plural marriages. As I was taught to comprehend the Sealing Power of Elijiah by the late L.D.S. President Harold B. Lee, the Sealing Power of Elijiah in all Utah-based Mormon groups, is more than a Divine ability to "bind" or, "seal" only the relationship of husband/wife and/or parent/child. It is, he said, "more...far reaching" [than a priestly order] is currently understood today.

Joseph Smith, Jr. claimed to literally have Elijiah's power "to bind on earth" and "in heaven" –and, supposedly, it is the same *power* that, the line of Catholic bishops also claim, from the same Sources: The ancient Peter; James and John; the apostles of the Early Christian Church of the 1st century c.e. All Catholics claim it has been given from one man to another, for centuries, in a long line that exists today in all Catholic Bishops. But, on the other hand, Utah-based Mormons claim it was lost when the original Twelve Apostles died off, to be restored by the, literal, original Elijiah—in "a glorified body" (for, he "did not taste of death") in the 1830s in their Kirtland, Ohio temple. (The Kirtland Temple, is today owned by Community of Christ—another faith community that claims Joseph Smith, Junior as their founder—headquartered in Independence, Missouri. This denomination has no teaching on the Sealing Power of Elijiah).

But, as I understand the teachings of the Prophet Joseph Smith, all of his words on the Sealing Power of Elijiah were saying that this special aspect of their priesthood history is far more than an investiture of priestly authority. In the words of the late L.D.S. President Harold B. Lee, when he laid his hands on my head and, bestowed the L.D.S. Sealing Power of Elijiah on me in 1973 in the L.D.S. Temple in Los Angeles, California; "it is a power" or, an energy that, is "more far reaching...than, it has since been" institutionalized to be. If that were not the case in the mind of this L.D.S. President then, why would he even make such a comment to me when he bestowed the Sealing Power of Elijiah on me as he advised me to study five sections in the Doctrine and Covenants? If that were not the case then, why do polygamous Mormons also teach it as such? This is the original theology on the Sealing Power of Elijiah.

Yet today, the L.D.S. Church—headquartered in Salt Lake City, Utah—limits the use of their Sealing Power only to heterosexual marriage and to parent/child adoption. I am suggesting here that, the greater, late 19th century social context is the reason why the Utah-based Mormons today aim to limit its use to only their evolved ideal of appropriate marriage and adoption. The fact is that, this historical social context is when all of America was steeped in slavery. Because the theology evolved from the early 1840s in the American Midwest and then, became solidified in the final decade of the 19th century when America had gone through the Civil War and through the federal prohibition of Polygamy in Utah, the Sealing Power of Elijiah became a doctrine about human genetics. The theological separation of the races and the forced L.D.S. conformity to American judicial judgments are the sociological motive in the Mormon minds who followed Brigham Young to Utah. Because of their 1890s political need to conform to the overwhelming social forces against them, and because they were steeped in 19th century theologies about the need to maintain pure genetic lines ["all Negros" were then, "prohibited" from "any and all priesthood" L.D.S. sacraments—not only from priestly ordination but, they were prohibited from the most sacred marriage in Mormonism], Utah-based Mormons needed to find new ways to understand their then, evolving theology. If one considers its greater social/political context then, their final version of their theology on the Sealing Power of Elijiah became crystallized as it is today, during the eugenics craze in America at the turn of the last century. It was not at the beginning as it is today.

The current L.D.S. theology was solidified as late as 1912, when the "International Manifesto" was first published by the L.D.S. First Presidency. When the L.D.S. Church solidified its current and, official doctrine on "Temple Sealings," Mormons were seeking ways to not only maintain their belief that their Twelve Apostles all descended from Jesus [*a'la* Arthurian mythologies] but, were also evolving in a context wherein the 20th century political demands required a new vision of the human races. Evidencing this social origin, their Genealogical Society of Utah was founded in 1895 for this exact purpose, and significantly, it is precisely also when the L.D.S. temple "sealing of men to men" was terminated; for, sealing men to men didn't make any sense to the Utah hierarchy in the late 19th century (when the evolving L.D.S. cosmology had become more centered in patriarchy than, in the day of the founder Prophet).

The result is that, today, Utah-based Mormons only perform Temple Sealings on legal heterosexual marriages and on parent/child relationships. But, as a student of the L.D.S. theology on the Sealing Power of Elijiah, I learned from older Mormon Sealers, including some who were ordained Presidents and Apostles in the L.D.S. Church. Now, in my 20/20 21st century hindsight, the L.D.S. <u>Doctrine and Covenants</u> marriage theology "for time and eternity" that originates in Sections 131 and 132 –"or, Temple Sealings"– to me, logically, is only one kind of human relationship, which their Sealing Power of Elijiah is capable of transmuting into a reality in the Worlds of Light. To me, this "power" is akin to the ancient *Toltec* Creative Agreement ideal. Students of Utah-based Mormon History and their Temple theology on the Sealing Power of Elijiah are also referred to <u>Doctrine and Covenants</u>; [L.D.S.] Section 132: Verses 1-18.

"If we consider that the civil marriage archive is, often, the only permanent record of an honest family then, to overtly act to omit an entire population group is, actual, *historical genocide*. It is an institutionalized dynamic that denies an entire people the right to have their existence as honest families recorded in the state's most permanent records of our civilized society. Contrary to patriarchal ways to envision, same-sex couples have lived and loved in all times and in all societies of our civilization. But, we don't know that, only because Queer folk have not been recorded in the permanent record of marriages that form our documented genealogies. This is true *historical genocide* in the same way as many others were denied a civil record of their coupling on the sole basis of their race or ethnic background in America prior to the 1967 Civil Rights Act.. "

CHAPTER TEN

LIMITING MARRIAGE BY SEX IS "HISTORICAL GENOCIDE"

Marriage has always been a significant part of my adult life since the year of my life when I first became aware of The Holocaust and when Mrs. White had helped me in high school, to choose to study journalism. I played Ann's love interest in The Diary of Ann Frank in our community theatre that year, and wrote my first paper on the murder of my great-grandfather by self-proclaimed vigilante veterans of America's 19th century Army of The West. It was also the year I confirmed *his* paternal great-grandfather's assassination had also been committed by land lusting 19th century Mormon Battalion members when they had occupied Los Angeles.

The 1846-1850 Mormon Battalion had been assigned police detail in *El Pueblo de La Reina de Los Angeles* in March of 1843 "with orders" to give their "smallpox infected blankets" to my fourth great-grandfather, *Don Jose Francisco Feliz*. It was the same year I had learned that my own father had to fight *his* illegal deportation —*him*, an American-born citizen, *whose family was here well before there was even a nation called America, or before there was even a Mexico, for that matter*! Ethnic cleansing confronted me in 1958.[i]

Ironically, Mormon missionaries had helped Dad document his genealogy with marriage records and, thus, he avoided being erroneously deported to Mexico. That L.D.S. intervention allowed my sister and me to stay and retain our place, as the next generation of Los Feliz of Los Angeles. Yes, that year I had learned a lot about *that* ugly time when Los Angeles County had ignited the Zoot Suit Riots by its ethnic cleansing of all of Dad's cousins. It was also the year that, *Terry* had started "coming on" to me.

In retrospect I'm sure that I was also impacted by a kind of self-loathing, common to religiously devout gays who discover that they are gay. It was also the year I'd had the epiphany,[ii] sealing my commitment to my church so, inner *cognitive dissonance* reigned in me. I reasoned: *My ancestors must have been in the wrong, surely 19ᵗʰ century Mormon Battalion church members wouldn't have done such things*! As told in Chapter One, my sixteenth year was when I fell into domesticated behavioral agreements with the heterosexual church.[iii] I'd thought I had no choice because of an experience I'd had at my first World Conference in Salt Lake City when I'd first met a Mormon Prophet/President. *That,* pivotal paranormal event gave me the will, or the sheer fortitude to *consciously choose* heterosexuality —an unnatural sexuality to me—as my chosen life path.

As if on a mythological quest, as the Earth Energy awakened my maleness in that fateful teen year, the burst of my true sexual awareness came in response to the man I call *Terry* in my books. But, *Terry* was manifest in perfect juxtaposition to my equally awakened propensity to experience paranormal giftedness! Later, friends said I'd had a classic "experiential initiation" into the old, "Sacramental School of Western Mysticism," and that, *that* mystical/theological tradition is also the historical root of our present Western marriage ideal in modern civilization. It had happened when I'd prepared to be ordained a priest—preparing me for a Mormon mission. Ironically, it was when I became aware of the Utah based Mormon theologies, on plural marriage, that had flourished under Brigham Young and his Utah successors. So, starting that year, I studied marriage from my contradictory domesticated, patriarchal worldview that, by then, had usurped my inner, *natural* sexual reality.

So, it's no accident that almost the entire first chapter of Out of The Bishop's Closet takes place within an L.D.S. Temple as I'd prepared to perform a sealing of a marriage. My whole life up to that one moment in my thirties was a series of training experiences meant to prepare me to become vested with the Sealing Power of Elijiah. Simply called, "The Sealing Power," this is *the* L.D.S. marriage priesthood order which, *only a living President of the Utah based Mormon Church may bestow on any*. Since my domestication had forced me to deny my *natural* attraction to *Terry,* and to only envision heterosexuality as being *natural*, I purposely set out to conduct a journalistic/theological study of marriage, *per se*. I'd determined in my sixteenth year to emphasize the historical, and the social, or the organizational marriage behaviors of Christian religious institutions.

In fact, a pivotal element of that first book dealt with the research I did on a 19ᵗʰ century sealing that, eventually, led to my leaving the Utah based Mormon Church. As reported in that book, this spiritual journey began in the L.D.S. Church Archives in Utah when I first discovered the "sealing" performed by the founder of the Mormon churches, which was for *two men*. Indeed, I have made the study of marriage my work in the ensuing thirty years since that watershed moment. Finally, as if I were a knight in an old Arthurian legend, I was guided to live with and learn loving ways with six *Meshica* families in Mexico in 1990 who changed my life. As told herein, because of them, I transcended my domestication.

So I guess, it is no surprise to me that I've come to see the issue of marriage equality by looking at marriage *philosophically*. I endeavor to perceive the institution of marriage from as many diverse cultural ways to envision it as I know how. As a result, I view diverse marriage forms *as metaphors, each with a reference* from which to learn. Yet, *collectively*, they are a different metaphor altogether and, being composed of them all, *that* metaphor is meant to be understood by the entire *universal* mass collective! This is the way of metaphor.

Metaphor is the language of all those who seek unity in diversity, and this is a key defining aspect of one who is on the way of open souls. We, seekers after peace, understand our marriage forms are all cultural. We see each institutional form as only a stem of one great ancestral tree of sacred stories. We know that, unless we learn to interpret our sacred stories as metaphors from which to learn, we won't attain social and political peace in today's "globalized" village. We know that interpreting our divergent sacred stories only through the lens of one's own, inherited worldview—whatever that is—has never led us humans to increased social and political pluralism. We know a *just pluralism* is *still* only the American Dream. Herein, I focus on aspects of this consistently reinforced awareness.

Naturally, all that travel the way of becoming open souls share in that same awareness. We all seek the path that celebrates human diversity, while we work for increased social and political unity by using various universal systems—like music—that, are all culturally labeled as a manifestation of love. We understand that the politics of love in the civic microcosm demands a *universal* social equity; for, the issue of social harmony is, ultimately, always about love, itself. Whether in the microcosm or, in the macrocosm, *in all inter-relationships of lovers, social equity universally begets inter-respectfulness, which is one key manifestation of love.* This ideal manifests in the full acceptance of all its citizens in its collective life, by *any* given community, precisely as is the case in the microcosm of a healthy personal inter-relationship, which we might call, "lovers."

Thus, in Becoming Open Souls then, I have here tried to tell personal experiences in relationship to my fellow sojourners on the same journey, by using myself as an example of one *microcosm*. In doing so, I have revealed that my fellow travelers also learned that envisioning social issues with the language of metaphor does allow for a *universal* reference to be gleaned from the public dialogue on any issue on how a citizenry inter-relates as a civic body —especially on the issue of civil marriage *per se.*

Because of several personal turns in my personal journey on either side of the much-debated civil marriage issue—as a social/ civil issue—marriage equality *per se* is a perfect example of my point here: My own second womb environment, after all, was a religiously rigid, and a highly patriarchal social group—one that has a notorious history of social experimentation in marriage. Yet, as I tried to tell in my first book, Out of The Bishop's Closet—and, now, in Becoming Open Souls—my personal journey evolved, and it has morphed me. It, thus, naturally transformed my personal worldview on marriage, as an institution of modern civilized society.

Moreover, the LGBT community has not remained static. We've labored hard to let America gain a more complete vision of the diversity of us Queer folk! In the defiant, adolescent phase of the earliest days of American "Gay Liberation," the term "homosexual" only conjured up the affect imagery of promiscuous nudity in hot Pride Day parades. America then, chose not to consider that, as any hormonally charged adolescent personally knows—whether Gay, or not—becoming sexually aware, with one's hormones raging, makes for the rush of sexual experimentation with newly opened freedoms. Well, America's perception of us has matured over the decades of my life. Other Americans now see that our community has always had "conservative" people too, *monogamous* LGBT couples!

For example in 2004, on Valentine's Day, I was fated to celebrate the Queer Mass Soul in our United States of America with many others of America's ordained. We, the speakers on the steps of the California State Capitol, covered the religious spectrum from synagogues to mosques, to churches. Speakers even included a few high profile, elected, political figures whose involvement seemed to underscore our progress toward the civic pluralism we've achieved. But this journey actually began twenty years earlier for me: I was at the 1984 Conference in Phoenix, Arizona of a LGBT social/support group "Affirmation, Gay and Lesbian Mormons"…

****

I had relocated from the Kansas City, Missouri area only months earlier. Bob Swoffer[v] and I had organized the social and support group for Gay, Lesbian and Bi-sexual former and current local members both the L.D.S. and the R.L.D.S.[vi] churches. He had baptized me in the old Stone Church in Independence, Missouri, but I had seen that—back then—my new community of faith "was not ready yet for my kind of Latter Day Saint."[vii] So I'd relocated back to California and Bob Swoffer happened to be attending the [L.D.S.] Affirmation annual Conference in Phoenix, Arizona.

Being whisked away, in a red convertible with the top down, by other guys who had just met him—Bob was awesomely good looking—he waved to me saying, "Hey Tony! We organized the old group into a purely R.L.D.S. group since you and all the other L.D.S. members have moved away…!" With that, he had announced the genesis of GALA,[viii] and the rest is history.

That was the last time that I saw Bob. I was on my way to a meeting of the Board of Directors of Affirmation—and, he was having lots of fun in that red convertible—so, we didn't take time to talk. Anyway, I was in a whirl over what I would say to the general leaders of this—very L.D.S.—support group for excommunicated Queer Mormon folk. My mind was on prepared remarks for them...

Within minutes, roughly fifteen people (including the man whom I called "Larry" in my first book and I) were sitting around a long table and I was speaking to the group. They had invited me to inform them on why I had begun to perform "holy unions" of same-sex couples and why I'd participated with several other members of Affirmation Gay and Lesbian Mormons in applying for recognition as a new religious group in California. The Affirmation leaders did not want to be seen as "an apostate group" by the Utah based church leadership, and needed reassurance by me that our goal was not to change our Los Angeles based Affirmation group into a church.

"First," I began, "we, in The Restoration Church, don't claim to represent Affirmation Gay and Lesbian Mormons at all. We just happen to all be members of Affirmation, as is everyone else in this room..."

"Tony," the chair interrupted, "tell us why you've legally organized a church in California? We'd heard you'd joined the RLDS church. We're a little confused. If you are now RLDS then, why start another church out in California?"

"All *I'm* trying to do is a *marriage ministry*. I still consider myself RLDS. But, I'm inundated with requests to do sealings in the L.D.S. tradition of a Mormon Temple."

"But Tony, the theology that we all here understand about L.D.S. Eternal Marriage teaches us that a temple is needed for those rites to be administered by a sealer. What good is a new church without a temple?"

"Well, I'm still a sealer. It's like being ordained a bishop; once a sealer, always a sealer. Some of you know that, I received the sealing power to perform all temple sealings from President Harold B. Lee in 1973 in Los Angeles, California. But, it is true, I no longer have access to any temple. So, in order to access a temple, we have to be legally able to tithe our members in order to build a new temple or, to buy a building to consecrate as one. We *had* to legally register with the state as a new religious organization for that purpose. A new church is only *to let us gain access to a temple,* and of course, *we all know* that Affirmation isn't a church!"

A board member asked, "Then, organizing a church was *not* the primary goal but, *a means to an objective* because of state laws?"

"Yes, in order to extend temple marriage—as we've known it in our common upbringing—we legally organized a separate 501c3 non-profit from this one, or from any other. That's all. We're not competing with Affirmation! We won't even proselytize anyone! Our new group even accepts all the RLDS revelations! All we want to do is to be legally able to seal couples who want a sealing. I'm about a marriage ministry here, nothing more."

Another elder with me added, "we, as a group, feel moved to provide the many same-sex couples who've sought out Tony to seal their unions as soon as they find out he's a Temple Sealer! We tell them: 'We can't seal you without a temple to seal in...' and then, they usually answer us back, 'Then, we'll start a new church to have a temple where same-sex Temple Sealings *can* be done. Tony just wants us to do it correctly!"

"But, Tony," another voice began, "isn't all this an apostate idea in the eyes of the one man who presides over all valid temple sealings from his offices at, 47 East South Temple Street in Salt Lake City, Utah?" He was speaking of the L.D.S. President in Utah.

Suddenly, I felt an indignant emotion rise within me, "Who really left the path first blazed by the Prophet Joseph Smith? Isn't *The Church in Utah* the real one in apostasy? It is *They* who refuse to take the "everlasting gospel" to "*every people*"—excluding all gay people, worldwide! Sealing same-sex couples is totally defensible, theologically, because as I..."

Another board member interrupted, "so why not just do it *quietly* without all the fan-fare, Tony? Why go through all the effort to make a public fuss that gets Affirmation involved? Just do it in your *home*."

Calming down a little, I went on, "Let me be clear, we are *not* a part of Affirmation. But, after a lot of soul searching in response to all the requests that I get to do sealings of same-sex couples, I had to join this group because they'd already begun to organize themselves to 'do what's right.' Eventually, the new church they were bound to organize would perform their own sealings of same-sex couples. So, it feels right for me to lend them a hand because of my expertise in the ritual, that's all."

Silence.

Then, I felt that familiar surge begin within me as it usually does and then, I added, "Don't you guys see? The water has already poured out of the bottle! You can't put it back in, anymore! This work is bigger than we even imagine! Why do you think it is written that, 'one of the prophesied signs of the Latter Days' would be, 'and they shall marry and be *given in marriage?*'[ix] '[G]iven *in marriage...*' here, denotes *non-*traditional marriages. Just think on it: This verse distinguishes what we Gays do, '*giving in marriage*' from what the heterosexual church does. This work is prophetic, it signals these 'Latter Days.' Hear it! Mark my words*, same-sex marriage is about to become one of the most important political issues of our time...*!"

Suddenly, raucous laughter broke, *everywhere.* Everyone was, laughing *at me!* After the laughter died down one said, "Come on Tony, it's 1984! You're crazy! That's not going to happen for another hundred years!"

"Guys!" I said, "The Church still refuses to even preach the gospel to gay people, yet, we're elders—we're still called to take '...the everlasting gospel...*unto every people.*' Most of you served on missions, and you know the verse well: That's *Every People!* When I saw that the 'everlasting gospel' was the doctrine related to the Sealing Power of Elijiah then, I knew I had been given the sealing power to bless *my kind of human being*! So, I had no choice: We just *had* to organize legally in order to, eventually, own a temple in which, to *then,* perform the first, 'everlasting' sealings of devout couples; couples that, the heterosexual church will not even send its missionaries to, yet! It's time to at least offer the saints of God all the options that Joseph Smith Junior offered the new Mormon faith in *his* 19th century dispensation! That is why today—in the old 19th century restoration tradition—we also plan to even dedicate our lands[x] for the preaching of the 'everlasting gospel'[xi] to Gay and Lesbian *people* because The Church refuses to preach to us Gays—as a social group! Then, theologically, as a new church, we'll be able to do the sealings of committed gay couples!"

Silence still reigned over the whole group. Then a woman whom I respected said, "Why, Tony! You make it sound as if you and these other elders with you, actually, '*opened a new Dispensation of the Gospel*' and…"

"Hey guys," I said, "this is about doing what's right. In fact, the day will come when this work will even be written about, and it will be spoken about, as far away as the streets of the great city of Amsterdam!" I marveled at the words that had just come out of me…

In the midst of more laughter, another said, "that would be nice Tony but, in the mean time, Affirmation is getting bad publicity in Salt Lake! Tony, don't you see? We're trying to put our best foot forward to the General Authorities. You're simply ruffling too many feathers!"

Then, twenty years passed—*not* "one hundred years"—and we, those former elders who had later begun that 1985 marriage ministry, had dedicated both Southern California and also Northern California in the formal way of 19th century Restoration Movement apostles.[xii] We had performed a host of temple rituals extending the sealing blessings vested in me to same-sex couples.[xiii] Then later, the events revealed within Chapter Two of this book, "From Power To Agreement" happened, and then a little later, Hawaii happened. So in 1993, from the comfort of my old Salt Lake City home by fax machine, I helped those fighting for the freedom to marry in Hawaii.

Moreover, for several years, I encouraged clergy in other faiths to do the equivalent of marriage in their own church, mosque, temple, and/or synagogue.[xiv] Then, my time in 1990 with *Meshica/ Toltec* friends in Mexico brought me new insight into our Marriage Equality movement. That's when I first understood that the Marriage Equality issue was only *our* focus but that, the core objective was to *increase in some by-product* in *its own* mass, and in *its own* scope. Eventually, I saw that, "*that something*" was our fellow Americans *learning or, practicing love toward us,* so that, *the proven Gandhian principles of Satyagraha could inspire compassion toward us* from America's non-gay citizens. So, *our actual objective then became to elicit today's current empathic public response*! Over the years, I'd observed the growing Marriage Equality movement, and I could see that it provided a way to increase a truly empathic response from our American citizenry.

Then, our State Assemblyman Mark Leno spoke to us at the September, 2004 GALA retreat in Santa Cruz, California. Later, I told him how I'd, years earlier, submitted my sworn testimony before the San Francisco Human Rights Commission public hearings on what was then, the first pending domestic partnership legislation. So in 2004, I joined the movement and was scheduled to speak at the 2004 Valentine's Day rally sponsored by MECA (Marriage Equality CA) on the steps of the California Capitol.

That event was scheduled for one day after San Francisco Mayor Gavin Newsom was to do "the unexpected" by authorizing his City Clerk to issue marriage licenses to same-sex couples in San Francisco! Then, the next day, a caravan was to leave that city en route to Sacramento for the planned rally. That event moved me to offer *Meshica/Toltec* wisdom as my medicine for Americans toward becoming open souls by using the issue of Marriage Equality as a vehicle, driving us all collectively, through new Agreements—new Agreements on what marriage, actually *is*, after all.

I knew that my words at the 1984 Affirmation general board meeting had been vindicated when, as if some cosmic present came to me right on my birthday: On June 26th of 2003, happily, the United States Supreme Court ruled against a state sodomy statute because of "rights of privacy guaranteed in one's home." At the GALA retreat that following September, I would declare: "We've already won! Now, we'll all just watch it play out!"

In 2003 the news had hit the airwaves about all the *civil* action legislated in California and elsewhere, and the final watershed event was the Massachusetts State Supreme Judicial Court ruling that in their state, same-sex couples shouldn't be denied licenses. It was that state's public dialogue that—in turn—led to San Francisco's same-sex marriages, and *rather than still being only my vision*, as they say, "the rest is history":

"S.F. set to defend marriages in court"–San Francisco Chronicle, February 17, 2004; "High Court Halts Gay Marriages" –Los Angeles Times, March 12, 2004! And, "so on, and so on...!" Today, it is one of the "...important political issues...!"

But, I believe that my friend, Dr. Joel Federman, has penned the best record of what is actually happening all around us today, a thing only visible to us through the public dialogue on marriage, *per se*. He posted the following on his web-site, "www.topia.org":

"Regardless of their legal outcome...Valentine's weekend weddings are akin to the moment that Rosa Parks refused to move to the back of the bus. For the first time, gay people simply claimed their rights to marriage...instead of merely protesting for them, as they had done...

"...[H]owever...the best case for gay marriage was visible in the faces of some 2,000 couples getting married in the San Francisco City Hall rotunda over the long Valentine's Day weekend.

From the lens of the outside world, these events may have looked at first like political statements taking place. But, for the couples getting married in these ceremonies, and to the friends and families gathered there with them, the marriage ceremonies were deeply personal testaments of their love and devotion. To paraphrase what Martin Luther King, Jr. said about inter-racial marriage, homo sexuals don't get married, people get married.

"In nearly every alcove around the huge City Hall rotunda over the weekend, a marriage was taking place; in the larger balcony areas, sometimes two or three. Some were officiated by clergy, others by city officials and prominent gay (and straight) politicians. Circling the rotunda, one could attend ceremony after ceremony, each profoundly personal and private, though infused with an awareness of the larger political and social significance of what was occurring....

"Until now, gay marriage was just a political idea to most people in this country. The San Francisco ceremonies put a human face—a few thousand faces—on that idea for the first time; much like what Rock Hudson or Magic Johnson announcing they had AIDS, did for that epidemic. The couples getting married demonstrated that gay marriage is not fundamentally about sex, but about love, and that by getting married, gays are not threatening the institution of marriage, but rather are celebrating it and enlarging its reach.

"The political meaning of the events of the Valentine's weekend marriages was trumped by their personal significance. The lines to enter City Hall may have resembled a march, but those who emerged after-ward did so two by two."[xv]

For me, the 2004 Valentine's weekend events also held a host of personal meanings. My first kiss by a man was in Sacramento,[xvi] and as told in earlier chapters in this book, I have had to experience the death of two companions. Pondering on that loss, walking around the California State Capitol grounds after speaking at that statewide Valentine's Day rally, I was shocked when a strikingly beautiful woman walked up to me. She held a perfectly formed, long-stemmed, royal iris in her right hand and extended it out to me. She had an almost angelic look in her face. She simply handed the long stemmed flower to me. Now, I don't recall if she said it, or if I quietly felt the words in my inner self but, I seemed to hear her say, "I have read your first book, and I know that, at least, one of your former companions is no longer with us. Here, he wants you to have this to remember him on this special day..."[xvii]

Taking it, I wept softly looking at her as she then, simply walked quietly away into the crowd. I couldn't even speak out loud to thank her, and lately, it's often that I sense a definite presence and then, I wonder...

The following months were filled with: Radio talks shows, public speaking events and book-signings on my second book, The Issue Is Pluralism, *An Urgent Call To Greater Pluralism In Civil Marriage Law. That,* kept me hopping! In fact, to make it to two sequential events I, actually, *flew* instead of traveled by AMTRAK train, as has been my personal choice since 1989! Those who know me well, know of my in-flight experiences and the huge personal change this was for me. I hadn't flown since 1989 because of five near disasters I'd experienced in five separate incidents. *That change* shows the significance of these events to me. A radio talk show and press conference in Kansas City (allowing me to attend the bi-annual World Conference of Community of Christ in Independence, MO) were all scheduled only one day after a big West Hollywood wedding I'd agreed to witness, had all combined to force me to fly again!

But, when I arrived at the Independence gathering, delegates from all over the world to the bi-annual World Conference had begun to work proposals before the global gathering of my faith community —proposals about priesthood ordination of gays, and about same-sex marriage in the Community of Christ! The prophet/president of the Community of Christ had submitted an inspired document prior to my arrival as, "Words of Counsel," and it was being considered by the Conference for inclusion in the book of revelations. I read it carefully. The revealed words called us to: *"let The Spirit breath"* and to, *"listen together to one another..."*

After several days of the legislative sessions, I had witnessed the tone of the gathering go from opposing opinions being expressed from the Auditorium Chamber floor to a sudden breakthrough in the *palpable Spirit* sensed by us all. What impressed me the most was that the youthful delegate who successfully amended the proposal that was adopted by the Conference regarding homosexuality was the spiked hair leader of the "Youth Caucus." After that, a devout, and respected Tahitian, literally, "outed himself" as a Gay man on the Conference floor! That is when the tone of the dialogue abruptly changed into a collective, and a loving empathic response. *Empathy* guided the body to take two years to *"listen together to one other..."* —as the "Words of Counsel" had advised—before a final decision on how to respond to America's on-going evolution toward increased civic pluralism that now, increasingly, includes us Queers.

In the process of the week of World Conference events, I often felt guided to meet and chat with delegates from my global community of faith. I met many: A sister from South Africa, that Tahitian brother and another man from the Republic of Georgia and then, there were the two sisters from The Netherlands!—*from The Netherlands*, of all places!

I especially enjoyed the intelligent and articulate way of those two women. Both expressed "patience with the rest of the church" that, one said, "has not, historically, seen human sexuality as is our Dutch way to understand same-sex couples." One of them asked for my card and...:

In my core, suddenly, *I knew*—I knew she would bring about the fulfillment of my old words to that Affirmation General Board back in Phoenix Arizona in 1984. Somehow—*somehow*— she will create a day *"...when this work will even be written about and it will be spoken about as far away as the streets of the great city of Amsterdam!"* Giving them both one of my business cards, I felt the tear of joy flow down my face.

****

What is the lesson to be had from all the above? When limiting marriage on the basis of sex is seen as metaphor, what is its reference? Without focusing on the "prophetic" aspects of these stories, what's their lesson? They teach us three ways *to discern love*:

(a) Any true politics of compassion will focus on truly empathic responses to pressing social issues of any time and society.

(b) Human rights are all about personal sovereignty and secular societies demonstrate their ability to manifest love through their empathic civic responses to those who do not fit their *external* norm in the form of their, respective, civil statutes.

(c) Likewise, because our human rights are always about personal sovereignty, religious societies also manifest their ability to love through their, respective, empathic institutional or policy responses in the form of their sacramental theology and policy, regarding those who do not fit their *external* norm. This is the way to know whether compassion, love and empathy are the behavior of any, particular, civil or religious society.

Hopefully, the stories in this book have illustrated these three points because this way of understanding our divergent sacred stories is critical to our survival in the 21st century because we'll soon have many new opportunities to learn more how to practice our love. I say this, because the *Toltec* Calendar—mostly known as "Aztec" and "Mayan"—ends at noon, December 23, 2012; which, ironically, is Joseph Smith Junior's birthday![xviii] The traditions of my mother's ancestors tell that the coming of the end of the *Fifth Sun* or, the fifth life cycle of this planet has arrived. According to today's masters of *Toltec* wisdom, we have *already* entered the SIXTH SUN, together with all of its predicted physical Earth transformations!"

So, today, we are now in what would be known as the SIXTH SUN, or the sixth cyclical epoch of our planet's existence. In other words, Mother Earth has gone through five earlier cyclical seasons controlled by our sun, and now modern scientific data supports this more ancient understanding about our planet's cyclical solar epochs, for, there is evidence of these cycles.

Basic to our ancient *Toltec* tradition is the knowledge that Father Sun responds to evolutionary transformations of our human Mass Mind and, as mentioned earlier in this chapter, the human Mass Mind is now quickly maturing! This is because the SIXTH SUN brought a change in its solar energy. This is why we humans are now experiencing major shifts in how we humans perceive. Today, we are all witnesses to the shaking death rattle of the dying fear-based worldview, and ancient *Meshica/Toltec* oral traditions also say that, "with the death of fear-based envisioning then, *natural* changes will accompany the new cycle, the SIXTH SUN." What we call *disasters* are inevitable. What will come, will come. We, humans can't stop it. What will happen is not about humans. It is about *all of planet Earth*.

So, to you who are still fighting for the freedom to marry; I say: Those who oppose our struggle for equity in the civil arena and in other circles will be judgmental of our step by step progress toward political and social pluralism because they still come from a place of fear. When terrorism and disaster strikes, they will blame us for all the *catastrophes* because of our political efforts. When they do so, be courageous because our cause is about our *freedom to love openly —without hypocrisy, as Jesus of old taught*. The worst thing that can happen is death, and we all die! But, if we *love honestly* then, what is there to fear? One way or another, all "pass on" to an afterlife.

Love honestly! *"You who have any who love you, cling to them and thank your God! Surround yourself with loving hearts. Place your person in the company of true compassion. Unite yourself with others who seek solutions to solve the sadness. Strengthen the souls of all the seekers that, they may enlarge the resources for your mutual sharing. Speak kindly to each and all, with no judgement or condemnation. Let each one be as each is made to be. Be tender, generous, forgiving and gentle. In this way, let your honest hope, joy, love and peace shine out brightly to the rest of the people. They will then, see your example, and they will be blessed by it. Your purpose is about increasing love here, and now. The* SIXTH SUN *brings inner awareness. It dawned a New Age of light and hope and love is now replacing fear.*" So, faster than we now think it will happen, peace, joy and harmony will begin to be more extended throughout the world! This is nothing less than a spiritual revolution! We are revolutionaries of human spirituality!

Know that, as Wayne Dyre is prone to declare: "We are not human beings having a spiritual experience but, we are all spiritual beings having a human experience." Know that we are light beings, and our mortal death is nothing but a transition wherein, *thereafter*, we become cognizant that—*all along*—we have each existed multi-dimensionally! At that moment of transition, we each become aware that our physical body has, actually, been an *energy metabolizer* for that is how we function as part of the Planet. Leaving the body in death allows us to inter-relate freely with other light beings. This is because *then*, being disembodied, we continue living, in a dimension of light—as the "active *Intelligences*" that we each truly are!

With all of that as a base of awareness, now, recall the lesson of an earlier chapter in this book titled, "Science Aligns With Ancient Wisdom." Remember that, I believe in Albert Einstein's Unifying Field but, recall that, because of how I have experienced the mystical experiences, mysticism also informs my awareness and says that the Unifying Field is Love. In other words, exactly as astronauts need their space suites to provide them with "life support systems" in outer space, *it is Love that we must learn to acquire in order to gain the "life support systems" to sustain us as we continue beyond mortal death in a dimension that is totally made of Love.*

Hopefully, I have made a clear case for the imperative of our all becoming more practiced in Love—*as the only effective disaster preparedness* today, *"immediately after entering the 21ˢᵗ century."* Hopefully, we have learned from the old theological mistakes of my former mentors who still, today, judgmentally lead the heterosexual church in America, for, their common error is taking a purely cultural marriage ideal as the only norm of our much more diverse, secular society. The great theological mistake of The Church of Jesus Christ of Latter-day Saints is that—in the effort to distance the institutional organization from polygamy—the Utah based Mormons lost their way on the inclusive theological trail on marriage *per se* that, Joseph Smith, Junior, had initially blazed for all future saints.

So what is the hidden reference? What is the metaphoric meaning of the issue of Marriage Equality? Well, as written earlier, my former Utah based Mormon mentors re-fashioned their faith's cosmology after only the then, dominant heterosexual cultures of the Earth. But, *that* choice, in effect, has eliminated an entire, naturally occurring segment of the world's populations from being eligible for their brand of the Afterlife! It, in effect, extends an exclusionary culturalism from this world into a world that, *by every definition*, is beyond any given culture, clan or custom! Because personal sexual proclivities are all probably biological in origin, sexual diversity *is the norm* of all that will live in the Afterlife.[xx] Yes, there is sex there!

But, because of my awareness of the power of the human Mass Mind; to disqualify a naturally occurring segment of Earth's humanity from their Utah based vision of the Afterlife is a classic genocide of one, naturally occurring *universal* manifestation of life! The Utah based Mormons administer rites that—because of their institution's political behavior—reveal that they mean to eliminate an entire segment of Earth's people from their Afterlife! *They use Earth's marriage records*, with which to then, vicariously represent individuals for whom they then, perform ritualized, "sealings for the dead." The problem is that, they do this "temple work" while, they also work politically to eliminate an entire segment of humanity from all of the marriage records of civilization, so as to not mistakenly seal any same-sex couple, "as a couple," in *their* Afterlife! Like self-involved adolescents, they only act to benefit their unique vision of an Afterlife but, in the process of this brand of mysticism, their earthly *political behavior* does far more:

Their total behavior is not merely a religious organization's unique mysticism. Their related political behavior regarding civil marriage is institutionalized genocide. If we consider that the civil marriage archive is, often, the only permanent record of an honest family then, to overtly act to omit an entire population group is, an actual, *historical genocide*. This is an institutionalized dynamic that denies an entire people the right to have their true existence, as honest families recorded in the state's most permanent of records of modern, civilized society. Contrary to the old patriarchal way to envision, same-sex couples have lived and loved in all times and in all societies of our civilization.[xxi] But, we don't know about it because Queer folk have not been recorded in the permanent records of marriages that form our genealogies. This is true historical genocide in the same way as many others were denied a civil record of their coupling on the sole basis of their race or ethnicity in America prior to the 1967 Civil Rights Act.

In traditional Christianity, the sacrament of marriage was based on Original Sin. Anciently, the marriage sacrament was about making a natural thing, sex, into a sanctified thing. Sexual behavior became holy in the eyes of the church only by the rite of marriage. Significantly, *although same-sex coupling was very common in the ancient world around him*, the Master of Love responded, to those involved in sexual deviancy from the social norm of His time and society, with no comment from His lips on same-sex coupling!

To the contrary, if I read the Gospels correctly, what the Lord of Love condemned, far more than sexual deviancy, was hypocrisy. This personal observation helps me to imagine today that—in today's world—Jesus would probably advise sexual minorities to "come out" of their, respective, sexual "closet" and then, to "sin no more." But, to be equitable, same-sex couples should also have access to the same sacrament that allows them to also continue on, in "sanctified" relationships. So, what is there to fear about same-sex marriage? Is there something to fear about *same-sex monogamy*? Is *that*, the fear? But then, if marriage was good enough for Jesus to be part of one at Cana then, that gospel story together with His egalitarian treatment of women of His time and society, also inform me. They both tell me that, today, Jesus might view Same-Sex Marriage as a consistent and egalitarian response to these naturally occurring types of love also.

"[M]y journey has taught me that heterosexuality is only one of several sexualities that abound in nature—and that, all Creation is 'good' in God's eyes. I think of Mary Jane, and same-sex marriage becomes one of those "*close places through which the church must pass…*" This comment was a part of my second L.D.S. patriarchal blessing that guided me to discovering that the policy of The Church on "homosexuality" was one I could not agree to. So, I sought a way to better reconcile my truth with 'eternal principles'…" Among other things, Patriarch Bushnell's 1960s prophetic declaration had said:[xxii]

"…*You will see many broken homes…*' and, to me, those few words refer to all of the countless young men and women that I've counseled, whose natural families were inhospitable to them, only because they were Gay, Bi-sexual or Lesbian. Those words refer to the hundreds that I've counseled over the years, for having married heterosexually—only to discover that they are, in fact, also Gay or Lesbian. Yet, if there is any message that has come through to me over my life's years, it is the truth that: '…*of all the languages, the greatest is the language of love…!'* Indeed, the only healing response to the absence of anything is its presence. So, whenever a healing is needed because of the absence of love then, the only truly healing response is love—judgment is not good medicine in this case—the appropriate medicine then, is love. And, in our one, common, civic world, Love is treating one another equitably."

Finally, as simple as it may sound, to me it comes down to this truth: The actual core issue is *not* about us Queer folk, or our sexuality. The true core issue is, actually, *not* Marriage Equality or the genocidal ethnic cleansing that all we, otherwise good citizens, inadvertently conduct by not including same-sex couples in our most permanent civic records. It is *not even about* our personal lack of manifesting love by our mixing of church and state nor, even about the disdain some Queer folk have toward those whom they call *"breeders."* The core truth to be had in all of this is that, God is about empowering us all *through humanity's empathic responses because empathy is the presence of love of neighbor*—God's presence in us.

The true core issue is about we humans leaning to become more humane; Marriage Equality is merely a contextual opportunity. When a theology, doctrine, policy or law causes one group of us to treat, "one of the least of these," as being *less than* we consider ourselves to be then, *that* theology, doctrine, policy or law, is *not* from God. This is because things Divine are *never* about creating "second-class saints" but, rather, things Divine are about *love,* and love is an *empathic* response, or *treating others as one wishes to be treated.* Let's get beyond inherited behavior in marriage, for, it is the historical genocide of honest families. The call of the Loving Jesus was to eschew hypocrisy, and to avoid hypocrisy, *to live honestly.* Yet, from past generations, we've inherited the ethnic cleansing of a people, only *because they loved honestly, without hypocrisy!*

The major problem is that we've meshed church and state! Let us, instead, put into practice what Jesus advised: "Render unto Cesar what is Cesar's and, to God what is God's."[xxiii] A way to do this might be to allow the church, the synagogue, the temple or the tribe to celebrate whatever form of marriage each, respectfully, wishes and to no longer license religious groups to perform any *civil* marriages. Indeed, it might even be more equitable to no longer license any civil *marriages* but, rather only, *"civil unions,"* that are no longer defined by any gender-centric terminology. This allows all our citizens equal access to the permanent public record of their existence—the state civil records—as honest domestic units of our society. In this way, we let the state do its job while, letting religious groups do theirs.

But, whatever we do, let us all learn more how to practice love! If the opposite of love truly is fear then, let us acknowledge that there is nothing to fear about the changing way that society now perceives Queer folk. There is nothing to fear in Queer people being able to be *monogamous* as far as the public record is concerned! The fact is: In today's new world, envisioning the daily life of Queer folk is no longer limited to the graphic vision of the kind of sex that we practice. In this new century, being able to envisage that Queer folk are *also* monogamous, now, lets America think of LGBT people in relationship as committed couples *in love,* as opposed to only seeing us as couples *having Queer sex.* Now, if the fear is that America *will* respond with empathy to same-sex *monogamous* couples then, *the actual fear* is that, *we Americans fear love*, when responding to our differences charitably is what we Americans, actually, claim!

Remember; it is love that we seek! I affirm that only *our own individual practice of Love* will prepare any collective of us to survive that which, is about to happen! Remember; the marriage issue is only a symptom of what we all truly need to heal from. The marriage issue is merely *today's opportunity* to practice love through our collective's *empathic* response. And, the opportunity is extended in both directions—not only to those who would maintain the *status quo* but, it also extends to those who would change how America still responds to same-sex *long-time couples.* Those from the extreme of homophobia must practice love of Queer folk, and we Queer folk, must also practice a greater love of our opponents. More *practice at loving* is our collective opportunity. Love is our best healing balm!

If, by now, Marriage Equality does not seem to be that for you then, I urge you to find another opportunity to learn more how to practice love. But, if you haven't yet found another way to *practice more love* then, come on! Consider us! Join our *concord circles*[xxiv] as a way toward becoming a much more open soul, through the core creative principle of Agreement!

NOTES TO CHAPTER TEN

[i] See The Appendix to this volume.

[ii] See <u>Out of The Bishop's Closet</u>, *A Call To Heal Ourselves, Each Other and Our World* (Alamo Square Press, San Francisco, California, 2nd ed. Paperback 1992) Chapter One, "Personal Dichotomies"

[iii] See <u>Ibid</u>. and <u>Becoming Open Souls</u>, *Transcending Institutional Seduction & Cultural Rape* (Concord Press, International, El Dorado Hills, California, 2004) Chapter One, "The Seduction."

[iv] Until outlawed by Congress in the Edmunds-Tucker Law of 1890, plural marriage was practiced by members of the Utah based Mormon Church.

[v] The late Bob Swoffer was a local RLDS priest and the first to respond to a card I'd posted in a Kansas City gay bar saying: "LDS? RLDS? Gay, Bi or Lesbian? Let's meet. Call me:___-___." Bob Swoffer later baptized me in the old Stone Church across the street from the Temple, in Independence, Jackson County, Missouri.

[vi] Community of Christ, whose World Church has been headquartered in Independence, Jackson County, Missouri since Joseph Smith III (its succeeding prophet/president to the original founder, Joseph Smith, Junior who prophesied that his "seed" would lead the Nauvoo church back to the "Center Place" in Missouri). Joseph Smith III was Joseph Smith, Junior's eldest son and his mother, Emma Hale Smith together with his siblings, joined the 1860s Illinois and Iowa remaining Saints who hadn't followed Brigham Young to Utah.

[vii] <u>Op.Cit.</u>

[viii] Gay And Lesbian Acceptance grew out of the Kansas City group that began with our 1980s modest outreach and, although it is not an official entity of it, by 2004, GALA was affiliated with Community of Christ.

[ix] Matthew 24:37-38.

[x] This is in reference to a ceremony specific to the apostolic tradition of 19th century Mormonism still practiced by The Church of Jesus Christ of Latter-day Saints. Mormon Church History is replete with the sacramental practice of a formal priestly "Dedication of The Land For The Preaching of The Gospel." This was a tradition followed by the 19th century apostles of The Church of Jesus Christ of Latter-day Saints, when it was headed by, Joseph Smith, Junior in the 1830s and 1840s. It invokes the attention of beings "on the other side of the veil" to a new opening of missionary evangelism, to a new dispensing of the "everlasting gospel" to a new "*nation, kindred, tongue*" *or to a new "people*" and—in this case—the "people" in question was the LGBT community, as a *people* of earth.

[xi] Theologically, this was in reference to the symbolism invoked by a statue of the Angel Moroni on the top of many Temples of The Church of Jesus Christ of Latter-day Saints, headquartered in Salt Lake City, Utah. The Moroni identity of the Book of Mormon, attributed to the angelic image, suggests Moroni was the angel seen by John as it is recorded in the biblical Revelation. The statue's identity is marked by the angel blowing his trumpet with one arm, announcing on top of a globe [a symbol of evangelizing the world] that the "everlasting gospel" is established on this spot; i.e.: in this Temple. Thus, this image is a metaphor with a hidden

reference, and the hidden meaning is: the "everlasting gospel" is taught within their temples! But, temple rituals are not mentioned in the Book of Mormon at all and, thus, 20th century Mormons (who've forgotten the reason why a copy of the Book of Mormon in his other arm) are confused by it.

[xii] Insofar as the theology of the "Everlasting Gospel" which, is found in the Temples of the Utah based Mormons, historians and students of Mormon mysticism should study the timing of changes relative to "taking the everlasting gospel to every people." Personally, I believe it is revealing to search out the dates when the official policy of the Utah based L.D.S. Church changed toward LGBT people in its prohibition to proselytize "every...people" [meaning Gay people]. I affirm that the sealing power and the creative principle of Agreement is the same. The date of that change in L.D.S. missionary policy from "not preaching to...homosexuals" (see Manual of Instructions in the 1970s) perfectly correlates with the timing of these dedication ceremonies. The official written Dedicatory Prayer offered at each site where the original 1985 founders of The Restoration Church of Jesus Christ read the, respective, prayer and presided over the ceremonies is archived with The Restoration Church of Jesus Christ, now headquartered in Salt Lake City, Utah. As I reveal in this volume, I resigned from this group in 1987.

[xiii] The Restoration Church of Jesus Christ was legally registered with the State of California as a non-profit organization in 1985. Within months, a "Temple Enclosure" had been designed, constructed, dedicated and, I was recognized by the group as "vested with the Sealing Power of Elijiah to seal couples therein."

[xiv] Antonio A. Feliz, 1989 paper, Episcopal Divinity School, Cambridge, MA.

[xv] Dr. Joel S. Federman, *"Writings Toward Another World"* at "www.topia.org/marriageasahumanright.html".

[xvi] This coming out story is frankly related in my first book.

[xvii] In Out of The Bishop's Closet, I relate that my second partner had passed on.

[xviii] December 23, 1805, and he often equated a coming "Zion" with his birth date, although, this Pre-Columbian calendar had not yet been discovered by scientists.

[xix] Dr. Wayne Dyre *"The Power of Intention"* PBS Special, KCET, April 2004.

[xx] Spiritual medium John Edward often confirms that "sex happens there too."

[xxi] See Same Sex Unions In Pre-Modern Europe, by Dr. John Boswell, (Villard Books, New York, New York 1994) and also, The Spirit & The Flesh *Sexual Diversity in American Indian Culture*, by Dr. Walter L. Williams (Beacon Press, Boston, Massachusetts, 1986).

[xxii] In reference to the L.D.S. Patriarchal Blessing reported in Chapter Five.

[xxiii] Mark 12:17.

[xxiv] *Concord Circles* are an ancient *Meshica/Toltec* tradition. To register for a future Concord Circles event visit, "www.concordcirclesinstitute.org".

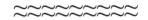

"Consider these two affect images: The Roman Catholic Virgen de Guadeloupe is set on top of the male symbol of two bull's horns, and Mormon Temple baptismal fonts sit on top of the male symbol of twelve horned oxen. In spite of the male-centric policies of these two religious institutions, their two *affect images* place the female principle on top of the male principle. Both are necessary, but according to the meaning of these *affect images*, the attributes which we attribute to femaleness must be seen by us as the better attribute because the female symbol dominates the male symbol.... "

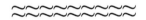

CHAPTER ELEVEN

OUR AGREEMENT MADE OUR TODAY

Any who seek peace, Love and harmony must also vibrate peace, Love and harmony, themselves. Any who seek to self-identify with the Universe, must likewise, attune themselves to the vibrations of the One Eternal Soul. This is because the same law that governs the smallest atom is also the law that governs the whole, including each human being. So, again, I reiterate: *as is the microcosm so, also, is the macrocosm.*

In the previous chapters, I have endeavored to show by a personal phenomenology that those laws referred to above, speak to all of us; that, The Universe is saying loudly to us that, we need to change the path on which we each, and also as a civilization, *journey.* At the beginning of this book, I also re-affirmed a statement that I'd made elsewhere that, the "...domestic enemies to our democratic society are racism and sexism, including heterosexism..." And [that,] "those laws that I say govern all that is, enable us to navigate our way." The Universe, *Itself*, is saying to us that, the way we are all now headed, as a society, does not enable us to take the path toward joy, hope, love, peace or, better social harmony for that matter.

No, we are not going toward those vibrations. Moreover, in light of the truth that, *everything is vibration*, we need to stop in our tracks, now, and vibrate in a new way. The wisdom of those who've led us here from past generations hasn't been sufficient to our present need. But, as stated before, hindsight is easy. So, we all need to study our past. As I personally do, we need to examine our collective past.

For the fact is, others will, eventually, also study our present choices. Some day, others who study us will record how we, today, experience the experience of living in our present culture, time and civic society. Those future persons, no doubt, will make their social commentary about us, by asking themselves the following question:

Had the 19th century Americans been more successful in their genocidal efforts of Indigenous societies then—what other wisdom would have survived until the beginning of the 21ˢᵗ century of their Christian era to meet the cyclical planetary cataclysm that had been previously survived by that centuries older, Indigenous wisdom?

The one message offered by all the stories told in this book has consistently been that none of us can survive, in any other way than, to magnify in our collective Love, by attuning to the vibrational frequencies of honest compassion born of true empathy. For, this is exactly the way in which the ancient ancestors of Indigenous peoples survived to tell the story of how, after it was over, they all "emerged" out of the earth. This is why the English, "emerged," is the word used by most translators of extant Pre-Columbian wisdom (the Indigenous wisdom of North, Central and of South America) to tell a common survival story of all of their, respective, beginnings. The same ancient survival story is lodged in all their mythologies!

So, recall that all myth is true metaphor. Evidently, a huge cataclysm drove their ancestors *into* the planet—*into* the Earth—in the first place. According to their ancient wisdom, there is a planetary phenomenon seen as cataclysmic by us that happens in cycles, like all the seasons of the planet. I'm saying that, the day will probably come when our own survival will depend on us also escaping back into the planet so that we may, eventually, also "emerge" out of it—after the Earth's magnetic polarity changes again—because the change of the Earth's polarity is *cyclical*, according to the legends.

When I first made that statement in a public setting I was then, accused of being, "nature-centric," as if saying it to me was to disparage me. But, I don't see that as a bad thing, at all. Moreover, the label may easily be correct. I hope it is. For, we all are nature, *all of us,* whether we like it or not. Oh, I know our inner selves are all made of light but, in terms discussed in earlier chapters, *everything else in nature is also light.* Our human chemistry is exactly the same as the sun's make-up, for heaven's sake! I'm saying that the perceived dichotomy between humans and nature is, actually, a false one. *We are all One being.* I embrace my self-identity as one being; one Who encompasses an entire world of light but, I do so while also embracing my self-identity as a complex physical being, one whom we call the Solar System: The Earth and all the other orbs in this system. Now, some would judge me, and say this "borders on psychotic."

Notwithstanding similar comments made by a few, who also disrespect my worldview, history shows that, there is wisdom in this more nature-centric worldview. For example: It is highly significant that upon discovering the Hawaiian people, Captain Cook recorded in 1768 that he had "never before encountered a happier people." It is equally significant that every member of the Christian clergy, that accompanied both Cortez in old Mexico, and Pizzaro in Peru—who also recorded their own "first contact" observations on encountering the Indigenous residents of the newly discovered land—also wrote similar commentary.[i]

There is a huge difference—*huge*—in how I experience the experience of life, now, since embracing my Indian way to envision. I assign great meaning to the context of all synchronicity now because, as physicist David Peat wrote, a synchronicity—or, an omen—is any "meaningful coincidence," or the "significantly related patterns of chance."[ii] All coincidence, to me, is now a *convergence*. An example of this kind of phenomenon is the *timing* of the first encounters with a far healthier wisdom than our own modern civilization's worldview. This is why the phenomenology of the conquest of America's Indian societies speaks so loudly to me now. To me, this phenomenology screams out to us all but, most of us don't listen to its message!

In my personal experience, I learn from observing the timing of a, seemingly spontaneous event, because *that* is the *context,* and in my personal phenomenology, it is an event's context that holds the great lessons taught to me by The Universe. So, I assign tremendous meaning to the clear fact that when each of the European explorers, respectively, landed on the shores of what is now Hawaii, Mexico and Peru, all the locals were each in the midst of their, respective, annual celebrations dedicated to some future arrival of "divinities." In each, respective, sacred story in Hawaii, Mexico and Peru the ring of their ancient prophetic wisdom was all about "the return of the tall, white, bearded ones" in their future to come. Their prophetic myths pointed to the way that was *ahead on the path, which they followed.* Had they changed course before the Europeans had come to America then, my sense is that a totally different history would have evolved. But, they had retained their oral histories in their myths.

The same concept applies to us today. The point is that *in each of the above historically documented events, the more ancient societies encountered by the European explorers were each expecting them*! Yet, in the arrogance of conquest, the invading conquerors saw the local ways with horror. The ancient wisdom, woven through the tapestry of their sacred stories, provided us multiple witnesses to their condition. If all prophecy is uttered through metaphor, and if it takes two witnesses to convince "beyond a shadow of doubt" in our courts of law then, why not *here*? Here, in our civilization's history, we have had three separate cultures teach us that they had each had prophets who foresaw the future in their, respective, language of metaphor. Tragically, instead of us learning from their prophets, we forced our theologies into them, and we tried to kill their wisdom in our nation's first federal detention camps. We still call them Indian Reservations and justify them by the American inbred and violent tradition, which we then called, "Manifest Destiny."

But, what about Americans today? What about our present civilization in the current context of a 21st century exploration of outer space? What will *we* encounter in, *"Their* outer space," if we don't change how we inter-relate before we encounter *Them*? The fact is: "Manifest Destiny knows no boundaries," as Dr. Olin Tezcatlipoca, a current leader of the *Meshica* Movement in Los Angeles, often says. Our problem is that we don't know if They, whom our immediate future generations will surely encounter, will be as kind, or be as benevolent and as loving as, say, the Hawaiians were to one, Captain Cook, a few centuries ago.

Global events today, especially since September 11, 2001, tell us all that our only security can truly be found in becoming open souls. In the open human soul, the soul's atoms are prone to mingle with other less harmonic vibrations, but they are *not* combined if the individual is truly in-sync.-with all of the rhythms of all of Eternity, including with the vibrations of the natural world because nature is also a part of the Eternal Round. This part, the synchronizing of the heart and the Earth, is crucial because the part of us that is nature is our body, and it has nothing to do with the mind. Unlike the human mind, the human heart is made of earth stuff, and as a result, the heart feels like the planet feels. Mind doesn't *feel*! Mind *thinks*.

Chemistry perfectly reflects this very logical differentiation. The difference in constitution between a molecule of oxygen, and one of, say, nitrogen; is imperceptible to us but their properties actually differ widely. Oxygen in pure air is mixed but, is not combined with nitrogen. Whenever these two gases are combined, according to their proportions, the result is a deadly poison. This is exactly the process that goes on within the human soul, which is made up of, not only spirit but, it's also a fleshy body with blood and mind. Indeed, *one's soul is actually, ones' entire world.*

I am saying the evidence shows that this dynamic exists on all levels of known existence. When the diverse atoms of the various parts of the entire Whole are mingled harmoniously in human social contexts then, the result is always physical, mental, emotional, social, and therefore, a spiritual wellness. When discord ruptures the rhythm of their vibrations and harmonious balance then, what we know as disintegration sets in. In the individual human, it's manifest as human physical and emotional disease. In society, as a larger collective, it is usually manifest as the mind-set of separateness.[iii] But, in both cases, the result is a manifestation of a sick condition. In earlier chapters, I wrote of this as a lack of Love; i.e.: *Fear.*

Here, it is crucial to recall that we human beings fear that which we do not understand, and while everything in the unseen dimension of spirit is made of Love, fear is the opposite of Love. As a result of fear, the illusion of separateness, eventually, becomes visible in our collective as destructive violence, and mental illness. It was seen at Columbine High School, in Afganistan's Taliban, and in Iraq's 2004 prisons run by our abusive troops! We humans can no longer continue in this way to be. We will not survive unless we change. Yet, we will not change unless we do survive! But, will we be able to change? That, I suggest, depends on our letting go of our literal –or *historical*– interpretations of sacred stories that all contributed to our present diseased state. Now, another example:

****

In 1997, I attended a "diverse gathering of some friends" of a friend. I was invited by him to this gathering by his words, "Tony, I want you to be your usual, honest self. Use language that is clear, concise and respectful and you can be open there."

In retrospect, I suspect that my friend, evidently, had not yet learned that I had an exercised ability to see in those of any closed community, a certain way of speaking in *encoded* language. How the world is, to someone like me, is not how others appear or speak, in words. I had learned far earlier in my life that a person's soul can be known by seeing into them, as I speak, and also by watching how they inter-relate in the common environment, as *others* speak. My B.Y.U. communications training had prepared me for this gathering.

At my friend's urging, in the course of the "gathering," I took the opportunity to voice my personal distrust of any god as violent, and as judgmental, as our present cultural idea of father-god. With no prior assumption—other than my friend's description—I had been as clear, as concise, and as respectful with my words as my upbringing allowed.

Afterward, I over heard some chitchat during a snack break, and listening to them, I discovered they were two who believed in the arcane, Hebrew, Enochian mythologies—mythologies, with which I was familiar from my Mormon up bringing. Utah based Mormons, in fact, believe they have a piece of Enoch's scripture that other societies do not, so I was confident that –from the words they used– they had acquired these sacred stories of Enoch and his fabled city, colored by generations of Hebrew storytelling.

But, the woman's outlook sorely pained me, or because of my own worldview, I received it with extreme emotional pain. I had overheard her asking her naïve question of a man standing with his back to me, "Will there be any place for the Native people who, like our visitor, identify as being part of the Earth, instead of identifying with Father Enoch and his heavenly city of glory? Will identifying so much with the planet allow them to leave it when The City of Enoch returns?"

To me, her question was born of the shackles of ignorance caused by someone's old cultural "rear view mirrors." Like any storytelling tradition, to me, her mythological tradition had signs of multi-generational syncretism. So, I pondered the unfolding of her world, by the words which she used. But, I'd responded differently –angrily– to the man who had responded back to her. She, at least, seemed to be a "true believer;" a devout disciple who only knew things about her tradition, by what her teacher had revealed. She did not have the benefit that I did, from outside of their spiritual relationship.

To me, his words contributed to what was –to my ears– her ignorant mind-set. He seemed to encourage her mental view as being "…more acceptable to…" her god than, would be that of a follower of "Native" traditions. I found relief, however, when I chose to see that he, apparently, had no actual awareness that things Native are totally about having harmonious relationships with all of Earth-life's forms, including all other human beings. Otherwise, his mal-informed and his most unwise counsel to her could only be interpreted as the evil of manipulating a disciple's perception.

That is when my own thoughts rang out my deep personal disgust of how they were both programmed by a kind of rigidness –a kind of fundamentalism– in highly literal interpretations of Enoch's mythologies. That's when I knew that the group had all the trappings of a cult group. I thought silently: The ideas of a heaven and of this Earth –of a heaven above this planet, and of Earth as a testing, or as a proving ground– both, make us loathe our natural selves, as if the Earthly self "is an enemy to god" *because* of our Earthness. If this mind-set is where our social ethics come from, I thought to myself, then; it is ultimately a good thing for our sick civilization to be done away with by some planetary cataclysm –by a planetary wobbling– expected by my Indian friends. In reciting their old stories, my Indian friends had said that, "the expected planetary wobbling" is a cyclical phenomenon that "is sure to repeat itself soon, as the seasons of the year repeat themselves cyclically." Now, science confirms this.[iv]

As the two continued in their conversation, I marveled at their myopic vision. She took comfort, as he reinforced her clear belief in Enochian fundamentalist interpretations, by his comment: "This is what being a 'chosen people' gives to us. Because we are The Chosen, we can escape the filth that this world is."

My own thoughts went on: Yeah, if our mind-set is that anti-Earth—anti-*nature*—then, ours truly is a self-loathing, ugly civilization that needs to die in order for part of humanity to survive their alien "visitation." My private, angry thoughts continued: A religion that despises nature is probably a schizophrenic, sick thing –in its core. Such a view sees things natural as unclean, disgusting, despicable and diseased. To me, it seems to spawn a cultural dynamic that objectifies all that is nature, toward self-destructive ends. Traditions of this kind do not comprehend our present condition. Truly, if this is civilization's origin then, we've all been led by blind guides!

That was when I first consciously thought that my unique, personal contribution to our present ugly condition was my simple, yet, honest awareness. It was the day I decided to publish to put these ideas out into the Chaos, for I'd seen Chaos Theory at work in my life.

****

The point is: All faith traditions—including my own— train their innocent children in their own private schools. In my experience, Mormons are no different than Jews, Catholics, Protestants, Muslims and others in this fact of tribal inculcation. This is why I voted against the 2000 school voucher initiative in my state. Like all, "faith-based programs," school vouchers can only add to today's inter-cultural problems, discussed within these pages. This fracturing of the mass consciousness of our school children into the tribal views of arcane traditions, taught in "faith-based" schools, will only exacerbate all the problems previously discussed. We all need to get away from the old institutions that have, traditionally, each provided us with our earliest social imprinting. It is no longer the time to go back to their bounded, ways of programming an arcane envisioning of one another. And, I'm confident that the reader can also identify her or his own examples of this polemic in the faith with which she or he is most familiar.

For example: In their formative years, all Mormon children learn to sing the hymns composed from their myths in the Book of Mormon. It is a matter of well-documented historical fact that this particular mythology contains divisive stereotypical themes, such as the racial concept with which I was confronted as a boy in my own Mormon Primary class experience, related in a story in Chapter One. From that experience on, I had been contaminated with the belief that my skin color was "a curse" from the very god whom we worshiped, because that is what the Book of Mormon said to us! Yet, in that faith community, there is no awareness of—nor, any sensitivity to—how damaging this myth can be to a developing little person of color.

To be balanced, I should say that, the Second Book of Nephi did say, however, that "the curse of a dark skin" would be lifted someday and that "they [Indians] shall be a white and delightsome people."[v]   But, this mythological device is the true origin –in my opinion– of modern manifestations of an almost irrational otherness in the deeply programmed *inner* psyche of the modern Mormon community toward all people of color. It is no accident that, the Christian separatist Church of Jesus Christ of The Arian Nation, was founded by one, Richard Butler—a former Mormon. To my vision, such is the unwitting result of any "faith-based" initiative.

In their version of that scripture, the Utah based Mormon Church has changed the original wording of this scripture—which they claim is "God-given"—to now read, "…a *pure* and delightsome people" from what had, originally read, "…a *white* and delightsome people."[vi]   But, I however, as a son of a *Meshica* woman, absolutely reject their teaching that, any of my ancestral heritage is not "pure," simply because (through this linguistic and theological device) the Mormon scripture, in effect, computes that one word, "pure" with a, "white" skin. This reveals a hidden, although—no doubt—a truly inadvertent, racism! I'm careful to say, "inadvertent" because Joseph Smith Junior, the author, was an abolitionist, after all.

However, in spite of the fact that I am no longer open to the view that these sacred stories of my youth are, indeed, the remnant history of my mother's ancestors; Lehi's Vision still holds a powerful meaning for me. *If I consider this story as a myth with a hidden reference then, it speaks loudly to me.* This has been my salvation in reconciling the theologies of Joseph Smith Junior.

As *metaphor*, the mythology of the Book of Mormon still speaks quite loudly, I believe, to anyone who reads it. This, I believe speaks far more of the authentic giftedness of Joseph Smith, Junior, than of the truth of original interpretations of a culturally influenced institutional religion; for, as has been most wisely observed by social anthropologist, Dr. David Knowleton, "syncretism has affected the evolution of even Mormon myth."[vii]

On the other hand, as with any good mythology, if it is taken only as a tool for the discovery of truth from within, rather than, as an externally imposed tool to use (like guilt is used to maintain a group's conformity) then, I am open to its wisdom. In this way, any canon of scripture is revelatory. Indeed, in this way, even a book like this can be revelatory!

All stories have a power to be genuine catalysts for personal revelation. This is because their inner meaning changes according to the constructs of each, individual reader. For example, although it was not written except as an honest telling of my personal experience, I received thirty-seven letters from readers of my first book who told me, that it was the catalyst that motivated them to actually convert to the Mormon Church. While, that was *not* my intent; like it is with any honest story, its readers found a personal meaning. So, to reveal my personal interpretation on it, I offer "Lehi's Dream" as an example of how personal any myth can be:

"And I beheld a rod of iron, and it extended along the bank of the river; and led to the tree by which I stood.

"And I also beheld a strait and narrow path, which came along by the rod of iron, even to the tree by which I stood; and it also led by the head of the fountain, unto a large and spacious field, as if it had been a world.

"And I saw numberless concourses of people, many of whom were pressing forward, that they might obtain the path which led unto the tree by which I stood.

"And it came to pass that they did come forth, and commence in the path which led to the tree.

"And it came to pass that there arose a mist of darkness; yea, even an exceeding great mist of darkness, insomuch that they who had commenced in the path did lose their way, that they wandered off and were lost.

"And it came to pass that I beheld others pressing forward, and they came forth and caught hold of the end of the rod of iron and they did press forward through the mist of darkness, clinging to the rod of iron, even until they did come forth and partake of the fruit of the tree.

"And after they had partaken of the fruit of the tree they did cast their eyes about as if they were ashamed.

"And I also cast my eyes round about, and beheld, on the other side of the river of water; a great and spacious building; and it stood as it were in the air; high above the earth.

"And it was filled with people, both old and young; both male and female; and their manner of dress was exceedingly fine, and they were in the attitude of mocking and pointing their fingers towards those who had come at and were partaking of the fruit.

"And after they had tasted of the fruit they were ashamed because of those that were scoffing at them; and they fell away into forbidden paths and were lost.'"[viii]

Mormons inculcate all their small children in various ways, especially by singing hymns that tell this story. I was once part of that programming. Back then, I learned institutionalized versions of the myth. I was taught that, "the rod of iron" is "the word of God." In this way, the original myth is distorted in a warp of the time and culture of all those who mold the minds of innocent children. Although the scripture, itself, *now* says that, the "iron rod" is "the word of God," *the fact that the Book of Mormon has been changed so much over nearly two centuries,* allows me to challenge that interpretation here. It is an institutionalized mythology, and significantly to me, Joseph Smith Junior said the biblical "word of God" was incomplete. How can "the word of God" be the "iron rod" when the "rod of iron"—a symbol of security—wasn't yet *complete*—for, to L.D.S., their canon is *open*?

Most live their entire lives believing that the only meaning of the iron rod can be their official canon. However, I now see that the written "word of God" has only gotten us to the place where we now find ourselves. My sense is that there is a clearer message in this myth than the, now, institutionalized challenge to "hold to the rod" because "it is the word of God." To me, early imprinting causes the Utah based Mormons –generation after generation– to miss the true reference of this metaphor! This interpretation, I am convinced –as the "man" who did the dictating of these legends warned– is only the work "of a man."[ix] Even if Joseph Smith, Junior, the self-proclaimed "Author & Proprietor" of the Book of Mormon [as was stated in its first edition] wrote that, particular, interpretation; he was a product of 19th century society. Thus, Smith, "a man," was as capable of making mistakes, as any other "man." After all, it was his very society, which gave us slavery and Manifest Destiny's conquering ways.

Before getting into it further, the reader should know that the Book of Mormon presents itself as stories from a few pre-Columbian civilizations. Personally, I take *that*, as a classic mythical essence. With that in mind then, here is how I view the reference of this sacred story:

1, because the placement of the rod of iron is grounded in Earth, *the rod of iron—itself—represents a grounding attribute is its reference.*

2, the path it follows is what I would call, The Way of All Opening Souls. It follows a path, a symbol of a spiritual *journey,* which is—

3, to *the side of the mainstream,* and in this way, it leads those holding onto the rod of iron to the final goal—Lehi's Tree of Life. However, this way is difficult (as in the straits of oceanic coastlines), and it is narrow, signifying that, *it is not the way taken by masses* of people because they would not fit in a "narrow" way. Also, with a narrow path that follows in the direction of the rod of iron, the seeker is made to not hold onto another seeker, but rather, onto a rod that is *grounded in nature, denoting the reference of a nature-centric theme.*

4, fountains are holy places because *water symbolizes spirit,* and *fountains then, are sources of spirituality,* like "energy vortexes" are to those in traditions, whom Zukav calls, "multi-sensory beings."

5, the large field is defined in the myth itself, as *"a world"* that is at "the head" of the fountain, or "the source of spirituality." To me, this reveals that the source of the fountain is, actually, *another world.*

6, the mist of darkness, to me, is the *cultural blindness* of the civilization to whom the myth is given. Those who seek the fruit of the tree must go through the mist of darkness but, they succeed by clinging to the rod of iron. Rather than interpreting this as a need to cling to a canon of scripture, my view is that *this is a warning to cling to what is grounded in Earth –in Nature, itself–* and in this way, attain the goal of accessing the fruit of the tree. In other words, *while we must go through civilization* (the mist) *in which we find ourselves, we can survive the journey by clinging to Nature* (for, the rod of iron is grounded in Earth).

7, the "large and spacious building" can only represent the illusion of our present condition. It is suspended in the air. In other words, like the man who taught of Enochian myths, earlier in this chapter, it is *not grounded* in nature. It is filled with the "beautiful people," with their propensity to mock and judge. *I can't imagine a better way to symbolize the institutional church, with all its external forms, proprieties and unholy judgments* of all those seen as the, "uninitiated." The contribution of this part of the myth is in *showing how we must not be* in our inter-relating.

This is how I would interpret this Book of Mormon story but, the point is: There are as many ways to understand sacred stories as there are persons. A particular way to assign meaning tells more about us than, it says anything about the myth or, the symbol, itself. For example, my father was the first person who taught me that the purpose of fire was to transform reality. Thus, fire has since then, represented transformation to me. However, I later understood this as evidence of Dad's mystic bent because, eventually, I discovered that most others consider other aspects of the Light of fire. For example: In order to *see* fire, first, requires a transparent medium to reflect the Light of fire. Yet, it was because of Dad's interpretation that I was able to perceive the significance of our natural atmosphere, as being a reflective medium, facilitating vision—much as mirrors reflect light.

Dad's rather mystical way of perceiving the Light of fire had focused my soul in a different direction than, most of us on the same life journey. In this way, it was easy for me to see the need for my clarity, honesty and integrity of soul in order to be able to know "by the Light of Truth" because, through a *transparent* medium, the light of fire reveals what *is*; i.e. Truth. But then, irrespective of any other way to envision what the Light of fire is, Dad was trying to enlighten my mind by focusing me on the *mystical* aspects of the Light of fire. For, he saw fire as mystical.

Nevertheless, in the example of how we see symbols, the Light of fire is truth because it is; it *exists*. All that exists is only true because *it is*. What doesn't exist –what is *not*– therefore, is not Truth. Moreover, light –by its nature– dispels the darkness and the light of fire, allows for our perception of the matter being transformed as the energy we call fire. Recall that dense, or opaque bodies can't transmit the light that falls on them. My point is: Here, Dad had taught me to know that, being clear, unclouded and lucid is about being centered in the cosmic vortex, which occupies the same, precise space as our own physical heart, and honesty is what brings about an opened soul. I know this today, because of how Dad had me focus on the nature of fire. Thus, I'm aware that being an open soul is a dynamic of *Nature* that engages the planet's transformation process because our honesty —*our transparency*—is Earth's defining essence, *Earth's vibration*.

But, since experiencing the wisdom of Indian friends, I now also compare the dynamic of our human transmutation to that of a budding flower that, eventually, comes to full bloom. They helped me to focus on things natural in ways that Dad did not. As a result, I know that, as it is with all of Nature, including human beings and all the beautiful flowers, our true soulfulness –our beauty– is deep within us, at first. Before the bud even appears, the fully bloomed flower already exists within the plant.

So it is with us all. If our heart –our very core– is grounded in Nature then, its inner beauty is revealed to us if we nourish that seed. When we each do this, like a developing flower of a plant, we also transmute into a beautiful soul. First, the petals of awareness show themselves. With that, the petals of true empathy, forgiveness and inclusion begin to form. But, it is not until the most growth is attained that, the almost fully bloomed flower radiates its awesome fragrance to all coming in contact with it. That fragrance references Love. Our practice of Love is how we humans evolve into compassionate—or humane—persons. While we focus differently on our most common symbols—*things natural*—we *still* attain peace and Truth! Because of all the above, the mustard seed parable on faith is pure perfection.

The great universal Truth is that *none of us will get out of our hell without becoming the kind of creature that does not belong in hell.* Recall that one of the names of the Devil is "The Accuser." If we want to get out of our hell then, we must eschew judgment of our others. The word "should," like those who pointed fingers at others from the great and spacious building in Lehi's Dream, is an idea that is often linked to the judgment of others. Judging others is merely about *external* stuff. Judging others is not spiritual behavior.

Judgment does little more than create conflict in all social groups. The truth is that our society has inherited "*judgment*" as a device for the staging of conflict as a means to manage sought-for goals. As discussed in a previous chapter, judging is a favorite tool of manipulators, by imposing guilt onto those who deem the accusing authority as a parental figure.

Moreover, the abstract concept of "should" makes the world into an illusion for nature-centered people because what "should be" is not *what is*. It is, therefore, not Truth, and thus, to them, *what should be* is illusion! As I see it, the old concept of "should" is our civilization's ugly, inherited technology for any externally engineered cultural change.

Yet, this *isn't* how nature works. All blossoming plants come from the unseen core of their species' seeds. Petals beautify our world from within the opening bud. Conversely, the concept of should is often used to create an *externally* imposed sense of shame. Let us remember what we have learned the hard way from Columbine High School in Littleton, Colorado. When an adolescent boy is humiliated, especially, by those with whom he only seeks to identify; his shame demands a defense because that inner response is what has been modeled to him from over sixty documented centuries of our human generations.

I cannot stress enough that the abstract concept of "*should*" is a language contextual device—a technology—for the controlling of and for the manipulation of one's own peers and all of society. It is a highly effective technology to which abstract theology is linked, which does not work today, as it did when patriarchs more overtly ruled (than today) by merely creating conflict. If a thing does seem to work in our civilization, either on the personal or on the social level then, it is often the result of some dominator staging a conflict.

Sadly, staging conflict is how our present civilization works. For example: It was not unusual for me to sit in presiding council meetings of some kind in any of my former faith communities, only to hear someone suggest that, "we needed to create a problem to solve the problem" at hand. But, the path which I would have all follow with me (along with many others) leads us in quite another direction. It's the way of becoming open souls. This way takes us all away from the uncreative and limiting propensity to stage conflict by judging another's religion; with the doctrine, theology or the tradition of one's own perspective of thei religion. It is time to turn away from anything that limits and makes others "less than."

Many years ago, I learned that there is nothing that is small, or limiting, about God. Negative judgment of anything or anyone —solely because it or they are seen as being *other*—is rooted in toxic and illusory attachments. Our attachments are all centered in cultural imprinting, and are, thus, all illusory in nature. This defines negative attachments, in my view, because our attachment produces negative judgment of any other's religion. The Divine, Who is wholly worthy of my Infinite worship, is about each of our individual empowerment, not about any of us being "less than." In my way of seeing, *if a teaching makes our neighbor into one of a different class then, it limits us to only our cultural ways of inter-relating with them.* That, to me, is a clear signal that the teaching does not come from Eternity; for, God truly is Love. Rather, *that* way of envisioning our neighbor comes from only a limited, or a culturally based view.

Because I have been motivated from my youth by the dream of a Millennium of Peace and Harmonious Love, my focus is toward a much more inclusive way to be in the world. Harmony, *itself*, tells me that such a future time will be about pluralistic, tolerant and diverse societies. I affirm that it is early cultural and other social imprinting that distorts and otherwise, warps the cosmic signal which otherwise assists in the search for self-knowledge. Before we can do, on the social level—as Zukav advises readers to do on the personal level— to align our *mass* personality with our Spirit *Mass*, we must *first* be aware of who and what we, collectively, are. We must acknowledge that the dominant culture has created the present illusory condition, or as Don Miguel Ruiz says, "the dream of the planet."[x] Clearly, we need a new dream!

This book's theme is the dignity of spiritual dissent from all theology. The Sanctity of Dissent is another book that teaches about human dignity. This great book speaks clearly to our common human dignity. As cited earlier, in The Sanctity of Dissent, Toscano defined Patriolatry as the "worship of a false god..." I am discussing our agreements here, and Toscano added:

"Dissent is holy because without it there can be no consent. Consent is a voluntary meeting of the minds. It is the agreement of free individuals who share a perception of what is mutually beneficial or at least acceptable to them. Consent is meaningful only where dissent is permitted and protected. Consent draws its power from the possibility of dissent... by eliminating dissent, a community takes from its members the power to resist or contradict. It neutralizes opposition by abridging an individual's right to protest, to object, to cry out in pain. Such a system is a prison in which every act of kindness may be an exploitation, and every act of love, a rape…"[xi]

Accordingly, while to some my upbringing—reported in this book's Chapter One—was a loving kindness, I came to see it as my personal institutional seduction, and later, I saw it as my cultural rape, and rape is pathological. On the societal level, our civilization now manifests the pathology of our agreements. Even before September 11, 2001, the neurological systems of the macrocosm have proven to be dysfunctional and deteriorating, and our modern civilization's life-giving energy has been waning to the point of expiration. No, you are not the crazy one when you came near to expressing your road rage in the summer of 2001, rather, all of us collectively, have become the victims of an inherited lunacy. Like the insane man I've encountered from time to time on the streets between my home and the gym I use, we –in our civilization– choose to wallow in our own mire. It is as if, in a spiritual or metaphysical manner, *we've drawn the present terror to ourselves.*

So, what is that mire I say has metaphysically magnetized the terror to us? Well, when we discover "infidels" in our towns and society, like crusading knights of old, we today kill for justice and our religious ethicists count us among the "righteous" for our behavior. There is a reason why seventy per cent of gratuitous violent acts on the screen are played out by the hero. It is because writers have not learned to be more creative than the ancient scribes of the bible. Our writers seem driven to glorify the character who's role it is to, "kill for justice." For example, in Mormon mythology General Moroni is glorified because he led his armies with their blood oath written on a banner in their battle against the supposed ancestors of modern day American-Indians.[xii] Yet, the Utah based Mormon Church mentions relatively little about they who, "buried their weapons of war," and who then, reportedly, allowed "themselves [to] be trodden down and slain" because they would "not lift their swords against" their true enemies.[xiii] This kind of attitude is in our sub-conscious mind, and it is still largely unchecked in our various states of induced social insanity. The insane collective, that greater society is, demands our insanity as a coping mechanism –although we're not actually, *clinically* insane.

In this light, it is a mistake for us to believe that the root cause of violence is merely a, "boy's insanity," or even an, "arcane warlord's insanity," with no further study. My sense is that we are all too much like our pets. We all crave an external approval programmed into us by the imprinting of cultural father figures. We mimic what we have had modeled to us by those parental figures. This is the process that causes "nice boys", and also, Afganistan's Taliban "boys" to act as they do—or any other "boys," who bully their peers, for that matter. These are our ugly agreements, agreements that rule our behavior.

Let us not forget that the word, *Taliban*, literally, translates into the English words, "school of religion." So, it behooves us all to take a final critical look and examine our own collective contexts; for, the Afgani's, is as regimented a religious context as those unfortunate American souls who endeavored to kill their peers because their peers do not respect them because they are different. Our common cultural insanity arises out of a programmed domestication into a classist way of envisioning. This was revealed to me in this way...

****

It was 1989. I walked briskly through the morning streets of San Francisco carrying my travel bag and brief case. Everyone was busy and somewhat hurried. Since my apartment was on Nob Hill, my route toward the city's Muni, the underground subway, took me through the notoriously crime ridden, Tenderloin District. This was no longer the "middle" America of my youth.

Homeless people were everywhere on the sidewalk in lines for some food at the Catholic parish hall. Suddenly, as if an audible voice had said it quietly in my ear, I sensed the words, "These are they who are America's lower class, the disposable throw-aways of your society." I'd often walked through this area, and some of their faces were familiar to me. "Hey!" I said, walking by one, whom I had recognized.

The man asked back, "where ya off to with yo' bags?"

"Would you believe," I answered back, as I kept up my pace walking down the hill, "the Geraldo Rivera Show in New York!"

As the man waved to me, like he was watching a parade, he yelled out, "Give 'em hell for me!"

Soon, I boarded the underground, and there I came in contact with others, such as I, who could afford the minimal cost of public transportation. As I smiled to a woman whom I often saw on that line, the comforting voice came from within, "These are they who are truly America's upper-lower, and lower-middle classes. These are the working class, who are in effect, the servants of all the upper classes." My eyes met another face. She was in a light-blue waitress uniform, apparently on her way to serve those who could easily afford the cost of eating in a public restaurant.

When I got off the underground, I boarded BART, the mass transit train that would take me under the bay and toward the airport in Oakland. On that train, I sat down with those who could afford to live on the peninsula and work away, in the east bay suburbs. The voice again made itself felt within me, "These are the so-called middle and upper-middle class. These are they who financially sustain all of the traditional American institutions through their income, property, and sales taxes as well as with religious tithes and charitable offerings."

Then, after the comfortable ride across the bay in the tunnel and on the rails above the freeway, I got into a taxi. On the way, I began to sense a certain isolation that I hadn't felt earlier that morning. "This is the isolation of the upper classes of America," the voice said quietly. The taxi driver had spoken in a very congenial, yet, distant manner. That's when I first realized, that I was no longer being treated as an *equal* by others with whom I had conversed that morning. I felt obliged to give my driver his expected gratuity, because of what it is the cultural symbol of the taxi patron's superior place in relation to the social rank of the driver in our much denied American caste system.

Then, handing my luggage to the airline employee at the airport, I pondered on the English word, "patron." I wondered if its linguistic root was the Latin; *patre*, as for "*patron*," because it's the Spanish word for the traditional paternalistic boss who is the source of salary raises as well as official supervisory reprimands. I thought to myself, *patronage* has always seemed, to me, like a dynamic of alien social constructs. With that thought, I recalled that such a view was probably a result of my earliest social imprinting in the public schools of Orange County, California, as well as from my earliest Mormon Sunday school lessons.

The entire flight time on that jet, I felt haunted by a new and unfamiliar inner sensation. It was an uncomfortable feeling. Finally, as we began our descent, it came to me: I knew that I was haunted by the sense of being serviced by my fellow *equals*. Looking on either side of my aisle seat, I saw that the others in the jet were all dressed in what seemed, to me, to be the vestments of a higher order of a denied American caste system. As they put away all of their computers and papers, I remembered the clothes worn by the earlier street people –the homeless man– with whom I *had* spoken briefly only slightly under four hours earlier. The voice did not come this time, however. There was no need; I'd learned what it was trying to teach me. I could see on my own that, these around me in the jet, are they who are the upper-middle, and the lower-upper classes of America. None of us were speaking to each other. None of us had spoken to each other the entire three-hour trip on that jet! We'd all been engrossed in using cell phones, our reading material—both on-line, and on paper—and we'd all become even more isolated than I had felt earlier, *even* in the taxi.

Then, after landing in New York City, I was greeted by the uniformed limousine driver from the television show. The limo was stocked with snacks and drinks for my pleasure. As I enjoyed myself, I tried to talk with the driver, but the glass window kept us apart. I felt totally cut off from the other human being in the same vehicle! The ugliness of our classism became palpable to me. I could almost *feel* it. There was only separateness all around me in that dark night, in that all too lonely limo.

For the first time in my life, in my personal use of our diverse transportation system, I had an experience that reinforced what I had before come to know only in an intellectual way. That fact is, our modern American transportation system is a mirror that reflects how we Americans support, and otherwise, maintain the *status quo* of our classism alive, in our much-touted "classless" America.

The various social/economic classes are each kept separate and apart from each of the other classes by the design of our different transportation systems. This was before the nation of South Africa experienced their revolution against apartheid and I wondered to myself, *is this essentially any different from the ugliness of apartheid that is going on in South Africa?* This was a strong question to ask myself, because in those 1980s days, I was still under the Utah based Mormon illusion, thinking that America was better in these ways than *apartheid's* South Africa was in the 1980s.

****

This, is the kind of society that we have created. And, this awareness doesn't make me proud of our Mass Mind's ways because, historically, our national classism manifests itself when our American economy is in a downswing. It's when we, *Norte-Americanos*, close ourselves off from our equals of the lower classes of the American Native, African Native and the Asian Pacific Native cultures. We do this, through our imaginary lines of the class distinctions of nation states, and we choose to call these national class delineations our, "borders." Indeed, we have made classist agreements.

We have categorized nations according to how we perceive their economic systems in comparison to our own. Throughout most of my life, we've said: "We are the *First* World, while theirs is the *Third* World." The, "*Second* World," was the label, which, we had assigned to nations that were suspicious of the, "New World Order," because of their differing economic systems. This is pure classism on the level of nation states, and this mind-set of classifying humanity is culturally inherited. I've learned that such a way of seeing ourselves, each other and the world, is the child of a mind-set which views only itself as the, "chosen people," of the planet. As a result, my sense is that, social classism is the result of a cultural superiority complex, which is—*itself*—at the root of our civilization-wide schizophrenic cultures, which all seem driven to compete among themselves. To me, our classism is a social paranoia.

Where, we marshal our forces to keep "Them" out, tells *what* we fear the most. Like the ancient tribal Levite patriarchs, our own classism requires a certain level of cultural *purity*. If the alien does not play by the rules of our own cultural mainstream then, we will view them all with disdain. We see them all as "unclean." This is in stark contrast to cultures which are nature-centered, wherein diversity is a true given and wherein, the most undesirable species of the planet is considered the sibling of us all! An examination of our history reveals, to me, that our pattern of derision of alien peoples is usually focused on those whose culture is not an Anglo-Euro ethno-centric culture. To me, America's class distinctions mirror the harsh reality that our mainstream body politic still tests positive. As difficult as it may be for all of us to admit; we are, collectively, terminally infected with the virus of *a perceived-supremacy* over other people.

This is reflected clearly by what we, collectively, do. We believe refugees from an area of economic chaos would be a drain on public welfare systems. We, Americans, conveniently forget that any economic chaos, whatever its cause, *results in eliminating all class distinctions*. We know that this is true, yet, we act as if we forget that all refugees –whether war is being waged on their homeland or not– are fleeing the aggressions of alien forces precisely because all present delineations of class will vanish with economic chaos. And, what's worse, a case can be made for the view that the economically powerful nations are, actually, the cause of economic chaos in the less developed nations because of how today's, now increasingly global, economic system works, and "job out-sourcing" is part of this.

The history of the European Union nations speaks loudly to this. Historically, for the privileged classes of Europe to survive, they ardently avoid the elimination of class distinctions among themselves by war. Today, we are no different here because America's economic mainstream is Euro-centric. Yet, our aggression isn't fixed in only the environment of two or more embattled nations. Culturally based economics are only used *as a tool* by all aggressive cultures. *Today's aggressing on the planet is waged by our cultural forces, not by our economics.* The *Meshica,* taught me that economics is merely a tool of cultural domination—that like religion, economics is an excuse for war—that, "multi-national corporations devour the diverse cultures."

In other words, culture dominates today mainly by the *use of* economics, but what it is that multi-national corporations dominate are, actually, earlier cultures. For example, in ancient lore, it is said that the reason the Hebrews were enslaved by the Egyptian Pharaoh

—in the *first* place—was because he used pure economics as a tool to dominate other societies. The scripture says that Pharaoh had stored seven years of a wheat surplus prior to the great famine that caused the legendary Joseph to receive his brothers into Egypt's economy. In effect, ancient Joseph was Pharaoh's C.E.O. of an ancient Egyptian equivalent of a multi-national corporation. In modern America, we point to the example of how our, "national interest," is tied to cultural worldviews that perceive that we, as proprietors of the planet, actually, own other living beings. This, in fact, is the usual reason given by our Presidents for going to war against any who would inhibit America's economy. We value our proprietary economy, as if the ownership of property –whether living or not– were an "inalienable right." We forget that, "the pursuit of *property*" is not a Constitutional guarantee, but rather, "the pursuit of *happiness*" is the, actual, guarantee.

Moreover, I learned in the experiences related in this book that, this Constitutional guarantee was a commonly held perspective of those cultures that already existed here, when our current economic system replaced their earlier nature-centered cultures. Indeed, it is property economics that drives our American consumption of all other cultures which we see as being "less than" ours. Historically, we aggress against societies which do not see reality in the same way that we do. It is as if we do not consider them worthy of co-existence with us. In our corporation-centric eyes, this is only the capitalism of our free market economy, and we account it to our practicality. But we are in denial, so we regularly go off to war.

We refuse to see that a mentality, which is represented by the politics of an old cowboy western movie, is –even today– centered in Manifest Destiny. We learn in school that Manifest Destiny was a 19th century phenomenon but, all around, today, we see that it is alive and well. As the world's superpower, we used international diplomacy with Madam Albright, the savvy Secretary of State in the Clinton Administration, wearing a cowboy hat as she traveled about forcing our worldview on the rest of the nation states. Why else did she use cowboy affect imagery? With all of her fine attributes, sadly, Madam Albright only mimicked male behavior. Then, our arrogance was rebuffed in 2001, when the U.N. dropped us as a part of its Human Rights Commission, and we were replaced with the Sudan! In 2003 President Bush, naturally, used cowboy hats as affect imagery in his own foreign visits. Sadly, these are our American agreements.

Conversely, it is still often noted in the world media how Jacqueline Kennedy's far softer approach won over a hard-minded Kruschev in the 1960's using a more feminine diplomacy. Likewise, I can see that my mother was one Don Miguel Ruiz might call a *Toltec*.

I never thought of her as a mystic, but in her quiet way, Mom was a deeply spiritual and centered woman. She wasn't motivated by force, or the threat of force. Mysticism was always Dad's *obvious* obsession but, to me, he seemed to be a little lost somewhere in a need to climb socio-economic ladders. Mom, on the other hand, quietly used her faith in the mystical principle of Agreement, to bless me in my times of serious dilemma. At first, I had thought that it was her Christian belief—her faith—but, today as I look over how I then experienced knowing her, I realize that Mom was a dream master! If I understand Ruiz's work, Mom was, actually, a Master of Intent…

****

It's 1967, and I have now been back from my mission in Peru in South America for over a year. I am a sophomore at Brigham Young University, while so many of my old high school friends who did not go on to any college are now being drafted into the United States Army. Although sensing some guilt because I wasn't enlisting, while some of my old friends are, I know enough about myself to fear that, if I do, I will not be able to retain my acquired personal sexual values in the military environment. I know in my heart that, if I do, I'll die in Vietnam, or I'll die to my faith community because of my inner, hidden need to be with another man. I know I still haven't reconciled this aspect of myself with the rules of my Mormon community. This fact was especially brought to my stark awareness the other day when I first saw Bobby Kennedy, when he had appeared on television. In that single moment, I saw that I'd never before seen a more beautiful face. That did it! I *can't* be drafted.

I've never shared my most inner turmoil with my mother. But, I know I need to find a way to access her faith on my behalf. After the fiasco in high school over the JFK campaign, I've learned to keep my politics to myself.

Our church leaders, whom we Mormons believe are God's holy prophets, actually, support the war in Vietnam. The Church's other involvement in the corporate oil, and coal industry, has also begun to speak louder to me than the rhetoric of their public talks on Temple Square in Salt Lake City, Utah.[xiv] I have learned to project feigned conservative Republican views on current issues because our prophet, after all, is Republican. The point is that, other than Mom, nobody else knows that I'm a conscientious objector to the Vietnam War—that, privately, I'm really determined to avoid the draft. All of Mom's brothers served honorably in the 2nd World War so, I am a little apprehensive of her response to my dilemma…

I visited Mom recently during a break, and in her room I said, "I don't want to get drafted. I know if I go to Vietnam, I won't come back alive!" Now, although we were Mormons, Mom still had her old rosary.

After some silence, she opened the box and picked up her rosary, and after she ran it through her fingers while she closed her eyes, she put it back in the small box. Finally, she answered my statement with, "then, *Mijo*, what we have to do is agree that you will not be in the military."

"I agree," I said quickly, "I won't go to war."

Then, she opened the old box again and got the rosary again, "No, *Mijo*, you won't go in the military. I agree to that." Silently then, she continued running the rosary through her fingers and added, "*Mijo*, if you really do get the letter drafting you into service, you call me right away, okay?"

"Okay," I said simply, and with that she put the rosary back into the little box. I knew at that moment that I would, somehow escape the draft. I had no idea how it would happen but, because of my experience with Mom, I know that there is something about her faith that will keep me from the horror, which *I know*, will greet me, if I do get drafted.

Weeks passed…

Today, I got the dreaded letter and without even opening it, I called Mom. "I got the letter from the government, Mom," I said into the telephone.

Her strong voice volume and the definite tone of her speech still resound in my soul, "when are you supposed to get inducted, *Mijo*?"

I struggled to open the envelope.

"Hello? *Mijo*, are you there?"

"Give me a minute. I still have to open the letter." After I got it open, I told her the day, the date and the appointed hour of my physical examination stated in the letter. I also read the sentence instructing me to meet a bus. "If I have to go into the Army, Mom, I don't know what kind of man –what kind of person– I'll become as a result!" The fear was not yet on the surface, but I was sure that she could hear my terror in my words.

But, her powerful resolve came through in her response, "*Mijo*, remember that we already made an agreement. I will be thinking of you that whole day. Now, tell me, what time do you have to report to the bus you mentioned?"

I answered her question and added, "I will go. I will get on that bus because I don't want to go to jail either."

"Are you saying, *Mijo*, that you will go into the military, after all?"

With that, my own will grew to match her resolve, "No, Mom. That will not happen because you and I have agreed that we do not will it." The words had no sooner left my lips than I felt the sweetness of a comforting peace fill up the whole of my person, as if entering through my head, and I knew everything would be okay!

Two weeks later, I was on that bus with fifty-one other men, students from BYU. As the bus took us all up to the military base in Ogden, Utah, for the physical examination for our induction, I looked out of the window at all the passing scenery with Mom's presence making itself known to me as I saw my face reflected on the bus window. Within two hours, I was standing in a large barrack building with hundreds of other guys. All of us had stripped down to our underwear. We stood at ease, military style with all our legs spread slightly. My only sensation was that of my bare nipples responding to the fans that were all blowing on our almost totally naked bodies. I felt a chill.

There were four men at the end of my line, to my far right. One was taking quick notes on some kind of an official document, another was obviously the medical doctor, and the other two were clearly there only to enforce the procedure. One of the two enforcers yelled out, "Drop your shorts." His voice was brutally harsh.

I began to pull my briefs down around my hips. All the time I was silently praying that I wouldn't get aroused with all the nudity...

The harsh voice burst out, "I said, 'Drop your shorts' and turn your punk face to your left. When the doctor comes to you, cough three times..." His yelling was the most brutal way anyone had ever spoken to me. Even Dad had never before spoken in that crass and ugly manner to me.

Following his loud instructions, I pulled the only covering I had down to my ankles—utterly aware of my stark nakedness.

Some of the others weren't fast enough I guess, because the two men who were yelling at us began, "Do I have to pull them off you?"

I felt unbearably humiliated, exposed in that gross fashion was horrifying to me because I still had an overwhelming fear that I would be sexually aroused. Wearing only briefs, and then to be verbally harassed into pulling them down to my ankles by a man in uniform, somehow, felt deviant to me. I wondered could I control, myself?

With that fearful thought I noticed a strange sound coming from deep within my chest. This stuffed, tight sensation, I thought to myself, must be chest congestion. It felt familiar, but I hadn't had asthma since my twelfth birthday. The wheezing got very loud, the pressure I felt in my chest became worse and I wondered what would happen. After what felt like a full half-hour but, was probably only minutes, the sound of my difficult breathing was all around me. My wheezing was completely unexpected, and my skin was suddenly all cold, and clammy.

The doctor, who was now only about six men away from me, looked up at me. He said to the man making his notations, "Four-F that man."

The one making the record said to me, "all right young man; pull your shorts up, fall out now, and go get dressed." Then, added, "Go on!"

As I pulled my briefs up over my cold knees, I knew Mom was thinking of me at that moment. I knew in my soul, that our agreement had changed reality because the wheezing then, stopped the moment we all boarded the buses to take us back to Provo, Utah, where we all lived.

****

The fact that I have not had a bout with asthma since that day, informed me for the first time that, Agreement is a powerful force. I did not, however, know how powerful. I have since come to know that, indeed, it was the agreement made between my mother and me that had impacted the chaotic nature of the Universe. In my soul's core, I then, understood that it was not mere prayer or Mom's simple belief. Later, a spirit-written message confirmed to me that, group prayer only manifests any prayer's inner, "active ingredient," which is *agreement among two or more who love each other*. That was the first of many other experiences in my life, when I've experienced the experience of re-creating my own world, by making uniquely *strong* agreements with others of like mind—with two or more *who have Love between them*. Another example comes to mind:

****

The man who'd helped me do the final formatting of my first book was a deeply spiritual influence in my changing world. I call him Don in this book. When we had first met, it was one of those "aha" moments at the first touch of our hands. Mormons are the most hand-shaking people that I've ever known, and by that electrifying sensation, I knew that this man would, somehow, become highly significant to my future life's journey...

When we finished the final edit work on the book, we had a finished product, but we had no real knowledge about how to get it published. I knew the project was groundbreaking, since I was the only ordained Mormon bishop –or Temple sealer of marriages for that matter– to have written such a biography. So, having assigned a portentous meaning to telling the story of my coming out, I again asked Mom to help. But, this was not all. Mom didn't know what I had, actually, written so; I decided to include Don and Jon, another close friend, to join in the agreement. I'd reasoned; since both of them are not only aware of the contents of the book but, both also know that my intent is a healing purpose, that would ensure a cosmic connection for purposes of a truly creative agreement...

We had just finished packing Don's U-Haul truck, "Well, that's it, you guys," he said. Then, pulling the rear cargo door down, he added, "I'm ready to roll out of here. Thanks for your help."

Jon was the first to ask, "When do you drive off?"

"Oh," Don said, "I think that, say, about nine in the morning I'll be crossing the Bay Bridge tomorrow, on my way out of the City."

"So," I said, "the moment of truth has, finally, come. I have something to ask both of you to do for me."

Don answered, "sounds ominous, Tony," locking the pad lock on the cargo door.

I was the first to get down on the concrete driveway.

"Remember the conversation, which we all had about how agreement is the core principle of creation?"

Relaxing, all of us now on the concrete behind the truck, both of them nodded in agreement.

"Well," I continued, "how about us making an agreement right here, that—by the time that you leave California, Don—I will have all the necessary resources to publish the book *myself*?"

Don just stared at me for the longest time before he finally answered, "You really are serious." Then, looking at Jon, he added, "you know he isn't joking, don't you?"

Jon responded, "Tony and I have had a long dialogue on this principle for several years now." With that, Jon turned to me and added, "I agree that you will have the necessary resources to publish the book," and then, he turned to Don saying, "by the time you leave California."

"Hey, hey!" Don said with his intoxicating smile, "Oh, I agree! Of course, I agree!"

With that, as we all sat there in the darkened driveway with my arms crossed so that my hands could be in that three-way handshake, I knew something wonderful was about to happen. More than anything else from that moment, I can still remember the glow in both of those two faces in front of me, as we all laughed in joy about what we were so absolutely sure was about to happen.

Later that night, alone, I called my mother and told her about our agreement, "...so, Mom, will you..."

Before I could tell her any of the details about our prior agreement, she interrupted, "*Hay Mijo*! Of course, now, tell me *Mijo* what is the exact agreement you made."

"That I will have the necessary resources to publish the book by the time my friend, Don leaves the state."

"When will that be, *Mijo*?"

"Well, he should be on the Bay Bridge tomorrow morning at nine."

"Okay, *Mijo*," she said softly, "I'll be thinking of you all the time now, but especially, tomorrow at nine in the morning."

At nine a.m. the following day, I found myself standing in the lobby of the building Jon and I were living in, and Jon was looking at his watch.

I looked at Jon, "so, what time is it?"

"It's time, Tony."

Nervously, I looked up at the large clock in the lobby...

At that precise moment, the building manager opened the door to his apartment, and he slowly came out into the hallway, "Oh, Tony," he said scratching his matted hair, "you're just the person I need to see."

"What's up?" I said, walking toward his door.

Jon followed with me.

With his eyes squinting hard from the morning light, he went on, "Tony, I don't know what it is that you're writing, but it must be pretty important."

"I think so," I said calmly, "why do you say that?"

"You're not going to believe this..."

Jon's smile had been growing, "Oh, go ahead," he said.

I felt my anticipation rise up from the core of my torso and looked right into his eyes.

"Well, you know, it's really the strangest thing, but Tony, all I can afford is..."

My world began to swirl around me. I tried to talk, but no words came out of me at first. Finally, all I could get out was, "why?"

The manager went on explaining, "I just had...a...uh...a dream. In the dream, Jesus came, and told me to give you the money you needed to publish your book..."

Jon's mouth was wide open. After a moment, Jon added, "Tony, that's exactly the amount you said you needed, isn't it?"

I hadn't heard the amount that the manager had said. My boundless joy had clouded my environment, somehow. But, what I knew clearly, was that we'd re-created our shared reality by a simple agreement. The absolute irony of the experience was overwhelming, and I began to laugh out loud.

Jon wouldn't stop patting my back.

Then, it hit me. "But," I said to the manager, "I don't know how I can ever pay back that amount of money. You know I don't have..."

"Don't think of it that way," the manager said, "Jesus told me to give it to you. It's not mine anymore."

****

Most people to whom I've related the above story miss its point. They don't seem to get that –on any level– *the human spiritual journey is always about spirit stuff, and spirit stuff has absolutely nothing to do with preserving established institutional forms.* In our religious forms, we mix apples with oranges—so to speak—we inter-mix the Eternity within us all, with mere institutional forms, or what is only external to us. The obstacle to civilization's healing is still lodged in how we've been programmed to respond to institutionalized stuff. The point is: My reality was re-created—not by prayer but—by the *operating principle* of group prayer: "Whatsoever any two or three of you agree, who are gathered together in my name." So, what does "in my name" mean? Well, it is written that, "God is love" so, to "*agree...together in*" Love is the story's meaning.

But, there is more: In an insightful discussion with a chemist friend, I was powerfully reminded that in prescription medicines, many ingredients go into whatever pill or tablet a physician might prescribe to a patient, yet, he also said, "*each medicine has its own active ingredient*"—or, its core ingredient— "without which, healing would not take place." Similarly, if two or three are, "gathered together," in, "the name of," the One who is credited with these words then, that is to say that, *they agree in Love* because it's written that, "God is Love." So, irrespective of the religion, the one essential ingredient is to *agree in love*. So, the religious institution one is, or is not a member of, is unimportant.

We use religious institutions as vehicles of personal spiritual development. Yet, we do not easily see that all the institutionalized religions of today's world are each –in truth– merely *institutionalizing* the human experience of the universal supernatural experience. We deny that our institutionalizing of the supernatural, in effect, is a psychic effort to warp our perceptions. We blindly trust our religious institutions to, first and foremost, be about our spiritual evolution. That is their claimed mission but, that is not what they commonly do. *All institutions are each, actually, about the institution's preservation.* They only preserve past customs, public ritual and hierarchies. To "institutionalize" means to preserve *things*—preserving the words used—the form, as it may have occurred in some prior event. There is a time-encased element inherent to all mythology and liturgy. The same truth applies to meditation as well: Its form is unimportant. Seen in this light, all institutionalized form is evil, *when it causes us to avoid our own living, human, spiritual evolution* because it removes individual *living* will from us. Let us recall that, the word "evil" is "live"—when it is spelled *backwards*. Evil, therefore, is about non-life. Institutions are not alive!

But, human beings are *alive*! In the end, all the evils from which all humanity suffers, are not eternal but –like all myth or ritual– all evil is confined to the limits of time. Thus, evil diminishes—and its intensity decreases—in the same proportion as humanity expands its life, both in space and time. The end of all evil will be its ultimate disappearance by evil being reduced to what our physicists call the "infinitely little." My sense is that it will happen in the same way as would be the case if a pound of salt were thrown into a bucketful of water: It would strongly salt it, while if it were thrown into a much larger container, it would only very slightly salt it. In a pond, the taste of salt would probably not be noticeable, and absolutely nothing would remain of its effect if it were thrown into a large, rushing river. I affirm that this is correct. I affirm that all of humanity's evils will disappear in the infinity of space, and in the Eternity of time. I am totally convinced that this is our ultimate, collective, destiny—as *humans*—and, therefore, as the planet, which I affirm we all are.

For example: I am confident that in years to come, it will be as uncommon for any of us to criticize a spiritual disability as it is today to criticize a physical one. Even today, in our presently diseased social condition, well brought up children would not laugh at a blind person, or at a lame one, nor would they make fun of the deaf either. Yet, does it ever occur to any of us that, whatever the misbehavior, crime or vice of a fellow citizen may be, if it awakens in us any other feeling than, our genuine, and empathic compassion then, it is precisely because we are not like "well-brought-up children" on the plane of spirit? At the very least, the obvious answers inform us that we have not yet matured. Happily, however, we will not remain stunted in our spiritual immaturity. Rabbi Gewurz has taught:

"The holy Qabalah teaches that every thought and emotion is represented structurally in invisible substance, the highest and purist aspirations and emotions consist atomically of bisexual human beings dualized in their mental nature and patterned after the shape of primal man."

I ask: Can *this* be what is manifesting in the, now growing, incidence of the inter-sexed phenomena, mentioned earlier? Well, regarding the inter-sexed who are much like my old friend Mary Jane —of whom I wrote in an earlier chapter—Rabbi Gewurz insightfully wrote a powerful truth:

"Time and space are the remedies which can cure evils afflicting mankind...Adam (the group soul)...had to be divided in space, in order to be healed and for the sake of his reduction and division *ad infinitum* by means of time.

"Until man understands this bi-une arrangement of his internal make-up, and, understanding it, strives to awaken and deepen the Divine Consciousness within himself...to become continually and increasingly aware of his duality, there is little chance of transcending the level of ordinary humanity."[xv]

This idea flies in the face of fundamentalist prejudice against the inter-sexed, or others like Mary Jane mentioned in an earlier chapter, or trans-gendered persons. It flies in the face of institutional decrees against the legalization of loving unions of same-sex couples also. So, what are we going to do about our present sick condition? My call is to choose a healthier way of inter-relating, and I invite you to come into agreement with what I've related in this book. Agree with us, who work for the day when our civilization will become transmuted into the promised new age of the harmonic and chordant ways of our inter-relating with our others—even if their genitalia *is*; "ambiguous genitalia."

The alternative to the above vision of Rabbi Gewurz is the sure demise of our, still recklessly adolescent, 21st century society. Mainstream American culture must come of age, as a body politic, or the disease of suicide –so prevalent among our teenage population– will spread, and become the contagion that finally takes the life of our beloved America. We all desperately need to become more adult in our way of approaching those: Who also breathe the same air as the rest of us; who also eat at the same restaurant tables as the rest of us; who also sit on the same public rest room toilets as the rest of us, and who also get buried in the same cemeteries as the rest of us. We need to grow up, and come of age now, in how we envision. If we don't then, truly, all will be for naught.

If the amazing way that I experience the experience of living has taught me anything, it is that the transmutation of our world is already engaged! It's now fast becoming common knowledge that, as the ancient Joel is recorded as having prophesied about our time, more and more of us "dream dreams" and "see visions." My sense is that this is why media reports of paranormal experiences seem to be on the increase today...

****

I'd heard of such things happening, but nothing quite like it had happened to me. This kind of experience had had no expression in my life until that night, when I got up from bed to use the bathroom. I know I was awake when it happened. The shock of the cold water that initially came out of the washbowl tap on my hands would have awakened me if I'd still been asleep. My *Meshica* friends in Mexico had told me that this would happen when I was ready for it but, it had never happened. Once, the *Meshica* dancers in Los Angeles had also mentioned this kind of phenomenon but, it had never happened to any of them, not even to sixty-year-old *La India,* who's the elder/mother of their little dancing band...

I enjoy sleeping with my bedroom window open all the way. It has been important for me to position my bed near a window facing east so that the light of the dawning sun awakens me *naturally*, since the days I spent with the *Meshica* Indians in Mexico. So, as I pulled the covers back further in order to get back into the bed, I leaned over the head of the bed, and standing between the bed and the window, a light caught my attention out of the right periphery of my sight. My neighbor across the street and I had struck up a good conversation the day before about his artistic cactus and rock garden, and I thought that –maybe– he was just out early in his yard with a flashlight. What's happening? I wondered to myself, maybe the neighbor can't sleep. But, what if it's a prowler?

So, I sat up on the bed, and I tried to focus on a blue glow coming from behind a large tree in my neighbor's yard across the street. As I watched, the glow seemed to move behind the tree. I thought of how the city had taken out another tree that had been next to it, just days before. I suddenly recalled seeing an elderly woman look all around before she had taken one of the pieces of wood that still lay on the earth near the place where there had been a large tree before. I remembered how she seemed to be hiding the fact that she'd taken the wood because of how she had put it under her coat before scurrying quickly back across the street, and into our gated apartment complex. Now, the glow seemed to move.

With that recent memory of the woman who wanted to keep a piece of that big old tree for herself, my persistent observation was rewarded. The glow from behind the tree suddenly got brighter than before. The brightness increased until –at first– a hand and an arm reached out from behind the tree. But, the astonishing thing is that I could see the fingers, the hand and even the forearm well enough to see that they were made of light! They were the perfect form of a human appendage but, as I'd experienced before on other occasions, it was made of white-blue light.

I was wide-awake now, for sure. So, sitting straight up now, and leaning toward the open window, I saw the clear form of a little youthful woman come very slowly out from behind that tree. She was about four and one-half feet tall, with long, flowing, platinum hair –hair that was *luminous*– wearing, a bright, flowing *translucent* dress down to her mid calves that was either very sheer, or it was also made of light. It had full, shiny, flowing ruffles over the shoulders, and at her hemline. In a frail way, she was uniquely beautiful; and she seemed to, literally, be *prancing*—artistically *prancing*—in a circle around that remaining large tree across the street. It was as if the beautiful youthful lady was in her own world.

The features of her face were so delicate, she reminded me of an Audry Hepburn film that I'd seen years earlier. She didn't appear to be interested in anything around her because, although she was just dancing gracefully around the big tree, she didn't look at anything in particular. Her face seemed pleasant, happy and totally into whatever it was that she was actually doing. Then, after she had finished her graceful prancing, she disappeared back into the other side of the tree, as suddenly as she had appeared. All I could see was that same glow of white-blue light that I had seen at first. And, there was no sound throughout the entire experience.

What did it all mean? I wondered to myself, why did that little woman of light make herself seen by me? Did she know that I had seen her? Had anyone else seen her? I looked up and down the street below. There was no other person anywhere around. Then I got up, and I went into the living room to see a clock. It was three o'clock in the morning.

Later, I lay in bed and recalled another presence. About three years earlier, I'd been enjoying a conversation with a good friend on my patio in a former apartment due east of where I now reside. He'd been rather open with me about his own belief in the reality of the spirit world around us all. As we had talked about such things calmly, I had been suddenly overtaken by a very strong sense of a presence. "Gustavo," I had said, "would you run into my bedroom and get my camera?" When he'd gotten back to me with my camera, I had said, "Okay, here. Take a snap shot of me, sitting over there, would you? And, be sure to get the plants I have in front of me in the picture."

"Okay," he had answered, aiming the camera. "What's this for?"

"Oh, I have a feeling that there's a plant spirit right about there, where that large plant is," I had said, pointing to the small, seemingly empty space directly between me and the plant I'd pointed to. "She's a healing spirit, Gus."

When I'd developed the photographs, I showed the snap shot to a photographer friend first. When he saw the deeply red figure resembling a woman covered in a long, Afgani *birka-like* style of dress, between me and the plant, he asked me; "what's that?"

"Oh, that's the spirit of that plant," I responded as calmly as I could, and slowly walked out of the photo shop in order to avoid further discussion. I didn't know how he'd take such a comment.

When Gustavo came over I'd asked, "Hey, Gus, remember this?"

Taking the photograph, "Wow," he said simply, "there really was a spirit there, Tony! But, why is it red? Don't spirits appear to us as other then just red? I mean, I thought that, spirits appear to us in a white color."

"Remember, Gus, this is a plant spirit. She's a plant's energy in this photo, and the energy of vegetation is seen by us as red in color."

****

There is a tradition among my Indian friends, about the way the spirit of a tree or of a plant manifests to us. Trees are a vortex for spirit beings. This is why some of us enjoy tree hugging. When one is on a vision quest, and the vision is granted of the spirit of a great tree, that spirit will often manifest as an innocent female spirit. In some traditions, She is not only seen as the spirit of that tree but, a personification of the Earth, *Herself.* It is said that, when one actually sees such a being, it is a sign that the spirits are comfortable with the seeker—the seeker soul has attained a sought-after spiritual comfort zone. Since the beautiful young woman of light of my neighbor's tree appeared to be made of a white-bluish light, my training tells me that, She was not a "plant spirit." She may even have been what Christian tradition terms a departed spirit!

Whatever She was, I knew that –if nothing else– the union of the mythological heaven and earth had again been confirmed to *my personal* awareness. I say, "again," because this is only one example of many other such experiences that I've had. The legendary promise has been fulfilled for me! As on other occasions, this time, I'd *seen* the beautiful Lady! Even if She were a creation of my sub-conscious, to my vision, She was from a world of light—as were all the rest, also!

Many of our traditions teach us that, the day will come when those beings from the world of light will freely engage us. In the Christian canon it is written that, the new heaven will bring a new earth which, will be "as a sea of glass." But, we are already in "a sea of glass!" Is it clear to you, the reader, that Paradise is, actually, now all around us? Can you, the reader, envision in such a way as to know that our planet's atmosphere is merely a less dense –a less opaque– environment than is, the vast sea that lies beyond the coast? I am saying that, whatever the context of the metaphor on what is known as the "end time," in today's world, the metaphor works.

Metaphor is the language of all prophecy. In other words, if the new earth does become "as a sea of glass" to us then, that is not to also say that its inhabitants will only dwell on its surface! Consider those perspectives other than the ones from your personal place of reckoning. As glass has the usual characteristic of allowing sunlight to, not only pass through it, can you see that, the only difference between us now and this way to see, is exactly that –*how we envision*? Are you ready to be able to now know –from your own experience in the experience– that we are already *immersed* in "a sea of glass?" Are you ready to see that *Paradise is, actually, already all around us,* and that *you are not traveling in a hell,* after all? Can you *imagine* it? Being aware of our present condition is a matter of our ability to discern it, and we do discern it because we are open to see it. Can you see that, transcending is, actually, *changing how we see*?

My first undergraduate academic degree was in the art and science of manipulating mass perceptions through television and radio broadcasting at Brigham Young University. From that early and impacting beginning, I've continued to study the absolute power of television, as a medium for the manipulation of the Mass Mind of humanity. This is probably why this book has focused on the human process of envisaging. All television and commercial films are one global way to cause human beings to learn new ways of seeing. Yet, it is today abundantly clear to me that; all of these media of electronic communication—along with the Internet—are tools for manipulating the Mass Mind that *must* be judiciously used.

For example: America's and Britain's 2003-2004 War against Saddam Hussein's Iraq was the first time that, real time—live—war was seen by masses of human beings as it took place. Until that war, taped and filmed news reports of military combat took days, weeks and, often, even months to be viewed by the masses. This kind of immediate, raw, global mass communication of modern, shocking war imagery had not been experienced by humanity before the 2003 American and British military leaders had "embedded" mass media reporters with their, respective, troops. Since 2003, the chronicling of war has become *"reality"* war reporting.

I have focused on the imagery created in our Mass Mind by the hypnotic, and the repetitive telling of, often violent, sacred stories in our temples, synagogues, churches and mosques during our week's holiest hours. Yet, that does not compare with global humanity being subject to a mass mental manipulation by today's world's mightiest military war chroniclers. Thus, it is imperative to be judicious about how these ways of seeing are controlled. Some say; "it is good that we all see what is truly happening *as it happens*." Yet, my caution is: to be aware that it is corporate programmers, who determine whether a given audience is able to access those images. Such power over all others in the hands of a few can have the effect of us perceiving events out of context. Remember; to imagine is to put an *image-in* our mind.

So, come, travel with us—we, who desire to remain on this path—for, we have left the old way of illusions. Let's imagine peace! In this way, you choose to be in a paradise, by being the kind of person that belongs in a paradise, to be in the kind of society that, Dr. Joel S. Federman calls, "Topia;"[xxvi] a place where "joy, hope, love and peace" abound. A paradise would be a place where its inhabitants sing out the joyously chordant, harmonious ways of equity in diversity. Can you truly envision yourself as being the kind of person whose ways of envisioning also sing out the song of happiness for those who *don't* have the same beliefs, customs, traditions and/or *external* moralities of your own second womb? Attaining a personal vibrational level of a harmonic human energy, allows each of us to sing out the sweet songs of concord because our inter-personal concordant behaviors then, truly do manifest Love. *This*, way makes Love! *This* way is all about making Love *increase*.

Love's *Universal* pattern exists in many traditions, and that *Way*—that Truth—is revealed in the Christian Gospels as Jesus, the Christ. The reason it is written there that, it is; "the only name given under heaven whereby man may be saved," is because, in the Greek, the term that translates into the English word "...*name*..." means; "*office* or *function*." The message is: Christ's *behavior,* or *how* it is that sacred stories report He *functioned,* as re-told in those Gospels, is how *he* lived. *His* is The *Way* to be—or, the "*name*"—the "*function*" we must do, in order to become open souls; i.e.: His vibrational way.

Now, whether manifested to a particular society as a Krishna, a Buddha, or Christ, the *only* Way is Love, and His personal energy can, literally, be felt by us, human beings. It is an *inner way of being.* It is felt by any as a human emotion that I herein call Love but—more importantly—His energy is manifest to us in our world only by *our behavior also,* as we inter-relate with our environment, including our fellow human beings. This is why His peace among us humans is a vibrational frequency—Love is the true '*Keys*' of the Kingdom! Keys of Priesthood are many yet, if they are conceptualized in metaphor as that of One cord of musical keys then, harmony may be created.

The archetype of creation is shown *in the placement of* the first verse of a Gospel;[xvii] "In the beginning..." it declares "...was the word" (KJV). A *word* will evoke a mental affect image to our mind. The point is; *thought* precedes all behavior. So, at the risk of being accused of "wresting" the scripture, I'd paraphrase that verse: "*In the beginning was the [Thought], and the [Thought[was with God, and the [Thought] was God. The same was in the beginning with God.*" In other words, we personally decide whether our collective future behavior is centered in only the brute force of the male principle. We do it by our thoughts, which are vibrational frequencies *preceding* our behavior. If we want our behavior to only be based in a balance of both the male and the female principles then, all of our *affect images* —especially sacred, sacramental rituals of a faith community—will include all those seen as *non*-men even though they are anatomically, male, and also all those who behave as men, while being anatomical female. Otherwise, our inner frequencies will be out of balance.

Irrespective of whether sacred stories come from the Torah; the Koran; the Christian Bible; the Book of Mormon, Doctrine and Covenants or even the Utah based Pearl of Great Price; the sacred stories of our mainstream are all stories about the inter-relating of only a part of us! It is, after all, a fact that all of these texts tell the tales of men, with only a minute mention of all the women in their worlds. Such a context is far too arcane for today's more enlightened and, now increasingly, egalitarian and quickly evolving social constructs. So, learn to envision beyond the warped moralities of old men who have, consistently, proven to secretly be child molester, male hierarchies. This difference; in how we balance these two principles—at least, in our hearts—compared to our culture's spiritual ancestors, is what will change the world because this is a New Age in which we all now live. In this age, we have the benefit of modern science, which informs us on the chromosomal, biological roots of human sexuality. Indeed, it is the New Age of Becoming Open Souls!

Our openness *does* manifest the female principle in our inter-relating behavior, and our openness impacts how we all inter-relate. In the feminine way, we are open to the vast volumes of vision and unknown wisdom that has always existed in cultural worlds, outside of our own. In openness, we are open to take into us, not only our own wisdom but, also the wisdom of other open souls. We are open to be impregnated by another's clearer vision, rather than, still remain in civilization's unhealthy and inbred state. We are open to this, by an understanding of our sacred stories—not, as history nor, literally but, instead—as mythic metaphor that is meant to inspire *universal*, inner references within the seeker soul.

So, consider these two affect images: The Roman Catholic *Virgen de Guadeloupe* is set on top of the male symbol of two bull's horns and Mormon Temple baptismal fonts sit on top of the male symbol of twelve horned oxen. In spite of the male-centric policies of these two religious institutions, here, their two *affect images* place the female principle on top of the male principle. Both are necessary, but the attributes which we attribute to femaleness must be seen by us as the better attributes by which to live.

Thus, responding to modern terrorism against us only with more of the same—only by us making *war* on terrorists—only uses those attributes we assign to the male principle. What I have tried to say in this book is that; what is needed today is for us to respond to darkness with light, not with more of the same. On the last page of the final chapter of my first book, I wrote; "*Evil is the absence of light. Light is the only healing response to evil: the remedy for absence is presence…*" What is needed now is to add more of what we attribute as female traits to our responses to terror. War is not the answer!

It will happen by our use of words. Recall that, words carry specific energy vibrations. For example, although the first name of our Department of Defense was, originally, the War Department, this bureaucracy is still used, only for waging war. Then, in 2003 Ohio Representative Dennis Kucinich, in his campaign for the Presidency of the United States, was the first to promote establishing a new "Department of Peace" in the federal bureaucracies. Hopefully, we are realizing that, *a critical balance is needed in our use of words* in our elimination of 21st century terror. Truly, we must respond to the *absence of peace* with the *presence that is absent* in the competitive acts of all who—because of the illusions of separateness—feel that they are still under siege by others. Throughout this book, I have suggested a key that is a word-based solution because *all words carry a vibrational energy*: We must use this awareness by use of *universal* references of our divergent sacred stories, and religious affect images. Would it not be more effective for America to wage the war against terrorism with the use of the mass media, rather than, with weapons of mass destruction? Let us change the world with affect imagery!

So I invite you, the reader, to join us; we, who try to travel by understanding the *universal* reference of myth, rather than, only its historicity. Join us: we who focus institutional policy on the way we go, rather than, only on our cultural rear view mirrors. Join us: we, who use past interpretations only as a field or, as *a context of universal references*. This is an invitation to hold to the rod that is grounded in *nature*; for, it is in the *natural* world, where we all journey. This path will lead all of us away from *external* ways of judgment and harsh barbarity, and will lead all toward "a new heaven" and "a new earth" of "joy, hope, love and peace!" This is *our* agreement.

Do you see why I wrote earlier that even the Christian book of Revelation doesn't say that "a new heaven…" would necessarily come about because of any *deity*? Do you see that it is *we*, who can choose to bring a paradisiacal world of light into existence, *now*, in *our* dimension, by being the kind of beings that dwell in such a world? So come, walk the path that we walk. Come out of the mythological cave, for the sun is shining at the opening of the cave in which we now find ourselves!   ▣

NOTES TO CHAPTER ELEVEN

[i] Finger-Prints of The Gods, *The Evidence of Earth's Lost Civilization* by Graham Hancock (Crown Trade Paperbacks, New York, NY., 1995). See also, American Holocaust, *The Conquest of The New World* by David E. Stannard (Oxford University Press, New York, NY., 1992).

[ii] Synchronicity, *The Bridge Between Matter and Mind,* by F. David Peat (Batam Books, New York, NY., 1987) page 1.

[iii] Confronting War, *An Examination of Humanity's Most Pressing Problem,* by Ronald J. Glossop (McFarland and Company, Inc. Publishers, North Carolina, 1987) Part II "Causes of War," Chapter V. Group Competition and Group Identification. I agree with what Glossop offers on page 58 as a solution to this problem because the cultural reality is: America celebrates competition:

"...Catholics and Protestants may experience less tension if they perceive themselves as Christians struggling against Moslems. In turn Christians and Moslems may have less conflict with each other if they view themselves as believers in God struggling against atheistic Communists. Perhaps believers and Communists could in turn see themselves as humans struggling together for survival against the forces of nature, including the psychological forces within themselves, which threaten their continued existence."

I simply add: In the 21st century, all humanity would better benefit from seeing ourselves as part of the forces of nature because nature is a world of mutuality.

[iv] NOVA, PBS Special, May 11, 2004.

[v] Book of Mormon, II Nephi, Chapter 30: verse 6.

[vi] Ibid, 1981 edition of the Book of Mormon, II Nephi, Chapter 30:6.

[vii] Sunstone Magazine, "Syncretism" 1988, by Dr. David Knowelton.

[viii] Op.Cit., I Nephi, Chapter 8: verses 19-28.

[ix] Ibid., Mormon, Chapter 8: verse 17.

[x] The Four Agreements, Don Miguel Ruiz (1997) pages 98-103.

[xi] The Sanctity of Dissent by Paul James Toscano (Signature Books, Salt Lake City, UT. 1994).

[xii] Op.Cit., Alma chapters 48-62 and Helaman chapter 15. This is the story of how this legendary Nephite General raised the "Standard of Liberty," which amounts to a blood oath taken by his devoted soldiers who covenanted saying: "We covenant with our God, that we shall be destroyed...if we shall fall into transgression; yea, he may cast us at the feet of our enemies..." while the pacifists "buried their weapons."

[xiii] Book of Mormon, Alma Chapter 24: verses 17-26. See also the entire chapter.

[xiv] The Mormon Corporate Empire, by John Heinerman and Anson Shupe (Beacon Press, Boston, MA., 1985). Specifically, Chapter 3, "LDS Incorporated" lists the oil investments of Zion's Securities Corporation,

an investment division of The Corporation of The President, the sole proprietor entity that is The Church of Jesus Christ of Latter-day Saints known as the Mormon Church. Some listed were the American oil companies at risk in the Saudi Arabian Peninsula, during the 1990s Gulf War, as in this millennium's Iraqi-American conflict.

[xv] The Hidden Treasures of The Ancient Qabalah, by Elias Gewurz (Yogi Publication Society, San Francisco, CA., 1918) pages 38 & 78.

[xvi] Visit Joel Federman's Internet Web-site, at: www.topia.org

[xvii] John 1:1. Elsewhere I have affirmed that reading the canon as metaphor is the key because from the beginning, inspired scripture has used the language of metaphor as exemplified by the *placement* of this verse by an ancient scribe at the start of the sacred story of the biblical Christ.

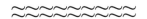

"My own 1990s research and our family's oral histories, kept from generation to generation, inform me on *why* the promised future millennial epoch has not yet come to be. There, waiting for the event to begin in the holy Temple, I was suddenly struck with the idea that, it is no different for my collective of opening souls -for the Community of Christ- than it is for any other institution, including the City of Los Angeles. Peace will not come for institutions that fail to listen to those whom they exclude. I thought silently: It is as if All Eternity, or some unseen Force knew that I had chosen as I did at every juncture of my path...."

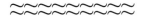

IN THE TEMPLE IN 2002
AT INDEPENDENCE, MO

I waited for the plenary session to begin in the Temple at the 2002 Peace Colloquy. I thought to myself, now, *this* building truly is a temple! Its architectural symbolism speaks to me: While, the *external* form of the structure is a single spiral—an ancient symbol of the Male Principle—the *inner* form or the Temple sanctuary's high ceiling, has the appearance of a spiraled opening that, does not appear to have an end—an affect image of the open, the receptive Female Principle. My mind was mesmerized, staring up. Looking up into the spiraled ceiling, I whispered to myself, it's as if…as if we *are* in…in…like we're in the cosmic *Womb of Eternity*!

Then, it hit me: *The ceiling* …it's…it's the same symbol as my old T-shirt, the one that I felt that I *had* to buy for myself! It's the same as that old pictograph on that T-shirt which, to me, seems to be saying to, "follow the sun." Then, I thought, what amazing thing will happen now?

Sitting there, I thought of the fact that I was on a sacred spot of early Mormonism. The venue was the Temple of Community of Christ, built on the Temple Lot that had been designated in the 19th century by the then, new church's founder, Joseph Smith, Junior. So, I pondered on the journey that had brought me to Mormonism's most holy historical place; Joseph Smith Junior's "City of Zion," his *New Jerusalem*:

I thought of my return to California in 1994… I knew that I had to research in libraries, archives and other depositories of history within Los Angeles. I didn't know why but, I knew it would be research about my paternal ancestors, Los Feliz of the 18th and 19th century *Californio* days—prior to the conquest of California by the 19th century American Army of the West. So, I had done this research when I had settled in a senior citizens apartment complex east of Los Angeles, where I began to do the final work on this book's manuscript prior to its final editing.

Then, 1999 had been when all my earlier visions of the future were played out in the world. The news media then, finally, reported what I had known for years—and, spoken out about every time I had been at events involving Utah Mormons—yet, nobody else had seemed to listen to my warnings. So, that second book had interrupted the publication of my major work in progress at the time: *the present* work, Becoming Open Souls.

I thought of what happened in 1989 before that second book was published: I had voiced my warning in my testimony before the City of San Francisco's 1989 Human Rights Commission as part of proceedings investigating the then proposed "domestic partnership" city ordinance. Then, later, there was the 1993 March On Washington: Roughly five hundred thousand of us had crowded on the Capital Mall! I thought of how I'd given out new copies of my first book and that 1989 written testimony to members of the Congress of the United States with very little positive response from the L.D.S. elected representatives. On a 1994 promotional tour through central Utah, this same written testimony was subsequently presented at the First Unitarian Church in Salt Lake City, Utah under the title, "The Issue Is Gender Equity." But again, only a few had heeded, or even understood my dire warning, and then, the Affirmation Gay and Lesbian Mormons executive leadership had also ignored all of my recommendations.

My thoughts continued in The Temple as we waited—by 1996 America had begun to, literally, tear down our recently won state civil domestic partnership laws with their behind-the-scenes political and financial backing of my former colleagues at the LDS Church Offices in Salt Lake City, Utah. Incensed by the blatant efforts of my former mentors in the hierarchy of The Church of Jesus Christ of Latter-day Saints in trying to block the progress of pluralism in civic law to include same-sex families in the State of Hawaii, I'd decided to publish my testimony in book form. Since, I'd arranged to self-publish Becoming Open Souls, my financial backer for this book then, agreed to help me publish it first, because I had felt such an overwhelming and ominous urgency about the ugly direction that, America's late 1990s political processes were taking.

The new book was titled The Issue Is Pluralism. It responded to the February 13, 1994 official letter from the Utah based Mormon First Presidency, calling on all Mormon Americans to fight against the inclusion of my *natural* community in civil law in my own State of California in 2000. Mormons in several other states also responded.

As if in a vision, *the future was on fire* to me because it now seemed the American electorate had re-birthed the climate of pre-Hitler Germany! As with Hitler's Gestapo, in the 1990s America began with us, Gays...

So, I had added a section to my old written testimony, and sub-titled it "A Warning And A Promise." The 2000 Election Day was fast approaching in California and in Nevada—where key ballot initiatives were pending. That little seventy-page book had come out in 2000, and its first printing sold out before the summer of 2001. Published before September 11, 2001, and prior to the 2003-2004 War with Iraq—I had warned what I inwardly saw was about to befall America. In spite of a booming economy, before the "stolen" November 2000 Election that had put the Religious Right back into office, I could envision what the future—like a javelin—would throw back to us. If we did not stop what amounted to a legitimized civic tyranny of all of us who are, actually, American sexual *minorities*, I had said a "horror" would come to us. In that small and hurriedly released 2000 book I'd warned as many as I was able to reach by writing:

"The major difference between us as the new century began— and, the voters of pre-Hitler Germany is our booming economy. If our economy suffers a massive downtrend—with restrictive civil laws in place—then, we will have re-birthed the climate of Nazi Germany ...With the clarity of my new mentors, I can see that we—as a nation— are on the same way toward the ugly stench which destroyed Bosnia, Kosovo and other nation states. Unless we choose to envision ourselves as more inclusive than only the ethnic culture of our rearing, then we will suffer the same fate as any nation, which fails to address the cries of its under classes.

"We need to leave our old ways of inter-relating with one another. We don't see that our way of being is a modern American version of civil apartheid. We are in denial. But, I see the future on this path that we are currently following if we don't change our direction. The only way to avoid what I see in our future right now, is for us to turn, and go another way.

"Take note of what I say: If we do not change course—away from limiting civil liberties to some without establishing an equivalent system—then you will witness the horror, about which I warn now. I am not a prophet of doom. I have great trust in the inevitable death of our classist paradigm. I also, however, see that we can make a non-violent transition, if we choose better today than we have before."

In under three years after I had written the above warnings, and only over two years after that little book was sold out, the following circumstances had became part of televised recorded historical fact:

We had all been attacked by Muslim fanatics who saw America as an "evil," occupying their sacred Saudi Arabian lands. Our entire nation had been turned into a terrorist war theatre for the first time since our 19th century Civil War. So as I sat in the Temple, waiting for the event to start, I recalled the words in a "spirit written" message: *you will yet stand before throngs of cave dwellers.*"

Here, in the Temple—waiting for the first plenary session to begin—a decade had passed since the last time that I had attended a bi-annual World General Conference of our church on these holy grounds. Although, I had given up on any religious group's ability to impact the issues I espoused; by then, an old 1992 experience in the Auditorium had been a spiritual anchor for my soul. I had often pondered on that pivotal 1992 event in my life that had taken place, there—across the street, on a most sacred historical land of the Restoration Movement —the Center Place. Several friends and I had traveled there to attend that General Conference...

Now, other than Utah-based Mormons, our church is the largest denomination that claims Joseph Smith, Junior as its founder. Made up of those who didn't follow Brigham Young to Utah, our World General Conferences are different from the Utah Mormons'. Through the years, I had often remembered details about that communion service and the business sessions that we had all experienced there. *Everything*: The way all the delegates freely debated the issues, the sacred music, the powerful waves of Spirit that had washed over me as I had sat in awe of the sensation bathing my person. Over the past decade, I had often pondered on that conference as the church prophet/president had read his then, latest revelation. I especially recalled that—as we had walked down the ramps when the communion service had ended—I had tried to speak to my close friends of what I had felt in the balcony but, *I'd been rendered speechless—me*! I could only open my mouth but, with no words coming out of me!

I'd been struck dumb! I had never experienced such a stunning loss of speech before! Now, anyone that *knows* me knows that this was not normal. Even when I'd known the whispers of those unseen spirit beings in the L.D.S. Los Angeles Temple[iii]—when I had sat in the room called the Celestial Room—I'd never been rendered speechless, as in the Auditorium after that R.L.D.S. communion service. So, all the time that I was away from my—then, new community—over the next ten years, that memory of speechlessness had been my spiritual anchor...

So, it had been no surprise to me when, on October 2, 2002, as I sat at my computer in my home, I felt directed to surf the World Wide Web to visit the web-site of the Reorganized Church of Jesus Christ of

Latter Day Saints. But, I did not know that, the name of the church had since been changed. So, while my computer was booting up, I thought it was odd that, my mind went to that "spirit-written" message that had announced to me that the day would come when "*churches, as…*" I had known "*…them, shall cease to be, by and by.*" Now, I'd heard through the grapevine that, my church was "in a dialogue" on the name of its institution, however. Then, as if an Intelligence had orchestrated it all, October 2, 2002 just happened to be the first day that, the April 2002 message from the current President of the Community of Christ[iv]—its new name—was available to me on my home computer.

To my absolute surprise, the President's counsel had dealt with the things that had driven me away from Community of Christ when it had been called "Reorganized Church…" He wrote of "inclusion" and "diversity," as if he and his entire First Presidency were all united in an acceptance of people like me. It was then, that I felt the tears flowing on my cheeks. I'd been overwhelmed with a powerful sense of calling; my soul was stirred to sustain this message from a President of my church.

So, what had eventually taken place in the immediate days after that experience resulted in the paper that I'd prepared for the 2002 Peace Colloquy. Research of my paternal Feliz family history in 19th century California had already resulted in several papers, which I had written over the previous four years. I had written for the City of Los Angeles, Department of Recreation & Parks; first, about the murder of my great-grandfather and then, later, on the decades earlier murder of his own great-grandfather by 19th century Protestant and Mormon beneficiaries of their conquest of what became the State of California.

In those four papers, I named the rut of religious resentment —that led to a violent retribution for past injustices—as the root of urban gang related murders, and as the key reason why I believed that violence would "rise in Los Angeles." Characteristic of my manner in speaking truth to the powerful, I'd warned the Los Angeles City Council in April of 2002: "…a rise in urban gang homicides will befall Los Angeles." I had said that, "historical economic causes of the revenge" sought "by youth"—who feel they have a just cause—are not yet being addressed by the City of Los Angeles.

I had seen that, the City's civil distresses have a retributive root and—since the assigned theme of the 2002 peace event in the Temple of the Community of Christ was "Toward Economic Justice?"—my paper was focused on my own Feliz family's 19th century loss of lands to the occupying American Army of the West, as a parallel to the 21st century violence involving Palestinian land and the occupation of *that* land by today's Israelis. To me, the peace colloquy's theme was incidental to the retributive issue that I saw at the root of why our global civilization is still at war. What had happened to us, was still happening to others...

My own 1990s research and our family's oral histories—kept from generation to generation—inform me on *why* the promised future millennial epoch has not yet come to be. There, waiting for the event to begin in the holy Temple, I was suddenly struck with the idea that, it is no different for my collective of opening souls—for the Community of Christ—than it is for any other institution, including the City of Los Angeles. Peace will not come for institutions that fail to listen to those whom they exclude. I thought: It is as if All Eternity, or some unseen Force knew that, I had chosen as I did at every juncture of my path.

I was excited! I looked at another man's watch, and it was time for the plenary session to start, right here—in the Temple. Suddenly, in my right periphery, I saw a very familiar face. Slowly, coming up the right side Temple sanctuary steps, was none other than our faith's sixth Prophet/President, Wallace B. Smith—a direct paternal descendant of the prophet Joseph Smith, Junior. He had just entered the Temple, and was making his way to a seat before the event was to begin. As if fate had planned it all, he then, took a seat right next to me! Then, after a very brief exchange of pleasantries with him, I looked back up at the awesomely high, spiraled ceiling of the Temple in which we all waited for the event to begin.

I thumbed through the printed program. There I was, listed on the program to present the following day. I suddenly recalled the words of my L.D.S. patriarchal blessing because they had prophesied this day! I thought: Here I am, in historical Jackson County—in *the Temple in Missouri*—sitting next to a direct descendant of Joseph Smith, Junior —the sixth President of our whole church—and I'm going to present a *"scholastic work"* on world peace in our present time of violence and vengeance. I looked at the printed program. Nobel Peace Prize laureate, Oscar Arias—the former *President of Costa Rica*— would be tomorrow's keynote speaker. My second patriarchal blessing had, indeed, foreseen all of this!

Then, the next day—to my absolute surprise—although I'm not ordained in this church, I was introduced as "Elder Antonio Feliz" in the Temple as I approached the pulpit. As I breathed in before starting to read, I thought to myself, this day was definitely foreseen. Although I was now in *a completely different* church, it had been a Utah based Mormon patriarch that prophesied of a *"scholastic work"* that would someday be mine to perform:

"The day will come when you will be called to a...scholastic work that...will bring you in contact with the leaders of the nation and of the earth, as well as one that will also bring you in contact with the leaders of the church..."

My undercurrent of thought was, I'm in awe of the *integrated wholeness* of it all! In spite of all the exclusionary theologies of "the *heterosexual* church" of my upbringing, and the ugly terror filled times in which we live today, I feel complete joy, hope, love and peace! Even though Community of Christ does not yet extend all of its sacraments in equity to its Queer members, like me, I feel peace about this institution's current policy regarding people like me. And then, my paper was well received by those who were at my session.

As the Peace Colloquy went on during the rest of the weekend, I attended presentations of other papers, and I was consistently in awe of the wisdom, the clarity of purpose and the spiritual giftedness that was obvious to me in the other presenters. As I sat in the Temple sanctuary, listening to the daily prayer for peace later on in the week following the Peace Colloquy, my mind silently wandered again...

Tears flowed freely down my cheeks because I found that my silent thoughts had taken me to another temple, in another community of faith, where I'd sat reverently many years earlier. With that memory, I looked up at the beautiful, huge spiral ceiling above me—seemingly swirling upward—and my inner self heard a familiar phrase from that long ago memory. Faintly, as if it were mere background music for this memory that flashed itself in my mind's eye, the majestic organ music seemed to paint *colors* before me. I thought, how strangely odd this is—music in *colors*—and, without any psychidelic substances!

Then the sacred teaching, my *Meshica* friends taught so many years earlier, seemed to vibrate within me: "...follow the sun...I am the center." Again, I mused on the amazing journey that my past life's choices had taken me on so far. What will happen now?

Suddenly, another old phrase from my memory banks became abundantly clearer to me. It was a phrase I had heard over and over again in other sacred spaces: "...God is so small that He can dwell in your heart...His center is everywhere, but His circumference is nowhere..." I'd always wondered what those words actually meant but, I'd never understood...

Then, wiping the wetness from my cheeks, I felt a now familiar sensation welling up deep within my core, and the words began to take shape quietly within: *The human Spirit Mass is accessible within you. This is why all holiness begins by going within first; for, did not Joseph write that, "the first principle of..."* the journey is *"to know the true nature of God?" The Universal Spirit is His "center"—and yet, is it not true that no Spirit Mass has a circumference?* With that idea ringing within me, as if to punctuate this message, the massive pipe organ of the Temple sanctuary suddenly blasted out its rich, powerful music!

Spirit Mass? There—in the holiest Temple, prophesied of in the 19th century to be built on this holy land prior to the opening of the Latter Day pre-millennial era—I couldn't hold back my tears of joy. An idea then, popped itself into my mind and I wondered, are all we human beings, actually, *making* soul by our daily choices in living? Is our term, "Mass Soul," merely a *new* way of naming what my old *Meshica* friends in Mexico called the Great Spirit? Yet, they'd also taught that, "the world of Mind is separate from the world of Spirit" and that our daily choices, actually, "*make* soul." So there, sitting alone—because everyone else had already left the Temple's sanctuary—I thought: Is there?...is there a generative relationship between the universal human Mass Mind and the creation dynamic of its own Mass Soul? Is there a generative process going on that few of us are aware of? As we each live out our sovereign daily lives, is there a creative dynamic going on of which, few of us are even aware? That was the first time such an idea had occurred to me. And, I don't know how long I sat there, alone in my thoughts…

As I got up, and slowly walked down the ramp, I recalled the old happening, so many years ago, that had happened across the street in the domed Auditorium when I had been, literally, struck dumb after that awesome communion service in 1992. In spite of excommunication from the church in 1982 wherein I had received the promises, and my disagreements with some policies of the church I was now a baptized member of in 2002, the entire phenomenology said loudly to me: All these things are happening exactly as they are all meant to. I marveled at my journey's absolute consistency.

I went on thinking to myself, as I walked through the Temple doors; all prophecy is, indeed, a multi-dimensional creative dynamic. Which way, and where a prophecy is ultimately fulfilled, is a product of the choices we make along the journey of life. This day was prophesied about me in the Utah based church but, it was, *fulfilled*, in this Missouri based church in this event. Walking on the grounds of The Temple, I looked up, and the night sky was completely clear. Stars twinkled as if in song! *Integrated wholeness?* Well, I thought—as I put on my warm top coat—now, *that's* an understatement, if I've ever heard one!

NOTES TO EPILOGUE

[i] The Temple Lot is land that was designated by Joseph Smith, Junior, founder of what have become numerous Mormon denominations, worldwide, as "The Center Place." It is traditionally considered by Saints who derive their spiritual tradition from Joseph Smith, Junior, as the future place of the "City of Zion," and from which it is written that; "…the law shall go forth from Zion and the word of the Lord from Jerusalem." It is significant to this author that, The Matrix film trilogy makes this metaphor central to its screenplay; teaching the ideal of Topian living as the, actual, meaning of the ancient mythological term, "Zion."

[ii] While, Utah based Mormons hold their semi-annual World Conference in their Conference Center; the Independence, MO based Community of Christ holds their bi-annual World Conference in their Auditorium. Both denominations also have a temple built next to these facilities. However, only Community of Christ has a Temple on the sacred Temple Lot that the, respective, canon of each calls the "Center Place," or from where a "future" City of Zion "will be established."

[iii] This experience is related in my first book, Out of The Bishop's Closet *A Call To Heal Ourselves, Each Other and Our World* (2nd ed. Paperback Alamo Square Press, San Francisco, California 1992).

[iv] W. Grant McMurray

[v] Antonio A. Feliz to Los Angeles City Councilman Tom LaBonge, April 11, 2002 and; Antonio A. Feliz, *The Nine Generation Los Feliz Memory Compliments Other Documentation as an Oral History of the Adobe at El Campo de Cahuenga Historical Monument Site* (A Paper For Use by The Department of Recreation & Parks of the City of Los Angeles). See also; Antonio A. Feliz to Greenwood & Associates, *Solving the Murders of 1847,* 22 April 2002, Addendum to El Campo de Cahuenga Conclusions…So Far, Revised 30 June 2002, and Antonio A. Feliz, *Los Feliz de Los Angeles,* October 10, 1958 in A Mi Familia, (Editorial Los Feliz, Los Angeles, California 2000) pages 6-7.

APPENDIX

Full text of paper by Antonio A. Feliz
Presented November 9, 2002.
At the 2002 Peace Colloquy sponsored by Community of Christ in
THE TEMPLE
INDEPENDENCE, JACKSON COUNTY, MISSOURI.

"19th Century American Mormons Verses 19th Century *Californios*: A Parallel To Current Conflicts Between Israelis And Palestinians"

I am the fourth Antonio Feliz, and in this sacred place, I invoke the spirit of my martyred ancestor who's namesake I am. My great-grandfather, Don Jose Antonio Feliz, was executed at *La Rumurosa* because he would not bow to the new laws of the usurping people. My Feliz Family stories teach me that it was "former Mormon Battalion members," turned vigilantes, who killed him, claiming they had done 'a good thing'…

PARRALEL CONFLICTS OF ECONOMIC SYSTEMS & RELIGIOUS VISION

Current events in the Middle East are strikingly parallel to the early history of the United States of America, of the State of California and of the City of Los Angeles,[i] in particular. Since the State of Israel was established —and earlier—the core disagreement between Palestinians and Jews has been about the land that each party to the conflict claims was "given by God" to their ancestors. Some claim that the different economic systems of the two states, have exacerbated the extremities of economic failure for Palestinians and of economic success for Israelis. Some point to the issue of scarcity, which —they affirm—is brought on by the 'imposed curfews of an occupying Israeli government.'[ii] Although referencing on a broader level, social theorist Dr. Joel S. Federman explains, 'the presence of hunger, malnutrition and starvation…is not caused by insufficient…foodstuffs but rather the mal-distribution of those foodstuffs.'[iii] So, applied to this specific situation, the issue of scarcity in the current Middle Eastern conflict is more about bad management than, it is about a given economic system, *per se*. It is also not only that Palestinians are not as much a free market society as the Israelis but, their contrary religious visions.

The 19th century conflict in California, in particular, was also about land that had been 'granted' by God to devout Roman Catholic Spanish subjects for their colonizing service. By the mid 19th century, these estates had evolved in tandem with the Spanish communal *Californio* Roman Catholic Franciscan Mission system in a bartering based economy that dated back to feudal Europe. But, it was in that exact time that, Manifest Destiny motivated 19th century East Coast capitalists to promote migration into what—to that point—had operated in a largely feudal system inherited from Spain. This included three Mormon incursions into what, by then, was sovereign, *Mexican* Territory: Brigham Young's colony to the Great Basin; Lyman Wight's Texas mission to establish a temple, and a third flank was an army Battalion of Mormons who became the mid 19th century police of America's Army of the West in *El Pueblo*. As in the case of modern Palestinians being governed by today's Israel, the then, newly occupied Roman Catholic *Californio pueblos* and *ranchos* were suddenly being governed by 19th century anti-Catholics—including Protestants and the Mormons—who then deported local ethnic *Latinos* from what had become a new capitalist society.

EXAMPLE OF LOS FELIZ OF LOS ANGELES, CALIFORNIA

This writer's grandfather[iv] had been assassinated by late 19th century vigilantes motivated by the 'lust for land' that continued into the early 20th century.[v] As late as the 1940s, his father was forced to prove that he did not 'come to America' but that, 'America came to him' in order to avoid being erroneously deported to Mexico.[vi] Among the *Californio* Spanish *dons* that had colonized large estates [called *ranchos*] by the mid 19th century, was this writer's direct paternal ancestor; whose large, expansive land had been granted to him by the Spanish Roman Catholic monarch ruling under the 'divine right of kings.' Don Jose Vicente Feliz was the first, longest serving *comisionado* [mayor/city manager] of Los Angeles, affectionately known by his 18th and 19th century fellow *Angelinos* as 'the little father of *El Pueblo*.'[vii] *Rancho Los Feliz* had been granted to him for his long service to the Spanish crown, and because he led the original colonists out of the 18th century outposts of New Spain to what is today, Los Angeles, California.[viii]

As a six year old boy, this writer's early memories include sitting on the living room floor of a house owned by a powerful grandmother, surrounded by adults who told the old stories about the loss of 'God given' estates by 'corrupt politicians' and the 'trickery of land developers.' Then, as a teenager, while cousins were being shot to death in ethnic gang warfare, his concerned parents relocated for survival away from what had become a *Mexican barrio* —a ghetto, in effect.[ix] As an earlier convert to The Church of Jesus Christ of Latter-day Saints, this writer was, eventually, employed by the LDS Welfare Services in the 1970s. Being in a position of respect in the family, he was called upon to perform certain familial duties, and he found himself presiding over the funerals of more recently converted *Angelinos* who had not received the benefit of being assimilated away from a 'borderlands' mentality into the mainstream. More recently, though, personal research into events surrounding March 1847 Los Angeles, has revealed the striking parallels that exist between this writer's familial history and that of the more present 21st century frustrated Palestinian 'suicide bombers.' In both cases, 'retaliation and retribution for past injustices are at the root of knee jerk responses of rebellious adolescents.'[x]

THE PARRALELS IN CONFLICTED RELIGIOUS VISIONS ARE STRIKING

In both of the two exponentially explosive conflicts, religious vision has been used as a justification for terrorism and bloodletting on both sides that echoes the ancient sacred story of Samson as their archetype. To those who are immersed in urban gang violence in the *barrios*, there is no difference between Los Angeles urban conflict and recent happenings in Bethlehem or Jerusalem. Both Palestinian terrorists and this writer's *Angelino* relatives, envision those in political power as usurpers, who stole their rightful lands by corruption and economic tricks. The model provided by the old story of the biblical Samson, is one of retribution, and it is mimicked by our *Angelino* urban gangs. Gang members know that urban warfare is a loosing enterprise, that they face an ominous established political power. They know it will only result in a more economically depressed *Latino* community, in urban destruction, continued personal incarceration, increased bloodletting, and ultimately, in yet, much more death. Nevertheless, gang activity is seen as almost a religious duty.

Urban gangs are motivated by urban myths. One urban myth teaches that, the term '*Latino* originated in 19th century California to allow for open discrimination against' Roman Catholic 'religious practitioners.'[xi] Conquered *Californios,* were called Latinos because they used the Latin language in their public religious services while, Protestants did not. This 19th century linguistic device is a historical reality that, sadly, reflects religious tradition as a basis of today's Los Angeles urban warfare: Being unsophisticated in articulating the biblical canon because of a religious context that celebrates its tradition more than its canon, urban gangs of East Los Angeles don't look to scripture for their symbolism. Urban gangs in Los Angeles use symbols from their Roman Catholic heritage in tattoos of the Virgin of Guadeloupe, cross insignias on low rider cars, and also in shirts and other clothing that use colors which denote a Mexican Indian *Zapotec* warrior. Indeed, urban gang justifications of their urban terrorism are, in their core, religious. Thus, while the basis of religious vision is undeniable in both cases, in the Palestinian case, it is more visible to those more familiar with the biblical canon than with the Roman Catholic, or *Mexica* tradition. And, the Bible (KJV) is clear on the issue of how to deal with injustices done to 'the righteous':

'Then the lords of the Philistines gathered them together for to offer a great sacrifice unto Dagon their god, and to rejoice; for they said, Our god hath delivered Samson our enemy into our hand...

'Now the house was full of men and women; and all the lords of the Philistines were there; and there were upon the roof about three thousand men and women, that beheld while Samson made sport.

'And Samson called unto the LORD, and said, O Lord GOD, remember me, I pray thee, and strengthen me, I pray thee, only this once, O GOD, that I may be at once avenged of the Philistines for my two eyes.

'And Samson took hold of the two middle pillars upon which the house stood, and on which it was borne up, of the one with his right hand, and of the other with his left.

'And Samson said, Let me die with the Philistines. And he bowed himself with all his might; and the house fell upon the lords, and upon all the people that were therein. So the dead which he slew at his death were more than they which he slew in his life.'[xii]

So, unlike modern urban gangs, in the conflict between Palestinians and Israelis, the essential factors of the sacred canon are followed carefully and exactly in their terrorist activities. Like the biblical story says of the archetype Samson, attacks are often made at religious celebrations being held by those perceived as being their oppressor neighbors. For example, recently, a Jewish Passover celebration was attacked by a 'suicide bomber' in order to precisely mimic the ancient modeling of Samson. Accusatory justifications by radical Palestinians point to this biblical hero of ancient Israel as their model for behavior that typifies the homicidal barbarism of the present. Similarly, the retaliatory reactions by the policy of present leaders of modern Israel seem to mirror the same canonical model of violent retribution. Yet, religious duty isn't the only justification used by Palestinians, or by Los Angeles gangs, for that matter.

ECONOMIC DISPARITY AS A JUSTIFICATION FOR TERRORISM

Both conflicts have a root basis in past injustices that are mentioned in the oral histories, as is exemplified in Los Feliz of Los Angeles, mentioned above. Palestinian teens specifically point to economic disparity between their communities and those of their neighboring Israelis as justification for their 'suicide bombings.' Indeed, both sides seem to be blindly focused on past injustices, as if unable to find a way out of the repetitive rut of retribution. In Los Angeles, the city's Protestant powerful are, likewise, seen by urban gangs as usurpers of their rightful lands, as the occupying social force, and as the immoral beneficiaries of an unjust economic system that, to them, is socially oppressive. Again, in both cases, this has its root in historical realities that are maintained through oral histories passed down from generation to generation.

MULTI-GENERATIONAL ORAL HISTORIES MAINTAIN ENMITIES

Los Feliz oral histories told, generation to generation, retain an old memory of being victimized by 'land lusting gringos' and 'corrupt politicians' who 'conspired' to take away estates and political influence that was once centered in the Roman Catholic community. Los Feliz of Los Angeles were the local civic leaders, the opinion leaders, the landholders and the respected citizens. From his toddler days, this writer evolved in a virtual second womb of memory that was a multigenerational hold back to a time when '...the Mormons raped our women, pillaged our property...' and otherwise '...took because they could.'[xiii] These are harsh formative mental attitudes in which to evolve as a member of a civic society that speaks a language that is not spoken in the home. As a devout L.D.S. teenager, this writer researched the genealogy

369

of his second great-grandmother *Dona* Josefa Peralta—the legal *Californio* heir to *Rancho Santiago de Santa Ana*—and discovered his heritage. Josefa Peralta is listed third in the first baptismal register of old St. Boniface Roman Catholic Church in Anaheim.[xiv] He asked the parish priest how the name of the town got changed to Anaheim from the name of the *rancho* that had been owned by his Peralta, Feliz and Yorba ancestors. The priest did not know but, later, his grandmother provided the answer:

'Oh, that's an easy question, Antonio. The problem was that the Americans' law did not at all recognize the right of women to own property —contrary to the older *Californio* way—and in their lust for land, the invaders confiscated our family *adobes*, they sought out and killed the propertied men and their male heirs, including your namesake, Don Jose Antonio Feliz. I remember the old stories about how the Americans [the Army of the West's Mormon Battalion] forced our women to take refuge in our old Mission San Juan Capistrano.'[xv]

The distinguished UCLA historian, Neal Harlow, in his truthful book California Conquered, The Annexation of a Mexican Province 1846-1850, related the above experience as he gleaned it from documents that collaborated her memorized oral history. He wrote: 'the women...closed the doors and shutters as...[the invading] 'army went through the small village...'[xvi] This writer's grandmother was often heard by him to say that 'denying women the right to own property was how [Americans] justified taking lands that they saw as deserted.' [It should be remembered here that, women could not even vote in America, until the 20th century.] According to Los Feliz oral histories, the *Californio* men fled to 'hide for their lives in the canyons...' because members of the 'Mormon Battalion' were searching them out '...to kill them for the lands.'[xvii]

Under siege by the usurpers, the women were forced to gather near to what, eventually, replaced the refugee sanctuary of the 18th century Roman Catholic Franciscan Missions. Then, when all the missions were lost to us, 'our women took refuge for their safety due south of old St. Boniface Catholic Church' then, under construction on the newly designated 'Center Street' in Anaheim, California. A German colony was invited by the new government to settle on the lands, and wanting to avoid calling their new settlement after a Roman Catholic Saint, they renamed the township '*Ana-heim*' [German for, Ana's home]. During a visit to the old cemetery in Yorba Linda, California [east of Anaheim] this writer heard his aunts and mother discuss how 'in those days we were all Catholic and then, suddenly, everyone around was Protestant and spoke only German!'[xviii] It was in a subsequent experience that, the same women gave their oral histories about the 'cross burnings in the 1940s in the neighbor's front yard on old Clementine Street in Anaheim.'[xix] Evidently, as late as the mid. 20th century, some descendants of *Californios* were still being terrorized in efforts to get them to move out of what had been their lands only two brief generations earlier. Historical realities make for long memories of economic injustice.

"ALL HAVE SINNED AND COME SHORT OF THE GLORY OF GOD"

As a result of these realities, one thing quickly becomes apparent to rational observers of global history, of world cultures, societies and nation states. That is, at one time or another, we have each been the conqueror, and each has been the conquered. So I, for one, here confess:

'I was also once domesticated. Indeed, issues of colonization—so very important to my people—have now converged in me. My Spanish ancestors conquered my Native ancestors. My family includes the oppressors and the oppressed. As if genetically predisposed by my DNA, my Mormon experience found me playing the roles of both, the excommunicator, as well as that of the excommunicate. But, I've transcended my domestication. I forgave our 19th century conquerors and their descendants, and I've forgiven myself for my own invasive deeds. For, as a Mormon missionary, I actually coerced a Roman Catholic to break all of her images of her virgins and saints in my presence before I'd sign her recommend form to be baptized by us. I now see that this was not the best way for me to be...my soul was not yet open....

'I am one in whom all the above ugliness ends. I have turned my back to the mentors of my youth. In the language of metaphor, I now follow the sun. I am not stuck in my past like Lot's Wife because my four directions are now: Above me, Below me, From where I've been, and Where I am going. My new mentors now are so diverse that, the places I enjoy in the journey of life, are now no longer the context of the same consciousness that created the ugly, violent, ethnic genocidal behavior of all my generations...

'Thankfully, I now envision differently. I now envision myself as the kind of person whose way of seeing others, sings out the song of happiness for those who don't have the same beliefs, customs and moralities of my second womb....Today, I sing the concordant American Indian song of a "two spirit man."'[xx] For this song, is the song of living peacefully.

Indeed, we have, respectively, each been those who oppressed others as well as those who were the victims of oppression. There is probably no human group on the face of the entire planet that has not played both the victimizer and the victim. If we research back far enough into our common planetary history, this uncomfortable reality becomes clear. The only solution to this condition is to try another way than, the way that we have all taken to arrive at the present juncture in human evolution. Eventually, we must come to understand that any who seek peace, must choose to finally vibrate in the song of peace themselves—to truly live the behavior of the peacemakers—first. Choosing to make peace first is the only way to truly transcend an injustice.

THE ONLY JUST SOLUTION AVAILABLE TO ALL PARTIES IN CONFLICT

Peacemaking efforts are, increasingly, focusing on ways to frame peacemaking dialogue in such a way as to now articulate present sensibilities, rather than, to continue to focus only on the envisioning of arcane sacred stories from the past. For example, more recent apparent efforts to change this kind of envisioning by those embroiled in today's Middle East conflict, include making reference to Israel's violent attackers as 'homicide bombers,' rather than, as 'suicide bombers.' In Los Angeles, urban gangs are now being urged by local neighborhood mothers and other concerned citizens to consider their children, their own younger siblings, and ultimately, the gang members' own personal fates. Notable among these efforts is the *Madres* Movement in Echo Park in Los Angeles. The famous Seeds of Peace events in the Middle East are also efforts to envision past injustices in a new way. Many now quote Gandhi who said, 'An eye for an eye only ends up making the whole world blind.'

So, a rational 21st century person might ask today: 'What *is* justice, anyway?' This writer recently asked this question of Dr. Joel Federman, who was the keynote speaker at the 1992 Temple School's Conference on Global Community and World Peace held in Los Angeles, California in October of that year. This question on justice was prefaced by a reference to how our communities of faith have a tendency to only celebrate the positive in our, respective, histories and then, deny the negative. For example, the wonderful Festival of Lights that is celebrated within the Jewish tradition is a way to remember the Miracle of Lights in Jewish history.

It is said that, it took place when sufficient oil was in a miraculous way provided by Divine Providence for the lighting of the Temple Menorah when it was thought that there was not sufficient oil for the ceremony's duration. Devout Jews celebrate this event every year throughout the world. Yet, while it recalls the contributions of the Maccabees to the conquest of the enemy of Israel, the annual celebration fails to note that the term '*macabre*' is derived from the French, and that, it has reference to the grotesque way in which this family of Jewish militants retaliated. Dr. Federman responded:

'…That's where I believe nonviolence comes in…I believe there are many creative, nonviolent ways of catching the world's attention and seeking political ends. I believe that the rule of action needs to be to keep the means you choose as congruent as possible with the ends you seek, since—again, to quote Gandhi—"the means are to the end as the seed is to the tree." If you seek peace and justice, you need to accomplish that through peaceful and just means…we start to create a real problem, I believe, when we use unjust means to achieve our ends, however just.[xxxi]

Most of us had this emblazoned in our psyche after September 11, 2001. Peace, itself, is the only way open that will lead us to world peace. Most of us had the rational sense to suddenly see that this is civilization's only solution to our present way of behaving as a species. We need to focus on the way we travel, on the prophesied 'Millenium,' rather than, on what some call our cultural 'rear view mirrors.' As I have discussed in each of my own books, by its very definition, the Thousand Years of Peace and Love will be global. The Bible (KJV) records that, the 'everlasting gospel' is for 'every nation, kindred, tongue and people.'[xxxii] The Millenium of Christ is going to include 'every' *nationality,* 'every' *race and ethnicity,* 'every' *language* and 'every' *social group*—for, that is what the above scriptural terms translate into. The key word is; 'every.' The glory of the Prince of Peace is unconditional love because His love is Infinite Love.

OUR TRADITIONAL AFFECT IMAGERY—OUR SYMBOLS—MUST CHANGE

Eventually, all of us must come to comprehend that all holiness is about wholeness. The Zion of God must be universal, it must include 'every people' or, it is not zionic at all. So, our envisioning needs to now become transformed. Our own historical judgment of others is rooted in old symbols that must become transmuted into new symbols if we, *ourselves*, are to truly be transmuted. For example, Sunday mornings are still the most segregated time in all of middle-American weekly activity. Each denominational grouping is competitively separated and apart from all others, according to its religion and/ or denomination.

Ronald J. Glossop provided an answer in his book, <u>Confronting War</u>. His solution was for us all to find ways of viewing ourselves as not being in competition with others and, wrote:

'War is large-scale violent conflict between organized groups that are or that aim to establish governments…The alternative to war must consist of some type of nonviolent resolution of such conflicts concerning decision-making power…Whatever serves as a focus of competition between groups may become a cause of war…The main things for which groups compete are the same things for which individuals compete: propagation of their ideas, acquisition of goods, and status…wars are fought ultimately for power over others…'[xxiii]

I suggest that the greatest single obstacle impeding the Millennium of The Christ is this competitive dynamic, and therefore, we must all find ways to envision, which do not have their root in *competition, per se*. For example: institutional religious symbols used to comprehend priesthood theology and policy, are yet encased in envisioning from the past. The terminology we use in reference to priestly orders—whether in this church, in the Roman Catholic or the Mormon or any other church—creates an image of 'keys.' This is an *affect image*. We get a picture in our minds when we use or hear that word, 'keys.' We envision keys, as in keys that one would use to open doors and unlock locks. Even the coat of arms of His Holiness, the Pope has an image of keys that one would use to open or unlock—or to close off—access to sacred sacraments. Sacred Keys, understood with only this external affect image, are about exclusion because a group's exclusiveness *truly is* about inter-group competition. Thus, this kind of affect imagery is not Infinite. Infinite is without limits. We must not limit God. Indeed, God does not need to compete.

So, how much more effective would our peacemaking efforts be, if we all began to envision the term 'keys' in making reference to Priesthood Keys as in keys of a chord of musical sound? Is not a chordant, harmonious musical vibrational sound made up of a full range of diverse keys of music? Isn't music a better affect image for any peacemaking that is about inclusion? I suggest that a small change such as this, is far more powerful as an affect image than all of the verbiage of sermons, dialogue and papers that we practice so well. This writer is not the first to see metaphor as a better key than literalism. However, when the idea was spoken to this soul's core through merciful, benevolent Spirit giftedness, a way out of our common hell became clear.

On the day that this vision came into my heart, I was conflicted because of my family's history. It was a day when I wept openly over the pain of our past generations. Thankfully, however, it was also the day when I was lifted out of the hell of my past generations by a new vision of the term 'keys.' All of us, looking with a new vision—toward a future symbolized by musical keys—is a truly harmonious way to perceive. Seeing Priesthood Keys as we see musical keys—as attaining inner personal vibrational levels of a harmonic human energy—allows us to sing the sweet songs of concord; because interpersonal concordant behavior manifests love. Christ is Love. His personal energy is felt by us. It is the emotion of love but—more importantly—His energy, is manifest to us in our world by *our humane behavior*. This is why peace among us humans—or a love vibrational human frequency—truly is the very '*key*' of the holy Kingdom! Keys of Priesthood are many, yet, if they are conceptualized in metaphor as that of a full cord of musical keys then, harmony is created. The archetype of all creation is *the placement of* the first verse of the Gospel: '*In the beginning was the word…*'[xxiv](KJV)—words, are symbols that evoke *affect images*. *Thought* precedes behavior. So, what can we do?

A FINAL BLESSING AND CHARGE TO ACTION

Our sacred stories all contain within them *affect images* that engage behavior. Because all *affect images* are the conveyors of behavioral impulses, examining our sacred stories and our policies by using metaphor as a tool of inquiry is a good step on the way of peace. If Community of Christ is to be transmuted into *Universal Attunement* then, music, *The Universal Language*, is the language to use to engage, *to understand the very nature of*, Priesthood Keys—with all that such imagery implies. Our careful examination of our limiting interpretations on all people, *indeed, on* 'every' *nationality*, 'every' *racial/ethnic group,* 'every' *language,* 'every' *social group* would powerfully engage the *universal* zionic community in the collective unconscious—a place that, today's physicists label as '*enfolded*' reality.[xxv]

Study the Priesthood Keys metaphor as a cord of musical keys. It may be the way, the pattern, the template of how the Holy Priesthood is to be on Earth. Using an affect image—of *inner* chordant human vibration, rather than, of *external* keys that lock and unlock—changes exclusion to inclusion. It *does* take 'the everlasting gospel' to 'every nation, kindred, tongue and *people*.' My blessing for us all is that, the Community of Christ will swiftly see that music 'transmutes human emotions'[xxvi] and that, the metaphor of Priesthood Keys as a chord of diverse vibrational keys may be the visual energy that transmutes our own Community of Christ. Perhaps, in this way, we will become more able to truly fulfill our corporate mission: Global joy, hope, love and peace! ⌘

ENDNOTES

[i] Throughout this paper, the City of Los Angeles is also referred to as *El Pueblo de La Reina de Los Angeles,* and as simply *El Pueblo.* This is the 18th and 19th century name of the city prior to the annexation of the sovereign state of California into the United States of America in 1850. The official founding date of the present City of Los Angeles is in the Spanish era of what is commonly referred to as the *Californio* period made famous by legends of *El Zorro,* who, according to our oral history, was a cousin of my paternal ancestors.

[ii] ABC News, September 2, 2001 Special Report.

[iii] Joel S. Federman, *The Politics of Universal Compassion,* Dissertation Presented to the Faculty of the Graduate School, University of Southern California, Political Science, August 1999, 181-182.

[iv] Don Jose Antonio Feliz, heir of *Rancho Los Feliz*, son of *Juez* Manuel Celestino Feliz [c.1850].

[v] Antonio A. Feliz [1916-1978] to Antonio A. Feliz [1943-], *An Oral History*, February 2, 1978.

[vi] Ibid.

[vii] W.W. Robinson, *Los Angeles From The Days of The Pueblo* (The California Historical Society, Los Angeles, California 1981).

[viii] Ibid.

[ix] Antonio A. Feliz *A Mi Familia* (Editorial Los Feliz, Los Angeles, California) 6-7.

[x] Antonio A. Feliz to Los Angeles City Councilman Tom LaBonge, April 11, 2002, and Antonio A. Feliz, *The Nine Generation Los Feliz Memory Compliments Other Documentation as an Oral History of the Adobe at El Campo de Cahuenga Historical Monument Site* (A Paper For Use by The Department of Recreation & Parks of the City of Los Angeles).

[xi] Alfred Acosta [1956-1974] to Antonio A. Feliz, August 15, 1972. It should also be noted that the 19th century was a time of extreme enmity in America between the Protestant majority and an American Roman Catholic minority. Many East Coast newspaper editorials of the time commonly used the term "papist" in an open derogatory effort that was anti-Latino. The social American climate between Roman Catholics and Protestants was then, more like Northern Ireland's 20th century social climate than America's social climate is today, in the 21st century.

[xii] Judges, 16:23,27-30.

[xiii] Antonio A. Feliz, *Los Feliz de Los Angeles*, October 10, 1958; see also Antonio A. Feliz to Greenwood & Associates, *Solving the Murders of 1847,* 22 April 2002, Addendum to El Campo de Cahuenga Conclusions...So Far, Revised 30 June 2002.

[xiv] Lista de Bautismos, Libro Primero, *St.Boniface Roman Catholic Church Archive of Baptisms, Old St. Boniface Parish Church,* Anaheim, California.

[xv] Oral History of Nicasia Acosta V. de Tafoya, journal date: June 26, 1957, by Antonio A. Feliz.

[xvi] Neal Harlow, *California Conquered, The Annexation of a Mexican Province 1846-1850* (University of California Press, Berkeley, California 1982), 330.

[xvii] Ibid.

[xviii] Antonio A. Feliz, *The Issue Is Pluralism* (Editorial Los Feliz, Los Feliz Village, Los Angeles, California 2002) 67.

[xix] Feliz, Op.Cit. A Mi Familia, 14.

[xx] Ibid. 16-17. Also: Walter L. Williams, *The Spirit and The Flesh, Sexual Diversity in American Indian Culture* (Beacon Press, Boston Massachusetts 1986) an excellent discussion on the "two spirit" tradition of many ancient American Indian and existing nature centered American Indians. While, Williams uses the French derivative, *berdache*, because of his source text vocabulary; in a conversation this writer had with him October 4, 2002, he used the "two spirit" terminology.

[xxi] Joel S. Federman to Antonio A. Feliz, 25 April 2002.

[xxii] Revelation, 14:6-7.

[xxiii] Ronald J. Glossop, *Confronting War* (Macfarland and Company, Inc. Publishers, Jefferson, North Carolina, 1987) The Causes of War, 40-50.

[xxiv] John 1:1 (Elsewhere I have affirmed that reading the canon as metaphor is the key to understanding its reference or, meaning. I have said this because, from the beginning, inspired scripture has used the language of metaphor as exemplified by the placement of this verse by a scribe of the 1st century Christian Church at the start of the sacred story of the biblical Christ in John's gospel.).

[xxv] Michael Talbot, *The Holographic Universe,* (HarperCollins Publishers, New York, New York, 1991) 46-48; 84;188.

[xxvi] Ibid.

BIBLIOGRAPHY

Joel S. Federman, *The Politics of Compassion, Dissertation Presented to the Faculty of the Graduate School, University of Southern California,* Political Science, Los Angeles, California: August, 1999.

Antonio A. Feliz, *A Mi Familia,* Los Angeles, California: Editorial Los Feliz, 2000.

Antonio A. Feliz, *The Issue Is Pluralism,* Los Angeles, California: Editorial Los Feliz, 2000.

Ronald J. Glossop, *Confronting War,* Jefferson, North Carolina: Macfarland and Company, Inc. Publishers, 1987.

Neal Harlow, *California Conquered, The Annexation of a Mexican Province, 1846-1850,* Berkeley, California: University of California Press, 1982.

Old St. Boniface Parish Church, *Lista de Bautismos, Libro Primero,* Anaheim, California: St. Boniface Roman Catholic Church Archive of Baptisms, 1850.

Michael Talbot, *The Holographic Universe*, New York, New York: HarperCollins Publishers, 1991.

W. W. Robinson, *Los Angeles From The Days of The Pueblo,* Los Angeles, California: Los Angeles Historical Society, 1981.

Walter L. Williams, *The Spirit and The Flesh, Sexual Diversity in American Indian Culture,* Beacon Press, Boston, Massachusetts, 1986.

For information on Concord Circles events
visit : www.concordcirclesinstitute.org

ABOUT THE AUTHOR

Antonio A. Feliz is a ninth generation paternal descendant of *Don* Jose Vicente Feliz, the 18th century founder, and the first Spanish *comisionado* (mayor/city manager) of *El Pueblo de La Reina de Los Angeles* at the place known by the *Yanya* Indians inhabiting it then, as *Yangna*. Through his mother, Antonio A. Feliz is also a descendant of Mexico's ancient *Mexica* (Aztecs) and also their 19th century French conquerors. An ordained, L.D.S. bishop, high priest, and a Mormon Temple marriage sealer, today, his energies are occupied in promoting *Mexica/Toltec* ideals in non-Indian contexts.

A member of Community of Christ (formerly, Reorganized Church of Jesus Christ of Latter Day Saints) headquartered in the city of Independence, Missouri, he was one of the two founders of the Kansas City, Missouri group that later evolved into GALA (Gay And Lesbian Acceptance) now, closely affiliated with Community of Christ. The author follows an ancient *Mexica/Toltec* tradition, as told in this book. In 1990 he apprenticed under the *Mexica/Toltec* wise man he mentions within Chapter Seven of this work, and the author practices "plant spirit medicine," as is evidenced by the photograph on the following page.

A 1969 communications graduate of Brigham Young University, today, the author works for world peace, global community and for social/political pluralism. He uses a diverse ancestry, his experience as one of America's ordained, and the awareness of a "two spirit" man [a Queer man, in our vernacular] to foster increased social, and political justice in today's global society. This, he does through the work of the Concord Circles Institute.

AUTHOR PRACTICING
"PLANT SPIRIT" MEDICINE
A TRADITION OF "CIRCLES" CEREMONIES

Taken with a throwaway camera, this image is of a "plant spirit" after it had made its presence known to the author, as told in this book. Note that the color of the entity is red, denoting it, as a "botanical earth energy" in contrast to energies not bound to botanical life forms. Other colors would indicate a non-botanical entity. *Mexica/Toltec* tradition is replete with stories of this kind of image as a "spirit" manifestation of the "plant" to which it is bound. Communion between practitioners of "plant spirit" medicine and the, given, "plant spirit" is essential for a healing through this healing tradition.

In "plant spirit" medicine, a spirit of an indigenous plant is able to heal human beings that ask it to process the cleansing of the energy field of the human seeking a healing. In the tradition of the ancients, the modern practitioner of "plant spirit" medicine uses sunglasses in order to allow the "plant spirit" to consider her or him as a peer, "for plants have no eyes." In the nature-centric worldview of *Mexica/Toltec* Indians, "it is necessary to" first, "bond as an equal with the plant spirit" before one can "gain sufficient agreement with the plant spirit" to allow it to engage the human energy field for healing to occur. In this way, "empathy is attained with the plant spirit" allowing it "to agree to perform the adjustment" in the energy system of the person who is seeking the healing. Of necessity, all healing in this tradition is because of inter-species respect and friendship.

"... The disciples asked: Oh, Master; when will the kingdom come? Jesus said: The kingdom will not come by expectation; they will not say, see here, see there. The kingdom of the father *is spread* upon the earth, and *men do not see it*."

> —Gospel of St. Thomas, final verse
> [Italics not in original]
> Dead Sea Scrolls

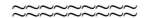

TREE SHRINE IN SALT LAKE CITY
AS IT APPEARED DURING WARM WEATHER

    Taken by the author with a throwaway camera, this image is in a tree, as it appeared in the 1990s warm summers. Note the aromatic, pink water flowing out of what Roman Catholics in Salt Lake City believe are "Our Lady's heart and womb" areas. Local Indians do not, however, see this image as "Our Lady of Guadeloupe," as do the Roman Catholics. *Mexica* oral history is replete with an ancient tradition of this image as a manifestation of their "revered mother," the Earth Mother, known by their pre-Colombian ancestors only as, *Tonantzin*. *Tonantzin* was, originally, a *Toltec* figure that had been absorbed into the *Mexica* pantheon after the *Mexica* conquest of the ancient *Toltec* Indians.

    In the nature-centric worldview of the *Mexica/Toltec* Indians, it is not a full image of a woman, much less, of a virgin. In their eyes, this image is, actually, the long-awaited sign of the most compassionate *Tonantzin* that, reveals Her as oral histories foretold, approximately 500 years ago, by her *natural* image; "the archetypal vulva, in full erotic passion." It is said among the *Mexica* that, "the sign of woman will exemplify the love and compassion of *Tonantzin,* as a model for all." Ancient myth further tells that, "when it appears in a tree, it will mark the generation that ends our 500 year penance" for the sin of human sacrifice committed by the ancients of the *Mexica* Indians of Mexico.

TREE SHRINE IN SALT LAKE CITY
AS IT APPEARED DURING FREEZING WEATHER

As told in this book, originally, the first image became visible to a devout Roman Catholic woman as she rode a city bus, going to her job as a Salt Lake City, Utah domestic employee. But, as shown above, during freezing Utah winters, the water from the tree stops flowing, and then the image changes to how it is revealed above. So, in winter months, the image appears like that of a man instead of that of a woman or, of a Catholic virgin, for that matter. This has caused some to believe that this is not an image of *Tonantzin,* after all but that, rather, it is an image of another pre-Columbian figure; a *Mexica* "deity" that, the conquering Spanish priests said was often depicted as being "*both male and female.*"

To modern Indian followers of ancient *Mexica/Toltec* ways, their 16th century Indian ancestors suffered conquest by the Spaniards because of their ancestral practice of human sacrifice. Thus, they believe that the imposed conquest by others is a 500-year penance and that, now, this natural sign foretells their penance is about to be lifted. This is why the appearance of this particular image has given some reason to think that they should now "militantly rise up against the European occupiers of *Aztlan*" because "now, the 500 year penance is soon to be over." Along with other American southwestern states, Utah was a part of the ancient traditional lands from where the *Mexica* migrated: *Aztlan.*

TREE SHRINE IN SALT LAKE CITY
AFTER 2002 EFFORTS TO DESTROY THE TREE

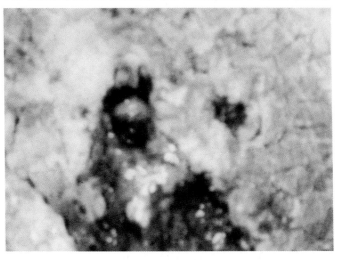

When the image first appeared in the 1990s, it caused some local Mormon neighbors to believe that it was "evil." They believed that "it must have a demonic origin" because "after all, it is an unexplainable phenomenon," and as such, "it must be from something other than our Heavenly Father." Local Mormon neighbors tried to chop down the tree with their home garden tools, only to have the city's mayor declare it a "protected site." Today, the tree is a sacred shrine to many. So, it is now a tourist attraction to pilgrims and, thus, economics became its salvation!

For now, the various and disparate theological enmities remain beneath the surface of local community sensibilities. So, whichever way the tree's natural image is taken; Utah Mormon, Roman Catholic or Indigenous, the fact is that its appearance is formed by the *natural* organization of the trillions of living molecules that make up the living tree, its soil and some underground water source. Affirming that, "all coincidence is actually convergence" the author argues in this book that the natural phenomenon is a message "in the language of *beingness* from a High Intelligence" to us all. After the efforts by some to destroy it in 2002, the image, now, appears to bleed from the image's wounded left side, with its left arm raised up—as if, to painfully say: "Stop all the violence and the hatred!"

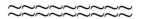

"**J**esus said, 'I am the light which, is above them all. It is I who am the All. From me did all come forth and to me the all extends. *Split a piece of wood and I am there.* Lift up the stone, and you will find me there.'"

—Dead Sea Scrolls (NHC II.46.23-38)
[Italics not in original]
The Origin of Satan by Elaine Pagels